MASTERING
STRATEGY

FINANCIAL TIMES

MASTERING STRATEGY

The Complete MBA Companion in Strategy

IN ASSOCIATION WITH

University
of Michigan
Business
School

SAID

BUSINESS

SCHOOL

MASTERING STRATEGY

CHICAGO GSB   The University of Chicago Graduate School of Business is at the forefront of bringing a discipline-based approach to the study of business. Chicago GSB is known for its world-renowned faculty, which includes more Nobel Prize winners than any other business school. Chicago GSB is also known for its strength in a number of areas, including strategy, finance, entrepreneurship, international business, general management, economics, accounting, marketing and its innovative MBA program, which has campuses in Barcelona, Singapore and Chicago. Through its Center for Decision Research, Chicago GSB was the first business school to emphasize behavioral decision making in its MBA and PhD curricula. The School offers seven programs leading to an MBA degree, in addition to executive and corporate non-degree programs, and a PhD in business. Approximately 350 Chicago GSB graduates hold key faculty posts at business schools and universities. More than 50 serve as deans.

INSEAD   In just 40 years, INSEAD has grown from a modest European educational start-up to one of the world's leading business schools, with more than 650 MBAs, 5,500 executives and 40 PhDs from over 75 countries passing through its programs every year. Participants are taught by an internationally recognized faculty of 124 professors from 26 countries. The institute's extensive alumni network is present in 122 countries and represents more than 20,200 MBA and executive alumni.

INSEAD was the first business school to offer the one-year MBA in a genuinely international environment. Renowned for its exceptional diversity and multicultural outlook, INSEAD realizes that to stay at the forefront of management education, it must continue to innovate. The most recent example is the launch of its permanent, fully fledged Asian Campus in Singapore. Its concept of "one school, two campuses" will give participants the opportunity to study on its European campus, Asian campus or both.

University
of Michigan
Business
School

In *Business Week* magazine's bi-annual survey of corporate executives, the University of Michigan Business School (UMBS) was rated the most innovative business school in the United States. In the same survey, UMBS was one of only two schools rated in the top ten in each of the four functional areas of business the magazine ranks. The *Financial Times* called UMBS "one of the most international business schools in the US.

UMB's MBA and undergraduate programs blend the School's unusual across-the-board academic prowess with intensive development of applied skills and capablities for results-producing leadership. This powerful combination has made UMBS a standard-setter among business schools and one of the most heavily recruited campuses in the world. Top employers of UMBS graduates include technology, consulting, consumer goods, manufacturing, and financial services firms.

In addition to degree programs, the Executive Education Center at UMBS offers a wide range of public and customized programs for working executives. More than 5,000 people participate in these programs each year, both on the School's campus in Ann Arbor, Michigan, and in overseas locations. Executive education participants reap immediate benefit from UMBS's high-impact blend of rigorous, cutting-edge knowledge, big ideas, and a focus on producing results.

At the heart of all of UMBS's progams is a thriving enterprise – high-powered faculty who produce important insights and new knowledge. Through the Mastering Strategy series, a portion of that valuable asset is being brought to *FT* readers.

SAID

BUSINESS

SCHOOL

The Saïd Business School is the business school of the University of Oxford, and the newest department in one of the world's oldest universities. The school was established in 1998 through an initial £20m benefaction from Mr Wafic Saïd and matching funding from the University. It specializes in high level research into international business topics, including strategy, finance and corporate governance. The school also offers MBA, undergraduate and research degrees to an international student body.

Executive editor Tim Dickson

Subeditor Ken Pottinger

Website editor James Pickford

FT Mastering co-ordinator Laura Scanga

Graphics Graham Parish

School co-ordinators   University of Chicago Graduate School of Business: Rob Gertner, Allan Friedman
INSEAD: Gareth Dyas, Helle Jensen
University of Michigan Business School: Will Mitchell, Keith Decie
Saïd Business School, Oxford University: Anthony Hopwood, Jonathan Davis

PEARSON EDUCATION LIMITED

Head Office:
Edinburgh Gate
Harlow CM20 2JE
Tel: +44 (0)1279 623623
Fax: +44 (0)1279 431059

London Office:
128 Long Acre, London WC2E 9AN
Tel: +44 (0)20 7447 2000
Fax: +44 (0)20 7240 5771

Website: www.business-minds.com

First published in Great Britain in 2000

© University of Chicago Graduate School of Business
© INSEAD
© University of Michigan Business School
© Saïd Business School, Oxford University

ISBN 0 273 64930 2

British Library Cataloguing in Publication Data
A CIP catalogue record for this book can be obtained from the British Library.

10 9 8 7 6 5 4 3 2 1

Typeset by Land and Unwin (Data Sciences) Limited, Bugbrooke
Printed and bound in Great Britain by Redwood Books Ltd, Trowbridge, Wiltshire

The Publishers' policy is to use paper manufactured from sustainable forests.

Contents

Introduction

The *Financial Times Mastering* series has grown out of a unique partnership between the *FT* and some of the world's leading international business schools. *Mastering Strategy* is the seventh book to emerge in this way and brings together, in a fresh format, articles that first appeared in the newspaper over a 12-week period in late 1999.

As with its predecessors, *Mastering Strategy* combines the most important principles of this area of management with new thinking on what direction it will take in the 21st century.

Many books have been written about business strategy over the last 40 years, but few offer the variety of perspective and subtlety of interpretation as the contributions in this book. The dawn of a new millennium – with businesses striving to navigate the fast-moving currents of liberalization, globalization, and e-commerce to name but three – is surely an appropriate time for executives to stand back and consider the theory and practice of the strategic art.

The old certainties of central and long-term planning may have fallen apart long ago, but what exactly has replaced them? Should companies primarily be looking outwards at their external environment – or inside at their distinctive capabilities? How do managers choose from the competing schools of strategy – and is it possible to synthesize the different approaches which have been tested over the years into a coherent whole?

There are no easy answers to these and other questions but our hope is that the ideas in this book will better inform readers and stimulate them to develop the most appropriate model for their own circumstances.

Mastering Strategy has 16 modules – chosen in part to reflect the way the topic is taught in leading international business schools and in part for editorial expediency. As with the study of all management topics

these days, however, the reader should beware of over-neat functional distinctions. The 16 modules cover strategy as it relates to: history; micro-economics; the general business environment; globalization; organizational structures; technology; mergers and acquisitions; shareholder value/governance; risk management; leadership; people; sectoral approaches; alliances; knowledge; operations and manufacturing; and future challenges.

This is a rich mix of topics and readers will find everything from the dynamics of price competition and resource margin accounting to post-acquisition behavior and the perils of corporate "thought control." New thinking sits alongside useful definitions and discussion of more familiar but not always well understood concepts such as network externalities, strategic complements and scenario analysis. As with previous books in the *FT Mastering* series, the emphasis on case studies and examples ensures that the link with the real world of business remains strong.

Brief introductions to each module outline the main themes, and the summaries accompanying each article are intended to help readers quickly identify particular areas of interest. Lists of further reading should be helpful for those who want to delve deeper or look up references.

As with previous books in this series, the inspiration for and compilation of the articles in *Mastering Strategy* was a team effort, involving representatives of the four participating business schools: University of Chicago Graduate School of Business; INSEAD, near Paris; University of Michigan Business School; and Said Business School, Oxford University. All the co-ordinators mentioned on page vi provided invaluable support, but Rob Gertner and Will Mitchell deserve a special mention for combining consistently astute and encouraging advice with a burdensome individual writing role. The other heroes, of course, are the professors and other business school faculty experts who gave generously of their time to write the 60 or so articles around which *Mastering Strategy* is based, who stuck to deadline undertakings they no doubt later lived to regret, and who endured with surprising cheerfulness the editing peculiarities of the *FT Mastering* team.

Finally, if you enjoy this book, you will be glad to know that there are more Mastering books on the way. The next book in the series will be *FT Mastering Risk*.

Tim Dickson

Tim Dickson is executive editor of European Business Forum, a new print and online publishing business which aims to highlight Europe's perspective on global management issues. EBF is a joint venture established by the Community of European Management Schools (CEMS) and PricewaterhouseCoopers. Tim can be contacted at tim.dickson@europeanbusinessforum.com

HISTORY/STATE
OF STRATEGY

Contributors

John Kay is a director and founder of London Economics, a UK consultancy. He was the first director of the Saïd Business School, Oxford. His research interests include economics and business, business strategy and the social context of markets.

Bruce Ahlstrand is a professor of management at Trent University, Ontario, Canada. He is author of *The Quest for Productivity* and co-author of *Human Resource Management in the Multi-Divisional Company*.

Henry Mintzberg is the Cleghorn Professor of Management Studies at McGill University and visiting scholar at INSEAD, France. He is the author of several books, including *Strategy Safari* and *The Rise and Fall of Strategic Planning*.

Joseph Lampel is professor of strategic management at the University of Nottingham Business School. He focusses on project-based knowledge-intensive industries.

Contents

Introduction

Mastering Strategy begins with two well-crafted essays on the history and meaning of strategy, a field which broadly concerns the matching of a company's internal capabilities to its external environment. The first article argues that history is in part a lesson in the mistaken belief that we could control the future – strategy today is better understood as a set of analytical techniques for influencing a company's position in the market place. In the second article, the authors identify ten views of strategy – from "design" and "planning" to "cognitive" and "cultural" – and reflect on whether these are really different approaches or merely different parts of the same process. Academics and consultants tend to focus on narrow perspectives, but business people will do best if they see the bigger picture.

Strategy and the delusion of Grand Designs

by John Kay

It is the early 1960s. Robert McNamara, recruited from Ford, the US carmaker, to run the US Department of Defense, is managing the first stages of the Vietnam war on computers in the Pentagon. John Kenneth Galbraith, detesting the world McNamara represents, writes of the New Industrial State, in which giant mechanistic corporations run our lives.

The Soviet Union is ahead in the space race and while most of the West loathes the Russian empire they do not dispute the claims made for its economic success. Every newly independent territory emerging from colonialism looks forward to the realization of its development plan. Harold Wilson, Britain's Prime Minister, talks of the white heat of the technological revolution: George Brown, Deputy Prime Minister, gives Britain its first, and only, national plan.

It is in this environment that the idea of business strategy is created. The early texts were by Igor Ansoff and Ken Andrews (*see* Suggested further reading). Its leading journal is called *Long Range Planning*. It is founded on an illusion of rationality and the possibilities of control.

It is a world that will soon fall apart. McNamara will be translated to the World Bank, but history will note the failure of each of his careers – CEO, Secretary of State, international statesman. Half a million hippies will gather at Woodstock to celebrate the demise of the New Industrial State; and – although few people saw it then – the Soviet Union is on an unstoppable path from totalitarianism to disintegration.

Yet the delusion of control has continued to define the subject of business strategy. In the heady 1960s, no major company was without its strategic plan. Few are without them today, although few devote the resources to them they once did. They contain numbers, neither targets nor forecasts, which purport to describe the evolution of the company's affairs over the next five years.

But planning and strategy are no longer conflated. The delusion of control has changed its form if not its nature. What matters are vision and mission. Charismatic CEOs can transcend the boundaries of the company. Their achievements, and those of the companies they inspired, could be restricted only by the limitations of their executive imagination.

Vision as cliché

But companies are not restrained only by imagination. They are limited by their own capabilities, by technology, by competition, and by the demands of their customers. So visionary strategy has been succeeded by an era in which the cliché – "formulation is easy, it is implementation that is the problem" – holds sway. If strategizing consists of having visions, it is obvious that formulation is easy and implementation the problem: all substantive issues of strategy have been redefined as issues of implementation.

As organizations stubbornly fail to conform to the visions of their senior

5

executives, we should not be surprised that organizational transformation has become one of the most popular branches of consultancy.

Or perhaps the CEO's vision is of the external environment, rather than the internal capabilities of the company. The future belongs to those who see it first, or most clearly. But this is rarely so. It is not just that forecasting is hard – although that difficulty should not be underestimated. Even if you do see the future correctly, its timing is hard to predict and its implications are uncertain.

AT&T, the US telecoms carrier, understood that the convergence of tele-communications and computing would transform not only the company's own markets but much of business life. It was a perceptive vision, not widely shared. But the company failed to see – how could it have? – that the internet was the specific vehicle through which the vision would be realized, or that its merger with NCR, the US business machines manufacturer, was an irrelevant and inappropriate response. While there are many examples – take General Motors or International Business Machines – of companies that suffered from failing to see the future even after it had arrived, there are almost none of companies building sustainable competitive advantages from superior forecasting abilities.

Thoughtful strategy, then, is not about crystal balls, or grand designs and visions. The attempt to formulate these at the level of national economies is now seen to have been at best risible and at worst disastrous – as with Soviet economic planning, Mao's Cultural Revolution, or the improvement strategies of almost all developing countries. What has been true for states is also true for companies.

No one has, or could hope to have, the necessary knowledge to construct these transformational plans. Nor, however totalitarian the structures they introduce in governments or corporations, does anyone truly enjoy the power to implement them.

The subject of strategy

Business strategy is concerned with the match between the internal capabilities of the company and its external environment. Although there is much disagreement of substance among those who write about strategy, most agree that this is the issue.

The methods of strategy, and its central questions, follow from that definition. The methods require analysis of the characteristics of the company and the industries and markets in which it operates. The questions are twofold. What are the origins and characteristics of the successful fit between characteristics and environment? Why do companies succeed? How can companies and their managers make that fit more effective? How will companies succeed?

I once thought that these core questions of strategy – the positive question of understanding the processes through which effective strategies had been arrived at, the normative question of what effective strategy should be – were quite separate. I now believe that they are barely worth distinguishing, and that the conventional emphasis on the vision is the product of the illusion of control.

Strategy is not planning, visioning or forecasting – all remnants of the belief that one can control the future by superior insight and superior will. The modern subject of business strategy is a set of analytic techniques for understanding better, and so influencing, a company's position in its actual and potential market place.

Evolving modern theory

Strategy, as I have defined it, is a subject of application, rather than a discipline – rather as, say, geriatrics is to underlying disciplines of pharmacology, or cell biology – and the obvious underpinning disciplines for strategy are economics and organizational sociology. Still, this is not how the subject developed in practice.

When the content of strategy was first set out 30 years ago, industrial economics was dominated by the structure–conduct–performance paradigm. This emphasized how market structure – the number of competitors and the degree of rivalry between them – was the principal influence on a company's behavior.

Market structure was determined partly by external conditions of supply and demand, and partly (unless antitrust agencies intervened) by the actions of companies to influence the intensity of competition.

This was a view of markets aimed at public policy, not business policy. It was correctly seen as having little relevance to the basic issues of business strategy. Its neglect of the internal characteristics of companies is obvious and explicit. While some of the strategic tools developed by consultants in the 1970s – such as the experience curve and the portfolio matrix – might advantageously have had an economic basis, in practice micro-economic theory was largely ignored.

Not until 1980, with the publication of Michael Porter's *Competitive Strategy*, did economists attempt to recapture the field of strategy. But this was ultimately to prove a false move. Porter's work – essentially a translation of the structure–conduct–performance paradigm into language more appropriate for a business audience – suffered from the limitations of the material on which it was based. Porter's "five forces" and value chain are usefully descriptive of industry structure, but shed no light on the central strategic issue: why different companies, facing the same environment, perform differently.

Much of the organizational sociology of the 1960s addressed strategic issues. Alfred Chandler's magisterial *Strategy and Structure*, or the empirical work of Tom Burns and G.M. Stalker, addressed directly the relationships between organizational form and the technological and market environment. But academic sociology was largely captured by people hostile to the very concept of capitalist organization. The subject drifted into abstraction, and further away from the day-to-day concerns of those in business.

More recent insights into the nature of organizations have come either from economics or from the accumulated practical wisdom of which Charles Handy and Henry Mintzberg are, in different ways, effective exponents. Porter's attention ultimately reverted to the public policy concerns of his former mentors in the Harvard economics department. This is seen in his book *The Competitive Advantage of Nations*.

Strategy today – rents and capabilities

At about the same time as Porter first wrote about strategy, the *Strategic Management Journal*, today the leading journal in the field, was established. The currently dominant view of strategy – resource-based theory – has been principally set out in its pages. It also has an economic base, but has found its inspiration in different places and further back in history. It draws on the Ricardian approach to the determination of economic rent, and the view of the company as a collection of capabilities described by Edith Penrose and George Richardson.

Economic rent is what companies earn over and above the cost of the capital employed in their business. The terminology is unfortunate. It is used because the central framework was set out by David Ricardo in the early part of the nineteenth century, when agriculture dominated economic activity. Economic rent has been variously called economic profit, super-normal profit and excess profit – terms that lack appeal for modern business people. Most recently Stern Stewart, a consultancy, has had some success marketing the concept as economic value added. The problem here is that value added – the value added that is taxed – means something different. Nor does my own attempt to call it "added value" help. Perhaps economic rent is best. The title doesn't matter. The concept does.

The objective of a company is to increase its economic rent, rather than its profit as such. A company that increases its profits but not its economic rent – as through investments or acquisitions that yield less than the cost of capital – destroys value.

In a contestable market – one in which entry by new companies is relatively early and exit by failing companies is relatively quick – companies that are only just successful enough to survive will earn the industry cost of capital on the replacement cost of their assets. Economic rent is the measure of the competitive advantage that effective established companies enjoy, and competitive advantage is the only means by which companies in contestable markets can earn economic rents.

The opportunity for companies to sustain these competitive advantages is determined by their capabilities. The capabilities of a company are of many kinds. For the purposes of strategy, the key distinction is between distinctive capabilities and reproducible capabilities. Distinctive capabilities are those characteristics of a company that cannot be replicated by competitors, or can only be replicated with great difficulty, even after these competitors realize the benefits they yield for the originating company.

Distinctive capabilities can be of many kinds. Government licenses, statutory monopolies, or effective patents and copyrights are particularly stark examples of distinctive capabilities. But equally powerful idiosyncratic characteristics have been built by companies in competitive markets. These include strong brands, patterns of supplier or customer relationships, and skills, knowledge, and routines embedded in teams.

Reproducible capabilities can be bought or created by any company with reasonable management skills, diligence, and financial resources. Most technical capabilities are of this kind. Marketing capabilities are sometimes distinctive, sometimes reproducible.

The importance of the distinction for strategy is this: only distinctive capabilities can be the basis of sustainable competitive advantage. Collections of reproducible capabilities can and will be established by others and therefore cannot generate rents in a competitive or contestable market.

Matching capabilities to markets

So the strategist must first look inward. The strategist must identify the distinctive capabilities of the organization and seek to surround these with a collection of reproducible capabilities, or complementary assets, that enable the company to sell its distinctive capabilities in the market in which it operates.

While this is easier said than done, it defines a structure in which the processes of strategy formulation and its implementation are bound together. The resource-based view of strategy – which emphasizes rent creation through distinctive capabilities – has found its most widely accepted popularization in the core competences approach of C.K. Prahalad and Gary Hamel. But that application has been made problematic by the absence of sharp criteria for distinguishing core and other competences, which permits the wishful thinking characteristic of vision- and mission-based strategizing. Core competences become pretty much what the senior management of the corporation wants them to be.

The perspective of economic rent – which forces the question "why can't competitors do that?" into every discussion – cuts through much of this haziness.

Characteristics such as size, strategic vision, market share, and market positioning – all commonly seen as sources of competitive advantage, but all ultimately reproducible by companies with competitive advantages of their own – can clearly be seen as the result, rather than the origin, of competitive advantage.

Strategic analysis then turns outward, to identify those markets in which the company's capabilities can yield competitive advantage. The emphasis here is again on distinctive capabilities, since only these can be a source of economic rent, but distinctive capabilities need to be supported by an appropriate set of complementary reproducible capabilities.

Markets have product geographic dimensions, and different capabilities each have their own implications for the boundaries of the appropriate market. Reputations and brands are typically effective in relation to a specific customer group, and may be valuable in selling other related products to that group. Innovation-based competitive advantages will typically have a narrower product focus, but may transcend national boundaries in ways that reputations cannot. Distinctive capabilities may dictate market position as well as market choice. Those based on supplier relationships may be most appropriately deployed at the top of the market, while the effectiveness of brands is defined by the customer group that identifies with the brand.

Since distinctive capabilities are at the heart of competitive advantage, every company asks how it can create distinctive capabilities. Yet the question contains an inherent contradiction. If irreproducible characteristics could be created, they would cease to be irreproducible. What is truly irreproducible has three primary sources: market structure that limits entry; company history that by its very nature requires extended time to replicate; tacitness in relationships – routines and behavior of "uncertain imitability" – that cannot be replicated because no one, not even the participants themselves, fully comprehends their nature.

So companies do well to begin by looking at the distinctive capabilities they have rather than at those they would like to have. And established, successful companies will not usually enjoy that position if they do not enjoy some distinctive capability. Again, it is easy to overestimate the effect of conscious design in the development of companies and market structures.

The evolution of capabilities and environment

Strategy, with its emphasis on the fit between characteristics and environment, links naturally to an evolutionary perspective on organization. Processes that provide favorable feedback for characteristics that are well adapted to their environment – and these include both biological evolution and competitive market economies – produce organisms, or companies, that have capabilities matched to their requirements.

Recent understanding of evolutionary processes emphasizes how little intentionality is required to produce that result. Successful companies are not necessarily there because (except with hindsight) anyone had superior insight in organizational design or strategic fit. Rather, there were many different views of the corporate capabilities that a particular activity required; and it was the market, rather than the visionary executive, that chose the most effective match. Distinctive capabilities were established, rather than designed.

This view is supported by detached business history. Andrew Pettigrew's description of Imperial Chemical Industries shows an organization whose path was largely fixed – both for good and for bad – by its own past. The scope and opportunity for effective managerial strategic choice – good and bad – was necessarily limited by the past. This is not to be pessimistic about either the potential for strategic direction or the ability of executives to make important differences, but to reiterate the absurdity and irrelevance of using the "blank sheet of paper" approach to corporate strategy.

New paradigm

The resource-based view of strategy has a coherence and integrative role that places it well ahead of other mechanisms of strategic decision making. I have little doubt that for the foreseeable future major contributions to ways of strategic thinking will either form part of or represent development of that framework. After 30 years or so, the subject of strategy is genuinely acquiring what can be described as a paradigm – to use the most overworked and abused term in the study of management.

Summary

There may be much debate on the substance but most commentators agree, says **John Kay**, that business strategy is concerned with the match between a company's internal capabilities and its external environment. In this introductory article he argues that strategy is no longer about planning, visioning, or forecasting – all remnants of a mistaken belief that we could control the future. Rather, it is a set of analytic techniques for understanding and influencing a company's position in the market place. The author focusses particular attention on the concepts of economic rent, competitive advantage, and distinctive and reproducible capabilities.

Suggested further reading

Andrews, K.R. (1965) *The Concept of Corporate Strategy*, Homewood, IL: Irwin.

Ansoff, H.I. (1965) *Corporate Strategy*, New York: McGraw Hill.

Barney, J. (1991) "Firm resources and sustained competitive advantage," *Journal of Management*, 17.

Kay, J.A. (1996) *The Business of Economics*, Oxford: Oxford University Press.

Strategy, blind men and the elephant

By Henry Mintzberg, Bruce Ahlstrand and Joseph Lampel

We are all like the blind men and the strategy process is our elephant. Everyone has seized some part or other of the animal and ignored the rest. Consultants have generally gone for the tusks, while academics have preferred to take photo safaris, reducing the animal to a static two dimensions. As a consequence, managers have been encouraged to embrace one narrow perspective or another – like the glories of planning or the wonders of core competences. Unfortunately, the process will only work for them when they deal with the entire beast, as a living organism.

We outline below ten views of the strategy process that have been popular over the years and remain deeply embedded in our thinking about the process today, all too often disconnected from each other. We suggest how this might change.

1 The design school

The original view sees strategy formation as achieving the essential fit between internal strengths and weaknesses and external threats and opportunities. Senior management formulates clear and simple strategies in a deliberate process of conscious thought – which is neither formally analytical nor informally intuitive – so that everyone can implement the strategies. This was the dominant view of the strategy process, at least into the 1970s, and, some might argue, to the present day, given its implicit influence on most teaching and practice.

2 The planning school

The planning school grew in parallel with the design school. But, in sheer volume of publication, the planning school predominated by the mid-1970s and, though it faltered in the 1980s, it continues to be an important influence today. The planning school reflects most of the design school's assumptions except a rather significant one: that the process was not just cerebral but formal, decomposable into distinct steps, delineated by checklists, and supported by techniques (especially with regard to objectives, budgets, programs, and operating plans). This meant that staff planners replaced senior managers, *de facto*, as the key players in the process.

3 The positioning school

The third of the prescriptive schools, commonly labeled positioning, was the dominant view of strategy formation in the 1980s. It was given impetus especially by Harvard professor Michael Porter in 1980, following earlier work on strategic positioning in academe and in consulting (by the Boston Consulting Group and the PIMS project), all preceded by a long literature on military strategy, dating back to 400BC and that of Sun-tzu, author of *The Art of War*. In this view, strategy reduces to generic positions selected through formalized analyses of industry situations. Hence, planners became analysts. This proved especially lucrative to consultants and academics alike, who could sink their teeth into hard data and so promote their "scientific truths" to both companies and journals. This literature grew in all

	Design	Planning	Positioning	Entrepreneurial	Cognitive	Learning	Power	Cultural	Environmental	Configuration
Sources	P. Selznick (and perhaps earlier work, for example, by W.H. Newman), then K.R. Andrews.	H.I. Ansoff.	Purdue University work (D.E. Schendel, K.J. Hatten), then notably M.E. Porter.	J.A. Schumpeter, & others in economics.	H.A. Simon & J.G. March.	C.E. Lindblom, R.M. Cyert & J.G. March, K.E. Weick, J.B. Quinn, & C.K. Prahalad & G. Hamel.	G.T. Allison (micro), J. Pfeffer & G.R. Salancik, & W.G. Astley (macro).	E. Rhenman & R. Normann in Sweden. No obvious source elsewhere.	M.T. Hannan & J. Freeman. Contingency theorists (e.g., D.S. Pugh et al.).	A.D. Chandler, McGill University group (H. Mintzberg, D. Miller, & others), R.E. Miles & C.C. Snow.
Base discipline	None (architecture as metaphor).	Some links to urban planning, systems theory, & cybernetics.	Economics (industrial organization) & military history.	None (although early writings come from economists).	Psychology (cognitive).	None (perhaps some peripheral links to learning theory in psychology & education). Chaos theory in mathematics.	Political science.	Anthropology.	Biology.	History.
Champions	Case study teachers (especially at or from Harvard University), leadership aficionados, especially in the United States.	"Professional" managers, MBAs, staff experts (especially in finance), consultants, & government controllers – especially in France & the US.	As in planning school, particularly analytical staff types, consulting "boutiques," & military writers – especially in the US.	Popular business press, individualists, small business people everywhere, but most decidedly in Latin America & among overseas Chinese.	Those with a psychological bent – pessimists in one wing, optimists in the other.	People inclined to experimentation, ambiguity, adaptability – especially in Japan & Scandinavia.	People who like power, politics, & conspiracy – especially in France.	People who like the social, the spiritual, the collective – especially in Scandinavia & Japan.	Population ecologists, some organization theorists, splitters, & positivists in general – especially in the Anglo-Saxon countries.	Lumpers & integrators in general, as well as change agents. Configuration perhaps most popular in the Netherlands. Transformation most popular in US.
Intended messages	Fit.	Formalize.	Analyze.	Envision.	Cope or create.	Learn.	Promote.	Coalesce.	React.	Integrate, transform.
Realized messages	Think (strategy making as case study).	Program (rather than formulate).	Calculate (rather than create or commit).	Centralize (then hope).	Worry (being unable to cope in either case).	Play (rather than pursue).	Hoard (rather than share).	Perpetuate (rather than change).	Capitulate (rather than confront).	Lump (rather than split, adapt).
School category	Prescriptive.	Prescriptive.	Prescriptive.	Descriptive (some prescriptive).	Descriptive.	Descriptive.	Descriptive.	Descriptive.	Descriptive.	Descriptive & prescriptive.
Associated homily	"Look before you leap."	"A stitch in time saves nine."	"Nothin' but the facts, ma'am."	"Take us to your leader."	"I'll see it when I believe it."	"If at first you don't succeed, try, try again."	"Look out for number one."	"An apple never falls far from the tree."	"It all depends."	"To everything there is a season."

Source: *Sloan Management Review*, Spring 1999

Figure 1: Summarizing the concepts of the ten schools

directions to include strategic groups, value chains, game theories, and other ideas – but always with this analytical bent.

4 The entrepreneurial school

Meanwhile, on other fronts, mostly in trickles and streams rather than waves, wholly different approaches to strategy formation arose. Much like the design school, the entrepreneurial school centered the process on the chief executive, but unlike the design school, and in contrast to the planning school, it rooted that process in the mysteries of intuition. That shifted strategies from precise designs, plans, or positions to vague visions, or perspectives, typically to be seen through metaphor. The idea was applied to particular contexts – start-ups, niche players, privately owned companies, and "turnaround" situations – although the case was certainly put forward that every organization needs the discernment of a visionary leader.

5 The cognitive school

On the academic front, there was interest in the origin of strategies. If strategies developed in people's minds as frames, models, or maps, what could be understood about those mental processes? Particularly in the 1980s, and continuing today, research has grown steadily on cognitive biases in strategy making and on cognition as information processing. Meanwhile, another, newer branch of this school adopted a more subjective interpretative or constructivist view of the strategy process: that cognition is used to construct strategies as creative interpretations, rather than simply to map reality in some more or less objective way.

6 The learning school

Of all the descriptive schools, the learning school became a veritable wave and challenged the omnipresent prescriptive schools. Dating back to early work on "incrementalism" (the notion of a series of nibbles rather than one big bite) as well as conceptions such as "venturing," "emergent strategy" (or the growing out of individual decisions rather than being immaculately conceived), and "retrospective sense making" (that we act in order to think as much as we think in order to act), a model of strategy making as learning developed that differed from the earlier schools. In this view, strategies are emergent, strategists can be found throughout the organization, and so-called formulation and implementation intertwine.

7 The power school

A thin but quite different theme in the literature has focussed on strategy making rooted in power, in two senses. Micro power sees the development of strategies within the organization as essentially political, a process involving bargaining, persuasion, and confrontation among inside actors. Macro power takes the organization as an entity that uses its power over others and among its partners in alliances, joint ventures, and other network relationships to negotiate "collective" strategies in its interest.

8 The cultural school

Hold power up to a mirror and the reverse image seen is culture. Whereas one focusses on self-interest and fragmentation, the other focusses on common interest and integration-strategy formation as a social process rooted in culture. Again, here we find a thin stream of literature, with a concentration on the influence of culture in discouraging significant strategic change. Culture became a big issue in the American literature after the impact of Japanese management was fully realised in the 1980s and it became clear that strategic advantage can be the product of unique and difficult-to-imitate cultural factors.

9 The environmental school

Perhaps not strictly strategic management, if one takes that term as concerned with how organizations use their degrees of freedom to create strategy, an environmental school nevertheless deserves some attention for the light it throws on the demands of the environment. Here we include "contingency theory," which considers what responses are expected of organizations that face particular environmental conditions, and "population ecology," writings that claim severe limits to strategic choice.

10 The configuration school

Finally, we come to a more extensive and integrative literature and practice. One side of this school, more academic and descriptive, sees organization as configuration – coherent clusters of characteristics and behaviors – and so serves as one way to integrate the claims of the other schools: each configuration, in effect, in its own place; planning, for example, in machine-type organizations under conditions of relative stability, entrepreneurship under more dynamic configurations of start-up and turnaround. But if organizations can be described by such states, then change must be described as rather dramatic transformation – the leap from one state to another. And so a literature and practice of transformation – more prescriptive and practitioner oriented (and consultant promoted) – developed as the other side of this coin. These two very different literatures and practices nevertheless complement one another and thus, in our opinion, belong to the same school.

The beast today

This may look like a historical survey, but all of these views are very much alive and active today, even if some have been so internalized in practice that they are not recognized as such (for example, the design school).

Of course, in the affairs of writing and consulting, to succeed and to sell, champions have to defend their own positions. So they erect borders around their views while dismissing or denying others. Butcher-like – to return to our metaphor – they chop up reality for their own convenience, just as poachers snatch the elephant tusks and leave the carcass to rot.

To restate a key point in this article, such behavior ultimately does not serve the practicing manager. These people have to deal with the entire beast of strategy formation, not only to keep it as a vital force but also to impart real energy to the strategic process. The greatest failings of strategic management have occurred when managers took one point of view too seriously. This field had its obsession with planning. Then came generic positions based on careful calculations, now it is learning, and doubtless other perspectives, waiting in the wings, will be greeted with similar enthusiasm before making their exit.

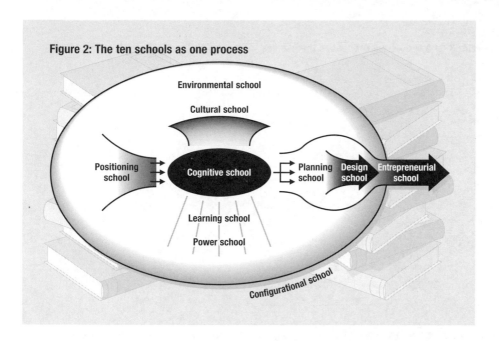

Figure 2: The ten schools as one process

Hence we find it pleasing that some of the more recent approaches to strategy formation cut across these ten schools in eclectic and interesting ways, for example learning with design in the "dynamic capabilities" approach of Gary Hamel and C.K. Prahalad.

Yes to both

Clear as the schools may be, one issue about them is not. Do they represent different processes – that is, different approaches to strategy formation – or different parts of the same process? We prefer to answer yes to both.

It is clear that some of the schools do fit in as stages or aspects around a single strategy formation process (Figure 2): the cognitive school in the head of the strategist, the positioning school to analyze historical data, and so on. Dealing with all this in the same process may seem like a tall order. But that is in the nature of the beast. Strategy formation is judgmental designing, intuitive visioning, and emergent learning; it is about transformation as well as perpetuation; it must involve individual cognition and social interaction, cooperative as well as conflictive; it has to include analyzing before and programming after as well as negotiating during; and all of this in response to what can be a demanding environment.

Yet, just as clearly, the process can tilt toward the approach of one school as it can to that of another: entrepreneurial in start-up or when there is the need for a dramatic turnaround, learning under dynamic conditions where prediction is difficult, and so on (Figure 3). Sometimes the process has to be more individually cognitive than socially interactive (in much of small business, for example). Some strategies seem to be more rationally deliberate (especially in mature mass production industries and government), while others tend to be more adaptively emergent (as in dynamic, high-technology industries).

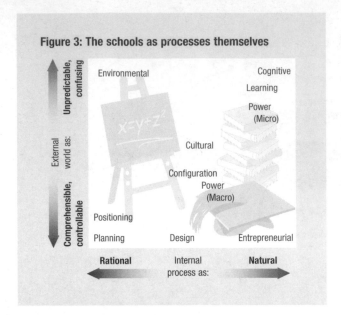

Figure 3: The schools as processes themselves

External world as:
- Unpredictable, confusing
- Comprehensible, controllable

Internal process as:
- Rational
- Natural

Environmental

Cognitive

Learning

Power (Micro)

Cultural

Configuration

Power (Macro)

Positioning

Planning

Design

Entrepreneurial

Conclusion

Scholars and consultants should certainly continue to probe the important aspects of each school, for the same reasons that biologists need to know more about the tusks, trunks and tails of elephants. But, more importantly, we must move beyond the narrowness of each school. We need to ask better questions – to allow ourselves to be pulled by concerns out there rather than pushed by concepts in here, whether in consulting or in research. In other words, we need better practice, not neater technique or theory. In addition to probing its parts, we must *pay more attention* to probing its parts, we must *pay more attention* to the integral beast of strategy formation. We shall never find it, never really see the whole. But we can certainly see it better.

Summary

Ten deeply embedded concepts typically dominate current thinking on strategy, say **Henry Mintzberg**, **Bruce Ahlstrand** and **Joseph Lampel**. These range from the early design and planning schools to the more recent learning, cultural, and environmental schools. Academics and consultants will no doubt continue to focus on narrow perspectives, but the authors suggest that business managers will be better served if they strive to see the wider picture. Some of strategic management's greatest failings, after all, have occurred when one point of view was taken too seriously. The lesson in all this is that there is a need for better practice, not neater technique or theory.

This article is based on the authors' book *Strategy Safari: A Guided Tour Through the Wilds of Strategic Management* (The Free Press and Prentice-Hall, 1998), summarized in "Reflecting on the strategy process," *Sloan Management Review* (Spring, 1999).

STRATEGY AND MICRO-ECONOMICS

2

Contributors

 **Austan Goolsbee** is an associate professor of economics at the University of Chicago Graduate School of Business. His research interests include the internet, taxes, executive compensation and government policy.

 **Robert Gertner** is a professor of economics and strategy at the University of Chicago Graduate School of Business. He teaches courses in strategic investment decisions and advanced competitive strategy. He is also principal of Lexicon Inc., a Chicago-based consulting firm.

 **Fiona Scott Morton** is an associate professor of economics and strategy at Yale University School of Management. She was formerly an assistant professor at University of Chicago Graduate School of Business.

 **Judith A. Chevalier** is professor of economics at the University of Chicago Graduate School of Business and a faculty research fellow at the National Bureau of Economic Research.

 **Luis Garicano** is an assistant professor of economics and strategy at the University of Chicago Graduate School of Business. His research interests include organizational design, contracts, specialization and strategy.

 **Thomas N. Hubbard** is an assistant professor of economics and strategy at the University of Chicago Graduate School of Business. His research interests include industrial organization, applied econometrics and economics of technology.

Contents

Introduction

Economics has provided numerous insights into the nature of organizations and their environment, and this module sets out to capture some of them. It discusses the tension between, on the one hand, economists who like to concentrate on the how and why of profit creation and, on the other, those who hand out "normative" advice and imply that somehow there is objectively a "best" way. Important concepts are introduced – the network effect, game theory, strategic complements, price competition and market entry barriers among them – and ways in which these have been applied in real situations are explored. The case of Herman Cortes, the Spanish conquistador who scuttled his ships, is colorfully described to illustrate the benefits of making an irreversible commitment.

Why the network effect is so striking

by Austan Goolsbee

One of the most important characteristics of many high-technology industries in recent years has been the prevalence of "network externalities" or "network spillovers." In simplest terms, a product has network externalities if the value to any one user rises with the total number of users who also utilize that product. A classic example is the telephone. It's not much fun if you are the only telephone subscriber in the country. The more people with phones, the more valuable yours is to you.

That some products are more valuable the more users there are must seem fairly obvious to most consumers and may appear to be a minor issue in strategy. In the last 20 years, however, both researchers and business people have noted the powerful impact that network effects have on strategy, industry structure, and company performance.

Being able to recognize and rapidly take advantage of network externalities has meant the difference between market dominance and complete oblivion in numerous industries in the last two decades. Indeed, network industries are emblematic of the "new" economy (that which some economists consider is being driven by information technology).

More recently, many business models created by internet companies are based on exploiting network externalities. This has generated even greater interest in the strategic analysis of such industries.

Three network types

There are three basic types of network externalities.

- The first is direct. This is most commonly associated with telecommunications products such as the telephone. The network benefit arises from the importance of direct connections. Industries like this include networks of fax users, networks of users who want to share word processor, spreadsheet, or similar files, or – more recently – networks of users of instantaneous online chat programs such as Mirabilis's ICQ. In each case, the value of a widely used product is greater than a less widely used one. A teenager wants the same chat program all other teenagers use. A business wants the same fax group all other businesses have. This is a direct network externality.

- The second is indirect. This is what economists would call demand side economies of scale. The classic example is the benefit that arises from using a computer system with the biggest network: more software developers will want to make products for the computer systems with the most users. Users benefit indirectly from the size of the network. A similar network effect is seen with auction-based websites like eBay, or other market creators such as the *Yellow Pages* commercial phone directories. The more potential buyers there are on eBay, the more likely sellers are to list products there (and vice versa). The more customers receiving the phone book, the more stores and services will want to pay to advertise in the book, and the more choices each customer will have. Indirect benefit for both sides tends to compound. This gives particular strength to the network externalities for online intermediaries.

■ The third is learning and word of mouth. This is somewhat unconventional, but has similar implications. In complicated high-tech products or in software, the bigger the network of people using a product, the easier it is to find out information about the goods or learn how to use them effectively. As a trivial example, the more people in your area that buy the Broderbund-manufactured computer adventure game Riven, the more people you can call to ask for hints when you get stuck. While similar to the other two, this third type of network effect is somewhat distinct. Jeff Bezos, founder and chief executive of online bookseller Amazon.com, has noted that this word-of-mouth effect is especially important for internet businesses. He says this is why Amazon spends so much time trying to improve the shopping experience for customers. Amazon is counting on consumers communicating with one another.

All three of these types of network effects can exist for the same product. Take the market for personal digital assistants (PDAs). 3Com Corp manufactures the market leader PalmPilot. It uses a different operating system to Windows CE-based devices, but nonetheless sustains market leadership. Much of this is due to the positive feedback that arises from the three types of network spillovers. The more people who own PalmPilots, the greater its value to each individual user. Part of this benefit is the direct connections that the PDA permits between users. Many PalmPilots have infrared beaming capabilities, so users can easily exchange their business cards or share software with one another when they meet. If everyone has the same system, new buyers want to be compatible. A larger part of the network spillover for the PalmPilot is the likely indirect benefit of more PalmPilot software resulting from so many PalmPilot users. Finally, the more PalmPilot users there are, the more people there are likely to be available for you to ask when you need help.

Industry differences

The main distinction between network industries and "normal" industries is that the former are much more likely to be dominated by a single company or standard. When there are network externalities, there is a positive feedback that makes current winners more likely to keep winning in the future. The bottom line is that you do not want to be playing catch-up in a network industry. The company with the installed base of customers has a great advantage. One important thing to note is that when there are major network externalities, the winning product does not necessarily need to be the one providing the best value, the most services, or the lowest price. The simple fact that a product has the largest installed base can make it the one that everyone wants to buy. Some have argued, for example, that Sony's Betamax format video-cassette recording devices were technically superior to JVC's VHS system, but they lost out. The conventional typewriter keyboard is thought by others to be slower than certain alternative keyboards, but once people learn to use the QWERTY format, it is quite difficult to get them or their companies to be the first to start using an alternative.

In some industries with network externalities, the dominant player may take some time to evolve, while in others this may happen at once. Either way, the role of positive feedback makes the power of the established customer base a very effective strategic barrier to potential new entrants to the industry, and ensures that competition between potential standards is particularly ferocious.

General strategies

All industries are different. There are some important general strategies, however, that are often employed by companies in network industries, as shown below.

Speed

The first and most important strategy in an industry with network effects is exploiting first mover advantages. Companies that can establish standards or gain an installed base in short order have significant advantages, because the value of their product will be that much higher for potential new customers. Getting patents, trademarks, and prized domain names are integral to this strategy. Sheer speed is a good strategy for industries with network spillovers.

In many ways, in the new economy there are only two kinds of companies: the quick and the dead. Although history is littered with early movers who did not succeed – Visicalc, the pioneering spreadsheet; Newton, Apple Computer's handheld organizer; Commodore 64, a product that helped fuel the home PC revolution in Europe – it is more cluttered with second movers who did not succeed. And there are many cases where companies, by developing an early, technologically adept product, created an established customer base that gave them a significant strategic advantage.

Buzz

Since the product customers want is the one that everyone else is going to have, expectations about the future are extremely important for strategic success. If a company can convince customers that its product will be the most widely accepted, this will tend to be self-fulfilling. This is where buzz comes in. Often the public is baffled by the intensity with which software or electronics companies trumpet future products that are not even close to actual production. Why should companies without a product advertise? The reason is that generating consumer buzz is a perfectly viable means of succeeding in a network industry. Before the field winnows down to a dominant player, there are many pretenders to the crown. Academic work done on strategy has shown just how important expectations about the adoption choice by future customers can be.

If e-Steel, the online steel broker, can convince potential suppliers and customers that it will be the primary selling venue in the future, it will be able to attract customers today and so gain those very network externalities. The role of marketing is especially important in this environment because coming back after falling behind is much more difficult.

Buzz is also a weapon used by incumbents in network industries when threatened by challengers. The process used is known as "vaporware." Existing players with good reputations announce that they will "soon" release a product that is even better than the new product on the market. The idea is to create doubt in the customer's mind as to whether they should consider buying the new product. After PDAs came on the market and consumers in droves began to adopt these handheld computers not based on the Windows operating system, Microsoft announced that it would create a new, scaled-down version of Windows called Windows CE. In doing so, it sought to convince some people that the new machine would not become standard. If it succeeds in convincing people to wait, it prevents the new product from gaining the early adopters it craves and the network externalities that these provide.

Reputation can also be considered a form of buzz in this sense. When International Business Machines announced that it would produce personal computers, many people figured that these would be the standard before IBM ever made a product.

Early adopters

Since the name of the game in a network industry is getting people to adopt in order to influence others, why not look for the most influential people you can find? When Silicon Graphics, now known as the broadband internet services group SGI, gets Star Wars film-maker George Lucas to use its high-end workstations, it is trying to cause important spillovers to other potential adopters. Sony believed that the main market for Betamax VCRs would be customers recording television shows. The VHS standard sought to get movies released on VHS.

Computer manufacturers try to get top computer science departments to adopt their machines (often through direct donations of equipment). All of these are examples of cases where the producer seeks to get high-profile early adopters to convince others that the product is good and will succeed.

Pricing and quality

A standard strategy in an industry with network externalities is similar to that in an industry with large economies of scale. It is penetration pricing. Every early adopter is a beachhead that will bring in others, so companies want to subsidize early use through low prices. Netscape, an early starter in web browsers, for example, gave the product away free to get people to adopt it, counting on establishing itself as the standard through network externalities among consumers. While often important, strategies such as penetration pricing are, by their nature, risky. Companies are competing for the right to dominate a market. The stakes, and potential profits, are much higher. The company that fails is likely to spend its early years losing money and then go broke. The successful company is likely to lose money in its early years and eventually become a dominant power.

There is also a great benefit to doing a better job building the product – either better quality for the same price, or lower manufacturing costs for the same quality. In many businesses with network externalities, the differences between the many products are relatively small. Innovations that lower cost allow manufacturers to charge less. In situations where there are spillovers from early adopters, this can make a tremendous difference.

Alliances

Since the companies in this area are effectively trying to set standards, it helps to have powerful allies when making strategic decisions. For companies trying to develop an internet-based personal computer that would be a non-Windows platform machine, it is important to get credible customers, credible hardware manufacturers, credible software makers, and so on to join the deal. Without this, there are no natural allies pushing for the new technology. In addition, sometimes groups can ally or merge to unite their installed bases to generate bigger network externalities. Certainly this was one motive for AOL's purchase of Netscape. It combined two of the most widely viewed sites on the internet.

When making alliances, though, it is also important to try to turn complementary products into commodities. 3Com, which makes the PalmPilot, has an incentive to get as many software developers as possible to create software for its equipment as inexpensively as possible. The cheaper these complements are, the more likely people are to adopt the Palm platform. The proprietary platform is where 3Com can make money.

Conclusion

In market after market, the last two decades have shown the immense and rising importance of network externalities. The gains from market victory have become larger, while so have the failure stakes. Recognizing network effects and responding quickly and effectively can make all the difference. Companies resistant to change or lacking a coherent strategy for making use of network externalities tend to argue that these situations are overstated. They say that there are few differences between the new and the old economy and that if they follow their well-worn course, their businesses are still likely to survive. Companies that use strategy to exploit network effects to the fullest have seen the potential gains inherent in this and decided that survival is not enough.

Summary

Network industries lie at the heart of the new, IT-driven economy – and they have inherently powerful characteristics, says **Austan Goolsbee**. From simple telephones to sophisticated personal digital assistants, the provider's advantage – as well as the value to customers – increases exponentially with the number of users. Networks therefore favor companies with a large installed customer base, but they penalize those trying to catch up. The author explains the different types of network "externalities" in today's market place, explores industry structures, and examines general strategies that can work. Speed, the ability to create buzz (basically a promise, not necessarily delivered, of greater things to come), and a focus on early adopters are among the key challenges. In the new economy there are only two kinds of companies: the quick and the dead.

Suggested further reading

Shapiro, C. and Varian, H. (1999) *Information Rules*, Boston, MA: Harvard Business School Press. An excellent business discussion of the issues involved with network externalities as well as other strategic issues for information-based businesses.

Why economics has been fruitful for strategy

by Fiona Scott Morton

The tools and techniques of strategy are changing. Instinct and experience remain important influences, but research in this area is moving away from normative lists of best practice toward discipline-based approaches such as economic modeling and the empirical testing of ideas. What disciplines such as economics and sociology offer is a coherent mental model of the world that permits structured "strategic thinking" about difficult questions.

Teachers of many of today's top MBA and executive students draw heavily on principles of micro-economics and its associated empirical work in classroom instruction. This article explains why the economic approach to strategy has been fruitful and how it differs from some other approaches.

Researchers in economics study the creation and distribution of scarce resources among people, companies, and governments. Many strategy researchers seek to understand a subset of this area – the process by which individual companies create and retain profits (meaning the monetary return to a resource, e.g. capital, land, over and above the competitive level, rather than accounting profit).

Strategy's two sides

Strategy has two sides, the positive and the normative:

- The positive side, understanding how and why profits are captured by certain parties, is straightforwardly a part of economics. It is therefore very natural that economists should make substantial contributions to strategy.
- The normative side of strategy involves researchers urging companies to follow their advice in order to earn higher profits, something that is also true of other academic disciplines like sociology and psychology when these have been used in studying management and strategy. The normative side is a less natural part of economics, and generates some tension between different types of research.

First I will explain how economists apply their tools to the positive questions and highlight the kinds of research insights that result. Then I will address the tension created by the strong normative implications of much research in strategy.

The "positive" approach

On the positive side we can ask the question: why are some companies successful? Answering this inherently involves telling a story. How can a storyteller, or modeler, create a story that is both convincing and true?

Economists create good stories by being simple, explicit, and plausible about three things: the actors involved, their goals, and the choices available to them. For example, we might want to set up a situation with two companies, one with higher variable costs than the other, where each can choose whether or not to differentiate its product for a new niche market. Serving the niche requires an investment in altering the product that will make it more valuable to a small group of consumers.

Both companies have a single goal – profit maximization. These actors, goals, and choices are starker than reality; no new entrant is allowed in this model, managers may not have other goals such as empire building, and the choice facing a company is "to differentiate or not to differentiate."

It is important to understand that no model will ever be as rich as the business world, nor would it be useful to create one that was. There is a trade-off between the complexity, and therefore reality, of the model and correctly interpreting and using the results. A good model deliberately leaves out the interesting and important features of the world that are not critical to the study at hand. The result is a crystal-clear understanding of a small piece of strategy. Interestingly, much of the debate about strategy approaches is really about the importance of factors left out across different disciplines.

A crucial part of the economic approach to strategy is the notion of equilibrium. The intuitive explanation of equilibrium is that *ex post*, if an actor could play the game again, he would not choose a different action; each actor is doing his best, given everyone else's choices and the options available to him.

To pursue the earlier example, the higher-cost Company H is earning lower profits than its rival on the standard product, and therefore finds differentiation an attractive option. Suppose that Company H will earn a higher profit by serving the niche, and so decides to invest. The lower-cost Company L will not differentiate, because it expects Company H to enter a niche that is not large enough for both companies. Now we have equilibrium: Company H will not stay out when the niche is empty. Company L does not want to enter, given that Company H is already entering. Each company is doing the best it can, taking the action of its rival as given. (NB: Many games have more than one equilibrium; changing a rival's action in order to bring the game to a different equilibrium is an exciting area of advanced strategy.)

Pause for a moment, to see why this condition is fundamental: if economists didn't have it, models could produce results where one party makes a mistake and the other's strategy works well in response to the mistake, but not under other conditions. In that situation, neither strategy should be generalized and recommended to managers! Economists focus their research on strategic interactions where all parties are achieving the most they can, and use the notion of equilibrium to avoid extolling mistakes or good luck.

Models and evidence

In short, economists have powerful tools: formal modeling, the assumption of maximizing behavior by agents, and the notion of equilibrium. Using these techniques produces crisp, testable conclusions. That is, of course, very important because we are trying to tell a believable story, which in turn depends on both the features of the model and the evidence. Do we see this strategy in the world around us? To answer that question, we first need a model with a clear prediction, and then look for data.

In a 1990 research paper, "The economics of modern manufacturing: technology, strategy, and organization," Paul Milgrom and John Roberts develop a model of complementarities among management practices. Their idea is that the profitability of a particular practice depends on what other practices are in place in the company; for example, giving workers lots of training is more profitable when the human resource strategy also empowers workers to control quality. If this is true, we should see companies using groups of complementary practices together.

Iain Cockburn, Rebecca Henderson, and Scott Stern, authors of the 1999 research paper "Balancing incentives: the tension between applied and basic research," test whether pharmaceutical companies that strongly reward academic publication are also the companies that provide a large incentive to researchers for generating useful patents. This would be the right way to structure incentives if drug discoveries by a cutting-edge researcher were more valuable than other drug discoveries. They find a positive relationship that validates the theory.

Nobel prize winner Ronald Coase, in his 1937 work "The nature of the firm," discusses how markets vary in their ability to handle particular transactions efficiently. If a free market functions well, there is less need to locate a transaction from that market inside the company. His theory implies that an inefficient market for a necessary transaction will cause the company vertically to integrate that function into the company. Kirk Monteverde and David Teece, in their 1982 paper "Supplier switching costs and vertical integration in the automobile industry," investigate which auto parts General Motors makes inhouse and which are outsourced. They find that the parts that are more complicated, where performance is harder to specify in a contract and that are therefore harder to buy successfully on the market, are those that it keeps inhouse.

The above examples are models and evidence of internal company strategy. Economics has worked longer, and had more of an impact, on competitive strategy, which studies how a company interacts with its competitors. Harold Hotelling's 1929 paper "Stability in competition" sets out the famous model of a "line" of consumers. This shows that when two companies can choose where to locate along the line, they both want to locate in the middle, nicely reflecting the location in the center by candidates for political posts seeking to capture votes from those standing between themselves and the extremes of their parties. Once prices are introduced, the situation becomes more complex. Locating close together now creates price competition, so companies will find that they can charge higher prices and earn more profit by differentiating, or separating. This is why we see more product variety in breakfast cereal than in politicians.

In his 1991 book *Sunk Costs and Market Microstructure*, John Sutton shows that in industries where advertising is important, companies affect the number of competitors in the industry. By using advertising to increase product demand, they increase the sunk cost of entry for others and therefore lower the number of companies that can "fit" in the industry. Such industries tend to have higher concentration and less competition than similar-sized industries. He tests this theory on a wide range of consumer products industries in different countries and finds that it holds.

Garth Saloner, in a 1987 paper "Predation, mergers, and incomplete information," describes a merger situation where a buyer engages in predatory pricing against its rival and target in order to convince the target that the buyer is a very efficient company. If the target believes that competition going forward will be fierce, it will lower its estimate of future returns for shareholders, and will agree to be acquired at a reduced price. In a 1986 paper, "Predatory pricing and the acquisition cost of competitors," Malcolm Burns studies American Tobacco's predatory behavior at the turn of the century; he examines the prices of American Tobacco's acquisitions and its behavior during these. He concludes that the cost to American Tobacco of using predation, and developing a reputation for using it, was offset by merger acquisition cost savings, so the strategy was successful.

Beware the cookie cutter

Although only discovered and tested as the discipline advances, economic principles hold across time and across companies. A manager can and should use them to find the best strategy for his or her particular situation. An alternative source of advice is the normative literature, the latest management "fads" seen on bestseller lists and in airport bookstores. Prescriptions in these books are too simplistic. They assume that most companies will benefit by following the advice, whereas economists tend to think that a company may have a good reason for not already following the advice. Rather than urging everyone to adopt a universally applicable strategy, the assumption underlying economic research is that, in general, the observed behavior of a group of companies is optimal. The researcher can understand the world better by finding out why one strategy was better than another for a company, not by determining which strategy was best and depicting the alternatives as a mistake.

The economic approach to strategy therefore emphasizes heterogeneity. This means that companies vary along one (or more) important dimensions that can be explicitly incorporated into the model. Characteristics such as physical assets, culture, brand image, and capabilities that distinguish your company from others also determine that the best strategy for your company is, again, different from that of others.

The cookie-cutter approach will not work, because finding a successful strategy is complex. It must work with the other features of the company. There is no "best" strategy, because a strategy must be applied to a previously existing organization, market, or product. However, although "best" will be something different in each case, the strategy is not divorced from economic principles. Instead, those principles allow a manager accurately to tailor the strategy to fit his or her company.

For the world of business this implies that when we look at an industry (or across industries), not all companies make the same strategic choices. Are some companies making mistakes? Not necessarily. Perhaps the right choice for one company is the wrong one for another. Sharon Oster, in a 1982 article "The diffusion of innovation among steel companies: the basic oxygen furnace," found that some steel companies adopted the basic oxygen furnace before others. Were those not adopting making a mistake in not pursuing the new technology? The author shows in fact that these companies had more efficient forms of the old technology and faced higher input costs if they used the new technology. Although the basic oxygen furnace was manifestly superior, these companies did not benefit as much from adopting it as new entrants, such as Japanese companies, because the former owned old plants with no other use. They maximized their profits, conditional on these old investments, by not adopting. (One could then go on to ask the more difficult question: was sinking those investments the right choice at the time?)

Andrea Shepard, in her 1993 article "Contractual form, retail price, and asset characteristics in gasoline retailing," has investigated why some retail petrol stations are vertically integrated with the oil-producing company and why others are independently operated. In some cases the petrol station has a repair shop. Because the quality of repairs is very hard to measure, it would be particularly difficult for a company to compensate, and offer good incentives to, the repair shop workers. The stations will be more profitable when the incentive to provide high-quality services is strong, so the stations are franchised or independently owned. My own 1997 work on turn-of-the-century British merchant shipping, "Entry and predation: British shipping cartels 1879–1929," shows the incumbent cartels would start a price war against some entrants but not against others. Why wasn't there one best strategy? Some entrants were financially stronger than others and the cartel correctly realized that a price war against a strong entrant would not pay off. Instead, they only fought weak entrants who could easily be driven out of the market.

This short list of work highlights an important feature of economic research in strategy: principles are enduring and do not change with management fashions, but companies are unique and must apply those principles to discover the optimal strategy for them.

Strategy is unusually normative for a social science field; the idea is not only to analyze how the world works, but to offer strategic recommendations to managers. It must therefore be the case that some managers are making mistakes and need advice from an outsider on what is the right strategy. This part of strategy has a tense relationship with an economics discipline that believes in differences between companies, efficient markets, and few wasted opportunities.

The twenty-dollar bill

A famous old joke illustrates this: two economists are strolling down the sidewalk together talking, when one of them catches sight of a twenty-dollar bill lying on the ground. One says: "Look, there's a twenty-dollar bill on the sidewalk over there." The other replies: "Don't be silly, there's no twenty-dollar bill. If there were, someone would have picked it up by now."

Competitive markets imply that economic profit, or excess risk-adjusted profit, is competed away wherever possible. Of course, there are moments when it is not possible for competitors to compete it away. For example, patents and regulations may allow a company to capture profits for some time. At other times there should not be excess profit because of the vigorous action of entrepreneurs and established companies in taking advantage of new opportunities. While a few twenty-dollar bills will always be found by chance, they should not be found in a fixed location. If this is true, what is the point of studying strategy?

One resolution of the conflict between economics and strategy lies in an observation by economist Friedrich Hayek in his 1945 paper "The use of knowledge in society." He pointed out that the fundamental problem in a market economy is the acquisition of information by the right person at the right time and place. Such information is valuable because it can be used to allocate resources efficiently, and allows the user to keep part of those gains as profit. A simple example of this is the entrepreneur who realizes that there is unmet demand for a particular product in a particular time and place. Another way to state the idea is that there are a lot of twenty-dollar bills (and some even larger) – not on the sidewalk, but available to a person with the right knowledge. For an economist, strategy is the knowledge allowing a person to find and recognize profitable information, and then make the best use of it (or sell it to someone who will). Economists in the strategy area attempt to increase our knowledge of the principles underlying the success of companies because that is the fundamental source of profit.

Summary

A lot of researchers into strategy – not to say airport bookstores – deliver prescriptions implying that those companies not following them must be making strategic mistakes. For the economist who believes in competition and efficient markets, however, this approach presents difficulties. Economics is a powerful force for analyzing strategy because it studies the creation and distribution of resources. This knowledge is crucial to creating and retaining profit, in its widest sense. Economists are therefore comfortable with the side of strategy that seeks to explain how and why businesses capture profit. But as **Fiona Scott Morton** explains, there is tension when it comes to handing out "normative" advice. Highlighting key findings from recent economic research, the author argues that there is no "best" strategy because strategy must always be applied to a particular organization, market, or product – the right choice for one company may therefore be the wrong one for another.

Suggested further reading

Brander, J. and Lewis, T. (1986) "Oligopoly and financial structure: the limited liability effect," *American Economic Review*, 76 (5).

Bulow, J.I., Geanakoplos, J.D. and Klemperer, P.D. (1985) "Multimarket oligopoly: strategic substitutes and complements," *Journal of Political Economy*, 93 (3), June: 488–511.

Burns, M. (1986) "Predatory pricing and the acquisition cost of competitors," *Journal of Political Economy*, 94 (2).

Chevalier, J. (1995) "Do LBO supermarkets charge more? An empirical analysis of the effects of LBOs on supermarket pricing," *Journal of Finance*, 50 (4).

Coase, R. (1937) "The nature of the firm," *Economica*, 4.

Cockburn, I., Henderson, R. and Stern, S. (1999) "Balancing incentives: the tension between applied and basic research," NBER working paper No 6882.

Garicano, L. (1999) *Hierarchies and the Organization of Knowledge in Production*, mimeo Graduate School of Business, University of Chicago.

Ghernawat, P. (1987) *DuPont in Titanium Dioxide, Case No 384140*, Cambridge, MA: Harvard Business School Publishing.

Hayek, F. (1945) "The use of knowledge in society," *American Economic Review*, 35 (4).

Hotelling, H. (1929) "Stability in competition," *Economic Journal*, 39: 41–57.

Milgrom, P. and Roberts, D.J. (1990) "The economics of modern manufacturing: technology, strategy, and organization," *American Economic Review*, 80 (3).

Monteverde, K. and Teece, D. (1982) "Supplier switching costs and vertical integration in the automobile industry," *Bell Journal of Economics*, 13 (1).

Oster, S. (1982) "The diffusion of innovation among steel companies: the basic oxygen furnace," *Bell Journal of Economics*, 13 (1).

Saloner, G. (1987) "Predation, mergers, and incomplete information," *RAND Journal of Economics*, 18 (2).

Scott Morton, F. (1997) "Entry and predation: British shipping cartels 1879–1929," *Journal of Economics and Management Strategy*, 6 (4).

Shepard, A. (1993) "Contractual form, retail price, and asset characteristics in gasoline retailing," *RAND Journal of Economics*, 24 (1).

Showalter, D. (1995) "Oligopoly and financial structure: comment," *American Economic Review*, 85 (3).

Spence, A.M. (1977) "Entry capacity, investment and oligopolistic pricing," *Bell Journal of Economics*, 8 (2).

Sutton, J. (1991) *Sunk Costs and Market Microstructure*, Cambridge, MA: MIT Press.

Game theory: how to make it pay

by Luis Garicano

Should Boeing, the US aircraft maker, lower the price of its 737 model in the face of competition from the European Airbus? Or should Wal-Mart, the US retail giant, enter the internet book-distribution business?

In answering these questions, Boeing and Wal-Mart would need to weigh the expected response of their rivals. Boeing must recognize that Airbus may react to its price cut with another reduction in price, possibly heralding an industry price war. Similarly, Wal-Mart must consider that its entry into the book-distribution business may generate a strong reaction from present incumbents Amazon.com and BarnesandNoble.com. In both cases, the tools developed by game theorists are likely to be helpful.

Before mathematician John von Neumann and economist Oscar Morgenstern published their pioneering book, *Theory of Games and Economic Behaviour*, in 1944, economists were ill equipped to make proper analyses of the strategic interaction between companies. Serious study was limited to situations in which there were either too many rivals for interactions to matter (what economists call perfect competition) or no rivals at all (the monopoly case). The arrival of game theory greatly expanded the scope of analysis not only in business strategy, but also in fields as diverse as litigation, evolutionary biology, and political science.

Analysis of simultaneous decisions

Suppose your company is one of only two in a mature consumer goods industry. The industry generates total profits of $100m, divided up equally between both of you. Your company must decide whether to undertake an advertising campaign, which will cost $30m. After some research, you conclude that since the industry is mature, an advertising campaign will not expand the size of the market. However, you find that consumers are very image conscious, so that if one company advertises and the other does not, market share at the company that advertises will increase to 90 percent. This results in gross profits exclusive of advertising increasing from $50m to $90m, an increase in net profits from $50m to $60m, and a corresponding reduction in profits for the rival company not advertising, from $50m to $10m. If both of you advertise, your respective market shares remain constant, with a reduction in net profits equal to the advertising expenditure. The table in Figure 1 (which is usually referred to as the strategic form of the game) presents the situation that both of you face. The figures in brackets represent the net profits that

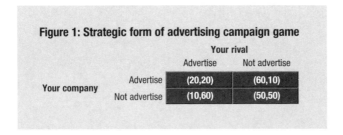

Figure 1: Strategic form of advertising campaign game

		Your rival	
		Advertise	Not advertise
Your company	Advertise	(20,20)	(60,10)
	Not advertise	(10,60)	(50,50)

you (the first figure) and your rival (the second figure) obtain in each one of the four possible outcomes.

No matter what your rival does, you are always better off if you do advertise. If your rival does not advertise, you do better by advertising and stealing some of the rival's market share (you earn $60m instead of $50m). If your rival advertises, your profits are $20m if you defend yourself by advertising, rather than $10m if you allow for the market share loss. In the jargon of game theory, advertising is a dominant strategy and not advertising is a dominated strategy: no matter what your rival does, you are always better off if you advertise.

Your rival's problem is identical to yours. He is also better off by advertising regardless of what you do. The game is solved by eliminating the dominated strategies. The outcome of the game is in the upper left corner of the matrix in Figure 1: both of you advertise, and get $20m profits. Note that this outcome is considerably worse than the $50m net profit you would have achieved if the two of you had chosen not to advertise.

Thus each player's individual incentives lead them to play a strategy that leaves both worse off. This unfortunate outcome is likely to take place as long as you confront each other only once, so that reputation considerations are not present. (The situation depicted is a collective action dilemma first formally analyzed in the 1950s in the classic prisoner's dilemma game, *see* p. 36).

Only changing the rules of the game would allow for a different result. A later article in *Mastering Strategy,* dealing with price competition, will review and discuss the ways in which companies and individuals can avoid falling into this kind of trap, particularly in the context of repeatedly confronting the same opponent.

That the advertising campaign game above resembles a prisoner's dilemma is a consequence of the structure of profits associated with the player's actions. Changes in payoff alter the strategy played and thence the outcome of the game.

Suppose, for example, your company is dominant in this $100m industry, capturing 70 percent of profitability. You are confronted with a small, growing rival. Your market research has shown that a $30m advertising campaign has a much larger effect on the sales of this "hip" upstart than on your own sales. If your rival advertises and you don't, your rival's share of gross profits is likely to increase by 40 percentage points, to $70m gross of advertising costs for a $40m net profit. Your own profits will simultaneously decrease by 40 points of the total profits to $30m. If you advertise and your rival does not, your share increases by only 10 points to generate profits of $80m exclusive of advertising costs, while your rival's profits decrease to $20m. If both of you advertise, your rival's share of the gross profits increases by 15 points with total profits exclusive of advertising costs of $45m ($15m net of advertising cost), while your own share of the gross falls from $70m to $55m ($25m net of advertising costs). The game matrix is now as follows (*see* Figure 2):

Figure 2: Strategic form of the asymmetric advertising campaign game

		Your rival	
		Advertise	Not advertise
Your company	Advertise	(25,15)	(50,20)
	Not advertise	(30,40)	(70,30)

You have a dominant strategy, which is not to advertise. If your rival does not advertise, you do better by not advertising and preserving your large advantage. If your rival does advertise, you still do better by not incurring the $30m advertising cost simply to recover 25 points of market share or $25m. This is a problem. Your rival, knowing that not advertising is your dominant strategy, needs to choose between not advertising and getting $30m net profit or advertising and making profits of $40m. Clearly, your rival will choose to advertise. The outcome of the game is on the lower left corner, and your profitability is $30m, instead of $70m.

Setting up the game makes it clear that if you do nothing to change the way the game is played, you are likely to end up very close to your worst outcome. What can be done about this? Imagine you could commit to advertise no matter what. If you could do this, your rival would choose not to advertise and the outcome of the game would be in the upper right corner – net profits of $50m for you and $20m for your rival. The problem is that such a commitment is not credible. Your rival knows that, faced with its ads, you will always choose not to advertise, since that leaves you *ex post* better off. Again, to make your move credible, your company needs to change the rules of the game. We discuss some ways to do this later.

Nash Equilibrium

Not all games can be solved through the elimination of dominated strategies. Imagine a new twist to your advertising problem. You need to decide whether you are going to use the ATP men's tennis tour or the US PGA golf tour as your promotion vehicle. Both you and your rival prefer tennis, since it has a larger audience. However, both of you prefer not to go head on against the other by picking the same vehicle, since the tour would then extract really high prices from your participation. Figure 3 presents the estimated profits, in millions of dollars, that you and your rival will obtain from each choice.

What is the solution to this game? First, note that no strategy dominates another. If your rival picks tennis (ATP) you would rather pick golf (PGA), since above all you want to avoid head-on competition. However, if your rival were to pick golf, you would rather pick tennis. In the jargon of game theory, the game is not "dominance solvable."

The solution concept that economists apply to this kind of game is Nash Equilibrium, named after its author and Nobel prize winner John Nash. A Nash Equilibrium is a pair of strategies such that each player can do no better by unilaterally shifting strategies. In other words, at a Nash Equilibrium, each player plays the best response to the other player's strategy.

In the game above, your choice of ATP and your rival's choice of PGA is a Nash Equilibrium, since neither you unilaterally moving away from ATP nor your rival unilaterally moving away from PGA can make either of you better off. Similarly,

Figure 3: Advertising vehicle game

		Your rival	
		Advertise in ATP	Advertise in PGA
Your company	Advertise in ATP	(10,10)	(40,20)
	Advertise in PGA	(20,40)	(5,5)

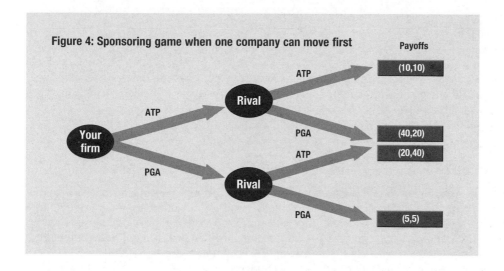

Figure 4: Sponsoring game when one company can move first

your choice of PGA and your rival's choice of ATP is also a Nash Equilibrium.

As in the asymmetric advertising campaign example, we can use our analysis of the competitive situation to come up with ways to improve outcomes. The way to do this is to change the rules of the game. Imagine that your company can grab the initiative and pre-empt its rival. For example, your company could publicly announce that it was going to advertise in the ATP. This would then lead to a sequential move game. To analyze such a game, we need to introduce some new tools.

Sequential games, commitments and credibility

Backward induction

Until now, we have analyzed situations in which the two players move simultaneously, in the sense that each of them reaches a decision without knowing what the other is doing. The game of selecting which tour to sponsor calls for the possibility that one rival can pre-empt the other by moving first. Although a suitably modified matrix along the lines of the one in Figure 3 could be used to present the sequential game, game theorists usually prefer to present sequential games with the help of an inverted tree diagram like that in Figure 4 (called the extensive form of the game).

To solve this type of sequential game, game theorists use "backward induction": you first determine what your rival will do in each case in the last period of the game and then decide what is best to do, given what it is doing. When you choose the ATP, your rival prefers sponsoring the PGA and so gaining $20m over competing head on with you and getting only $10m. If you advertise in the PGA, your rival prefers advertising in ATP and making $40m rather than facing you in PGA and earning just $5m. Thus you know that when you can move first, which is your best choice, you should announce that you will sponsor the ATP. In this case, your rival will certainly advertise in the PGA.

The Prisoner's Dilemma

The original story involves two criminals who are arrested after committing a serious crime. The police have no proof of their involvement except for a minor infraction. The prosecutor offers them a deal whereby the one who implicates the other escapes all punishment and the other gets a heavy prison sentence. If both implicate the other, both end up in prison for a long time. The dominant strategy is for each criminal to implicate the other. Consequently, they both end up getting relatively heavy prison sentences.

The battle of the sexes

The game in Figure 3 is an example of a paradigmatic game called "battle of the sexes." In these games, players want to coordinate their actions, but they have different preferences on where they want to coordinate. In the (politically incorrect) example that gives the name to this class of games, a husband and a wife want to coordinate their choice for an evening out. The husband prefers to go to a football game and the wife prefers to go to the theater; but they both prefer to do together any of the two activities than to do their preferred one alone. A notable business situation that has a similar structure is standard setting. Two companies want to coordinate on one standard, but each company prefers to adopt its own technology as the standard.

Commitment and credibility

We have transformed the interaction in a sequential interaction by allowing your company to move first. In practice, moving first in this context means that you commit to advertise on the ATP no matter what. If you can credibly bind yourself to advertising on the ATP, you will avoid a costly rivalry.

Just announcing your intention to advertise on the ATP is clearly not enough to convert the game in Figure 3 into a sequential game. A rival who doubts your intention could still try to force the other equilibrium outcome, knowing that faced with a true *fait accompli* you will retreat in the end. So to change the outcome of the game you need credibly to commit to your advertising strategy. How do you do this?

In *Thinking Strategically*, their excellent non-technical introduction to game theory, Princeton University's Avinash K. Dixit and Yale University's Barry J. Nalebuff propose a taxonomy of the ways in which actors can commit in advance to an action that could, after their rivals have made their move, be non-rational. They suggest, for example, writing contracts; building a reputation for never backing down; or burning your bridges and taking decisions that make it impossible to back down.

Entry deterrence

An important example of a sequential game is the problem of entry deterrence. Here, a potential participant in a new market must decide whether to enter or not. The entrant knows that the incumbent is most likely to accommodate the entry once confronted with the entrant. The incumbent's problem is then credibly to commit to a strategy that it knows will not be optimal later (such as lowering prices after entry has taken place), in order to alter the entrant's strategy and deter it from entering the market in the first place.

Games of entry deterrence have an identical formal structure to the "nuclear deterrence game" once played by the US and the USSR. The US needed credibly to commit to a strategy that was, *ex post*, glaringly irrational, such as blowing up the world for some "minor" invasion in western Europe. If the US could tie its hands in this way, it could avoid a first-strike invasion in western Europe by the USSR. In his seminal game theoretical analysis of nuclear strategies, *The Strategy of Conflict* (1960), Thomas Shelling noted paradoxically: "The power to constrain an adversary may depend on the power to bind oneself."

Information

The deterrence example raises most clearly a problem that we have ignored until now. Each player is often confused over where his or her rivals are at each point. The players are left with important uncertainty about questions such as: will my rival back down? Will he or she believe my threat? Most recent game theory research deals with games of "incomplete information," in which players have asymmetric information about payoffs. The box below on US airwave auctions gives a flavor of some of this analysis.

Game theory in action: designing the US airwaves auction

In 1993 the US Congress decided to auction off licenses to use the electromagnetic spectrum for personal communication services. This involved selling off thousands of licenses with different geographic coverage and at different spectrum locations.

Auctioning off the licenses was a break with the tradition of direct license allocation to those with a bigger "need." It required the Federal Communications Commission to set up a mechanism capable of efficiently allocating licenses to the bidder most valuing them. Game theory (and game theorists) played an important role in both the design of the actual auction mechanism used and in advising bidders on optimal bidding strategies.

Auctions are, *a priori*, an ideal method for allocating goods to those who place a higher value on them, as these people are likely to make the highest bid. However, research by game theorists has shown that the design of the auction matters, both for the efficiency of the allocation – does the good go to the person who values it most? – and the revenues earned for the seller. In this particular instance, Congress had asked the FCC to ensure that the spectrum was used in an efficient and intensive way, rather than simply to maximize auction income for the Federal Government.

According to an account in the *Journal of Economics Perspectives*, by two of the economists involved in the design (Preston McAfee of Texas A&M and John McMillan of University of California, San Diego), the designers considered the existence of complementarities between the licenses the most important threat to efficiency in this particular context.

For the bidder, the value of each individual license depends to a large extent on whether another license has been obtained so that several licenses can be grouped together to form a coherent region. The auction design needed to allow for the coherent aggregation of licenses, so that a bidder would not find himself bidding for a license as a part of a whole to discover that he is in fact awarded an incoherent entity of much smaller value to him or her.

Following the advice of several economic theorists employed by the bidders, including Stanford economists Paul Milgrom and Robert Wilson, plus McAfee and McMillan, the FCC opted for a novel design: a simultaneous ascending auction, in which the bidding for all the licenses remained open as long as bidding in any of the licenses remained active. The aggregation of licenses was facilitated by the fact that bidding and the observation of the bids were simultaneous.

For all the advantages, the simultaneous ascending auctions involved an important risk of implicit collusion between rival bidders. To avoid this problem, the identity of the bidder would remain hidden until the auction concluded. But it was still possible for a bidder to find ways to signal its intention in order to ensure allocation of the preferred license at low cost. In fact, as subsequent portions of the spectrum were auctioned off, complaints about this type of behavior increased. For example, Mercury PCS, a US telecoms operator, was accused of highlighting its interest in winning a specific license by ending the bid amount in January 1997 with the postal codes of the particular city in which it was interested.

On the bidders' side, the consultants to the bidders have not made public their recommendations. We can only speculate that game theory was used by bidders both to enhance the rationality of their bidding and to understand and influence the bidding behavior of the rival bidders.

First, game theory could introduce a higher degree of rationality in the bidding process by helping to design optimal bidding strategies. For example, game theorists have long understood that in auction settings bidding as much as one would be actually willing to pay for a good could lead to what is known as the winner's curse: imagine that a license will be in fact equally valuable to any firm, but that each firm has a different opinion about how valuable it is likely to be. Clearly, the winning bid is most likely to be from the most optimistic firm. But the most optimistic firm's estimate of the value of the audio waves will be biased upward – it will be too high – even when the estimate by each individual bidder is unbiased. In fact, if the highest bidder wins without taking into account this effect, it will overpay, and winning will be a curse. Developing an algorithm for bidding that takes into account this curse requires the use of game theory.

Game theory could also be used by a bidder to understand the incentives of rival bidders and formulate strategies capable of altering their behavior. In particular, if one could credibly commit to winning a license, one could win the license at zero cost, as the incentives for the rivals to bid when they know they are not going to win the license are likely to be low. An actual example of this could be the allocation in the April 1997 sale of wireless date frequencies of the licenses for several cities, like Minneapolis, for $1.

To sum up, by identifying the individual incentives of each player in each auction design, game theory helped the designers and consultants in understanding the impact of the rules of the game on the behavior of the actors. As McAfee and McMillan put it in their account: "The role of theory is to show how people behave in various circumstances, and to identify the trade-offs involved in altering those circumstances."

The uses and limits of game theory

Unlike other tools devised by economists that can be applied directly to produce numerical solutions (such as demand curves or the Black-Scholes option pricing model), game theory must not be used actually to "solve" the game and produce a numerical answer. The reason for this is that the solutions to the games are often too sensitive to the assumptions that the modeler makes about the timing of the moves, the information available to the players and the rationality of their decisions. The simple sponsoring game presented in Figure 4 makes the point very clearly. The extent to which one player can be assumed to have information about the other's irrevocable sponsoring decision before taking a decision crucially affects the outcome of the game.

Instead, game theory's greatest use is in obtaining insights about the structure of interaction between the players, not only to learn what is the right way to play the game, but also to understand existing possibilities and consequences of changing game rules.

If, for example, Boeing understands that its price competition with Airbus is a prisoner's dilemma, it can change the rule of the game to remove the incentives that both it and Airbus have to engage in a price war. Similarly, Wal-Mart, faced with a threat from Amazon to employ deep price cuts to discourage its entry into internet book distribution, needs to understand Amazon's incentives to follow through with its threat, in order to be better equipped for a decision. A later article in this book discusses how to combine game theory with scenario planning to develop a decision-making tool for complex strategic interactions and sensitive to its limitations.

Summary

Unlike many other tools devised by economists, game theory should not be used to produce numerical answers to a problem. It is most beneficial, says **Luis Garicano**, in obtaining insights into the way players in a market interact in specific circumstances. Such an approach can help participants not only learn the "right" way to play, but also understand competitor behavior, and what is likely to happen if they alter the rules. Game theory has greatly expanded the scope of analysis for business strategy, sharpening corporate competitiveness and advancing policy. It has also spilled over into fields like litigation, evolutionary biology, and political science.

Suggested further reading

Baird, D.G., Gertner, R.H. and Picker, R.C. (1994) *Game Theory and the Law*, Cambridge, MA: Harvard University Press.

Brandenburger, A.M. and Nalebuff, B.J. (1996) *Co-opetition*, New York, NY: Doubleday.

Dixit, A.K. and Nalebuff, B.J. (1993) *Thinking Strategically*, New York, NY: W.W. Norton & Co.

Gibbons, R. (1992) *Game Theory for Applied Economists*, Princeton, NJ: Princeton University Press.

Kreps, D.M. (1992) *Game Theory and Economic Modelling*, Oxford: Oxford University Press.

The dynamics of price competition

by Luis Garicano and Robert Gertner

Nothing wipes out profits like price competition. Companies in industries such as personal computer retailing and book selling earn little money, largely because of intense price competition. Despite its strategic importance and central place in economics, it remains difficult to predict differences in price competition across industries and over time within industries. There are no simple, robust rules. Yes, price competition is on average less intense in more concentrated industries, but the relationship is surprisingly weak. There are many concentrated industries – like commercial aircraft – where price competition is intense, just as there are unconcentrated industries that have limited price competition, credit cards for example.

In most industries, companies choose the prices at which they sell. Of course, this is constrained by the actions of competitors and consumers, but nonetheless it is a choice. Yet the press often refers to the "outbreak of a price war" as though it were a contagious disease rather than the result of conscious decisions by companies believing that they are acting in their own interests. The intriguing reality, as we shall explain, is that price wars often lower or destroy industry profits.

Price wars

The logic of price competition was first captured in a simple model by nineteenth-century French economist Joseph Bertrand. The model is as follows. Suppose that your company and another company are the only producers of a certain good. There is only one potential client, who would be willing to pay up to $50 per unit for a contract of 10,000 units of this good. The good costs $10 to produce, including a normal economic return on the capital employed and on managerial time. The company offering the lowest price wins the contract; if the price is tied, the contract is shared between the two.

You could both charge $50, and divide up the contract. Each one would make $200,000 profit on it. This strategy is not, however, individually optimal. If your rival charges $50, you can reduce your price to $49.90, win the contract, and increase your profits to $399,000, leaving your rival out of the market. Clearly, the same thought occurs to your rival. At any price higher than $10, the two of you can improve your individual situation by undercutting the other and obtaining the entire contract.

Only when both of you are charging $10, and getting a return just high enough to make you stay in the market, is there no incentive for either of you to undercut the other. In the language of game theory, $10 is the only Nash Equilibrium of this game – the only price at which either of you cannot individually improve his or her own situation by reducing prices. But if the two of you charge $10, you are much worse off than you could have been had you shared the contract at $50.

Although the game that Bertrand analyzed is a simplified version of the pricing problem confronted by companies in markets with few competitors, the logic of the example still applies when some of its assumptions are weakened. It is generally the case that the individual incentive to cut prices by each participant in the industry leads to prices that leave each participant collectively worse off. For example, if two competitors sell products that are imperfect substitutes, undercutting one's rival by a small amount will not steal the entire market. This mitigates the incentive to cut price and avoids the stark results of zero profits, but still leads to prices below levels that maximize the joint profits of the two companies.

Price reactions

The most important oversimplification of the Bertrand model of price competition is its one-shot, static set-up. In fact, virtually all price competition includes the possibility to react to a competitor's price decisions. A simple example of two adjacent retail petrol stations in a town illustrates the basic dynamics. For simplicity, we will assume that there are no other petrol stations in town and that the town is somewhat isolated. To customers, one station's petrol is a perfect substitute for the other, so that if prices are unequal, the lower-priced station will attract all the demand. Assume that both stations initially charge the full monopoly price (that price maximizing the joint profits of the two stations). What happens if Station A, following Bertrand's logic, lowers its price by one cent per gallon? The manager of Station B will observe the price change as soon as his rival manager gets out a ladder and changes the sign. Knowing that this small price difference will reduce sales to zero, Station B's manager will surely respond by matching the price cut. Station A's manager, anticipating this response, should not lower his price in the first place. The outcome is the exact opposite of Bertrand's result – full monopoly pricing, rather than fully competitive pricing.

We have oversimplified, but the example does demonstrate a fundamental logic of price competition. A company considering a price cut should bear in mind the entire impact of the price cut on profits. This includes the impact of any anticipated competitive response. If a company can anticipate price matching or even a more aggressive punishment by a rival, a price cut may be unprofitable.

Questions that the potential price cutter must answer include: by how much can I increase market share before rivals respond, how will rivals respond, and what impact will the post-response set of prices have on my profits? The petrol station example involves a set of assumptions that make it easy to answer these questions and so predict a cooperative outcome. Among such assumptions are: price starts at the monopoly level, both competitors implicitly agree on what that level is, each observes the other's price immediately and without cost, consumers observe both prices simultaneously and at no cost, there are only two petrol stations and no relevant substitutes, and price changes are inexpensive.

However, most markets have more complex features than this gas station example, making prediction more difficult; the key is understanding how to answer our basic questions in more complex environments. We now explore these issues.

Industry conditions that affect the degree of price competition

If all companies in an industry could get together and negotiate binding contracts setting each company's prices and production, and also including payments across companies, it is possible that they could reach an agreement that maximized industry profits. Such an agreement might be difficult to achieve as each company angled for a greater share of the profits. Of course, no court would enforce such an agreement, the very discussion of which probably violates antitrust laws.

The problem of coordinating at monopoly prices without violating antitrust laws is much more difficult, although a dynamic strategy such as tit-for-tat could achieve this outcome. The coordination process may be especially difficult when the objective is a price increase rather than prevention of a price cut. This is seen in the back-and-forth behavior of the airlines after an attempt at raising prices (*see* Table 1 on p. 42). We discuss here some of the factors that will make more likely implicitly cooperative outcomes through the use of variants of such strategies.

1. The number of companies in an industry

Cooperative pricing becomes more difficult as the number of companies increases. Coordination becomes more complex and less likely. Imagine the problems of coordinating price and quantity choices among many competing companies when communication is severely limited by antitrust laws.

The presence of many companies may lead to reduced incentive to punish a price cut. A company that cannot achieve a large market share may be able to avoid a response, because the impact on other companies may be small relative to margins lost from responding. Also, observation of a rival's prices may become more difficult as the number of companies grows. As we explain below, differences among companies are likely to increase as the number of companies rises. An example of the difficulty of maintaining cooperation with large numbers of players is the Organization of Petroleum Exporting Countries, the oil cartel. Despite being able to raise prices and assign quotas in a manner that would be illegal if undertaken by individual producers in a country, OPEC has on each occasion finally failed to maintain high prices, in spite of occasional periods of success. One reason is that for any individual producer nation, increasing the amount of oil it pumps beyond its quota is profitable, as the reduction in its own revenues on the units it has already sold (not the revenues of the cartel, which do not enter this calculation) is more than offset by the increase in revenue due to the increase in the number of barrels sold.

Table 1: A variant of tit-for-tat in the airline industry in 1998

Date	Action
• March	Northwest begins sale on 14-day advance purchase fares. Others match.
• April	Continental tries to raise leisure fares $20 round-trip twice. Other carriers match, but Northwest blocks both attempts.
• May	Northwest initiates 25% sale on 21-day advance-purchase fares. Others match. Later, Continental tries a 5% increase on non-sale leisure fares. United, American, Delta and USAir all match, but not Northwest. Increase is rolled back.
• July	Continental raises leisure fares $20 round-trip; Northwest blocks.
August 11	Delta and American raise fares by 4%, Northwest blocks.
August 14	American raises fares by 4% in markets not served by Northwest; carriers other than Northwest match.
August 17	Delta rolls back the increases; other airlines follow.
August 18	Northwest raises fares by 4%. All other carriers match the increase.
August 19	Northwest rescinds fare hike; US Airways and TWA match same day.
August 20	American, Delta, Continental match reversal; other carriers follow.
August 21	Northwest hikes fares by 4%, other carriers match.

Source: PaineWebber Airline Research, *WSJ*, authors' elaboration.

2. Differences among the companies in an industry

Unlike our two petrol stations, no companies are exactly like their rivals. Companies differ in cost structure, capacity, product quality, existing market share, product characteristics, and product range. These differences make coordination more complex. The OPEC problem is not just a result of the number of member countries, but of differences in extraction costs, levels of reserves, wealth, refining interests, and political motives. Of course, as the number of companies increases, the differences among them are also likely to proliferate.

If companies differ, they may not even agree on a single cooperative price – a low-cost company will prefer all companies to charge a lower price than a high-cost company. If companies differ, one company may find that it can cut price without inducing a response from rivals, or one company may prefer low prices even if there is a competitive response. A new entrant into a market where market shares are quite stable may have an incentive to enter with low prices for either of these reasons. An incumbent may not respond because the loss in margin on all its customers may be greater than the small loss of share to the entrant. Even if all incumbents match the entrant's low price, the low price may attract new customers to the market. The entrant may get a disproportionate share of the new customers because they have no ties to the incumbents. An example of price cutting by entrants is in the US wireless telephone market, where PCS companies, the first generation of digital wireless carriers, have entered with prices well below those of the two incumbent carriers.

The prisoner's dilemma in practice: tit-for-tat in the First World War trenches

The "price war game" is an example of the general game a *prisoner's dilemma*. In these games, the individual incentive of each player to defect (in the pricing game, to reduce prices) leads both players to a situation that leaves them collectively worse off. The original story involves two criminals who are arrested after committing a serious crime. The police have no proof of their involvement except for a minor infraction. The prosecutor offers them a deal whereby the one who implicates the other escapes all punishment and the other gets a heavy prison sentence. If both implicate the other, both end up in prison for a long time. The dominant strategy is for each criminal to implicate the other. Consequently, they both end up getting relatively heavy prison sentences.

When the game is repeated, however, cooperation can be sustained implicitly through dynamic strategies. In his classic book *The Evolution of Co-operation*, University of Michigan political scientist Robert Axelrod studied empirically and experimentally the strategies that lead players involved in prisoner's dilemma-type situations to cooperative outcomes. His starting point was an unexpected experimental result. When experts were asked to submit strategies for repeated prisoner's dilemma games and these strategies were matched with each other in a computer tournament, tit-for-tat, the simplest strategy, won. This was a strategy that simply started cooperating and then did to the other player what that player had done to it previously.

Axelrod's analysis of the data found that tit-for-tat had four properties making a strategy successful. A successful strategy should be nice: confronted with a cooperative player, it should reciprocate. It should also be provocable: faced with an uncalled defection, it should respond. It should be forgiving: after responding to a defection, it should go back to cooperation. And it should be *easy to understand*: other players should be able to anticipate the consequences of their actions.

Axelrod presents a surprising example of the usefulness of a variant of this strategy: First World War trench warfare. Here is a summary of his account:

"The historical situation in the quiet sectors along the Western Front was a [repeated] prisoner's dilemma. At any time, the choices of two small units facing each other are to shoot to kill or deliberately to shoot to avoid causing damage. For both sides, weakening the enemy is important because it promotes survival. Therefore, in the short run it is better to do damage now whether the enemy is shooting back or not.

"What made trench warfare so different from most other combat was that the same small units faced each other in immobile sectors for extended periods of time. This changed the game from a one-move prisoner's dilemma in which defection is the dominant choice, to an iterated prisoner's dilemma in which conditional strategies are possible. The result accorded with the theory's predictions: with sustained interaction, the stable outcome could be mutual cooperation based upon reciprocity [emphasis added]. In particular, both sides followed strategies that would not be the first to defect, but that would be provoked if the other defected.

"As the lines stabilised, non-aggression between the troops emerged spontaneously in many places along the front. The earliest instances may have been associated with meals which were served at the same times on both sides of no-man's land. An eyewitness noted that: 'In one section the hour of 8 to 9 a.m. was regarded as consecrated to private business, and certain places indicated by a flag were regarded as out of bounds by the snipers on both sides.' In the summer of 1915 [a soldier noted that] 'It would be child's play to shell the road behind the enemy's trenches, crowded as it must be with ration wagons and water carts, into a bloodstained wilderness, but on the whole there is silence. After all, if you prevent your enemy from drawing his rations, his remedy is simple: he will prevent you from drawing yours.'

"The strategies were provocable. During the periods of mutual restraint, the enemy soldiers took pains to show to each other that they could indeed retaliate if necessary. For example, German snipers showed their prowess to the British by aiming at spots on the walls of cottages and firing until they had cut a hole." (*Extracted from Chapter 4 of* The Evolution of Co-operation, *by Robert Axelrod, 1990, Penguin Books. © Richard Axelrod, 1984. Reproduced by permission of Penguin Books Ltd.)

3. The short-run gain from cutting prices

To the extent that the benefit of undercutting high prices is small, the temptation to "cheat" on an implicit high price agreement by lowering prices is also small. Two main factors may reduce the gains from short-run price cuts: high capacity utilization and high product differentiation. If little or no excess capacity exists, then little benefit in the form of higher sales can be derived from cutting prices. On the other hand, if a company has excess capacity, there is a large incentive to reduce price and use additional capacity, particularly if the company enjoys a low marginal cost relative to prevailing prices. For example, the return to an airline from filling an empty seat, or a hotel from filling an empty room, creates a strong incentive to cut price.

Similarly, a large degree of product differentiation between competing products also reduces the gains from undercutting the prices of rivals. If product differentiation is high, the increase in sales that a company may derive from reducing its prices is small, as consumers of the other products are less likely to switch to a product that they do not perceive as a close substitute to the one they consume.

4. Price transparency

In order to respond effectively to a rival's price cut, one must know that a price cut occurred. If secret price cuts are possible, matching of price cuts is slow or non-existent, and the incentive to cut prices is higher. The incentive to cut prices is smaller the more transparent the market, as price cuts are more easily matched in such a case. As a consequence, markets where prices or other sale conditions arise out of complex, private negotiations are less likely to result in monopolistic pricing. Implicit coordination becomes especially difficult when companies cannot observe their rivals' competitive actions – a company must infer a rival's actions from market outcomes. It is only after losing many sales that you may be confident that a rival is pricing aggressively. The longer the price cuts go unpunished, the higher the incentive to cut prices.

There are market features that may affect the ability to infer rivals' actions. Frequent demand shocks, for example, make detecting price cuts by rivals more difficult. If one of the players observes a sudden decrease in sales, is he to conclude that the rival is undercutting his prices, or might it just be a "bad month" (or year)? Alternatively, if there is natural product or geographic segmentation, a company will learn if a competitor is trading aggressively by the loss of sales that "belong" to it.

To sum up, industries in which there are few companies, transparent prices, and stable demand conditions, some easy way to implement tacit coordination and high product differentiation are the most likely to be conducive to high price outcomes. But there is no simple formula for combining these elements to make predictions when different features work in different directions. Attempts to predict the extent of price competition in internet retailing offer an interesting case study of this problem. (*See* Price competition box on p. 45.)

Changing the rules of the game

Companies may embark on actions to change the rules of the game, by creating conditions that will lead to high prices.

The most common of these tactics usually involves making the market more transparent or decreasing the short-run gains from price cuts, mainly through an

Price competition in internet retailing

Internet retailing is a new and fast-growing market place characterized by shopping convenience and low entry costs. The benefit to consumers from better information, reduced search costs, and access to a wider variety of goods and services is dramatic. This benefit for consumers need not necessarily translate, however, into higher long-run profitability for firms. Whether it does or not depends on the extent of price competition.

On a first approximation, it would appear that internet retailing is like our petrol station example – consumers can easily shift to a low-priced seller and transaction prices are transparent to competitors. This suggests that pricing competition may be limited. A small number of similar firms competing for sales on the information superhighway would probably compete on price less aggressively than the same number of firms competing on an asphalt highway, as they would expect their price cuts to be immediately matched by their rivals, with no gain in market share.

This is not the whole story, however. Entry costs may be very low. It is possible to access large numbers of potential customers at a small fraction of the costs of telemarketing or the mail system and it may be possible to find and target specific segments of the population without the purchase of expensive lists. This should increase the number of firms and the differences among them, making high prices much more difficult to sustain. A small entrant with no brand name or reputation and few existing customers will find it necessary to compete on price to get a toehold in the market.

Moreover, the reduction in search costs and the relative ease with which shoppers can compare prices on the internet would encourage consumers to switch to the low-cost producers. In fact, the cost of switching in comparing is so low that there is a real possibility of negotiated prices being the norm. It may be much easier for a consumer to play competitors off against one another when one can get price quotes through electronic mail and make offers and counteroffers among a large number of sellers at very low cost. For example, playing one car dealer off against another is already quite easy thanks to the internet.

increase in product differentiation. The antitrust treatment of such actions is very complex, so none of them should be taken as a strategic recommendation by the authors.

Companies have used many different tactics to increase market transparency. These include: attempts to create market segmentation, commitments to published price lists, advanced announcement of price changes, and price leadership by a company that, being larger than the rest, can play the price-setting role, leaving all the other companies simply to imitate it.

Also, as we have argued, the short-run gain from price cuts depends on the degree of product differentiation in the market. If differentiation increases, consumers are less likely to react to price cuts. An example of an action taken exclusively to increase the degree of product differentiation in a market is an airline frequent flyer program (FFP). If a customer is a member of the American Airlines FFP, he is less likely to respond to a low tariff offered by KLM on the same route. Thus KLM has a smaller incentive to cut prices, as do all other airlines. Higher ticket prices result.

Other ways exist to lower the temptation to cut prices by decreasing the short-term gains from cutting prices. Among them is the use of most favored customer clauses, which we discuss in the box on p. 46.

Most favored customer clauses and price competition

When a firm uses a most favored customer clause (MFC), it promises each customer to give him or her the best price that the firm gives to anyone. The impact of such rules seems to be favorable to consumers, as each consumer gets the best possible treatment. In fact, such clauses decrease price competition, by making it very costly for firms to give discounts to their customers. Suppose that a firm is negotiating a price with a particularly large customer. In the absence of an MFC, the firm may be tempted to reduce prices in order to gain this additional business. Now suppose the firm has an MFC clause: this means that if it gives a discount to this customer it will have to cut the prices to everyone. The trade-off now involved in reducing prices is cutting prices to all customers and decreasing the margin on all of the units sold, in order to increase the quantity sold to this particular customer. Clearly, the incentives for the seller to cut prices are now smaller, making it likely that the prices paid by every consumer will increase.

In a 1997 study published in the *Rand Journal of Economics*, Yale School of Management professor Fiona Scott Morton studied empirically the effect of a version of this clause introduced in the Medicare reimbursement program in 1990. The genesis of the change was the frustration of the US Congress in seeing that powerful health maintenance organizations obtained better prices from drug manufacturers than the government Medicaid program did. In the 1990 Omnibus Budget Reconciliation Act, Congress legislated that manufacturers were required to sell branded drugs to Medicaid for the best price anyone paid for the drug or 87.5 percent of their average manufacturer price. The government expected prices to decrease as a result of the program. Scott Morton found that, in fact, the prices of branded drugs in competition with generics rose by 4 percent as a result of these new rules.

Why this unexpected effect? The program gives incentives to manufacturers to raise prices. As the director of drug purchasing of Kaiser Permanente, America's largest HMO, put it (as quoted by Adam M. Brandenburger and Barry J. Nalebuff in their book *Co-opetition*), "In the past we'd offer a drug manufacturer 90 percent of our business, maybe $10m in additional business, and get really low prices. Now, no one wants to go below the Medicaid floor." By adding an MFC provision to the law, the US Congress reduced the incentives of drug manufacturers to compete on prices, resulting in higher overall market prices.

Summary

Pricing has an important strategic role in economics, but the dynamics of price competition is frequently misunderstood. **Luis Garicano** and **Robert Gertner** focus here on the incentives that companies have to use price as a competitive weapon, the situations in which price cutting can pay off, and the conditions that lead to higher prices being charged by all companies in an industry. Changing the rules of the game so as to avoid price wars can raise antitrust issues and needs to be approached with caution, the authors warn. They explain why price setting in future is likely to be buffeted by the ease with which customers can indulge in comparative shopping on the internet.

When it can be good to burn your boats

by Judith A. Chevalier

Maintaining the flexibility to change its course of action might seem a valuable requirement for a business at all times. But there are situations in which making irreversible commitments can have important strategic value. In this article I consider two types of commitments: commitments to being a "tough" competitor and commitments to being a "soft" competitor.

Commitments to be tough

The classic example of the strategic value of commitment comes not from business, but from war. In 400BC Sun-tzu in *The Art of War* wrote: "At the critical moment, the leader of an army acts like one who has climbed up a height, and then kicks away the ladder behind him."

The Spanish conquistador Hernán Cortés took this advice to heart in 1519. On landing in Mexico, in preparation for his invasion of the Aztec city of Tenochtitlan, Cortés sunk most of his ships. As Cortés's companion Bernal Diaz de Castillo wrote: "We could look for no help or assistance except from God for we now had no ships in which to return." Clearly, the sinking of the ships would have provided extra motivation for the army. However, it also sent a powerful signal to the opponent. It was clear to the Aztec king Moctezuma that resistance to Cortés's invasion would lead to a bloody fight to the death, not to the retreat of Cortés's men. The Aztecs chose not to resist Cortés's invasion of Tenochtitlan. Thus the commitment to act aggressively engendered the desired passive response from the opponent. Quoting Sun-tzu again: "The skillful leader subdues the enemy's troops without any fighting."

Reversibility

A strategic commitment, like the sinking of a ship, is a decision that is difficult to reverse. When companies build factories, sign contracts, and launch advertising campaigns, they are making decisions that might be difficult to go back on. This irreversibility can have both benefits and costs. The main benefit of an irreversible commitment is the effect it has on competitors.

Consider this example. A new trucking company is contemplating entering two local markets to haul agricultural products. Suppose the two local markets are identical in every respect, except for the identity of the incumbent company operating in the market. In the first market, the incumbent company is a railroad. The incumbent spent $20m to construct the railroad and the operating cost of hauling grain for the railroad is $0.20 per ton-mile. In the second market, the incumbent is another trucking company. The trucking company has $20m worth of trucks operating on the route. The operating cost of hauling grain for the incumbent trucking company is $0.20 per ton-mile. Which market is the new trucking company more likely to enter?

At first, the conditions in the two markets seem identical. However, there is an important difference. Most of the costs in constructing the railroad relate to clearing the land and laying the track; these are irrecoverable should the railroad decide to shut down. In contrast, if the incumbent trucking company decides to close, it could almost fully recover its $20m investment. Trucks obviously are easy to move from place to place, and there is a fairly liquid market for them. Thus, for the incumbent trucking company to want to remain in the market, it needs to cover its operating cost, and earn a return on its investment in the trucks. If it is not earning an adequate return on its trucks, it will sell them or take them elsewhere.

For the incumbent railroad company to choose to stay in the market, it needs to cover its operating cost and earn a return only on the (relatively small) scrap value of the railroad. The track investments are totally irrecoverable, or "sunk," and thus the railroad does not consider their value when deciding whether or not to stay in business. Should prices and quantities fall in the market, it is quite likely the railroad will wish that it had never made the investments in laying track. However, as the track is there, unless market conditions are extremely poor, it makes sense to continue operating the railroad. Thus, the entrant will have a much easier time inducing the trucking company to exit than it will have inducing the railroad company to exit. Entering the market currently occupied by the trucking company is, therefore, more attractive.

The irreversibility of the railroad's investments acts as a commitment by the railroad to stay in the market, and may deter the entrant from entering the market. Thus, the commitment allows the railroad company to "subdue the enemy's troops without any fighting."

Commitments to be soft

When thinking about commitments in the context of strategic management, a manager has first to determine what kind of commitments might be valuable and then determine whether the strategic advantages of commitment outweigh the benefits of retaining flexibility. The types of commitments that managers might want to make fall into two broad categories: commitments to be "tough" and commitments to be "soft."

A company might benefit from a commitment to be tough when it wants to deter entry into its markets, encourage a rival to build only small capacity, or even induce exit. The Cortés and railroad examples above are instances of commitments to be tough. Alternatively, a company might benefit from a commitment to be "soft." If two competitors are competing by setting prices in a market in which exit is unlikely, commitments to be "soft" might be valuable. Consider, for example, the fierce competition between mass-market discount department stores. A number of these are now adopting "frequent customer cards" and other loyalty programs. In order to encourage the customer not to shop around, these programs give rewards to those who accumulate a large number of purchases with the retailer. However, introduction of such programs raises a question to outside observers: wouldn't the cost of the awards and the infrastructure for the program be better spent simply lowering prices? Wouldn't customers appreciate this just as much or more than prizes?

Club Z

Customers might appreciate lower prices just as much as "loyalty rewards," but the effect on competition would be very different. Consider the largest, and perhaps most successful, retail loyalty program in North America. Approximately one-third of all Canadian residents belong to Club Z, the loyalty program for the Canadian mass merchandiser Zeller Stores. Eight out of ten of Zeller's shoppers are estimated to be members. What signal does the adoption and maintenance of this loyalty program send to Zeller's competitors?

At first one might guess that the fact that Zeller has customers who don't like to shop around is unambiguously bad news for its competitors, such as the US retailers Wal-Mart and Sears Roebuck. However, Zeller's customer loyalty also has a positive side for its competitors. As Zeller's president Thomas Haig noted in an issue of *Discount Store News*: "We can position ourselves a bit above Wal-Mart in price." If Zeller's customers are loyal and unwilling to shop around, this would tend to make Zeller reluctant to compete fiercely by cutting prices.

After all, cutting prices might help Zeller to pick up a few new customers, but it would be giving up margins on all of the customers who were willing to pay a bit more. Thus, its strong customer loyalty program serves as a commitment on Zeller's part not to cut prices too fiercely. How should Wal-Mart respond to this? Wal-Mart will surely choose prices that are lower than Zeller's prices, but it will not compete as fiercely on price as it might otherwise. After all, it will be very costly to dislodge those customers from Zeller who don't shop around much. And, if Zeller isn't competing too hard to attract those "non-loyal" customers, Wal-Mart doesn't have to charge extremely low prices to capture them. Wal-Mart competes less aggressively due to Zeller's loyalty program, and this less aggressive competition benefits Zeller.

In considering what kinds of commitments to make, it is important to figure out what one's objectives are and how competition is taking place in the market. For example, Zeller's loyalty program is a good strategy because the company is engaged in price competition with a competitor that it cannot hope to try to induce to exit. Maintaining "soft" price competition is probably the most profitable tactic for Zeller. However, if it were trying to induce Wal-Mart's exit, the loyalty program might prove a hindrance. Suppose Zeller cut its prices to try to persuade Wal-Mart to exit. Wal-Mart would probably stand firm, knowing that the existence of loyal customers who are willing to pay higher prices makes price cutting a very expensive strategy for Zeller. Wal-Mart knows that Zeller won't want to keep up a price war for too long. Foreseeing that Wal-Mart can see through its motivations, Zeller would probably never attempt to cut prices to induce Wal-Mart to exit.

It is important to stress that an easily reversible decision does not function as a credible commitment that will alter a competitor's behavior. Moctezuma might not have been impressed had Cortés merely announced, "We will not return to Cuba." The scuttling of the ships convinced Moctezuma that even if the invasion turned out very poorly, making Cortés want to retreat to Cuba, he could not do so. Moctezuma would not have considered an announcement by Cortés to be credible. In June 1999, for example, online bookseller Amazon.com announced that it was building a new 800,000 sq. ft distribution facility in the state of Georgia that would employ 1,000 people. While this represents a measurable capacity expansion for Amazon, it does not represent a commitment to expand. A distribution facility's infrastructure does not tend to be specialized, and the site could easily be sold as a distribution/warehouse facility for some other type of business. Thus, when competitors consider whether to expand into Amazon's markets, they would not consider the distribution facility as a commitment on Amazon's part not to reduce capacity in the future.

One might argue that Zeller could easily discontinue its loyalty program. However, it has made considerable investments in setting up infrastructure for this program. These investments are unrecoverable. The loyalty program functions as a commitment because it affects Zeller's incentives in the future. Zeller understands, and its competitors understand, that having created loyal customers through this program, maintaining this loyalty by continuing the program is relatively cheap. The loyal customer base that Zeller has created functions like an asset that it has purchased and that has very little scrap value. The fact that the major investments in creating a loyalty program have already been made means that the company is likely to remain on the path of promoting customer loyalty rather than switch to that of fierce price competition.

CD technology

Commitments, then, can often be valuable in altering a competitor's responses. However, when considering a commitment, it is crucially important to consider the value of the flexibility forgone by undertaking the commitment. Harvard Business School professor Anita McGahan considers an example of a company facing the decision of whether to build a large factory ahead of demand, in an article entitled "The incentive not to invest: capacity commitments in the compact disc introduction." In 1982, on the eve of the launch of its compact disc in the US market, the Dutch electronics group Philips NV had to decide whether to build a large local facility immediately to press discs. As the innovator of the CD, Philips could bring a facility into production in 1983, much faster than any rival presser could enter the market. If the compact disc achieved US acceptance, Philips's lead in moving down the learning curve and its large installed capacity might deter others from building their own pressing facilities. By moving early, Philips might be able to deter others from entry and protect itself from destructive price competition in the future.

However, there was an important downside to this option. In 1982, it was not at all clear that CDs would achieve popular acceptance. After all, consumers already had record players and libraries of LPs. The next innovation, digital audio tape, was only a few years down the line. Should the CD not catch on, Philips would be saddled with a $25m facility with almost no alternative uses.

Excluding the possibility of competition, it seemed to make sense for Philips to import CDs from existing facilities in Europe and not to invest in US capacity until it became clear that CDs would be accepted in that market. By waiting to see whether US consumers would be attracted to the CD, Philips could preserve the valuable option not to invest if acceptance were too low.

Philips, fearing that popular acceptance of the CD might be low, chose to wait and see how the US CD market evolved. Unfortunately for the company, however, Sony built a CD facility in the US in 1984. CDs were, of course, a great commercial success, and Philips and others entered with rival plants soon after.

While CD prices themselves have held fairly steady over the years, the prices charged to the record labels by the pressing facilities have declined precipitously, due to overcapacity and fierce price competition in the pressing market.

An earlier move by Philips might well have resulted in a different market outcome. However, opting for flexibility may have been the right decision given the information available at the time. This example illustrates the difficult trade-off between undertaking a commitment strategy and maintaining flexibility. While both strategies can be valuable, neither strategy provides insurance against later regret.

Summary

Irreversible commitments can have an important strategic value, explains **Judith A. Chevalier**. In this article she describes two broad categories of commitment – the "tough" and the "soft." The tough approach can be used to deter a competitor from entering a market or to force it out. The soft approach may be more appropriate where exiting the market is not an option for a competitor and no players would benefit from heavy competition on price. The benefits of making a strategic commitment – never more dramatically illustrated than by the Spanish conquistador Hernán Cortés's decision to scuttle his ships – need to be weighed carefully against the advantages of maintaining flexibility. Neither strategy provides insurance against later regret.

The pros and cons of entering a market

by Judith A. Chevalier

Introductory economics textbooks generally tell us to expect new entrants into an industry whenever the incumbent companies are earning profits greater than their cost of capital. Furthermore, we are told that entry will occur until profits net of the cost of capital are driven to zero. Obviously, this view of the world is too simplistic. We can think of many examples of markets with no regulatory barriers to entry in which incumbent companies are making high profits, yet little or no entry occurs.

For example, in a 1999 working paper, Boston University economist Marc Rysman estimates that the profits of US *Yellow Pages* directory publishers average 35 to 40 percent of revenue. Despite this, relatively few independent publishers have entered the market to compete with local telephone companies in providing *Yellow Pages* services. In contrast, we can think of several examples of markets like online bookselling where, despite the virtual absence of profitability, many new companies seem to be starting up. In this article, I will explore some of the factors a company should consider when deciding whether or not to enter a new market. In doing so, I will try to reconcile the entry patterns we observe in real business with the basic principles of economics.

Basic economics of entry

Consider the textbook case of entry dynamics. A company enters a new market and finds it profitable. Typically, that market will then attract further entry, eroding the pioneer's profitability. Profits are eroded for two reasons. First, the pioneer loses market share to new entrants. Second, the presence of the entrants often brings vigorous price competition, eroding margins on each unit sold.

The case of Rollerblade skates, now owned by Italy's Benetton Sportsystem, conforms fairly well to the textbook example. Rollerblade introduced inline skates in the US market in 1980. At the same time, the company invested considerable resources in popularizing the sport. It was successful; the market for inline skates exploded in the late 1980s and early 1990s. Participation in the sport in the US rose from 3.1m in 1989 to more than 20m in 1995. However, the explosion of the market for inline skating did not escape the notice of others. While Rollerblade did have patents for features of its skate boot, it did not have a patent for the basic idea of lining up skate wheels. This idea had been around for a long time. Indeed, inline skates had been a fad in the 1860s. Thus, Rollerblade could not prevent entry into the market. In the late 1980s, Rollerblade had virtually all of the market and its cheapest model sold for $90. The company's only competitor at that time, First Team Sports, sold its skates for about 15 percent less than the comparable Rollerblade models. By 1994, approximately 30 companies had entered the inline skates market. Rollerblade's market share had dropped to about 40 percent. The cheapest skates on the market sold for $29.99; Rollerblade's cheapest skates sold for $69.99.

As mentioned before, the erosion of profits through entry occurs at differing speeds in different markets. Economists use the term "barriers to entry" to describe situations in which incumbent companies are earning profits in a market and yet entrants do not find it worthwhile to enter that market.

Barriers to entry

Legal barriers to entry

Some markets have legal barriers to entry. For example, entry into a market can be blocked by government regulation and by patent protection. However, even when patents exist, they might not stop competition, depending on the breadth of the patent protection.

A 1987 survey by Richard Levin and others in the *Brookings Papers on Economic Activity* asked R&D executives to rank the effectiveness of patents at preventing duplication of their innovations. Using a seven-point scale in which one represented "not at all effective" and seven represented "very effective," mean responses were 3.52 for process patents and 4.33 for product patents. The highest ranking for product patents, 6.5, was given by executives in the pharmaceutical industry.

While product patents are sometimes effective at preventing duplication, they don't prevent all forms of imitation, even in the pharmaceutical industry. For example, in the late 1960s and early 1970s, US pharmaceuticals company Eli Lilly owned the US market for cephalosporins, a type of powerful antibiotic. Its patented products, Keflin and Keflex, were both among the top-selling drugs in the US. While rivals could not produce the same chemical compounds as Keflin and Keflex until those patents expired, they could not be stopped from innovating powerful antibiotics using similar inputs that worked the same way in the body. By early 1982, the year in which the first of the two cephalosporin patents was to expire, Lilly's share of the cephalosporin market had dropped to 75 percent.

High minimum efficient scale relative to market size

Even in the absence of legal barriers to entry, other entry barriers are possible.

Entry can be prevented, for example, when the minimum efficient scale of production is large relative to the overall size of the market.

Consider, for example, Richardson Electronics, founded in 1947 as a distributor of vacuum tubes. A casual observer might regard it as extremely bad luck for Richardson that the company was founded only one year before the discovery of solid state physics – the basis for the transistor, an invention that made the vacuum tube virtually obsolete. In fact, however, the obsolescence of the vacuum tube turned out to be very good news for Richardson. While total sales of vacuum tubes declined dramatically during the 1970s, 1980s, and 1990s, Richardson's share of the market increased sharply as Western Electric, General Electric, RCA, Sylvania (a lighting company), and Westinghouse all exited the vacuum tube business. Since the 1970s Richardson has been the sole distributor available for many vacuum tube products, which means little price competition.

An example of Richardson's market position in the vacuum tube market is detailed in its 1998 annual report. An automotive company's rubber curing machines required replacement vacuum tubes. If the manufacturer could not find the replacement parts, it would cost nearly $1m to replace the machinery. Obviously, the value that the manufacturer placed on obtaining the vacuum tubes was high and Richardson was the only supplier in a position to help. Since the customer's only alternative to doing business with Richardson is often scrapping an entire machine, Richardson is in a strong bargaining position and can extract a substantial chunk of the cost of a new machine as the price of a replacement tube.

If the vacuum tube business is so profitable for Richardson, why have new entrants not come into the market? The answer is that it doesn't make sense for a competitor to enter on the scale that would be required to compete effectively with Richardson, whose inventories include thousands of types of vacuum tubes from all over the world in order to supply hard-to-find replacements quickly. The shrinking market for vacuum tubes is big enough to support one large player profitably; it probably isn't big enough to support two.

Large sunk expenditures

Some markets require large capital expenditures to enter. In and of itself, a large entry cost does not constitute a barrier to entry. Consider, for example, a start-up airline contemplating offering a shuttle service between Dublin and London. In order to begin offering this service, the airline has to make a large capital outlay for aircraft. However, the need to purchase the aircraft is not really a barrier to entry. Should the airline not find the route lucrative, it could probably sell the aircraft to another company for a price close to that originally paid.

The term "sunk" is used to describe investments that are unrecoverable once made. Entering the airline market requires a large expenditure of capital, but the expenditure is for capital goods that are relatively liquid. These expenditures are not "sunk" should the venture fail.

On the other hand, consider the Channel Tunnel. There, the expenditures required for entry are sunk (literally!). When revenues turned out to be lower and costs higher than initially forecast, the original investors must have wished they had not made the initial investments. However, the tunnel stays in business because the investment expenditures are unrecoverable.

If demand and cost conditions turn out to be favorable in a new market, it does not matter whether the entry expenditures are sunk or not. However, when conditions turn out unfavorably, the entrant cannot recover those entry investments that are sunk. Thus, given an industry in which entry requires making unrecoverable expenditures, aspirants are less likely to enter, even when incumbent companies are earning some profits.

Ascertaining whether entry expenditures are sunk is trickier than might at first appear. In order to determine this, one has to consider what types of uncertainties face the new venture.

Consider a company that wants to capitalize on the "microbrew" craze by marketing beer brewed from corn rather than barley or wheat. To do this the company has to purchase basic brewing equipment. If the primary uncertainty facing such a brewer is whether consumers will find corn brew tasty, then we should consider the brewer's entry expenditure not to be sunk. After all, should corn brew fail to catch on, the brewing equipment could be resold to another brewer at close to the price initially paid for it. However, suppose the primary uncertainty facing the brewer is whether the "microbrew" craze will come to an end. If this happens, the brewer may still want to close down, but there would then be little demand for used small-scale brewing equipment. The used brewing equipment would sell for a much lower price than the brewer initially paid for it.

Network externalities

Entry can be unattractive despite incumbent profits in a market characterized by network externalities. A network externality occurs when consumers value consuming the same product as other consumers. For example, consumers want to have JVC's VHS video-cassette recorder system rather than Sony Beta VCRs, because rental movies are only available for VHS VCRs. Thus they value owning the same type of VCR as other consumers.

The network externality may effectively create a monopoly for the incumbent if the incumbent company either has a cost advantage in producing its particular design or has legal rights to all compatible designs. Rysman's article suggests that a phenomenon similar to this explains the lack of new entrants in *Yellow Pages* markets. Consumers only keep and reference the *Yellow Pages* book for their local area that contains the largest number of advertisements. Thus, advertisers want to advertise in the same book in which everyone else advertises. It is hard for an entrant to break into this circle, because advertisers only want to advertise in the upstart book if they believe that others will too.

Incumbent first mover advantages

Entry may be difficult if the incumbent company in the market has important cost and demand advantages over potential entrants.

Incumbent first mover advantages generally derive from three sources: learning curve advantages, incumbent control of scarce assets, and customer switching costs.

Some production processes are simply difficult to master. Companies that enter an industry early have a head start when it comes to accumulating the knowledge necessary for production. For example, in a 1999 working paper, C. Lanier Benkard notes that a company's costs of producing commercial aircraft fall considerably with each new plane produced. New entrants might find this cost disadvantage relative to the incumbent to be a formidable barrier to entry.

Entry can also be difficult if the incumbent company controls scarce assets that are important to production. For example, the incumbent may have exclusive relations with important distribution channels, or may have long-term contracts with the only supplier of an important input. In this case, entrants are blocked from entry by the high costs they face in making or distributing their products. Because incumbent asset control can create entry barriers, the first mover in an industry often makes an effort to "lock up" supply or distribution channels. It is important to note, however, that these efforts have often precipitated the scrutiny of the antitrust authorities.

Finally, entry is impeded if customers would find it costly to switch to a new supplier. This exists to some extent in many markets where the incumbent's reputation and brand loyalty make consumers willing to pay more for the incumbent's product than for the entrant's product. However, the entry barrier is most severe when buyers have made some kind of investment in using the incumbent's product that would make it costly to switch to the entrant's substitute. For example, International Business Machines had difficulty achieving market penetration with its OS/2 operating system in part because users were unwilling to switch from the familiar Microsoft Windows environment.

The paradox of entry barriers

Obviously, the existence of entry barriers is good news for incumbent companies in a market. Indeed, when entering previously undeveloped markets, it makes sense to consider the magnitude of the entry barriers that subsequent entrants will face. For example, consider the strategy of Wal-Mart, the cut-price US retailer, when it initially marched across the US.

Wal-Mart built large discount stores in small towns that had never been served by large discount stores. Many of these towns were sufficiently small that they had "room" for one company to earn profits, but it would not be worthwhile for a second company to enter on the scale needed to offer the discounts and selection required to compete effectively with Wal-Mart. Thus, as the market pioneer, Wal-Mart certainly benefits from choosing markets in which there will be barriers to entry for subsequent entrants.

The existence of entry barriers might at first seem to be unambiguously bad news for a company considering entering an existing market. However, this is not entirely true. After all, if there were no barriers the market would be flooded with new entrants until profits equaled zero. The market could not truly represent much of an opportunity. Thus, paradoxically, entry barriers can be good for a potential newcomer because they keep other companies from entering.

However, a market with entry barriers only represents an opportunity if the potential entrant has skills or assets that enable it to overcome the entry barriers at a lower cost than would be required of other potential entrants.

"Fit" and entry

Novel product or business plan

When does a potential entrant have the ability to scale entry barriers? One example is when the incumbent has a truly innovative product or business plan. However, even here entry must be undertaken with caution. If the incumbent company can easily copy the product or business plan and would choose to do so, entry may not be worthwhile.

Consider Minnetonka, a small US manufacturer of consumer goods that used its innovation of attractively packaged liquid soap for the home – called SoftSoap – to enter the soap market in 1979. Minnetonka would have had a difficult time launching a mass-market bar soap product. The main incumbent companies, such as Procter & Gamble, Unilever, and Colgate-Palmolive, had relationships and contracts with distributors and retailers that gave them huge cost advantages over any potential entrant. By entering with an innovative product like SoftSoap, Minnetonka was able to overcome the formidable entry barriers and grabbed a 5 percent share of the US personal soap market by the latter half of 1980.

Minnetonka could not, however, prevent Procter & Gamble and the other incumbents from marketing their own liquid soaps. Indeed, at the time of Minnetonka's entry Procter & Gamble was holding "sleeping" patents for its own liquid soap formulations. By 1983, the soap industry giants all had their own liquid soaps. Minnetonka's share of this market fell from more than 80 percent in 1981 to less than 30 percent in 1983. Its operating profit of $11m in 1980 turned into a loss of $7m in 1982.

Synergies with existing products

A potential entrant may also have the ability to scale entry barriers if there is some synergy between the production of the new good or service and the goods or services already produced by the potential entrant in the entrant's existing markets. The potential for shared marketing or umbrella branding may be sufficient to encourage an entrant. Consider, for example, the case of eBay and Amazon.com. eBay is the largest internet auction site; Amazon recently started brokering auctions itself.

In some ways, it might seem that an entrant would have a difficult time entering against eBay. After all, customers want to sell their wares in the most populated auction markets; they do not want to sell in a market with very few buyers competing for their goods. As the first mover in the market, eBay would seem to have the huge advantage of a network externality, because it has established itself as the most liquid auction market on the internet.

While eBay's first mover advantage is important, Amazon entered the auction market in 1999. How did Amazon plan to get started against eBay? First, it used site advertising and emails to advertise its auctions to its existing large customer base. Amazon planned to leverage its strong brand name and reputation in an effort to obtain the market base required to compete effectively with eBay.

Although the principle of looking for synergies is important, one must not be overly optimistic. While the issue of auction market dominance has yet to be settled, eBay for now continues to have considerably more trade than Amazon.

Conclusion

In summary, the simple decision rule for a potential entrant is this: enter the market if the post-entry profits are expected to be greater than the sunk costs of entering. As noted in the examples provided, however, current profits being earned by incumbents are not necessarily an ideal measure of the post-entry profit opportunities, as incumbents can be expected to respond to new entry, just as Procter & Gamble and others responded to Minnetonka's invasion of the soap market.

Summary

How should a company decide whether or not to enter a new market? How do entry patterns seen in the real business world mesh with the basic principles of economic theory? According to the textbook, says **Judith A. Chevalier**, the profits of pioneering companies are typically eroded by loss of market share and vigorous price competition as new players arrive on the scene. In reality, however, incumbent businesses can be protected by barriers to entry. The author sets out some of the main examples – patent and other legal devices, control over scarce resources, sunk expenditures – and concludes with some strategic considerations for companies trying to break them down.

Suggested further reading

Available at www.nber.org (1987) "Appropriating the returns on industrial research and development," *Brookings Papers on Economic Activity*, 3: 783–820.

Benkard, C.L. (1999) "Learning and forgetting: the dynamics of aircraft production," National Bureau of Economic Research Working Paper, No. 7217, May.

Dunne, T., Roberts, M.J. and Samuelson, L. (1988) "Patterns of firm entry and exit in US manufacturing industries," *Rand Journal of Economics*, 19 (4, Winter): 495–515.

Rysman, M. (1999) "Competition between networks: a study of the market for *Yellow Pages*," Boston University Working Paper, September.

Sutton, J. (1991) *Sunk Costs and Market Structure*, Cambridge, MA: MIT Press.

Strategic complements and substitutes

by Fiona Scott Morton

What makes competitive strategy difficult is that the other forces in the environment are live – they can change their strategies at any time. A manager therefore has to chart the best course for the corporate "ship," avoiding fixed hazards like rocks while trying to avoid collisions with other moving vessels.

Before making a strategic decision in such a setting, it is crucial to understand how your rival will respond to an action. Advertising may be answered with more advertising, expanding capacity may cause a rival to build less capacity. Clearly, the advantages of a particular strategy will partially depend on reaction by others.

The essence of strategic thinking is to anticipate your competitor's moves. Knowledge of your competitor's reaction, or likely reaction, dramatically improves your ability to choose a strategy that will be successful. Some competitor reactions enhance your own profit, while others reduce it. The economic tools described below allow a manager to determine what a competitor's reaction will be and what kinds of initial action generate positive or negative feedback. Informed managers understand and can affect competitive interaction to their advantage.

This analysis only applies in markets where there are few major competitors – an environment in which the actions of any one company can noticeably affect the profits of the others. Such markets are known as oligopolies. (I will therefore ignore monopoly and perfectly competitive markets.) Competitive interaction can get complicated and very sophisticated. The models in this article are the basics, the first steps required before moving on to advanced competitive strategy. While they may seem simplistic in some regards, they make basic and fundamental points about how competition works. More elaborate strategies build on these insights, so it is important to understand them.

Assumptions

To figure out the most likely competitive response, a manager needs to know the rival's goal (this is usually to maximize profit), the possible actions available to that rival (enter a new market or not, raise or lower price), and the gains to the rival from choosing one action over another. While to an outsider many of these concepts seem difficult to estimate, competitors within an industry often have very good estimates of technical options, costs, and the profitability of their competitors. Identifying a goal such as profit maximization is important, because that is how we will predict a company's choice: if, for example, we know approximately what level of profit will result from two different actions, and the company's management team steadfastly pursues profit, we can guess that they will choose the higher-profit alternative.

How are profits determined? The "game" being played by the industry is of crucial importance. There are two basic economic models of competition, price games and quantity games, which I will discuss below. (This distinction was originally noted by Jeremy Bulow, John Geanakoplos, and Paul Klemperer in their article "Multimarket oligopoly: strategic substitutes and complements.") Both models are short term; they are specifically designed to reflect the profitability of current competitive tactics. Dynamic concerns such as building market share today in order to reap profits from it tomorrow are advanced refinements of these models.

Prices or strategic complements

The most common kind of competitive interaction is in prices. Coca-Cola and Pepsi, for example, are substitutes, yet consumers have different preferences for each. If Coke lowered its price in a particular city, some Pepsi customers would switch to Coke at that moment, while others would prefer Pepsi enough to pay its higher price. Coke would gain some customers who, until the price declined, were outside the soft drink market; it would also attract some former Pepsi customers.

In 1883, Joseph Bertrand developed an expression for the profits of a company based on this type of consumer demand. He showed that any company engaged in price competition – in our case Pepsi – has a best (profit-maximizing) response to competitor price changes. If Coke lowers its price, Pepsi does best by lowering its price also, although it may not match Coke's decrease in full. Why? Pepsi will lose customers to Coke when Coke's price falls. By lowering its own price, it prevents some of those customers from leaving. However, a lower price means a lower margin, so Pepsi finds that it is not worth exactly matching Coke's price drop, but prefers to preserve some margin on its existing customers instead.

Suppose the opposite case, whereby Coke raises its price. Pepsi would find that it could raise profits by partially matching Coke's increase. It could steal some customers from Coke – and serve them at a higher margin than before – if it

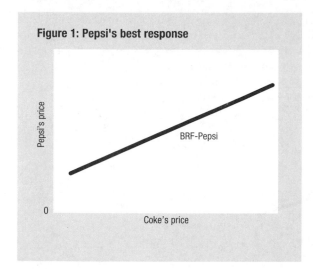

Figure 1: Pepsi's best response

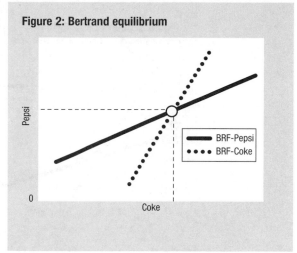

Figure 2: Bertrand equilibrium

matched only part of the price increase. This example illustrates that the best response in a price game is to imitate the original move of your rival. Pepsi's best response function is shown in Figure 1. In a price game a lower price inspires a lower price, while raising a price causes the other company to raise price; competitors' prices move together.

Coke also has a best response function (BRF), which is shown in Figure 2, along with the market equilibrium prices. Why is the equilibrium where the two curves cross? If both companies want to make best responses to the other's price – and that itself is a best response to their price – the intersection is the only option. A key feature of these markets is that both companies' choices and profits move together. Industry prices and profits rise, or industry prices and profits fall. In some sense, everyone is in the same boat. This is known as a strategic complements market.

Quantities or strategic substitutes

The other type of action is a strategic substitute. The classic example of a strategic substitute is a company's choice of production quantity. Clearly, if companies choose the quantity they will put on the market, they cannot also force a particular price. (Think of OPEC's decisions over production, not price.) Instead, consumer demand determines the price. Another Frenchman, Augustin Cournot, showed more than a century ago that in a quantity game you should do the opposite of what your competitor does. For example, if your competitor decreases the quantity it puts on the market, you should increase yours if you want to maximize profit. Why? Because your competitor's decrease drives up the (common) market price, which raises your margin on every unit. It is now worth producing more units. For example, when OPEC organizes lower production, the best response by other oil-producing countries is to produce more.

While quantity competition is the classic parallel to price competition, it is not very common. Commodity markets are some of the only examples. The most important strategic complements action is capacity choice. For example, increased levels of computer memory-chip capacity by one player lead others in the industry to

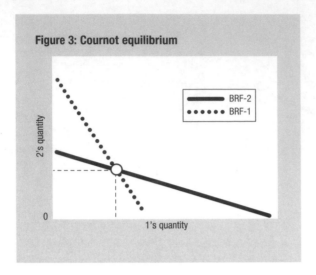

Figure 3: Cournot equilibrium

scale back. This is because increased chip production due to increased capacity will lower market prices. Lower prices lower the return on the capacity investment planned by other companies. Therefore, they scale back their capacity investments in memory chips. The best response functions for a strategic substitutes market are shown in Figure 3 where the equilibrium is marked.

Notice that in contrast to the first type of market, the best response to a competitor's move in a strategic substitutes game is to do the opposite. The pattern of profit changes is also different. Lower quantity goes hand in hand with lower profits; higher quantity with higher profits. When a rival increases output, your profits fall. While you can improve them somewhat by reducing your own output, you are still worse off, on balance. On the other hand, if a competitor lowers its capacity, your profits rise and will rise further if you increase your capacity.

Key difference

How do you tell when you are playing a price game rather than a quantity game? Simply that the company chooses to set the price component of the demand curve. Coke and Pepsi choose the price at which their products sell. In a quantity game, a company chooses what quantity (or capacity) to place on the market, but it is the market demand curve for the product itself that determines price.

Commitment

There are two types of strategic commitment a company can make. A commitment is either aggressive or nice, depending on whether it hurts or helps the competition. By strategic commitment I mean a choice that is both hard (or costly) to reverse, and that changes the best course of action for the company. Such a choice permanently shifts the location of a company's best response function by altering its underlying cost or revenue functions.

Let us examine price competition more closely. Suppose a company adopts a new technology that substantially lowers cost. With lower costs than it had before, that

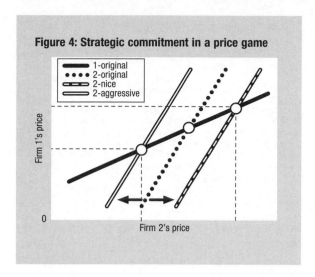

Figure 4: Strategic commitment in a price game

company will want to charge a lower price than it did before at each price its rival might charge. Its best response function has shifted down (to lower prices). Lower prices hurt the competition; they are aggressive. This strategic commitment is therefore aggressive. On the other hand, if higher local taxes increased a company's variable costs, at every price its competitor might set it would want to charge a higher price than it did before. In this case, government policy has committed the company to charge higher prices; its best response function shifts up. The higher prices that result improve the profitability of the competitor. Therefore, the government caused the company to make a nice strategic commitment. These shifts are illustrated in Figure 4.

Strategic commitments look somewhat different in a quantity game. Suppose a company signs a long-term contract (with penalties for breach) to deliver a large quantity of the next generation of memory chips to customers. The company now wants to build more capacity than it did before it signed the contract. Its best response function has shifted out; it will produce more chips. We know from the preceding discussion that the competitor's best response is to build less capacity. Recall that in a quantity game profits move with market share, so the competitor will earn lower profits. The original contract is an aggressive strategic commitment because it hurts the rival.

Imagine a case where one company is located in a developing nation and one in an industrialized nation. The industrialized nation passes a law raising pollution standards. The local company now finds that each unit of output is more expensive due to treatment and disposal costs that it did not have to pay before the law took effect. Its best response function has shifted inwards; its production falls, while its rival's production and profits increase. The government law actually caused the commitment; the company didn't choose it. However, the rival still benefits, so the final effect is a nice strategic commitment in a quantity game. *See* Figure 5 for a graph of the market.

To summarize, when the company's set of best choices shifts, the industry equilibrium also shifts. Obviously, the company making the strategic commitment

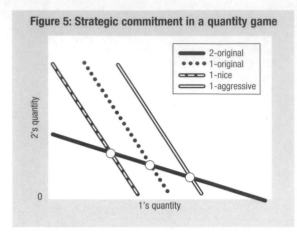

Figure 5: Strategic commitment in a quantity game

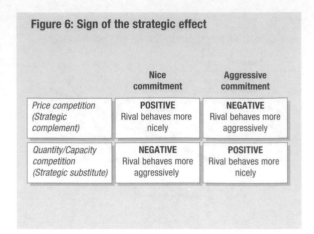

Figure 6: Sign of the strategic effect

	Nice commitment	Aggressive commitment
Price competition (Strategic complement)	**POSITIVE** Rival behaves more nicely	**NEGATIVE** Rival behaves more aggressively
Quantity/Capacity competition (Strategic substitute)	**NEGATIVE** Rival behaves more aggressively	**POSITIVE** Rival behaves more nicely

wants to change its price or quantity. Less obviously, its rival reacts and also changes price or quantity in a predictable way. Does the rival's reaction intensify or lessen competitive pressures in the industry? It depends on what kind of competition exists in the industry and what kind of strategic commitment is made. Figure 6 summarizes our analysis thus far.

As you can see from the figure, in a price game you get what you give: nice strategic commitments are returned with nice behavior, aggressive with aggressive behavior. In capacity games bullies have an advantage: aggressive behavior is met with a soft response.

Bluffing

If the rival is not convinced that the company's incentives have changed (for example, the commitment can be easily reversed), then commitment has no impact. For example, imagine that the memory-chip contract mentioned above was tentative; either side could change its features or cancel it with no penalties. In that case, the best response function of the manufacturer has moved much less, perhaps not at all. Everyone's strategies will stay the same. In contrast, real commitments (that are costly to change) alter incentives permanently. In turn, this changes the rival's expectations and its own choice. The industry "game" will have a different outcome due to the strategic commitment.

Direct costs and benefits of strategic commitment

While the preceding discussion has explained the strategic effect of various types of commitment, keep in mind that the commitment itself usually has a direct cost and a direct benefit, which we have not discussed. Figure 6 only shows the sign of the strategic effect. For example, building and using a new factory involves a direct initial capital cost, a direct long-run operating benefit, and a strategic impact due to the change in competitor behavior. The total impact of the new factory on company profitability is the sum of the direct and the strategic effects. Straightforward analysis of a project would consider only the direct effect and naively omit competitor responses. Because the direct and strategic effects can be either positive or negative, careful analysis is required to determine what signs they take, which is stronger, and whether the company will benefit from the move. A simplistic view of strategic commitments is that only the direct effect matters and the strategic effect is minor. This is not true. The strategic effect can be very important and can even overwhelm the direct effect in some cases.

Negative strategic effects

Imagine, for example, that a new factory would lead to lower costs and lower prices; internal corporate estimates suggest that the new greater price differential between the rival products will enable the company to steal a 20 percent market share from its main competitor. Missing here, though, is an estimate of the reaction of the competitor. The competitor will not keep price constant in the face of this change. Our framework says that the strategic effect (Price Game + Aggressive Commitment) is negative. The competitor will drop price in response to its competitor's lower price. As a result, the new factory will not gain the company as much market share as it had naively anticipated. This means that analysis of the total returns from a new factory should incorporate the strategic effect, namely the drop in the competitor's price.

Consider a situation where two companies, A and B, set production for sale in a common market; they are playing a quantity game. One of the companies, B, is involved in a long-running patent suit. One day, B finds out that it has lost the suit and will now have to pay a steep royalty on each future unit of production. A's costs are unaffected by the legal decision. What will happen to competition in the market? B's best response function will shift inwards. It will restore its margin by cutting back production and inducing a rise in the market price. This creates a negative strategic effect (Quantity Game + Nice Commitment). The legal decision has a negative direct effect on B (higher costs) but also imposes a negative strategic effect by forcing B to make a nice commitment in a quantity game. A's market share is now greater and its profits are higher, because B is forced into a weak competitive position by the lawsuit. When B was negotiating the outcome of the suit, it should have asked for equivalently sized annual payments instead of a royalty per unit output, because an annual payment would not create a negative strategic effect, benefitting Company A at B's expense.

Positive strategic effects

Suppose a new generation of semiconductor chip has just been invented. A Korean and a Japanese company are expected to split the market evenly and the Japanese company makes plans to build a manufacturing facility that will handle half the market demand. Unexpectedly, the Korean company finishes construction of a large facility before the Japanese company begins building. The capacity of the Korean facility is two-thirds of expected market size. What will the Japanese company do? Because marginal costs of chip production are so low, once a facility has been built, it is most profitable to run it at as high a utilization rate as possible. The Koreans made an aggressive commitment in a capacity game. That commitment is credible and irreversible because the facility is built, not just announced. The Japanese company will drive prices down if it builds according to its original plan; instead it will build a smaller facility. The new equilibrium (Figure 5) shows this outcome, with increased Korean market share and decreased Japanese market share. The strategic effect is positive, while the direct cost of the strategic commitment is negative: the facility is ready too early. If the additional profits earned from a higher market share outweigh the cost of entering early, then the strategic commitment is worth making.

In 1991, there was a change in the regulation of prices of pharmaceuticals sold to the Medicaid program in the United States. For some drugs, the government decreed that it would pay only the lowest price offered by the manufacturer to any other customer. Managers realized that a discount to a health maintenance organization (HMO) or large buying group could turn out to be the lowest price offered on the drug, and therefore would apply to Medicaid sales. Without the discount to the HMO, Medicaid sales would take place at a higher price. The law caused a nice strategic commitment in a price game (strategic complements), resulting in a positive strategic effect. My own research shows that equilibrium prices rose for companies affected by the legislation and their competitors; price competition softened. In this example, a substantial benefit of the legislation would be missed if a manager analyzed the direct cost and benefit of the law and ignored the strategic effect. The direct cost of the law was lower prices to Medicaid and some lobbying expenses. The strategic effect was higher prices on the remaining 90 percent of the market.

Conclusion

This article argues that understanding competition and how to affect it can significantly improve managerial decision making in oligopoly markets. When your competitors' behavior has an impact on your profits, it is crucial to manage the competitive relationship to your advantage. If you know whether you are playing a game of strategic substitutes or complements, and you understand whether your commitment is nice or aggressive, you can predict your competitors' response. This allows a manager to avoid harmful competitive dynamics and take advantage of profitable opportunities.

While the model is simple and does not encompass all situations of competitive interaction, it is a valuable first step. More advanced models of competition build on the insights of Cournot and Bertrand.

Summary

Understanding competition and how to influence it can significantly improve decision making in markets where there are few major competitors, says **Fiona Scott Morton**. In seeking to predict a competitor's response it helps to know which game you are playing – strategic substitutes or complements – and whether your commitment is nice or aggressive. The tools discussed by the author are relatively simple, but they represent a critical building block for more elaborate game theory tools.

Suggested further reading

Bertrand, J. (1883) "Book review of *Recherche sur Les Principes Mathematiques de la Theorie des Richesses*," *Journal des Savants*, 67:499–508.

Bulow, J., Geanakoplos, J. and Klemperer, P. (1985) "Multimarket oligopoly: strategic substitutes and complements," *Journal of Political Economy*, 93 (3):488–511.

Cournot, A. (1897) "On the competition of producers," Chapter 7 in *Researchers into the Mathematical Principles of the Theory of Wealth*, New York: Macmillan.

Scott Morton, F. (1997) "The strategic response by pharmaceutical firms to the Medicaid most-favoured-customer rules," *The RAND Journal of Economics*, 28 (2).

Spence, A.M. (1977) "Entry, capacity, investment and oligopolistic pricing," *Bell Journal of Economics*, 8 (2).

Integration strategies and the scope of the firm

by Thomas N. Hubbard

What lines of business should your company be in? Which of your inputs should you make yourself and which should you buy from outside vendors? Should you market your goods yourself or rely on outside wholesalers or retailers? Whether to integrate is one of the most important strategic decisions a company makes.

Integration is a risky proposition. In general, there are two key drawbacks. One is that integrated companies often bypass the opportunity to trade through markets. Well-working markets allow companies always to procure from their lowest-cost supplier and sell through the most appropriate distribution channel. When companies manufacture their own inputs or distribute their own goods, they are generally not completely free to do so. Procurement or marketing costs are higher as a consequence. The other is that integration spreads companies' managerial resources over a wider set of activities. Managerial decisions may suffer as a consequence, either because managers are in markets in which they lack expertise or because decisions generally become worse when managers have more responsibilities.

These drawbacks are particularly salient when companies are considering whether to integrate into an industry in which scale economies are high. Consider a supermarket's decision on whether to produce its own tomatoes. Even large supermarkets cannot sell enough tomatoes to support an efficiently scaled tomato farm. Were a supermarket to integrate backward into tomato growing, it would either have to operate an inefficiently scaled, high-cost tomato farm, or wholesale some of its harvest to other tomato retailers. The first option implies high procurement costs. The second involves expanding supermarket activities not just into tomato growing, but also into tomato wholesaling – spreading managerial resources even thinner and over less familiar territory. It is therefore unsurprising to observe that when supermarkets produce the goods they sell, they do so for goods for which scale economies are low, such as sandwiches.

Integration's risks are suggested by the "diversification discount" identified by corporate finance researchers. In a 1990 *Journal of Finance* article, Randall Morck, Andrei Shleifer, and Robert Vishny report that, on average, companies' stock prices decline when they announce plans to diversify into new businesses. In certain situations, however, integration's benefits can exceed its costs. This makes it an attractive strategy. The rest of this article discusses how a company's technological and economic environment affects the benefits of integration. Although much of the analysis applies to integration in general, the focus will be on vertical integration – the company's scope within a supply chain. This is because issues arise in such contexts that make integration a particularly interesting and difficult problem.

Synergies

Integration decisions are often justified by the synergies they create. Synergies, or complementarities, exist when assets are worth more when used in conjunction with each other than separately. Synergies can involve both physical and non-physical assets. One important class of the latter is human capital – individuals' skills or know-how.

Synergies of some form are essential for integration to be successful. Integration offers little or no potential benefits when they do not exist. The costs discussed above related to procurement or managerial inefficiencies are almost certain to exceed integration's benefits in such circumstances.

Synergies can exist for a wide variety of reasons. Production-related scope economies arise when production of one good lowers companies' costs of producing other goods. For example, Hollywood studios such as Paramount produce and distribute both feature films and television shows. This helps utilize their capacity at a high rate. Marketing-related scope economies arise when brand names can be extended over multiple products. Walt Disney Company is able to take advantage of cross-promotion effects among a wide range of industries, including film production, theme parks, and retailing.

But while synergies are necessary elements of successful integration strategies, it does not follow that integration is always the best way to capture them. For example, auto-assembly plants are worth more if used in conjunction with parts-making plants, but achieving production-related synergies does not require common ownership. As one observes in the auto industry, synergies can be achieved by way of a wide variety of organizational arrangements, ranging from simple spot arrangements to detailed contracts to integration. Similarly, many companies – including Disney – capture marketing-related synergies by branding items for which they subcontracted production. Usually, the difficult question is not whether synergies exist but whether integration is the best way to capture them.

Pricing and market power

This subsection focusses on circumstances where integration can help companies obtain more favorable prices.

Elimination of pricing distortions

Integration can allow companies to profit from the elimination of pricing distortions. Consider the case of a manufacturer and retailer, each of whom has some pricing power in their respective markets. Each company will set too high a price from the other's point of view, because neither accounts for its sales-lowering impact on the other's profits. Merging would allow the two companies to set a retail price that increases their collective profits because it unifies pricing decisions. This is one reason that "eliminating the middleman" can be beneficial. Some personal-computer sellers have based part of their overall strategy on this principle. For example, after observing that retail computer stores were selling its computers at higher prices than it would like, Compaq, the US computer group, began to sell computers directly to customers. Vertical integration into retailing allows Compaq to set retail prices on some of its computers.

Raising rivals' costs

Other integration strategies seek to improve companies' positions at their competitors' expense. One class of these raises rivals' costs. Foreclosure strategies are examples. Foreclosure is when a company integrates into another stage of the supply chain to eliminate competitors' potential suppliers or customers. Such

Brewers and pubs in the UK

Many pubs in the UK are "tied houses": establishments where only one brewer's products are sold. Some tied houses are owned by brewers and operated by their employee-managers. Brewers set retail prices at these "managed" pubs. Others are operated by individuals who lease the premises from brewers and run the pub themselves. At "tenant" pubs, owner-managers typically set beer prices themselves. In 1989, over half of pubs in the UK were tied houses owned by national brewers. Concerns that national brewers' pub ownership led to high beer prices and low variety led the then Monopolies and Mergers Commission (MMC) to recommend reforms. One of these required national brewers to divest some of their managed pubs. Most pubs that were divested remained tied houses, but became part of national pub chains. Unfortunately for

beer drinkers, the MMC's reforms appear to have led to higher prices. In a 1998 article in the *Economic Journal*, Margaret Slade shows that prices increased at tied houses relative to independent pubs after divestiture. She also provides evidence that profits in the industry decreased. Slade's findings strongly suggest that brewers vertically integrate to eliminate the pricing distortion that arises when brewers and pubs set prices independently. When brewers own pubs, this has the disadvantage of extending their managerial resources from beer production to beer retailing. Pub managers' incentives are weaker than at tenant pubs because they are employees and not owners. But integration appears to allow brewers to control retail prices better.

actions can soften competition and increase profits by raising rivals' costs. In extreme cases – such as when integration allows companies completely to control the supply of critical inputs – integration can enable companies to foreclose entry completely.

One well-known historical example is US Steel's acquisition of iron ore mining rights in the northern United States early in the twentieth century. This softened competition in steel markets by eliminating competitors' sources of supply. More recently, the proposed acquisition by Barnes & Noble, largest book retailer in the US, of Ingram Books, largest book distributor in the US, would likely have raised costs at Amazon.com, the e-commerce group, at least in the short run. Similar incentives appear in newly deregulated telecommunications markets. In the US, incumbent local telephone companies have an incentive to purchase cable television companies. By doing so, they could raise potential entrants' costs by controlling a channel through which entrants could supply local telephone service.

There are three significant hazards of integration strategies based on raising rivals' costs. One is that long-run success depends in large part on the existence of entry barriers in markets into which companies integrate. Controlling a competitor's existing suppliers or distribution channels is pointless if new companies would then enter input supply or distribution markets. Another is that situations in which these strategies are most attractive – when integration involves the acquisition of rights to a scarce resource – tend to be those in which they would invite antitrust or regulatory intervention. The Barnes & Noble/Ingram merger was scuttled after antitrust authorities announced their opposition, and legislation in the US currently prevents many local telephone companies from purchasing cable television companies. Finally, when integration strategies require companies to acquire scarce resources, the big winners may well be owners of scarce resources rather than integrating companies. The resource's owner has an incentive to hold out for the highest price possible. At this price, integration may not be profitable even if it allowed a company subsequently to raise its rivals' costs. Although US Steel's mineral right purchases may have foreclosed entry into steel markets, it is unclear whether it or the seller of these rights, the Great Northern Railway, benefitted more from the strategy.

Relatedly, companies may integrate in response to competitors' integration strategy. Integration may ensure access to critical inputs, thus reducing the prospect of foreclosure. For example, many US waste-management companies have purchased disposal facilities. Some companies' integration into disposal reflects concern that integration by their competitors would raise their costs by forcing them to distant facilities.

Why not contracts?

In many cases, companies can attain integration's pricing goals without the already mentioned drawbacks through contractual strategies. One may be able to eliminate the "successive monopoly" distortion via a contract that specifies minimum quantities that companies down the supply chain must order or sell. Exclusive dealing arrangements may work just as well as integration for the purposes of raising rivals' costs. Although it is sometimes difficult to mimic integration's pricing effects with contracts – perhaps because appropriate pricing strategies are complicated, difficult to articulate, or hard to enforce – managers should investigate thoroughly whether contractual solutions are feasible alternatives before embarking on integration strategies.

Because contracts are appealing substitutes to integration for affecting prices, economists and strategists have explored other rationales for integration. This work, building from early research by Benjamin Klein, Robert Crawford, and Armen Alchian (1978), Oliver Williamson (1979), Sanford Grossman and Oliver Hart (1986), and Oliver Hart and John Moore (1990), focusses on the fact that integration changes who controls physical assets. The following section describes how control changes affect investment decisions that are difficult to contract on. The profitability of integration depends on whether it enhances or diminishes investment incentives.

Specific investments

Companies and individuals sometimes make investments in specific assets. Assets are specific when there is a wedge between their value to their first and second highest-value users. Physical assets can be specific because of their physical characteristics or geographic location. For example, machines that produce a special part for a particular vehicle maker are specific to the vehicle maker; they are much less valuable if used to supply a different vehicle maker. Human capital – skills or know-how – can also be specific. Assets can be specific over different horizons, depending on how quickly they can be redeployed in other uses, but specificity is most important when it is long lasting.

Simple market arrangements do not work well when transactions involve investments in specific assets. The reason is that they fail to protect such investments from appropriation. Returning to the vehicle maker example, suppose a supplier were to build a machine to produce the special part. Once the machine is in place, the vehicle maker may be able to extract much of the machine's value from the supplier by demanding a lower price for the part. Demands to renegotiate may succeed if the machine is not easily redeployable – the part maker is "locked in" if it cannot use the machine to serve other vehicle makers. Foreseeing this, the part maker may do things to protect its interests: for example, it may refuse to customize the part to the degree the vehicle maker would like. Such decisions may be optimal from the part maker's point of view. But they decrease the potential gains from trade, and are thus value decreasing.

Successful strategies in these environments structure relationships so as to capture the gains from trade as much as possible. Contractual strategies are attractive when decisions and contingencies can be easily articulated. Integration strategies are attractive when they are not. Asset specificity's implications for integration strategies differ depending on whether specific investments are in physical assets or human capital.

When specific investments are in physical capital, integration eliminates incentive problems by vesting all investment decisions with one company or individual. If making a custom part requires a specialized machine, appropriation problems go away if the vehicle maker owns the machine and customizes it itself.

Integration thus can help streamline production or reduce transportation costs within supply chains. Integrating companies may be able to profit from capturing configuration efficiencies. A common textbook example of this concerns the production of steel. Making sheet metal out of raw steel immediately after the raw metal is produced avoids the cost of reheating it after it hardens. It is efficient to configure production such that the equipment that produces sheet metal is very near that which produces raw metal. In principle, separate companies could make raw and sheet metal and achieve configuration efficiencies by locating next to each other. But each would be fearful that the other would exploit them, and it would probably be difficult to alleviate these concerns with a detailed contract. As a consequence, steel makers produce both raw steel and sheet metal.

When specific investments are in human capital, however, it is impossible to solve appropriation problems by vesting all decisions with one individual: individuals must decide on human capital investments themselves. Integration can exacerbate incentive problems by making individuals less secure about such investments. For example, suppose making a customized part does not require a specialized machine, but requires the supplier to learn special techniques. If the vehicle maker were to own the machine rather than the supplier, this could leave the supplier in a precarious position: the vehicle maker could extract value from the supplier by threatening to deny the supplier access to the machine. Suppliers in such a position would be more fearful that they would not be able to appropriate returns from their learning investments than they would if they owned the machine. Integration would thus weaken investment incentives within the newly acquired company.

This work gives rise to a useful rule of thumb for integration strategies in environments where specific investments are important. Integration will be value increasing if the goal is to elicit specific investments in physical assets, but value decreasing if it is to elicit human capital investments within the target company.

Conclusion

Integration strategies are unsuccessful when companies pay insufficient attention to integration's costs. When companies integrate into competitive industries, this often constrains them from procuring inputs or marketing outputs through efficient channels. It also spreads companies' managerial resources over a wider set of activities. As a consequence, diversification often lowers the value of companies.

Integration is sometimes beneficial when markets are imperfectly competitive or specific investments are important. In imperfectly competitive markets, integration can allow companies to obtain more favorable prices. But doing so with contracts is often a viable alternative through which companies can obtain integration's pricing benefits without incurring its costs. Integration can help elicit investments in specific physical assets, especially when such investments are difficult to articulate in an enforceable contract. However, it can discourage investments in specific human capital investments within the newly acquired company by diluting managerial incentives.

Summary

Integration is a risky approach, warns **Thomas N. Hubbard**. If a company pays insufficient attention to the associated costs, integration strategy may fail. Risks include the fact that in bypassing market mechanisms, procurement or marketing costs increase. Integration also spreads managerial resources more thinly, so decisions may suffer. Diversification thus often lowers the value of a company. Integration may bring companies more favorable prices. But an often more viable alternative is to secure these through contracts, giving companies pricing benefits from integration without the costs.

Contributors

C.K. Prahalad is Harvey C. Fruehauf Professor of Business Administration and professor of corporate strategy and international business at University of Michigan Business School.

W. Chan Kim is the Boston Consulting Group Bruce D. Henderson Chair Professor in International Management at INSEAD in Fontainebleau, France.

Renée Mauborgne is the INSEAD Distinguished Fellow and affiliate professor of strategy and management at INSEAD in Fontainebleau, France, and Fellow at the World Economic Forum at Davos.

Aneel G. Karnani is associate professor of corporate strategy and international business at University of Michigan Business School. He focusses on global competition, strategic analysis and manufacturing strategy.

Thomas N. Gladwin is the Max McGraw Professor of Sustainable Enterprise serving jointly at the University of Michigan Business School and School of Natural Resources and Environment. He directs the University's Erb Environmental Management Institute and its Corporate Environmental Management Program.

Paul Verdin is affiliate professor at large at INSEAD and holds the Chair in strategy and organisation at Solvay Business School (ULB, Belgium). He focusses on strategic management of internationalization and the successful development of European strategies and organizations.

STRATEGY AND THE GENERAL BUSINESS ENVIRONMENT

3

Contents

Introduction

Companies need to understand global forces and to react quickly when designing their own business models. This module looks at the emerging business environment shaping strategy, notably the newly competitive landscape of the last decade, the switch from "production" to "knowledge working," and growing public concern about sustainable development. The challenge in all this after years of downsizing is to find new ways of growth – one way is to follow the "value innovators" who reject conventional practice, expand demand through strategic pricing and increase their profits by focussing on "target" costs.

Changes in the competitive battlefield

by C.K. Prahalad

It is hardly surprising that the conceptual models and administrative processes used by managers often outlast their usefulness. It takes researchers time, after all, to identify new problems and emerging solutions before they can produce theories about them. Then there is the time lag between the development of these theories and their conversion into common business practice.

Where management concepts are concerned, this time lag – often a decade – brings with it an interesting conundrum. In an era of rapid and disruptive change in the economic, political, social, regulatory, and technological environment, do managers have to discard established and tested analytical tools equally fast? How can they identify the on-going relevance of concepts and tools in a changing environment? In my article "Weak signals and strong paradigms," published in the August 1996 issue of the *Journal of Marketing Research*, I ask: what is the nature of the battle between strong and well-established paradigms and weak economic signals that herald a new and emerging competitive reality? In the current article, I propose to identify the nature of changes required in both the concepts used in strategy analysis as well as the process by which strategy is developed in modern corporations.

The heritage of strategy concepts

The most prevalent and widely used tools of strategy analysis are: strength, weakness, opportunities and threats (SWOT) analysis, industry structure analysis (five forces), value chain analysis, generic strategies, strategic group analysis, barriers to entry, and others of the genre (set out in Michael Porter's 1980 book, *Competitive Strategy: Techniques for Analyzing Industries and Competitors*, and also in his 1985 work, *Competitive Advantage*).

The concepts and tools – many of them the staples of economists – were adopted and simplified for the use of managers. The formalization of these concepts was instrumental in pushing strategy development from the realm of "the intuitive genius of the founder or a top manager" to that of logical process. However, most of these concepts were developed during the late 1970s and the 1980s. During this period, underlying competitive conditions evolved but within a well-understood paradigm. A major competitive disruption during this period, certainly for US and European companies, was the spectacular success of Japanese manufacturing in industries as diverse as steel, consumer electronics, autos, and semiconductors. The sources of competitive advantage, during this decade, accrued to those who could wrest significant efficiencies in operations through focus on quality, cycle time, reengineering, and teamwork. Operational efficiencies within a relatively stable industry structure paradigm became the focus. In fact, this focus on wresting competitive advantage through operational efficiencies led some managers to believe that strategy was unimportant and management was all about implementation.

The emerging competitive landscape

The 1990s witnessed significant and discontinuous change in the competitive environment. There is now an accelerating global trend to deregulate and privatize. Large and key industries such as telecoms, power, water, healthcare, and financial services are being deregulated. Countries as diverse as India, Russia, Brazil, and China are at various stages of privatizing their public sectors. Technological convergence – such as that between chemical and electronic companies; computing, communications, components, and consumer electronics; food and pharmaceuticals; and cosmetics and pharmaceuticals – is disrupting traditional industry structures. Whether it is Eastman Kodak, the US photographic giant, Sony, the global electronics group, International Business Machines, Unilever, the Anglo-Dutch consumer giant, Revlon, the US cosmetics group, or Ford, managers must come to terms with the nature of transformation that technological convergence and digitalization will have on their industries. Further, the impact of the spread of the world wide web and the internet is just beginning to be felt. Ecological sensitivities and the emergence of non-governmental organizations such as the green movement are also new dimensions of the competitive landscape. Are these discontinuities changing the very nature of the industry structure – the relationships between consumers, competitors, collaborators, and investors? Are they challenging the established competitive positions of incumbents and allowing new types of competitors and new bases for competition to emerge (e.g., Barnesandnoble.com and Amazon.com, both internet-based book retailers)?

We can identify a long list of discontinuities and examples to illustrate each one of them. However, that is not our purpose here. We need to acknowledge the signals (weak as they may be) of the emergence of a new competitive landscape where the rules of engagement may not be the same as they were during the 1980s. Strategists have to make the transition from asking the question: "How do I position my company and gain advantage in a known game (a known industry structure)?" Increasingly, the relevant question is: "How do I divine the contours of an evolving and changing industry structure and, therefore, the rules of engagement in a new and evolving game?" Industries represent such a diversity of new, emerging, and evolving games. The rules of engagement are written as companies and managers experiment and adjust their approaches to competition.

Strategy in a discontinuous competitive landscape

Strategists must start with a new mindset. Traditional strategic planning processes emphasized resource allocation – which plants, what locations, what products, and sometimes what businesses – within an implicit business model. Disruptive changes challenge the business models.

Four transformations will influence the business models and the work of strategists in the decades ahead.

The strategic space available to companies will expand

Consider, for example, the highly regulated power industry. All utilities once looked alike and the scope of their operations was constrained by public utility commissions and government regulators. Due to deregulation, utilities can now determine their own strategic space. Today, utilities have a choice regarding the level of vertical integration: "Do I need to be in power generation? Do I need to be in power transmission?" Companies can unbundle assets and can also segment their businesses: "Should we focus more on industrial or domestic consumers?" They can decide their geographic scope: "Should I become global, regional, national or just remain local?" And finally, they can change their business portfolio: "Should I invest in water, telecoms, gas lines, services?" Houston-based Enron is a good example of a traditional utility that has, in less than ten years, exploited deregulation and transformed itself into a global services powerhouse in energy, water, and other infrastructure industries.

The forces of change – deregulation, the emergence of large developing countries such as India, China, and Brazil as major business opportunities – provide a new playing field. Simultaneously, forces of digitalization, the emergence of the internet, and the convergence of technologies provide untold new opportunities for strategists. The canvas available to the strategist is large and new. One can paint the picture one wants.

Business will be global

Increasingly, the distinction between local and global business will be narrowed. All businesses will have to be locally responsive and all businesses will be subject to the influences and standards of global players. Consider, for example, McDonald's and Coca-Cola, held up as examples of truly global players unconstrained by local customers and national differences. In India, McDonald's had to change its recipe to serve lamb (instead of beef) and vegetarian patties (a radical departure from its normal western fare). Coke had to recognize the power of "Thums Up," a local cola (which Coke purchased), and promote that product. The need for local responsiveness, especially when global companies want to penetrate markets with different levels of consumer purchasing power, is very clear. On the other hand, Nirula's, a local fast-food chain in India, was, in its own restaurants, forced to respond to the cleanliness and ambience of McDonald's. This is a case of global standards being imposed on a local player.

Global and local distinctions will remain in products and services. Globalization may have as much to do with standards – quality, service levels, safety, environmental concerns, protection of intellectual property, and talent management. Needless to say, globalization will force strategists to come to terms with multiple geographic locations, new standards, capacity for adaptation to local needs, multiple cultures, and collaboration across national and regional boundaries in everything from manufacturing, product development, and global account management to logistics.

Speed will be a critical element

Given the nature of competitive changes, speed of reaction will be a critical element of strategy. At a minimum, it will challenge the yearly planning cycle. For example, consider the traditional strategic planning process in a large company. The process of strategy discussion and commitments typically starts in October. It identifies the strategic issues for the next calendar year and three to four years hence. What is the use of such a process in an internet-based start-up? What is the use of this process for a General Motors, or a Ford, as it approaches internet-based selling? Or for Lucent Technologies, the leading supplier of computer and telephone networking equipment, as it approaches internet-based service (following the very successful effort by Cisco Systems, the US-based market leader in data networking)? Speed of reaction, not tied to a rigid corporate calendar, is of the essence. Strategy must be a topic of discussion and debate all the time, not just during the planning sessions –

strategy making and thinking cannot be a "corporate rain dance" during October!

Speed is also an element in how fast a company learns new technologies and integrates them with the old. As all traditional companies are confronted with disruptive changes, the capacity to learn and act fast is increasingly a major source of competitive advantage.

Innovation is the new source of competitive advantage

Innovation was always a source of competitive advantage. However, the concept of innovation was tied to product and process innovations. In many large companies, the innovation process is still called the "product creation process." Reducing cycle time, increasing modularity, tracking sales from new products introduced during the last two years as a percentage of total sales, and global product launches were the hallmarks of an innovative company. Increasingly, the focus of innovation has to shift toward innovation in business models. For example, how does an auction-based pricing market (e.g., airlines, hotels) in an industry with excess capacity change the business model? How do you think about resources available to the company for product development when customers become co-developers of the product or service? The 400,000–500,000 people who will beta test Microsoft 2000 represent a development investment of $500m (at a modest $1,000 per person testing) outside the investment made by the company. Should we have an expanded notion of resource availability? What impact does mass customization or, more importantly, personalization of products and services have on the total logistics chain? Business innovations are crucial in a competitive landscape subject to disruptive changes.

Strategy in the next millennium

Given the dramatic changes taking place in the competitive landscape, I believe that both the concept of strategy and the process of strategy making will change. Older approaches will not suffice.

Managers will have to start with two clear premises:

- First, that they can influence the competitive environment. Strategy is not about positioning the company in a given industry space, but increasingly one of influencing, shaping, and creating it. What managers do matters in how industries evolve. This is not just about the reactions of large, well-endowed companies like Citicorp, Merrill Lynch, Hilton Hotels, IBM, or General Motors. Smaller companies can also have an impact on industry evolution. For example, E*Trade, eBay, Price.com, and Amazon.com (all new commercial enterprises created as a result of the internet) have significantly influenced the dynamics of well-established and traditional industries.

- Second, it is not possible to influence the evolving industry environment if one does not start with a point of view about how the world can be, not how to improve what is available but how radically to alter it. Imagining a new competitive space and acting to influence the migration toward that future is critical. Strategy is, therefore, not an extrapolation of the current situation, but an exercise in "imagining and then folding the future in." This process needs a different starting point. This is about providing a strategic direction – a point of view – and identifying, at best, the main milestones on the way. There is no attempt to be precise on product plans, or budgets. Knowing the broad contours of the future is not as difficult as people normally assume. For example, we know with great uncertainty the demographic composition of every country. We can recognize the trends – the desire for mobility, access to information, the spread of the web and increasing dependence of all countries on global trade. The problem is not information about the future but insights about how these trends will transform industries and what new opportunities will emerge.

While a broad strategic direction (or strategic intent and strategic architecture) is critical to the process, it is equally important to recognize that dramatic changes in the environment suggest that managers must act and be tactical about navigating their way around new obstacles and unforeseen circumstances.

Tactical changes are difficult if there is no overarching point of view. The need continually to adjust resource configuration as competitive conditions change is becoming recognized. A critical part of being strategic is the ability to adjust and adapt quickly within a given strategic direction. This may be described as "inventing new games within a sand box," the sand box being the broad strategic direction.

The most dramatic change in the process of strategy making is the breakdown in the traditional strategy hierarchy – top managers develop strategy and middle managers implement it. By its very nature, discontinuous change in the competitive environment is creating a whole new dynamic. People who are close to the new technologies, competitors, and customers appear as managers in the middle. They have the information, urgency, and motivation to act. They are also the ones who have direct control over people and physical resources. Top managers, in an era of discontinuous change, are rather removed from the new and emerging competitive reality.

For example, how many top managers have personal experience of the internet, video games, fantasy football, and chat rooms? Middle managers must take more responsibility for developing a strategic direction and, more importantly, for making decentralized decisions consistent with the broad direction of the company. The involvement of middle managers is a critical element of the strategy process.

Finally, creating the future is a task that involves more than the traditional stand-alone company. Managers have to make alliances and collaborate with suppliers, partners, and often competitors to develop new standards (DVD – digital versatile disc – technology, for example), infrastructure (like broadband), or new operating systems (like Java). Alliances and networks are an integral part of the total process. This requirement is so well understood that it is hardly worth elaborating here. Resources available to the company are dramatically enhanced through alliances and networks.

The new view of strategy

The emerging view of strategy contrasts dramatically with the traditional view. The difference is shown in Figure 1. The shift in emphasis in the concept of strategy and the process of strategy making is dramatic.

It is clear that the disruptive forces that have wrought this change are accelerating. It is time for managers to abandon the comfort of the traditional and tried-and-tested tools and concepts and embrace the new. Disruptive competitive changes will challenge the status quo. Those who take up the challenge and proactively change will create the future. The markets will decide the drivers, passengers and the rate of "road kill" soon enough.

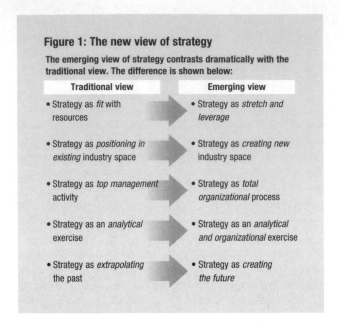

Figure 1: The new view of strategy

The emerging view of strategy contrasts dramatically with the traditional view. The difference is shown below:

Traditional view	Emerging view
• Strategy as *fit* with resources	• Strategy as *stretch and leverage*
• Strategy as *positioning in existing* industry space	• Strategy as *creating new* industry space
• Strategy as *top management* activity	• Strategy as *total organizational* process
• Strategy as an *analytical* exercise	• Strategy as an *analytical and organizational* exercise
• Strategy as *extrapolating* the past	• Strategy as *creating the future*

Summary

Many of the concepts used in strategy were developed during the late 1970s and 1980s when underlying competitive conditions evolved within a well-understood model. Japan's manufacturing success, with its emphasis on operating efficiency, challenged some of the traditional assumptions – but it is only in the last decade that a new competitive landscape has emerged and the rules of engagement have changed. While the canvas available to today's strategists is large and new, companies will need to understand global forces, react quickly, and innovate when defining their business models. **C.K. Prahalad** sets out to define the new paradigm.

Suggested further reading

Brown, S.L. and Eisenhardt, K. (1998) *Competing on the Edge: Strategy as Structured Chaos*, Boston, MA: Harvard Business School Press.

Hamel, G. (1996) "Strategy as revolution," *Harvard Business Review*, July–August.

Hamel, G. and Prahalad, C.K. (1994) *Competing for the Future*, Boston, MA: Harvard Business School Press.

Porter, M. (1985) *Competitive Strategy: Techniques for Analyzing Industries and Competitors*, New York: The Free Press.

Porter, M. (1985) *Competitive Advantage*, New York: The Free Press.

Prahalad, C.K. (1996) "Weak signals and strong paradigms," *Journal of Marketing Research*, August.

Prahalad, C.K. and Lieberthal, K. (1998) "The end of corporate imperialism," *Harvard Business Review,* July–August.

New dynamics of strategy in the knowledge economy

by W. Chan Kim and Renée Mauborgne

Despite the current passion for mergers and acquisitions, the companies that are creating much of the new wealth, jobs, and excitement are not those obsessed by getting bigger. They are those that challenge how existing businesses run and offer entirely new ways of thinking about an industry.

This applies not only in high-tech fields such as computers, software, and the internet, where the likes of Microsoft, Intel, Cisco, Yahoo!, and Dell are reaching new innovative heights. In other industrial sectors the ability to develop new business models extends to retailers such as Wal-Mart, airlines such as Southwest, home repair chains such as Home Depot, coffee shops such as Starbucks, brokers such as Charles Schwab, and bookstores such as Borders and Amazon.com.

For four years running, *Fortune* magazine has ranked Enron, the Houston-based energy company that operates in two of the oldest industries in the world – gas and electricity – as the most innovative company in the US. Today, Enron has as many traders, analysts, and rocket scientists – including a genuine ex-rocket scientist from the former Soviet Union – at its headquarters as it does gas and pipeline people. Enron exemplifies the transition from the production to the knowledge economy in which the proportion and value of ideas and innovation to land, labor, and capital are rising dramatically, even in the most basic industries.

Knowledge economy risks

This switch from production to knowledge economy has two consequences.

- It creates the potential for increasing returns. This can be seen in software where, for example, production of the first copy of Windows 95 cost Microsoft millions, while subsequent copies cost no more than the near trivial price of a disk. It is also evident in businesses as capital intensive as Enron's. Here, for example, the fixed costs of developing sophisticated financial risk-management tools for hedging gas prices can be spread across infinite transactions at insignificant marginal cost.
- It creates enormous potential for free-riding. This has to do with the non-rival and only partially excludable nature of knowledge.

A rival good has the property that its use by one company precludes its use by another. So, for example, Nobel prize-winning scientists employed by IBM cannot simultaneously be employed by another company. Scrap steel consumed by Nucor cannot be simultaneously consumed for production by other mini-mill steel makers.

In contrast, use of a non-rival good by one company in no way limits its use by another. Ideas fall into this camp. Thus when Chrysler's innovation in minivans took off in 1983, other car companies were able to make use of the concept without in any way limiting Chrysler's ability to apply it at the same time. This makes competitive imitation not only possible, but less costly – the cost and risk of developing the innovative idea are borne by the value innovator, not the follower.

This challenge is exacerbated when the notion of excludability is considered. Excludability is a function of both the nature of the good and the legal system. A good is excludable if the company can prevent others from using it, due, for example, to limited access or patent protection. So, for example, Intel can exclude other microprocessor chipmakers from using its manufacturing facilities through property ownership laws. And Starbucks can prevent other coffee chain start-ups from using its coffee beans by refusing to sell them to would-be copycats, i.e., strategically limiting access. However, what Starbucks cannot exclude from others is their ability to walk into any store, study its layout, atmosphere, and product range, and mimic the "idea" or "blueprint" for a chic coffee-bar concept. Thus the highest value-added element of the Starbucks formula is not excludable. Once ideas are "out there," there is a natural knowledge spillover which all companies can learn from. This lack of excludability reinforces the risk of free-riding.

Of course, were it possible to get a patent and formal legal protection for innovative ideas, the risk would be considerably lower. Pharmaceutical companies, for example, have long enjoyed the benefit of formal patent protection to prevent the free-riding of other drug companies on their scientific discoveries for a specified period. But how do you get a patent for a radically superior coffee store design concept like Starbucks, which has tremendous value but in itself comprises no new technological discoveries? It is the arrangement of the items that fundamentally adds new value, i.e., the way they are combined, not the items themselves. There is no black magic in making exotic coffee drinks, high-quality coffee beans can be purchased from multiple sources, placing chairs and tables in corner store outlets is easy enough, as is having stacks of free newspapers to read and nice background music with friendly sales staff to help. As with The Body Shop, the UK cosmetics retailer, Home Depot, Charles Schwab, Virgin Atlantic Airways, Amazon.com, Borders and Barnes & Noble, and Chrysler's minivan (imitated in Europe as the MPV or people mover), the Starbucks story is about value innovation. All offer buyers fundamentally new and superior value in traditional businesses through innovative ideas and knowledge.

Even value innovations in software face the risk of free-riding. While companies that write computer software can obtain copyrights that prohibit other companies from copying the specific coding in the program, the look, feel, and functionality of software are hardly patentable. This means, effectively, that any successful program can be copied. Competing companies need only write their own code, but what functionality the software is to perform, how the internal programming components should be structured, and how the software should look and feel to customers can all, as Netscape painfully learned, be imitated. The same can be said for Wal-Mart's valuable inventory-replenishment system.

Maximizing returns

The question, then, is how best to maximize rents from value innovation ideas that have the potential for both increasing returns and free-riding. Should value innovators follow the conventional practice of technology innovators that price high, limit access, and initially engage in price skimming to earn a premium on their innovation, and only with the passage of time focus on lowering price and costs to hold ground and discourage imitators? In most cases, the answer is no. The dynamics of competition fundamentally change.

In a world of non-rival and non-excludable goods subject to the potential of not only economies of scale and learning but also of increasing returns, volume becomes key, price becomes key, and hence cost becomes key in ways never seen before. The aim from the outset is to capture the mass of buyers and expand the size of the market by offering radically superior value at price points accessible to the mass of buyers. Hence Amazon.com's strategy, summarized by founder Jeff Bezos as "GBF" or "Get Big Fast."

We thus expect that value innovators should not follow the theory and practice of rent-maximization behavior used by conventional innovators, for two reasons:

- First, because a high price premium and restricted supply provide a huge incentive for others to act on the opportunity of free-riding and undercut the price of the innovator.
- Second, because pricing high and limiting volume in the interests of an image of exclusivity prevents the innovator from exploiting economies of scale, learning and increasing returns, thereby defeating the innate profit advantage of "knowledge-heavy" goods.

Indeed, we see successful value innovators following a market approach distinct from that of the conventional monopolists.

This involves:

- strategic pricing for demand creation;
- target costing for profit creation.

Strategic pricing can lead to high volume and a rapid and powerful brand reputation for unprecedented value. Target costing can help achieve attractive profit margins and a cost structure that is hard to match for potential followers. The combination of target costing and high volume is a high-profit, high-growth engine as economies of scale, learning, and increasing returns kick in.

Consider, for example, how Nicholas Hayek, the chairman of Swatch group (formerly known as SMH), used this market approach to launch the Swatch, a value innovation that revived the entire Swiss watch industry.

Swatch transformed the perception of a watch. It moved from being a functional, time-telling device to a fashion accessory embodying the joy of life. It combined punctuality, endless new designs, a powerful emotional message, and artwork into an innovative concept for a watch.

To capture the rents of this value innovation, Hayek set up a project team to determine Swatch's strategic launch price. At the time, the arrival of hundreds of cheap but high-precision quartz watches from Japan and Hong Kong was capturing a substantial part of the market. These watches sold for up to $75. To pull the mass of buyers, create new demand, and build a strong and rapid brand name, SMH aggressively set its price at $40.

This price would not only motivate customers to buy several Swatches, just as people do with other fashion accessories like clothes, hats, coats, or hair ribbons, but the price left scant if any room for Japanese or Hong Kong-based companies to copy and respond.

The directive to the project team was: the watch must sell for that price, not a penny more. The team then worked backward to arrive at target cost. This involved working out what margin SMH needed to earn to support promotion and advertising. The project team was then charged with devising a production system

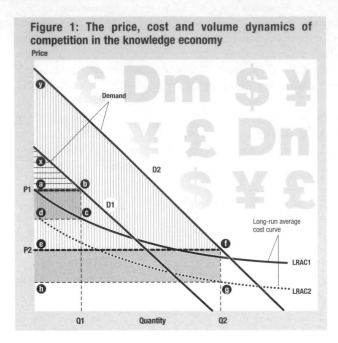

Figure 1: The price, cost and volume dynamics of competition in the knowledge economy

that could make Swatch at that cost and still earn the required profit margin. The result was that SMH was driven to innovate through automation of its design of Swatch mechanics, production, and assembly. This led to an unbeatable cost structure in the worldwide watch industry.

The price, cost, and volume dynamics of value innovation like that of Swatch can be graphically seen in Figure 1. Value innovation radically increases the appeal of a good, shifting the demand curve from D1 to D2. However, recognizing the non-rival and only partially excludable nature of its innovative good, the value innovator strategically prices the product from the outset to capture the mass of buyers in the expanded market. In the Swatch case this meant shifting the price from P1 to P2. This increases the quantity sold from Q1 to Q2 and builds strong brand recognition for unprecedented value. The value innovator, however, simultaneously engages in target costing to reduce the long-run average cost curve from LRAC1 to LRAC2, to expand its ability to profit and discourage free-riding and imitation.

Buyers receive a quantum leap in value, shifting the consumer surplus from **axb** to **eyf**. And the value innovator earns a leap in profit and growth, shifting the profit zone from **abcd** to **efgh**. The rapid brand recognition built by the value innovator as a result of the unprecedented value offered in the market place, combined with a simultaneous drive to reduce costs, allows companies to leapfrog the competition as economies of scale, learning, and increasing returns kick in. Hence the emergence of category killers and winner-take-most markets where companies earn dominant positions and customers simultaneously come out big winners.

Although value innovators do not always exercise low strategic pricing as in the case of Swatch, their market approach in pulling the mass of buyers is in many respects at odds with conventional monopolists. The extent to which the idea behind a value innovation is non-excludable has a bearing on the level of strategic price set by the value innovator. While, as we have argued, innovative ideas and processes are usually non-excludable or partially so, there are also value innovators whose ideas are patentable and hence excludable for a given length of time.

In such cases, value innovators may be inclined to set the strategic price of their product at the same level as, or even above, rivals' products and services. However, recognizing the powerful economies of scale, learning and increasing returns that come with high volumes of knowledge-heavy goods, the strategic price will still be set from the outset with the aim of capturing the mass of buyers.

Dyson Appliances, for example, created a value innovation in vacuum cleaners when it launched the Dyson Dual Cyclone in the UK. This was far easier to use and eliminated vacuum cleaner bags and hence the need to buy replacement bags for the life of the machine. In so doing, Dyson dramatically increased its vacuum cleaner's suction power against the industry average. However, given the radically superior value of its product and the fact that its value innovation was patentable, Dyson was strategically in a position to set its price relatively high while still capturing the mass of buyers. Although the vacuum cleaner was priced higher, it was still judged to be a leap in value and within the economic reach of the mass of buyers. Thus the conventional monopolists' practice of restricting supply through a high price premium is not followed even in these instances.

Dead weight loss

In the production economy, companies with dominant market positions adversely affected society's welfare in two ways:

■ First, in seeking to maximize their profitability, price would be set high, creating a dead weight loss for the mass of customers who, although desiring the good, would find it prohibitive due to unnaturally high prices.
■ Second, the lack of viable competition would encourage companies with monopolistic positions to be slack and not focus on efficiency, thereby consuming society's resources.

In the knowledge economy, however, innovative companies engage less in exorbitant price skimming. The focus shifts from restricting output with a high price premium to creating new aggregate demand through a leap in value and a price point accessible to the mass of buyers.

This creates a strong incentive not just to bring costs down, but to bring them down to the lowest possible level.

Summary

Vast new opportunities, as well as threats, are opening up as economies move from traditional "production" to a new model based on knowledge working, say **W. Chan Kim** and **Renée Mauborgne**. One is the potential for earning vastly increased returns; the other is the new potential for free-riding as new ideas are copied. The authors explain why successful "value innovators" reject conventional market practice, and follow a new dynamic of strategy. They expand demand through strategic pricing, and improve their profits by focussing on target costs.

Suggested further reading

Kim, W.C. and Mauborgne, R. (1997) "Value innovation: the strategic logic of high growth," *Harvard Business Review*, January–February.

Kim, W.C. and Mauborgne, R. (1999) "Creating new market space," *Harvard Business Review*, January–February.

Kim, W.C. and Mauborgne, R. (1999) "Strategy, value innovation, and the knowledge economy," *Sloan Management Review*, Spring.

Five ways to grow the market and create value

by Aneel G. Karnani

After years of restructuring, reengineering, and downsizing, many companies are now emphasizing growth. They are under pressure to do so from three directions: shareholders, competitors, and employees.

Shareholders have become more active and demanding not only in the US, but increasingly so in Europe as well.

Consider the number of companies that have fired or gently pushed out their CEOs in recent years: computer giants like Apple and Compaq, mobile phone makers like Ericsson, the Dutch electronics company Philips, Eastman Kodak of the US, US pharmaceuticals maker Pharmacia & Upjohn, and the list goes on. Even in Japan there are signs that companies are becoming more responsive to shareholder interests.

Shareholders demand value creation. This is closely linked to corporate growth. The obvious limits of value creation through cost cutting now make revenue growth essential.

Then there is the heat from competitors, particularly in industries such as banking, pharmaceuticals, automotive, defense, airlines, and personal computers, which are undergoing consolidation. Here growth is essential if economies of scale in technology development, operations, capacity utilization, marketing, distribution, and network externalities are to be captured. Those companies that fail to expand as fast as competitors will lose competitive advantage and enter a downward spiral. The only options then are expansion or a vicious cycle leading to oblivion.

Finally, employees are an important influence. Employees in an expanding company have greater opportunities for career advancement, financial rewards, job security, and job satisfaction. It is more fun to go to work every day and the collective mood is more upbeat in a growing company.

While growth is important, it is not easy. Asked about their target growth, companies in the US and Europe will respond that on average it is between 10 and 15 percent. As the overall economic growth rate of the countries in which they trade is about 2 to 3 percent, there is no way all of them can achieve their targets.

Put differently: add up the five-year projected market shares of all the competitors in an industry and you get a figure well over 100 percent. For every company that achieves its growth target, another will be well short. To count among the successful, a company needs a wise growth strategy. Developing this involves two major decisions: the direction and the mode of growth (see Figure 1).

A company can grow using any of 15 options shown in Figure 1; examples of both successful and unsuccessful companies are easily identified in each box. There is no one right answer fitting all companies. The chosen strategy needs to be based on a company's own resources and competitive position.

There are five possible growth directions:

■ from current business by gaining market share and increasing market penetration;

Figure 1: Growth strategies

		Direction of growth				
		Market penetration	Globalization	Vertical integration	Related diversification	Unrelated diversification
Mode of growth	**Organic/ internal**	Toyota: Lexus	Honda in USA	Enron: energy ind.	Disney: Cruise ships	TATA (India)
	Strategic alliances	GM + SAAB	Renault + Nissan	Acer + Texas Instr.	Disney + Infoseek	Siam Cement (Thailand)
	Mergers & acquisitions	Ford + Jaguar	Daimler + Chrysler	Merck + Medco	Disney + ABC	Vivendi (France)

- in the same business, but in a different geographic location;
- by vertical integration, either backward or forward;
- in another related business;
- in a different, unrelated business.

A company does not have to pick only one such direction. However, it is unlikely that simultaneous pursuit in all directions is wise. Instead, given limited resources, a company should determine the relative emphasis to place on each chosen growth direction.

This article analyzes the advantages and disadvantages of the five directions. The outcome shows that the most promising growth directions in today's environment are: market penetration, globalization (particularly where emerging country markets are concerned), and forward integration.

Conglomerates

The logic for growing in an unrelated business is that conglomerates can reduce risk. While reducing risk is a good idea, shareholders can directly diversify their risk much more efficiently than a conglomerate can, thanks to efficient capital markets. Shareholders should diversify their portfolio to reduce risk; companies should focus on developing and exploiting core competences.

These days, the dominant trend is away from conglomerates and toward more focussed companies. Consider the change in strategic direction by companies like Eastman Kodak and Westinghouse, the break-up of conglomerates like ITT, and the spin-off of non-core businesses by high-tech companies like Hewlett-Packard.

This trend toward more focussed companies has been slower to take hold in Europe, but is advancing there too. Nokia, the Finnish mobile phone giant, has shed various businesses to focus on telecommunications equipment; Philips has exited from several businesses; DaimlerChrysler is focussing more on its automotive business; Unilever, the UK consumer products group, sold its chemicals business; and Imperial Chemical Industries spun off its pharmaceuticals business.

While more US and European companies move away from the conglomerate model, the economies of much of the rest of the world – Japan, South Korea, India, Thailand, and Brazil are examples – remain dominated by it.

There are three main reasons for this: inefficient capital markets, the importance of political influence, and a shortage of managerial talent.

As these factors change – and they are – the role of conglomerates in these countries will also decrease. In places such as South Korea, conglomerates are under increasing pressure to concentrate on a few businesses; in Japan, major success stories are found among focussed companies like Sony, Honda, Bridgestone, the country's biggest tyremaker, and Canon, the copier and camera maker, and not in traditional conglomerates.

This is not to say that every conglomerate is performing poorly. Companies like General Electric of the US and Johnson & Johnson, the pharmaceutical maker, continue to perform very well. But the odds do not favor a strategy of unrelated diversification.

Vertical integration

This, too, is declining. Indeed, its exact opposite, outsourcing, is on the increase. Outsourcing allows the company to focus on activities that are the source of its competitive advantage. It increases flexibility and eliminates some of the organizational problems common in vertical integration. Companies are rapidly reducing the level of backward integration. The automotive industry, for example, is increasingly outsourcing components.

The car giant General Motors, one of the more vertically integrated companies, is spinning off Delphi, the world's biggest motor parts maker. Interestingly, while backward integration is decreasing, forward integration is, in many industries, offering opportunities for competitive advantage and growth. Economic clout is moving downstream, closer to the customer.

Automotive companies, for example, are playing an increasing role in distribution; pharmaceutical maker Merck & Co bought Medco, a large distributor of pharmaceuticals; LVMH, the world's biggest purveyor of luxury goods, acquired Duty Free Shops of the US. Internet use and e-commerce will certainly accelerate this trend toward reducing the layers in the value chain and toward direct distribution.

Those companies that increase outsourcing offer a growth opportunity for vendor companies. As the electronics industry outsources manufacturing, companies that do contract production – like Selectron Corp, the high-tech manufacturer, and Jabil Circuit, a maker of circuit-board assemblies – have grown quickly. As companies outsource information technology, International Business Machines, EDS, the US information technology group, and Andersen Consulting have built fast-growing businesses in IT services. As companies outsource logistics management, Federal Express and DHL, international courier companies, have grown.

The challenge is to identify products and activities that others are outsourcing. Competitive advantage often comes from developing close relationships with customers (the companies doing the outsourcing) and providing value-added services.

Synergy

A promising direction of growth is in a business related to the company's current business; competitive advantage comes from exploiting core competences and developing synergies. When successful, this is a very powerful growth strategy. Walt Disney Company has leveraged synergies among its various businesses (theme parks, movies, cartoons, merchandising, software, and cable TV) to achieve rapid and profitable growth. The problem is that synergy is a very seductive concept, much harder to achieve in practice than it seems. In their desire to diversify and expand, managers see potential synergies where none exist. Eastman Kodak found that there was no synergy between photography and pharmaceuticals. Even though both involve "chemicals," the key success factors in the two businesses are entirely different. Kodak also found no synergies between photography and copiers, even though both are in the "imaging" business.

Following the conventional wisdom that communications and computers are converging, AT&T, the US long-distance operator, acquired NCR, the IT hardware company, only to find no synergies between the two businesses. AT&T recently spun off NCR at a significant loss. The real issue in synergy is whether there is enough overlap in key success factors and competences required between two businesses, and not whether one can find overarching terms such as "imaging" and "convergence."

Even when there is real potential for synergies, companies should find the easiest way to exploit these. There is such potential between airlines and hotels: common customer base, one-stop shopping, reservation systems, and a shared service culture. Even though many airlines (for example Air France, Air Nippon, United Airlines, and SAS) have tried to diversify into hotels, none has succeeded. Instead of diversification, cross-marketing alliances and third-party-based reservation systems are easier ways to exploit the synergies.

Finally, to achieve synergies, different parts of the organization need to coordinate and work together – a rare phenomenon in large companies. For example, there is potential to exploit marketing synergies between the tobacco and food businesses in Philip Morris, one of the world's largest cigarette manufacturers. The tobacco division is strong in China, a market the food division is very keen on entering. Yet the food division receives no help from the tobacco division as it struggles to enter China entirely on its own. The problem is that top managers plot diversification and synergy strategies, but synergy is actually achieved in the trenches by middle-level managers. Companies are organized as vertical silos, with few horizontal linkages at lower levels, which makes it impossible to achieve any synergy.

Synergy is like heaven: more people talk about it than actually go there. Overall, if a company can avoid the above pitfalls, synergy can be a powerful growth engine. Disney, for example, realized revenues of over $2bn from the $50m movie *The Lion King* by leveraging synergies between the movie, video, and consumer product sales.

Globalization

This is clearly the growth strategy emphasized by most companies today. It is consistent with both the larger changes in the world economy (and politics) and with the current emphasis on focussed companies.

Even traditionally domestic industries, such as utilities, telecommunications, and retail, are going global. For example, retail companies have found that globalization, rather than diversification, is the direction for successful growth. In the past, the US retailing giant Sears sought growth through diversification into financial services – a strategy that failed and has since been reversed. Today, Wal-Mart and Carrefour, the French food retailer, emphasize growth through globalization.

Within this broader trend toward globalization, companies are placing increasing emphasis on growth in emerging economies (like much of Pacific Asia, India, Central Europe, and Latin America). The first reason is straightforward: the developed countries are growing at about 3 percent a year, whereas the emerging economies grow at about 6 percent on a long-term basis. Ford projects that the automotive industry will grow at 1 percent in developed countries against 7 percent in emerging economies. The sheer size of some of the emerging economies makes them very attractive. For example, China, India, and Indonesia alone account for 2.4bn people – 40 percent of the world population. Furthermore, the size of these markets is larger than suggested by the per capita income numbers. The financial exchange rates significantly understate the purchasing power of local currencies. Also, official figures do not take into account the substantial "underground" economy in many of these countries. All emerging economies suffer from very unequal income and wealth distribution. This is an important human, social, and political problem; but it does create markets. If everybody in India had income of about $400 per year, there would be no market for motorcycles and scooters. As it is, India is the largest market for such vehicles.

There is also a competitive reason to pursue emerging markets. Economic liberalization and globalization lead not only to the emergence of new consumers, but also to the emergence of new competitors. Some companies in these countries, such as computer giant Acer and Taiwan Semiconductor Manufacturing from Taiwan, and Cemex of Mexico, the world's third largest cement company, have emerged as strong international competitors. Local companies are learning about good management practices such as quality management, customer service, and marketing. In China, Legend, a local company, is the single largest personal-computer manufacturer, while Haier, another local company, is the largest home-appliance manufacturer. Not only are these companies getting stronger in their local markets, but they are venturing (or soon will) outside their local markets. Success in the emerging markets will become the prerequisite for global success in the future. The world's fourth biggest steelmaker, Ispat International (originally from India, now based in London), has become the fastest-growing steel company by emphasizing emerging economies and even poorer countries; having built enough scale through this strategy, Ispat recently acquired Inland Steel Industries in the US.

To succeed in the emerging economies, it is important to create new markets, not just sell to the market as it is today. The markets in emerging economies are like a pyramid, with many people at the bottom who lack the purchasing power to be consumers, a few people at the top who are rich and resemble the consumers in the more developed countries, and a large, emerging middle class. The real challenge is to sell not just to the wealthy at the top of the economic pyramid, but rather to the large middle class (*see* the box on defining the market on p. 91).

To succeed at globalization, a company should balance global leverage with local adaptation. Global companies can exploit economies of scale *and* exploit their global capabilities in manufacturing, technology, and marketing. At the same time, companies must localize, because too much standardization may alienate local consumers, vendors, and governments. McDonald's, the fast-food chain, understands this ideal balance. The company standardizes the overall concept of its restaurants: brand, core menu, quality standards, and work practices. At the same time, it adapts a part of the menu – for example serving beer in France, "rendang"

Define the market

Kellogg, the US food group, recently entered the market in India to sell cornflakes. The company, capitalizing on its brand name and superior product quality, quickly achieved success. However, three years later sales dipped significantly. What went wrong?

Cornflakes is an expensive breakfast (both the cornflakes themselves and the milk are expensive) and culturally alien to India. However, there is a market for cornflakes in India: the rich, urbanized, westernized part of the population – the tip of the economic pyramid. But it is a very small market. The better approach is to grow the "market" by defining the market not as "cornflakes," but rather as "fast, convenient breakfast," targeted at the growing number of middle-class families who value time and convenience.

Nestlé has seized this opportunity by creating a whole range of reasonably priced products that can be used to prepare a traditional Indian breakfast quickly. By combining its skills in food processing, marketing, packaging, and distribution with an understanding of the local market, Nestlé has created a new market where none previously existed. To succeed in emerging economies: grow the market!

Even if the market for cornflakes grows dramatically in the future, as the Indian population becomes more affluent, Nestlé is better positioned than Kellogg to seize it. Nestlé is establishing a strong brand name and building capabilities in India such as customer knowledge, distribution, sourcing of raw materials, and manufacturing operations. To succeed in emerging economies: grow with the market!

burgers in Malaysia, and spaghetti in the Philippines. Its target audience in rich countries is young children; hence the Disney link. By contrast, the target audience in poor countries is teenagers and young adults, who go to McDonald's to "hang out." This difference implies changes in restaurant size and location, pricing, advertising, and promotion strategies. Teenagers in Bangkok wear tee-shirts with McDonald's in large letters on the chest. In Bangkok the chain is "cool," whereas a McDonald's tee-shirt in the US would imply that one worked there! The key to McDonald's success is to standardize and localize simultaneously.

Market penetration

Many high-growth companies have discovered that the best avenue for growth is right in their current business. To achieve this kind of rapid growth, the company needs to gain significant market share – easier said than done. One of the best ways to do this is to invent a new way of doing business, a new business model. Southwest Airlines (in the domestic US airline industry), The Body Shop (in cosmetics), Ikea (in furniture), Nucor (in steel), Amazon.com (in internet commerce), and Dell (in personal computers) are a few examples of companies that succeeded by radically changing the business model. This is innovation at its best, and more sustainable than competitive advantage based purely on technological innovation.

A company can also achieve rapid growth in its industry by playing a key role in consolidating that industry. Many industries are fragmented at an early stage and become consolidated over time. "Bigger is better," and the challenge is to find the source of economies of scale. For example, billionaire entrepreneur H. Wayne Huizenga triggered the consolidation of the waste-management industry in the US, forming the company Waste Management (now called WMX). After selling that company, he started Blockbuster Entertainment, and consolidated the video-rental industry. He then sold that operation, and is now trying to consolidate the US car dealership industry through AutoNation USA.

Wal-Mart initially grew not by taking market share from rivals like K-Mart or Sears, but rather by out-competing the small, family-owned general stores in small towns. Other retailers have followed Wal-Mart's strategy and consolidated their industries: Home Depot, the largest US do-it-yourself retailer, Office Depot, the office-supply retailer, Best Buy Co, the consumer-electronics retailer, and Barnes & Noble, the US-based bookseller. Even in the mature funeral parlor industry, Service Corporation International has achieved high growth by pursuing a strategy of acquiring family-owned parlors and making them more efficient. It does so through purchasing power, sharing facilities among a cluster of parlors, and financial leverage. On a somewhat larger scale, industries such as pharmaceuticals, automobiles, banking, and defense are also undergoing consolidation. The force of industry consolidation makes market penetration (and globalization, if it is a global industry) the only sensible growth option. Companies in these industries face the stark choice: get bigger or get out.

Conclusion

Choosing the right growth direction is not easy. Coca-Cola, the soft drinks manufacturer, has emphasized globalization for many years. PepsiCo, its rival, chose to diversify into snack foods and restaurants. The latter recently spun off its restaurants and is refocussing on global expansion. On the other hand, Maytag, the US home appliance group, expanded globally with disastrous results. It is doing better now that it is focussed on the US market. Would Compaq, the US computer group, have been better off focussing on the personal computer industry rather than acquiring Digital Equipment? Ohio-based BancOne has grown rapidly following a strategy of acquiring local and regional banks all over the US. It is now shifting its emphasis to growth through internet banking. Even successful companies may need to change direction.

Summary

With tasks like restructuring and downsizing behind them, companies now need to concentrate on growth, suggests **Aneel G. Karnani**. Driving this is pressure from shareholders, competitors, and employees. Shareholders are particularly demanding. They want value creation and actively raise this cry in boardrooms around the US and in Europe. The author discusses some of the most promising routes for growth – including vertical integration, diversification, and globalization – and points out advantages, disadvantages, difficulties, and rewards. He warns that even successful companies need to change direction.

A call for sustainable development

by Thomas N. Gladwin

Most writers in *Mastering Strategy* have highlighted the economic and technological dimensions of corporate strategy, presenting their ideas as seemingly "value free." A few have examined social issues, but virtually none has related the topic to the natural world. Most have grounded their arguments in the instrumental realm of markets and efficient resource allocation, evading the exploration of how strategy relates to ultimate ends (i.e., human fulfillment and community) and ultimate means (i.e., the capacity of the biosphere to support life). Contributors appear implicitly to have assumed that continuous growth and technological progress are inevitable. They have tended to focus on rather proximate matters shaping masterful strategic management, rather than attending to the more systemic, non-linear, large-scale, long-term, and slow-motion processes set to shape strategy in coming decades. I would like to redress the balance.

The biases I have just mentioned are not atypical of management theorists in general. But a variety of dysfunctions arise when business in general, and strategy in particular, becomes detached from the biosphere, the full human community, and the principles of right conduct in the world. Our strategic sense making, for example, is channeled away from the fundamental interdependencies (and associated vulnerabilities) that ultimately determine organizational success and survival; our sensitivities are numbed to the moral injunctions, obligations, and accountabilities that stakeholders attach to the "responsible" mastery of strategy; our creative capacity to envision glorious corporate opportunities associated with fulfillment of basic human needs is constrained; and our search for genuine meaning and purpose in this world is impeded if weighty questions like for who, where, when, and what purpose we are "mastering strategy" are discouraged.

This article examines the business case for sustainable development and the leadership challenges that it implies.

Why it matters

Threats to the integrity, productivity, and resilience of both our natural and social "life support" systems have been widely highlighted by scientists in recent years (*see* Figure 1). Well-documented examples include the overexploitation of fish stocks, falling water tables on every continent, major rivers running dry, overgrazing, and soil erosion.

Concentrations of carbon dioxide are increasing in the atmosphere, global average temperatures are rising, extreme weather events are increasing in frequency and severity, nitrogen overloading is acidifying rivers and lakes, ultraviolet radiation is rising due to stratospheric ozone depletion, and toxic heavy metals and persistent chemicals are building up steadily in organisms and ecosystems.

The Earth's forests are shrinking, highly productive wetlands are vanishing, especially in coastal areas, coral reefs are dying, natural ecosystems are being lost thanks to exponential rates of land use change, invasions of non-native species are

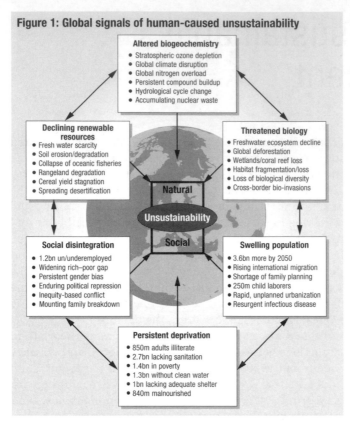

Figure 1: Global signals of human-caused unsustainability

Altered biogeochemistry
- Stratospheric ozone depletion
- Global climate disruption
- Global nitrogen overload
- Persistent compound buildup
- Hydrological cycle change
- Accumulating nuclear waste

Declining renewable resources
- Fresh water scarcity
- Soil erosion/degradation
- Collapse of oceanic fisheries
- Rangeland degradation
- Cereal yield stagnation
- Spreading desertification

Threatened biology
- Freshwater ecosystem decline
- Global deforestation
- Wetlands/coral reef loss
- Habitat fragmentation/loss
- Loss of biological diversity
- Cross-border bio-invasions

Natural

Unsustainability

Social

Social disintegration
- 1.2bn un/underemployed
- Widening rich–poor gap
- Persistent gender bias
- Enduring political repression
- Inequity-based conflict
- Mounting family breakdown

Swelling population
- 3.6bn more by 2050
- Rising international migration
- Shortage of family planning
- 250m child laborers
- Rapid, unplanned urbanization
- Resurgent infectious disease

Persistent deprivation
- 850m adults illiterate
- 2.7bn lacking sanitation
- 1.4bn in poverty
- 1.3bn without clean water
- 1bn lacking adequate shelter
- 840m malnourished

on the rise due to global traffic, and species are being exterminated about a thousand times faster than normal.

The knee-jerk reaction to such news is typically psycho-dynamic denial, repression, or rationalization. But "masters" of strategy need to acknowledge that human population growth and growth in resource consumption are altering our planet in unprecedented ways, at a faster pace and on a broader scale than previously. Scientists warn that we are eating up the planet's natural capital, crossing a range of sustainable yield thresholds, and fomenting conflict, within and across generations, over the growing scarcity of natural resources.

As shown in Figure 1, steady deterioration in the Earth's biophysical health and the stagnant or falling quality of life for a majority of humans are closely connected. A swelling global population, persistent deprivation, and growing social disintegration are just some of the problems. United Nations reports say that the world's human population, after soaring from 1.6bn in 1900 to a little over 6bn today, is projected (despite lower fertility rates) to reach 8bn in 2020, and perhaps stabilize at around 9bn to 10bn by 2050. In the time it takes to read this article, the planet's net population will have risen by 1800 people. An estimated 350m couples still have no access to family planning.

Population pressures and the associated economic/ecological/political decline fuel internal and cross-border migration. Rural to urban migration is producing mega-cities, especially in the developing world. Medical experts warn that the epidemiological environment is deteriorating. Old diseases like TB are resurgent and new ones, such as HIV-AIDS, emergent.

Global data on persistent human deprivation are even more distressing. An estimated 37,000 infants will die today from poverty-related causes; more than 260m children are out of school at the primary and secondary levels; 840m people are malnourished; 850m adults remain illiterate; 880m people lack access to health services; 1bn humans have inadequate shelter; 1.3bn people (70 percent female) attempt to live on less than $1 a day – up by 200m over the past decade; 2bn have no access to electricity; and 2.6bn lack basic sanitation.

This misery translates into massive social disintegration. Some 1.2bn adults are either unemployed or woefully underemployed below a living wage. This is one-third of the world's workforce and the highest percentage since the 1930s. More than 250m children between 5 and 14 years of age are working as child laborers. Income inequality is rising within and among all nations. The share of global income of the richest one-fifth of the world's people is now estimated to be 74 times that of the poorest one-fifth – a gap that has doubled over the past 30 years. *Forbes* magazine estimates that the combined wealth of the 225 richest people in the world now equals the combined annual incomes of the poorest one-half of humanity. The widening social gulfs breed anger, frustration, alienation, anomie, and hopelessness.

What is the relevance to *Mastering Strategy* and those engaged in global business?

An obvious answer is that if they go uncorrected, these trends imply greatly increased exposure to external risks of all kinds, and massive constraints on the global "operating space" available for business development. In many parts of the world, environmental degradation and growing resource scarcity, together with poverty and population density, are already contributing to economic disruption, forced migrations, ethnic strife, cross-border health crises, famine, fundamentalism, regional conflicts over resource use, weakened states, and even "eco-terrorism."

Such instability adversely affects the investment climate – furthering the downward spiral in socio-economic and environmental decay. Heavily populated swathes of the planet disappear from the strategic "radar screen" for business and market development.

Take a reality check on this point. The word Africa is mentioned just twice in this book. And while it is understandable that some people want to retain their sanity, it is not good enough for executives from the developed North merely to say: "Yes, but all of this chaos will be far away, and we will be OK here in our insulated fortresses."

All business – in any form, in any place, at any time – is directly or indirectly, immediately or eventually affected by ecological and socio-economic deterioration wherever this occurs. Business takes place within, and is thus dependent on, the vital "life-support" services provided by the biosphere. Corporate welfare is equally dependent on healthy social systems. Business worlds would cease to thrive without educated citizens, public safety and order, a supply of savings and credit, legal due process, or the observance of rights.

It would thus seem logical for business to protect, maintain and restore the integrity, resilience, and productivity of such vital life-support services – a premise that leads inexorably to a conception of the moral corporation.

To paraphrase Christian philosopher Albert Schweitzer: "It is good: to preserve, promote and raise to its highest value, life capable of development; it is evil: to destroy, injure, and repress life capable of development. This is the absolute fundamental principle of the moral. A man [business] is ethical only when life, as such, is sacred to [it]."

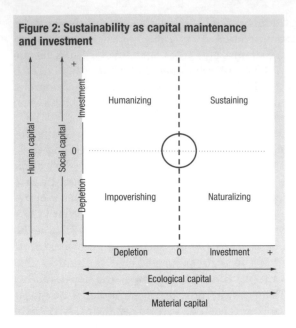

Figure 2: Sustainability as capital maintenance and investment

A model for strategy

The core idea of sustainable development was most influentially defined by the World Commission on Environment and Development as: "that which meets the needs of the present without compromising the ability of future generations to meet their own needs."

Hundreds of derivative definitions have followed, and the notion appears set to remain fuzzy, elusive or contestable for some time to come. This is to be expected during the emergent phase of any new, big and generally useful idea. There is broad agreement that ensuring future generations are no worse off than the present one requires the maintenance of welfare-yielding capital endowments. A sustainable society lives off the "income" generated from its stocks of capital, not by depleting them. There are differences of opinion over attempts to specify the exact assumptions, conditions, and rules for ensuring development paths that are both fair to different generations and efficient over time.

Figure 2 shows a "strong" model of sustainable development. This assumes that natural and social capital are complements of, rather than substitutes for, manufactured capital. Different types of capital must be maintained intact separately, for the productivity of each depends on the availability of the others (i.e., the model abandons the conventional neo-classical assumption of near-perfect substitution for different types of capital). We can thus appraise the workings of manufactured capital (i.e., stocks of producer and consumer goods such as factories, buildings, machines, tools, technologies, infrastructure, and products) according to their consequences for four types of primary (enabling or limiting) capital: 1) ecological (i.e., renewable, cyclical, biological resources, processes, functions, and services); 2) material (i.e., non-renewable or geological resources such as mineral ores, fossil fuels, fossil groundwaters); 3) human (i.e., people's knowledge, skills, health, nutrition, safety, security, motivation); and 4) social (i.e., relating to civil society, social cohesion, trust, reciprocity norms, equity, empowerment, freedom of association, orderliness, and so forth that facilitate coordination and cooperation for mutual benefit).

A truly sustainable society is one that organizes its economy to ensure the maintenance of its stocks of ecological, material, human, and social capital – at a base minimum hitting the exact center or "bull's-eye" of the grid in Figure 2, thus adhering to that prudent ancient wisdom of "not eating thy seed corn."

A society would become increasingly sustainable (boosting its capacity for continuance) as it organizes its economy to invest in and expand existing stores of primary capital (moving to the north-east of the grid). Such restoration lies at the heart of "natural capitalism," according to a 1999 book by Paul Hawken, Amory B. Lovins, and L. Hunter Lovins.

The two-by-two grid in Figure 2 yields four states of society, only one of which is sustainable. The south-west quadrant is the impoverishing zone, where society imprudently "lives" off a vanishing capital base. This is a society that maintains itself only through the exhaustion and dispersion of a one-time inheritance of natural capital (e.g., topsoil, biodiversity, groundwater, fossil fuels, and minerals), with no investment in conservation or replacement. This is a society (too common, sadly, today) that disinvests in its people, especially its children, and permits the forces of mobile economic capital, elite detachment, and special-interest politics to atrophy civic and social communities.

The south-east quadrant of Figure 2 is the zone of naturalizing, where the operations of the economy are increasingly brought into conformity with natural imperatives. This comes at the expense, however, of human and social capital, at least transitionally. Examples might include "eco-inspired" agricultural biotechnology that threatens traditional farmers with redundancy, or cleaner automated factories that eliminate assembly and manufacturing jobs. In the absence of alternative sources of sustainable livelihood, these supposedly "environment-friendly" developments could set in motion powerful forces of social decomposition and political upheaval. Naturalizing, in the absence of concomitant attention to the human condition, may be self-defeating.

A similar logic applies to the north-west quadrant of Figure 2, a zone of humanizing, where the operations of the economy are progressively endowed with a human character. This is at the expense, however, of diminishing natural capital. Examples might include the development of housing communities on drained wetlands, or logging that causes deforestation. Jobs or communities constructed on the basis of systemic depletion of natural capital will obviously be unsustainable over the longer term. Humanizing and naturalizing are fundamentally complementary.

This leaves the north-east quadrant as the only genuine sustaining zone. Economic and technological development here are simultaneously people centered and nature based. Damage to ecosystems is prevented, biological diversity and productivity are conserved, the entropic physical flow of energy and matter is moderated, and the economy is converted to rely on perpetual resources and resilient technologies. The sustainable society communalizes its civic order and decision making, democratizes its political and workplace environments, humanizes capital creation and work, and vitalizes human need fulfillment, ensuring sufficiency in meeting basic needs.

These macro-level principles of sustainable development unfold into myriad subprinciples, guidelines, and metrics for application at the micro level.

The ecologically sustainable enterprise would eliminate all harmful discharges into the biosphere; use renewable resources like forests, fisheries, and fresh water at rates less than or equal to regeneration rates; preserve as much biodiversity as it appropriates; seek to restore ecosystems to the extent that it has damaged them; deplete non-renewable resources such as oil at rates lower than the creation of renewable resource substitutes providing equivalent services; continuously reduce risks and hazards; dematerialize, substituting information for matter; and redesign processes and products into cyclical material flows, thus closing all material loops.

The socially sustainable enterprise would return to communities where it operates and sells as much as it gains from them; include stakeholders affected by its activities in associated planning and decision-making processes; ensure no reduction in, and actively promote the observance of, political and civil rights in the domains where it operates; widely spread economic opportunities and help to reduce or eliminate unjustified inequalities; directly or indirectly ensure no net loss of human capital within its workforces and operating communities; cause no net loss of direct and indirect productive employment; adequately satisfy the vital needs of its employees and operating communities; and work to ensure the fulfillment of the basic needs of humanity prior to serving luxury wants.

Transformational leadership

Sustainable development is an idea whose time has come, but it is important to acknowledge the extraordinary barriers that stand in the way of its general acceptance and achievement (for a detailed survey *see* "Northern elite mind" in Suggested further reading). These include: mechanistic thinking; conventional wisdom promoting growth; consumption and techno-fixes; institutional structures such as perverse governmental subsidy and tax systems; and the profound forces of inertia compounded by vested interests and denial. I am strongly encouraged by the emergence of a well-informed and visionary set of corporate leaders who have taken up the challenge of orienting their companies to support a sustainable human future. These transformational leaders can be found, for example, in family-led enterprises; entrepreneurial ventures into renewable resources; companies that have learned from public controversies; "culturally programmed" Scandinavian enterprises; and companies getting out of commodity businesses into more knowledge-intensive life sciences. For these and other first-movers, check out the World Business Council for Sustainable Development, SustainAbility Ltd., and *Tomorrow* magazine.

Large-scale organizational transformation toward sustainability is a long-term and multi-level challenge, entailing a range of reinforcing roles and tasks. Vivid images of sustainable futures must be painted. A sense of stretch must be instilled. Organizational purpose, identity, and meaning must be aligned with ecological and social contribution. Leaders must challenge embedded assumptions by asking tough questions like: what is our ecological and social footprint? Do customers really need our products, or just their functions or services? Are we focussing on "excessities" or necessities? Are we creating genuine value for society or appropriating value from it? What is our rightful place in the living world?

Implementation must be energized by dramatic changes in management incentives, internal information systems, and external performance reporting. Major in-house learning programs must be mounted to boost awareness, literacy, and strategic excitement. Supportive organizational values and ethical principles

Leadership voices

Some business leaders have made a case for becoming ecologically and socially sustainable:

Legitimacy – "Business . . . must take the lead in directing the Earth away from collapse and toward sustainability and restoration." – Ray C. Anderson, Chairman of Interface, the US carpet manufacturer.

Morality – "Institutions that operate so as to capitalize all gain in the interests of the few, while socializing all loss to the detriment of the many, are ethically, socially and operationally unsound. . . . This must change." – Dee Hock, Founder, President and CEO Emeritus of Visa International, the credit card organization.

Prudence – "Far from being a soft issue grounded in emotion and ethics, sustainable development involves cold, rational business logic." – Robert B. Shapiro, Chairman of Monsanto, the US multinational.

Reputation – "The gap between rhetoric and reality is increasing. I would tell multinationals they have to watch out . . . they are much more vulnerable, because they have to be accountable to the public every day." – Thilo Bode, Executive Director of Greenpeace.

Opportunity – "The sustainability agenda is developing faster than almost any other part of the business agenda . . ." – Livio D. DeSimone, Chairman and CEO of 3M Corporation, the US manufacturing conglomerate.

Performance – Explaining his company's forays into renewable energy and enhanced support for the communities where it does business: "These efforts have nothing to do with charity, and everything to do with our long-term self-interests . . . our shareholders want performance today, and tomorrow, and the day after." – Sir John Browne, CEO of British Petroleum/Amoco.

Personal meaning – "When my grandchildren first saw the big snapping turtle in the pond where I used to play and fish as a boy, they glowed with the same wonder and awe as I did. Without sustainable development, [the world's] going to be a less satisfactory place for my grandchildren to live in. For me, these are the stakes." – Samuel C. Johnson, Chairman of S.C. Johnson & Son, the US household cleaning, insect-control and personal-care products maker.

must be infused. High-impact partnerships with other companies and governmental/non-governmental organizations must be forged. Finally, leaders for sustainability must take on the hard work of lobbying for public policies and institutions that truly work on behalf of a sustainable future.

"Between the idea and the reality, between the conception and the creation, falls the shadow," said T.S. Eliot. The notions of sustainable development and enterprise currently lie in this shadow. The central task of corporate leaders moving into the next century, both through aspiration and inspiration, is to bring them into the light.

Summary

In this passionate plea, **Thomas N. Gladwin** argues that there is a long-term, multi-level, strategic challenge that business leaders must meet head on if we are to avoid a grim future. Socially responsible business people need to ask tough questions about their activities. Can they measure their ecological and social footprints? Do their customers really need their products? Might these be "excessities" as opposed to necessities? And are they creating genuine value for society? Problems occur when business and strategy become detached from the biosphere, the world community and rules of "right" conduct.

Suggested further reading

Gladwin, T., Kennelly, J. and Krause, T. (1995) "Shifting Paradigms for Sustainable Development: Implications for Management Theory and Research," *Academy of Management Review*, 20 (October), 874–907.

Gladwin, T., Newbury, W. and Reiskin, E. (1997) "Why is the Northern Elite Mind Biased Against Community, the Environment and a Sustainable Future?" in Bazerman, M. *et al.* (eds), *Environment, Ethics and Behavior*, San Francisco: New Lexington Press.

Hawken, P., Lovins, A. and Lovins, L. (1999) *Natural Capitalism: Creating the Next Industrial Revolution*, Boston: Little, Brown and Company.

The euro and market convergence

by Paul Verdin

Up to the eve of its introduction, surveys showed that most managers considered the euro to be mainly a technical and operational issue. Are these companies right? Is it just an operational nuisance? Or does it have strategic implications for businesses in "euroland"?

The following comments are based on our year-long research in a wide range of industries and companies which has alerted us to the broader ramifications that need to be considered.

In industry after industry, the most important question on the European scene still is: how much convergence is there already, how much do we need, and how much do we want in our markets and businesses in future?

Our research suggests that the effects of the euro on market convergence are not as overwhelming as some predicted, or as obvious as the simplistic slogans in the debate seem to imply.

There is a clear sense of *déjà vu* if you remember all the great predictions that were made ahead of the European single market deadline in 1992. Studies have now confirmed that the expectations raised by the internal market program were unrealistic and in many cases have not materialized. In many ways, we are still waiting for 1992 to happen.

Price convergence is a typical proxy for the degree of market convergence. But the assumption of price homogenization in the wake of the euro's introduction oversimplifies buyer behavior and the large number of persistent differences across Europe beyond the difference in accounting units. There are many good economic and strategic reasons – different distribution systems, labor costs, customer preferences, geography, culture, and history – why prices for the same goods will remain different from one place to another in the euro zone.

Pursuing convergence where differentiation is in order runs the risk of destroying rather than maximizing opportunities for creating and capturing value.

On the other hand, there are many perceived cross-border differences that keep inefficient fragmentation and duplication within companies in place; the interesting challenge for managers is to find out which ones are real and which are just an excuse for not adapting to more efficient ways of organization and cooperation on a cross-border level.

In short, the debate on how much cross-border integration we need in our strategy and organization in Europe did not start or end with the introduction of the euro on January 1, 1999. (Nor will it end on January 1, 2002, when notes and coins are introduced for the first time.) The euro will not make the European market integrated overnight.

Nor will it change the need for a continuous analysis and monitoring of the cross-border (pan-European or globalization) opportunities versus the localization pressures in your industry.

What new opportunities for (or threats to) value creation and value capturing will arise at the company level? Particularly, what opportunities for increased efficiency and cross-border segmentation can be expected in the euro zone?

Besides a few minor economies in certain aspects of the value chain (in finance and accounting, for example), we have failed to see companies reaping huge efficiencies from the introduction of the euro itself. Other more significant trends, like information technology, will have a much broader impact on the cost position of companies operating internationally. Market integration generally (as opposed to the effect of the euro by itself) may actually unleash opportunities for more rather than less segmentation or discrimination, and companies should beware a "one size fits all" strategy.

If the euro is the real reason to harmonize your strategy and pricing in particular, you are probably already too late. By doing so you are implying that your pricing and strategy were suboptimal to start with. If your competitive advantage is affected by the fixing of a new currency at levels that are not different from those prevailing before, should you not have started to worry much earlier?

In sum, we believe that for most non-financial industries the euro itself is likely to have only a small impact on market convergence or competitive advantage. This is not to say, however, that it cannot be made "strategic" by using it as a catalyst for European strategy evaluation or organizational development. It can be used as a trigger to push the implementation of an internal integration process that has not really taken off so far or that got stuck along the way.

Some long-established multinationals such as Proctor & Gamble Europe started the cross-border process early and took the long route (over almost 20 years). Others, like 3M Europe, prepared the change extensively and then completed the process much more quickly (through internal "shock therapy"). Others yet, after trying for many years, finally made the change when pushed against the wall in the context of an overall corporate restructuring, as was the case at International Business Machines Europe or Alcatel, the telecoms equipment group.

For some other companies, especially those that have been less active or successful in cross-border coordination, any excuse for pushing the internal convergence and company integration could be welcome. More proactive companies in this category will evaluate what organizational "learning by doing" they can extract from euro strategy discussion and euro team experiences.

Beware, though, of the "tail wagging the dog" syndrome. The danger here is that while the euro (and its focus on finance, accounting, systems, or pricing) is used to get to the bigger debate, broader top management issues are ignored.

If the euro is turned into a strategic project in this context, it should be conducted at the appropriate level in the company organization. Top management should ensure that:

- expectations are well managed and realistically formulated;
- the required competences and authority (say power) are in place;
- the relevant trade-offs (e.g., between the short term and the long term, between national market concerns and cross-border synergies) are properly identified and handled;
- the required resources are dedicated to implement decisions and ensure that integration actually happens;
- the process of integration is constantly monitored, energized and followed up.

Avoid pitfalls that can turn the euro exercise into a destructive or antistrategic phenomenon:

- With all the emphasis on operational issues, be careful not to be *distracted* from thinking about international strategy.
- Do not rush into *unwarranted mergers, acquisitions and other panic restructuring*. If a particular acquisition or merger did not make sense or was not particularly urgent before the euro, why would it then suddenly be justified because of a new currency?
- Avoid the *end-game fallacy*, as if after a given date all bets are off and business will stop! What one needs to do instead is constantly to re-evaluate the market and industry developments, pursue a long-term vision, and particularly pay attention to managing the process internally.

STRATEGY AND GLOBALIZATION

4

Contributors

Thomas C. Kinnear is Eugene Applebaum Professor of Entrepreneurial Studies, professor of marketing, and executive director of the Samuel Zell and Robert H. Lurie Institute of Entrepreneurial Studies at the University of Michigan Business School.

Joan Penner-Hahn is an assistant professor of corporate strategy and international business at the University of Michigan Business School. Her research interests include international research and development and the acquisition and evolution of firm capabilities.

Arie Y. Lewin is professor of business administration and sociology, director of the Centre for International Business Education and Research (CIBER), and IBM research fellow at the Fuqua School of Business, Duke University.

Mitchell P. Koza holds the Chair in International Strategic Management and is director of the Centre for International Business at Cranfield School of Management. He was on the faculty of INSEAD for over ten years.

Subramanian Rangan is professor of strategy and management at INSEAD. His current research focusses on global teamwork and global innovation within multinationals.

Contents

Introduction

Globalization has challenged many of the old strategic assumptions. The days of vertical markets, it is argued, appear to be numbered with companies better advised to concentrate on market segments defined by the consumer. In R&D the earlier focus on supporting marketing and production efforts in specific overseas countries has been replaced by a global hunt for regionally concentrated science bases outside the "home" territory. While assembling and animating the global multibusiness requires a quite different organizational approach from what was needed to run the traditional multinational and transnational forms of business. Going global, however, has drawbacks as well as attractions and a global business is no substitute for a sound business strategy.

Brave new horizontal world

by Thomas C. Kinnear

Consider the following senior management challenges, all based on real examples:

- A large UK-based consumer packaged goods company has historically been organized on a country-by-country basis. The country manager has the final say on all aspects of new product introductions, brand target segments, brand names, brand positioning, advertising, sales promotion, pricing, and so on. The senior corporate management in the UK has become concerned that: 1) major new product innovations developed in one country or in the central research and development laboratories are introduced in various countries in a very slow fashion or not introduced at all; 2) no global or even regional brand names have been developed; 3) common new products often have different segment targeting, positioning, advertising, and so on in different countries. For example, it took ten years for this company to introduce a major new household food product in the main EU countries. The implementation consisted of six different brand names, varied segment targeting and brand positionings, and related price points that ranged from "premium" to "bargain," and very diverse advertising and promotion programs.

- One of the world's largest global banks was a major player in credit cards in North America and Europe. It had some presence in Asian countries in commercial, mortgage, and retail banking, and had a few branches in major Asian cities. Senior management believed that there was a great opportunity to market Visa- and Mastercard-based credit cards across 16 Asian countries. In each country the bank faced varying degrees of competition from local bank credit cards, and from American Express. Virtually all of the bank's country managers opposed the introduction of credit cards in their countries.

- A major global marketer of industrial manufacturing robots, control systems, and related services had traditionally organized its marketing and sales activities around vertical markets based on industry type, such as specialty chemicals, automobiles, electronics, aerospace, and so on. Under this system each of its vertical divisions separately pursued technical product and service applications without regard to the other divisions. Senior management was concerned that this approach to the market ignored any synergies that might exist across vertical markets and divisions. In addition, this vertically based structure was combined with a country-based vertical structure similar to the UK-based packaged goods company described above. Its aerospace, automobile, and electronics divisions were all separately developing "visual" inspection systems. The research and development cost of developing these three projects were very high, as were the on-site implementation costs and customization required for specific industries across different countries. As a result, this was a very unprofitable set of product lines.

The meaning of market

All three companies believed that they were "market based." The UK packaged goods company was taking country differences into account, the credit card company allowed the country managers to do what was best in their countries given the competitive situation, and the robotics company was developing deep understanding of the specific industry requirements for its products. This type of "vertical" thinking is still commonplace in many global companies today.

The problem with this vertical approach is that in many situations it no longer represents the real market that it purports to serve. A truly market-based company organizes itself around market segments based on consumer needs. A market segment is a set of consumers with a common needs structure, not necessarily consumers in a specific country or a specific vertical industry. The problem with the vertical structure noted above is that it is unrepresentative of the needs-based market segmentation that has developed in many markets.

Real horizontal markets

Let us illustrate the horizontal nature of market segments related to the three situations at the beginning of this article. The packaged goods company discovered that the market for innovative yoghurt was not based on the countries that form the EU, but on four needs-based segments that existed to varying degrees in each country (see Suggested further reading). One such segment was the "health and innovative" segment. It comprised about 25 percent of yoghurt users in Denmark, Germany, and the UK, 18 percent in Ireland and the Netherlands, and only about 4 percent in France, Portugal, and Spain. Another segment, the "top quality seekers," was strongly represented across all EU countries. Thus we can see that the common nature of needs across these EU states generated an opportunity to place different brands and formulations of yoghurt horizontally in them.

Similarly, after intensive marketing research the global bank found that there was a usable needs-based segment for credit cards across Hong Kong, Singapore, India, Indonesia, Malaysia, Thailand, and Taiwan. This segment needed a card with flexible credit limits, available for international travel, and offering premium services such as airline club entry, insurance, and so on. The size of the segment in some of the countries would not support the required high cost of obtaining customers when taken a country at a time. However, across all countries as a whole, the cost–benefit was easily positive. There were enough total potential customers and great scale economies in logistics and marketing if the business was managed horizontally.

The tale is similar for the industrial robots company. In robotics-based visual inspection systems application there were a number of common segments across the vertical industries. In one instance, inspection for the presence of a part in an assembled product (rivet, chip, etc.) was common across automobiles, electronics, aerospace, and so on. The technological approach was similar and the company was able to develop more off-the-shelf products, with great savings in costs of customizing software.

Failure to understand and act on needs-based segments that are often horizontal has left many companies with declining fortunes. In contrast, where senior management has grasped this understanding it has had some legendary successes. International Business Machines eventually found that its vertically structured mainframe computer magic was unresponsive to the large group of both individual and corporate consumers who did not require and were not willing to pay for pre-sale education or full service installation for their personal computers. Dell and

Gateway, two US manufacturers of direct-to-consumer products, developed this understanding and put the appropriate logistical system in place to serve this horizontal segment.

Country borders mean little to "dot com companies" (one way of describing online start-ups that depend on business and consumer use of the internet for success) because they approach markets looking for the commonality across territories. For example, companies like E*Trade, the online securities trader, and Amazon.com, the online bookseller, have left traditional competitors wondering what to do with their vertically oriented infrastructures and whether they can operate both their classic vertical company and a new "dot com company" simultaneously. Merrill Lynch, the US brokerage business, spent years struggling with this dilemma. In the interim, the innovative companies have grabbed large customer bases and market position.

On the positive response side, Proctor & Gamble, the US consumer products company, saw the horizontal nature of markets arising in Europe almost 20 years ago. As a result, P&G can now introduce a new product globally in less than 18 months based on a horizontal approach. This contrasts sharply to some 15 to 20 years taken in the old days of omnipotent country managers.

Implementation challenges

The commitment to approach markets in a horizontal fashion raises many challenges. These include: identification of the needs-based segments; building horizontal teams to manage against the targeted segments; making appropriate use of vertically based specialists; determining the split between central and country or other vertically based authority; and designing an appropriate compensation system.

Identifying needs-based segments

The most positive aspect of vertical or country-based segmentation is that it is easy to do. For example, in the vertical world, one just need say we are targeting the "French market," or the "automotive market." Consider how much more difficult it is to identify and locate the "top quality seekers" for yoghurt, or the "inspection for the presence of parts" segment for visual-based robots. A horizontal organization is one committed to the discipline of marketing research in order to identify needs-based segments. Top management of these organizations also recognizes that needs-based segments change over time and that their organizations must change accordingly.

The role of teams

Managing the horizontal enterprise requires teams that are cross-functional and also able to cross geographic regions. These teams perform the critical integrating function. The development and acceptance by senior and middle management of a charter of responsibilities for these teams is critical. Their authority must be clearly understood. Typically, effective horizontal teams must enjoy senior management leadership and continuity of membership; they should comprise individuals who are responsible for critical functions and geographic regions and be prepared to stick to the area of responsibility mapped out by their charter.

Integration of specialists

One of the difficulties of horizontal teams is that they often lack depth in functional expertise, not least in marketing. Effective teams need easy access to a stable of functional experts in marketing research, marketing strategy, advertising, production planning, finance, and so on. The key is for these specialists to be effectively integrated into the group's decision making. Without these group integrators, the team will not deliver the whole enterprise. Without the effective use of specialists, the team is likely to perform shallow analysis and create marketing and other programs below par. The intention is to obtain the skills of the vertical organization along with the needs-satisfying aspects of the horizontal organization.

Central versus decentralized

The horizontal team structure usually exists alongside the functional vertical organization and alongside a country or regional manager's organization. What tasks should the horizontal team thus perform? One approach is to have the teams responsible for the strategic aspects and leave the details of implementation to the vertical functions and regional managers. No global team can competently make all the detailed decisions of implementation around such issues as advertising copy, promotional contests, price discount structures, and so on. However, the team can be instrumental in identifying and targeting the horizontal segments, selecting a positioning for the brand, setting general price levels, setting general tone for the advertising programs, and pushing product innovations. These are the critical strategic issues for the company. The charter for the teams must articulate the locations and nature of these responsibilities.

Compensation

We noted in the packaged goods and credit card examples above that the country managers tended to be resistant to horizontal initiatives. Reasons might include their belief that local knowledge about markets is superior, or political tensions with headquarters. Ideally, this sort of issue would be handled by the team charter. There is one issue, though, that is beyond the scope of the charter. This is the compensation for functional and country managers. That concern was the root cause of resistance to horizontal initiatives by the packaged goods and credit card country managers. They expected their bottom lines to be adversely affected by the costs of introducing the horizontal brand and by other decisions made by teams outside their control. Thus, since their bonuses were based on functional performance standards or country-specific measures, they were naturally hostile.

The sensible solution is to change the compensation system to reflect the true nature of their responsibilities. Thus some part of country managers' compensation must be based on their positive participation in the horizontal teams, the performance of horizontal brands across countries, along with the performance of the parts of the marketing and other functional programs that are specific to their countries.

Conclusion

All three companies discussed earlier implemented a horizontally oriented organization and strategy with resounding success. For example, the credit card business in Asia became the most profitable part of its banking business. The packaged goods company now routinely introduces brands globally within a few years and has experienced both increases in market share and cost savings. The robotics company effectively saved itself from bankruptcy. The days of vertical thinking as the dominant mode are numbered. The winners will be those senior managers who lead their organizations boldly into this brave new horizontal world.

Summary

The days of vertical markets are numbered. The winners in global business, says **Thomas C. Kinnear**, will be those who focus on market segments defined by the consumer. This is difficult even in the domestic market context. It is especially problematic when these segments exist in a global context across countries. In this article, the author addresses the issues of how companies learn about horizontal market segments; how to identify a go-to-the-market global strategy; and how to define the role of country and central management in a global marketing strategy.

Suggested further reading

Engel, J., Warshaw, M., Kinnear, T. and Reece, B. (2000) "Market segmentation and competitive positioning," Chapter 7 in *Promotional Strategy*, Cincinnati, Ohio: Pinnaflex Educational Resources.

George, M., Freeling, A. and Court, D. (1994) "Reinventing the marketing organization," *The McKinsey Quarterly*, 1994 (4).

Ostroff, F. (1999) *The Horizontal Organization*, Oxford: Oxford University Press.

Steenkamp, J.B. and Traill, B. (1994) *A Consumer-Led Approach to Marketing of Yoghurt in the EU*, Belgium: European Commission, Agro-Industrial Research.

Why R&D is increasingly international

by Joan Penner-Hahn

Before the 1980s it was accepted wisdom that research and development needed to be centralized in order to capture the benefits of the scientific and technological knowledge created. Limited R&D activities were established in other countries, primarily for the adaptation of products to a new market. This pattern followed the long-accepted foreign direct investment strategy of exploiting home-country resources in foreign markets. Market adaptation is still a motivation for the establishment of foreign R&D activities; a good example is the clinical laboratories that pharmaceutical companies establish to win product approval in a particular country market.

In the 1980s multinational companies, particularly those in technologically intensive industries such as pharmaceuticals, chemicals, and electronics, began to appreciate the opportunities for tapping into specific national scientific and technological areas of expertise. These "pockets" of expertise are geographic areas where a cluster of companies and other institutions focus on a particular scientific or technological area. Familiar ones include Silicon Valley for electronics, La Jolla in California for biotechnology, and Oxford in the UK for neuroscience. Multinational companies set up R&D activities there to gain access to the science and technology being developed. This strategy offers a way of extending and augmenting home-country technology, rather than simply trying to exploit existing skills.

Additionally, companies have begun to pursue international R&D as they realize they cannot support all areas of technology that might be important to them. One major pharmaceutical company's website states: "We realize no single organization has all the expertise required to produce the innovative solutions for the numerous unmet medical needs still present. Therefore, an integral part of our R&D strategy is to continue to seek out new research capabilities and high-potential drug candidates from external sources." Increasingly, therefore, such companies look for external sources of knowledge, wherever these might be located.

Tapping foreign expertise

Four routes are open to companies interested in tapping pockets of foreign expertise: buy technology from local developers; sponsor research at another company or institution; perform research and development cooperatively with a local company; or build or purchase laboratories in the foreign country.

Buy from local developers

This strategy may involve either technology licenses or marketing agreements and has proven expedient for a number of companies wishing to push new products to market. It has been the norm for decades in the pharmaceutical industry, where companies have made arrangements to sell drugs developed by others in their own markets. This is advantageous because most companies do not have the necessary resources to develop drugs in every medical category. They can, however, use their salesforce to sell a full product line. The drawback is that the company does not develop any technological competence of its own.

Increasingly, pharmaceutical companies are looking for technology trades, in the form of cross-licenses, to supplement any gaps in their own product lines. This implies that companies are able to develop technology that is desirable to others.

Sponsor research activities

This is where a company funds research at a university or, occasionally, by another company. Such projects do not involve research by the parent company (i.e., the company underwriting the cost). Instead, companies usually target sponsored projects for discovery of a specific product or phenomenon. Consequently, sponsored research activities often have a specified project duration. After licensing, sponsored research generally involves the lowest cost and requires the least knowledge of the local environment. However, sponsored research also tends to provide the least return, because the company is likely to learn less and may be unable to protect all of the benefits of the research conducted on its behalf. Sponsored research provides an initial step for companies to begin learning about a new country's research environment. Companies need to learn the scientific norms, the geographic location of specific research capabilities, and the strengths and weaknesses of specific research institutions. Only once a company has learned about a country's innovation system can it undertake its own learning within that context.

Cooperate with locals

Here a company enters a collaborative arrangement with local institutions or companies. Such arrangements can range from fully fledged joint ventures under a separately established organization, to short-term arrangements involving the training of personnel in foreign laboratories. Collaborative research projects require participation by company staff in foreign research activity, either through on-site relocation or dual-track research at home and abroad. Companies may undertake collaborative projects with universities or other companies. This option is most used by companies with deep experience in a particular science.

Build or purchase laboratories

Finally, companies wishing to obtain access to foreign scientific knowledge can establish or acquire laboratories abroad. Staff here may be foreign nationals. Often they will be researchers who have studied at academic institutions where the seminal knowledge in the field was developed. This, in turn, makes them part of the scientific network formed in the national "pocket of expertise." A company can also transfer scientists from its domestic operation to the foreign site.

Establishing or acquiring a laboratory requires a lengthy development and integration process. Controlled research activities are those for which the company establishes ownership. Controlled research offers the greatest protection and the greatest potential learning. However, it also requires the greatest commitment of money and managerial effort and the greatest knowledge of the local environment to realize the learning potential.

Thus, choosing the international research and development mode is a question of trade-offs in the degree of protection afforded the company and the amount of learning possible with each mode. Company choices are based on the ability to protect existing knowledge and the ability to capture new knowledge created. These choices are influenced by the company's previous experiences and its existing research capabilities.

The diversification path

In my study of Japanese pharmaceutical companies, I found that the traditional ones were most likely to start their international R&D activities with some form of collaborative activity. Companies attempting to diversify were most likely to use sponsored research activities. There are two reasons for this: first, companies already in an industry are best able to evaluate the opportunities available to them in the form of collaborations; second, a company in the industry is a more desirable partner for the collaborator, often providing complementary skills, such as development or sales and marketing, that are lacking in the partner company.

Beyond the choice of international R&D mode is the question of how to integrate the newly obtained knowledge into the company's repository of knowledge. Companies are currently experimenting with the best methods for coordinating their various worldwide research and development activities. There is broad agreement that, to be effective, research and development strategies must be integrated into the overall strategies of the company. This generally requires the active participation in strategy setting of a senior executive familiar with science and technology.

Guido Reger of the Fraunhofer Institute for Systems and Innovation Research says that Japanese companies involve senior executives in technology activities more than their European counterparts. There is also agreement that more knowledge coordination is needed to utilize the knowledge developed in a company's research and development activities effectively. Reger reports that Japanese companies have made greater use of meetings to help coordinate and integrate researchers in the different locations.

Does international R&D work?

Corporate enthusiasm for international research and development activities would seem to suggest that companies have found value in these investments. The amount of R&D funded by foreign sources has increased substantially since the late 1980s. There is some indication that companies have been able to increase their technological competences as a result of these activities.

The ability of companies to absorb scientific knowledge from foreign pockets of expertise has been illustrated by both Paul Almeida of Georgetown University and John Cantwell of Reading University (*see* Suggested further reading).

Both researchers examined patent data for companies involved in foreign research and development activities, with particular emphasis on the citations included in patents. Almeida found that foreign semiconductor companies tap into local knowledge in the US. Cantwell showed that technological leaders are becoming increasingly geographically specialized in their technological activity.

In research on the Japanese pharmaceutical industry, Myles Shaver of New York University and I have found some evidence of increased innovation on the part of companies that have established research and development facilities in foreign locations. However, only those with previously existing competence in research and development experienced increases in innovativeness. While this may sound like a case of the rich getting richer, we argue that it indicates a path to gaining competences. Companies need to develop skills in the basics before trying to gain an understanding of new sciences and technologies. Thus, there would seem to be no opportunities for leapfrogging, at least in the pharmaceutical industry.

Overall, international research and development is an increasingly prevalent phenomenon. While patent data indicates that companies are learning from their research activities, we have not yet established a conclusive link between research and actual products.

Summary

In earlier times, says **Joan Penner-Hahn**, the focus of foreign R&D activities was on supporting marketing and production efforts in specific overseas markets. But today, companies are involved in a global hunt to tap regionally concentrated science bases outside their home countries. Foreign R&D may be gathered through different modes – purchased, sponsored, collaborative, or controlled research – and each has its benefits and trade-offs.

Suggested further reading

Almeida, P. (1996) "Knowledge sourcing by foreign multinationals: Patent Citation Analysis in the US Semiconductor Industry," *Strategic Management Journal*, 17 (Winter): 155–65.

Cantwell, J. (1995) "The globalisation of technology: what remains of the product cycle model?" *Cambridge Journal of Economics*, 19: 155–74.

Penner-Hahn, J. (1998) "Firm and environmental influences on the mode and sequence of foreign research and development activities," *Strategic Management Journal*, 19: 149–68.

Penner-Hahn, J. and Shaver, M. (1999) "Does international research and development increase patent output? An analysis of Japanese pharmaceutical firms," submitted for publication.

Reger, G. (1999) "How R&D is coordinated in Japanese and European multinationals," *R&D Management*, 29 (1): 71–88.

How to manage in times of disorder

by Arie Y. Lewin and Mitchell P. Koza

"**B**usiness is more difficult today than it has ever been before." Surely this statement has always had its adherents. After all, have managers ever reported discontent because the business world is too comfortable or the market place is not challenging? As this book so aptly demonstrates, both the pace and direction of change have become increasingly uncertain and unpredictable. And the trend is for more turbulence and volatility, not less.

Companies are experiencing discontinuous transitions as they evolve from the "Industrial Era" and adapt to the emerging "Information Age." The macro forces of change driving and contributing to this transformation are now familiar. They include globalization of markets, interdependence of economies, falling trade barriers, the cyber revolution, massive population movements, deflation, and the like. These changes have produced an environment for today's managers that may be accurately portrayed in the current lexicon as chaotic.

They are big changes. But they are not as unique as some popular business writers would have us believe. In the transitions to the Renaissance and to the second Industrial Revolution there were similar discontinuities.

The mid- to late nineteenth century, for instance, saw the invention and spread of railroads, telegraphs, and telephones, massive population movements, the 1870 Franco-Prussian war and the Civil War in America, as well as the emergence of the modern multidivisional corporation. The political, economic, and technological forces propeling the transition to the Information Age are different from those that propeled the transition to the Industrial Age. But they are hardly unique in terms of transformational impact. The challenges of adaptation are not new, although the strategic and organizational solutions must be different.

As this book documents, perceiving the environment and establishing environmental "fit" will no longer produce winning strategies. "Silver bullet" solutions such as building in "customer value" or infusing "stretch" into companies sound good, but have often proved elusive in practice.

Assembling the global company

In our research and involvement with companies from many industries and from every continent, we have learned that managing in times of growing disorder requires a new managerial logic. Managers need to understand the importance of 1) assembling the global company, and 2) animating the self-renewal capacity of the total enterprise.

Assembling the global organization means recognizing that the modern large global company will consist of what Jack Welch, chairman of the US General Electric conglomerate, calls "multibusinesses." These new business assemblies are very different from the old multinationals or their modern variant, the so-called transnational corporation. The first addressed the need for diversification; the second responded to the problem of cross-divisional cooperation. The new challenge of strategic assembly refers to the imperative of simultaneously accessing geographic and product markets or market segments, managerial competences and skills, and technologies and brands. It involves the traditional vehicles of internal development and acquisition, as well as the full range of strategic alliances, partnerships, networks, and inter-company relationships necessary for success in the global market place.

However, the fundamental difference involves the managerial task. In the old multinational corporation and the traditional conglomerate form, the focus was on the allocation of capital across the various business units. In the transnational form, the new focus was on the transfer of learning and capabilities across the global enterprise. Managing the global multibusiness, however, involves the need continuously to animate self-renewal of the total enterprise. Leaders must first make the assembly choices but, even more important, must infuse the organization as a whole with the life force necessary for institutionalizing change. Animating the global organization means implanting and nurturing the ideal of continuous self-renewal.

Historically, companies seem to have followed the inevitable life cycle of growth, maturation, decline, rejuvenation, and back to growth again. Rejuvenation, as distinct from transformation, has entailed restructuring, rationalization, repositioning, cost reduction, and diversification. The anticipated new growth trajectory was expected to result from the redirection of resources into new opportunities, mostly through mergers and acquisitions, augmented by new internal investments. These restructurings were intended to achieve economies of scale and scope. In the new environment, counting on rejuvenation once decline has already set in risks being too late to combat ultimate extinction. The managerial challenge is to animate the company's internal rate of change to match or exceed the rate of change in its environment. This is the keystone strategy for countering the build-up of structural inertia, which is the root cause for the growth, decline, and rejuvenation life cycle trap.

Animating the company

How does a company animate change as a way of life and develop the capacity to compete on what complexity theorists call the "edge"? For the past 20 years, managers have been inundated with a barrage of management fads, from total quality management and reengineering to leaders as entrepreneurs and free agents, and companies as jazz bands and football teams. A succession of management gurus have exhorted companies to become "hypercompetitors," "learning organizations," "intelligent enterprises," "network organizations," and, most recently, "knowledge-based organizations." However, it is altogether clear that companies like Daimler-Benz of Germany (now DaimlerChrysler) and General Electric have eschewed the search for the silver bullet. They are learning to manage by adopting the new counter-intuitive maxim: "If it ain't broke fix it anyway."

Animating change begins with the fundamental insight that rationalization and transformation must be simultaneously balanced as on-going, intertwined and co-evolving actions. In our work we have used the metaphor of balancing exploitation and exploration. Exploitation implies a never-ending opportunity to improve, extend, refine, elaborate, and reduce the costs associated with existing products, technologies, skills, and competences. Exploration is about prospecting new landscapes and investing in new opportunities, generating new innovative products, technologies, and markets, and supplanting existing competences. Moreover, managers practicing the simultaneous balancing of exploitation and exploration also understand that in the long run, above-average returns cannot be realized from over-reliance on exploitation. Advantages from sources of efficiency can invariably be copied and will be competed away.

The ability of managers to sustain an on-going balance of exploitation and exploration has generally proved elusive. The primary cause is the asymmetric reward structure of the financial markets. This leads managers to prefer the more assured immediate returns associated with exploitation efforts, and to avoid the risk associated with the more variable returns attached to exploration activities. These preferences are self-reinforcing when companies experience the expected negative returns related to the typical "off and on" exploration behavior of most companies, which embark on exploration activities when times are good and retrench them when times are tight.

However, animating change as a way of life goes beyond learning to balance exploitation and exploration simultaneously. It also requires constant attention to managing the rate of change in these activities by, for example, benchmarking the rate of change of competitors, with the strategic intent of leapfrogging such rates of change. It requires managing all available sources of inducing change, like managing strategies of disruption and surprise, instituting flexible formal structures, keeping bureaucracy in check, nurturing emergent processes, and practicing a new leadership based on trust.

Self-organization

Sustained self-renewal requires leadership that understands the importance of anticipating and initiating new directions. This does not mean embracing every new management fad and changing for the sake of change. For example, in the 19 years that Jack Welch has been CEO of GE, he has unleashed a new change initiative at a rate of one every three years. These initiatives extended and reinforced earlier ones (e.g., Six Sigma followed Workout), thus conveying his priority of not standing still. But he has also directed GE into new strategic landscapes, such as investing in Asia following expansion into Eastern Europe, or, most recently, directing the move into e-business. Overall, the objective should be to pace change and institutionalize anticipation for change.

The new leadership logic accepts the tenet of self-organization. It requires that leaders and managers focus on articulating and teaching the frameworks that constrain and enable self-organization at each and every level of the organization.

Stimulating and nurturing emergent processes represents the most underutilized source of change and self-renewal. It implies the leveraging and supplanting of past competences to create new markets or new products, such as when Mercedes-Benz introduced the A Class model and the Smart car. It involves nurturing and supporting improvization, encouraging rule breaking, and rewarding change agents. It also requires the need to train and select leaders who are comfortable with managing ambiguity (e.g., all else being equal have a high tolerance for ambiguity) and are comfortable with the democratic implications of accepting and supporting emergent outcomes. Moreover, the new managerial logic requires managers to be trained and become proficient in articulating and establishing the boundaries and process controls that stimulate and enable emergent action.

Contingencies

The principles of managing the internal rate of change, balancing exploitation and

Figure 1: The logic of the new global multibusiness company

	Multinational	Transnational	Multibusiness
Growth logic	Diversification	Leveraging competences	Strategic assembly
Managerial task	Capital allocation	Interdivisional cooperation	Balancing exploitation & exploration
Control mechanism	Financial controls	Behavior controls	Enabling emergent process
Leadership	Command and control	Coaching	Animation

exploration, and utilizing emergent process are universal. However, the specific adaptation practices, and the character and direction of self-organization that companies pursue, will be contingent on and reflect such attributes as administrative heritage, industry, social and political context, and national identity and culture. In companies with an administrative heritage of strong top-down management, or in cultures where small managerial elites exercise hegemony, stimulating and nurturing self-organizing emergent processes will represent a particular challenge. Similarly, in a culture characterized by individualism, self-reliance, and high employee mobility, realizing the cumulative benefits of collective self-organization could be a limiting constraint (*see* Figure 1).

Conclusion

Managing the global multibusiness company in times of increasing disorder represents a major departure from the conventional wisdom of international management. The traditional multi-national followed the logic of diversification, centralized capital allocation, strong financial controls, and command-and-control leadership. The transnational form emphasized leveraging competences, fostering interdivisional cooperation, and applying complex behavioral controls, and expected managers to mentor and coach. In contrast, animating the global multibusiness organization requires a strategic assembly perspective, adaptation through the simultaneous and continuing balancing of exploitation and exploration, process controls that stimulate and enable emergent process and self-organization, and, most importantly, depends on leadership *sans* control.

In this article we have outlined some of the key elements underlying the emerging new managerial logic for animating and assembling the global multibusiness company in times of increasing disorder, as distilled from the practices of a few leading-edge companies.

Summary

Managing a global multibusiness company poses a major challenge for international managers, say **Arie Y. Lewin** and **Mitchell P. Koza**. They examine key elements for "animating" and "assembling" a global multibusiness company. These are techniques, distilled from leading-edge companies, for helping a business to adapt to the dramatically increasing disorder in the environment. The authors contrast the traditional multinational and transnational approach to management with what is needed in today's global multibusiness organization – including, critically, leadership without control.

Suggested further reading
In Search of Strategy (1999) Special issue of the *Sloan Management Review*, 40 (3).
Co-evolution of Strategy and New Organizational Forms (1999) Special issue of *Organization Science*, 10 (5).

Seven myths regarding global strategy

by Subramanian Rangan

Companies of all shapes and sizes are pondering global strategies. While there are many useful ideas and opinions on this topic, there are also unfortunately a number of myths. In this article I will highlight seven common ones and discuss them briefly below.

1. Any company with money can go global

The flaw with this is that going global and going global successfully are not the same thing. The Paris department store Galéries Lafayette went global with much fanfare, setting up shop in New York some years ago. However, success proved elusive and the store folded its operations after sustained losses, returning to its home base a wiser company. Expansion into Europe by Whirlpool, the US home appliances manufacturer, has not exactly been smooth either.

The reasons are rooted in an idea known as "the liability of foreignness." A company attempting to sell into a foreign market tends to face an inherent handicap relative to local rivals. Customer needs and tastes in the foreign market are likely to be different; obstacles may abound, from identifying good local suppliers to dealing with sceptical host authorities; and the very model of business may be different. Crucially, on all these fronts, local rivals are likely to have the home advantage. If a company is to succeed abroad, it must possess some valuable intangible asset that will enable it to meet and beat local rivals in their own home market. This could be advanced technology (as with Canon, the copier and camera maker); an appreciably superior value proposition (such as that developed by Ikea, the Swedish furniture group); a well-known brand name (e.g., Coca-Cola); low unit costs deriving from scale or process knowhow (e.g. Dell in PCs, or South African Breweries in beer); or some combination of the above (e.g., Toyota, L'Oréal and Citibank).

When Galéries Lafayette went to New York, it faced established rivals as diverse as Macy's and Bloomingdale's, as well as Saks Fifth Avenue, and it did not have any valuable intangible asset that would set it apart. Whirlpool faces similar challenges in Europe.

Implications: If the urge to expand internationally should strike your company, first study local rivals abroad and look for concrete evidence that you can beat them. A track record of solid and growing exports into the target market can be a credible sign that you can deliver value that local rivals either do not or cannot deliver themselves. This is why companies tend to export before they set up shop abroad. Also, ensure that you dominate your home market. As the foreign market poses inherent handicaps, you may not be ready for global expansion if you are not a domestic leader (if you are not, in other words, a Samsung, a Telefónica, or a Cemex). The broader point is that a global strategy is no substitute for a good business strategy. Also, remember that low growth at home is neither a necessary nor sufficient condition for global expansion. So, if your company does not possess valuable intangible assets, then, no matter how deep its pockets, expansion abroad is unlikely to be profitable (and hence should be postponed).

2. Internationalization in services is different

Companies in the services sector are indeed, in many important ways, different from companies in the manufacturing and primary sectors. Services tend to be less transportable (and, hence, less tradable), less storable, more regulated. Yet, when it comes to internationalization, services are no different. From hotels to healthcare, retail to real estate, financial services to fast food, service-sector companies are subject to the viability test stated above. That is, if a service company does not possess a valuable intangible asset, internationalization is not going to be profitable.

Before embarking on international expansion, service companies, as much as manufacturers, must also respond affirmatively to two other questions. First, is there sufficient and steady demand abroad (backed by purchasing power) for the service offered? French cuisine, Spanish bullfighting, and US football might not meet this test. Second, is the service experience replicable abroad? Disney may (with some difficulty) be able to recreate its theme parks in Japan and France, and Club Med can offer its convivial holiday village atmosphere not only in southern Europe but also in North Africa – but Virgin Airways, Toys "R" Us, and Indian diamond cutters may be less able to replicate their value proposition abroad. Reasons include regulatory hurdles, costly access to key inputs, and the difficulty of transferring competences abroad.

Implications: Internationalization in services is no different from that in manufacturing. A service company can internationalize successfully as long as it meets the intangible asset test, the effective demand test, and the replicability test. Companies as diverse as Blockbuster Video, the US video rental operator, Sodehxo Alliance, the French in-house catering company, and Goldman Sachs, the US investment bank, have met these tests and expanded abroad profitably. But fail one or more of the three, and expansion abroad is unlikely to be profitable.

3. Distance and national borders matter no more

Spurred by developments like the internet, some observers have proclaimed the demise of distance. Others, perhaps persuaded by the omnipresence (from Mexico to Malaysia, from Iceland to New Zealand) of the US-based broadcaster CNN and of McDonald's fast-food outlets, believe that national cultures have converged and can be safely disregarded when it comes to global business. In the latter view, the only culture that matters now is corporate culture; national borders are passé.

There may sometimes be some truth in these assertions, but they should, at least for now, be treated with skepticism. Indeed, besides being exaggerated they are plainly incorrect as generalizations. Take distance. In books and CDs, software and remote diagnostics, new technologies continue to shrink physical distance; but in most spheres of economic activity transport and telecommunication costs, small though they may have become, are still positive and still increase with distance.

Moreover, as every executive knows, reliable information is the lifeblood of economic decisions. And, even in this day and age, reliable information is acquired more readily and more reliably locally than from afar. This is partly why companies tend to cluster close to others in their industry – part of the explanation perhaps for the "home bias" that economists have documented in trade and investment. It is also why, even after controlling for transport costs, distance has a significant (and negative) influence on economic exchange.

National culture and borders are also still significant. National cultures shape national institutions and influence economic values and ethos. Although patterns are changing, economic organization in Japan still seems to favor business above labor and consumers; in parts of Europe labor comes first, followed by producers and consumers; in the US consumers tend to rank ahead of producers and labor.

Cultural values aid interpretation and are an input in business decisions. The relationship of a company to its customers, national and local governments, rivals, shareholders, financial institutions, and the local community, all tend to be influenced by national culture. From language to labor policy, punctuality to property rights, taxation to transfer pricing, accounting rules to supplier relationships, business still operates differently across nations and regions. As a result, companies that cross national borders tend to face sharp discontinuities, and those that disregard or fail to anticipate the latter are likely to see successful home-grown strategies meet a poor reception abroad (just ask Lincoln Electric Holdings, the welding systems equipment maker, or Otis, the lifts and elevators manufacturer).

National borders represent the combined forces of national history, institutions, and conditioning, and give potent meaning to the terms insiders and outsiders. Even the seemingly innocuous US–Canada border appears to operate in this way. Empirically, language and national borders show up as significant and large determinants of international trade and investment. Even in our increasingly digital and anglicized global economy, national language and cultural affinity are still a crucial determinant of trade and investment decisions. US companies still head for Canada first, Portuguese companies for Brazil, Spanish companies for Latin America, Japanese companies for other parts of Asia.

Implications: In view of the above, it continues to make sense to expand regionally before entering more distant markets; to head for familiar markets before unfamiliar ones. Companies that respect national borders and cultures are more likely to win back respect from employees, suppliers, customers, and national authorities. This hardly means forsaking "globality;" it just means placing added emphasis on being both local and global. Indeed, companies that embrace this ambiguity will more likely be rewarded with profitable growth.

4. Developing countries are where the action is

In much public discourse on globalization, there is a view that the big markets are in the large developing countries (such as Mexico, Brazil, China, and India). In fact, globalization is still very much a concentrated, rich country game. Of the 100 largest multinationals, only two are from developing countries. In terms of international trade and inward and outward foreign direct investment, ten nations – Canada, the US, the UK, Germany, France, the Netherlands, Sweden, Switzerland, Japan, and Australia – account for 50, 70, and 90 percent of respective world totals. Their purchasing power is still unrivaled despite recent economic convergence.

Implications: No company that wants to be counted as world class can afford to ignore developed country markets. Indeed, as Japan restructures its economy and recovers from a prolonged slump, it should not be surprising to see the US–European cross-border merger mania being followed by a similar Europe–Japan and US–Japan company-driven integration. The 1999 Renault–Nissan deal may only be a harbinger of things to come.

5. Manufacture where labor costs are cheapest

During the debate on the North American Free Trade Agreement or Nafta, the "sucking sound" hypothesis – that multinationals will shift their operations to nations where labor costs are lowest – was elevated to new heights. In reality, of course, the only sounds that low wages should stir are loud yawns. As every business executive knows, what matters first off is delivered unit costs and not just wage costs. Materials are typically a big chunk of total costs and by levying import duties and such, developing countries (that boast low wages) often make local manufacturing expensive. Second, where wages are low, productivity tends to be low too. Consequently, hourly wage costs may appear ridiculously low, but unit costs tend to be high. Lastly, it is generally optimal to manufacture in (or at least near) the big markets. Not only does such a strategy minimize tariffs, transport costs, and logistical problems; it also creates a structural hedge against unfavorable changes in real exchange rates. If, for instance, Mercedes had opened its plant in Mexico rather than in the US, it would have traded off its deutschmark–dollar currency exposure for peso–dollar exposure.

Implications: As a generalization (but not as a rule), make where you sell. For large companies that sell in the triad (Europe, Japan, the United States), this means operating in that triad. Young European managers might care to concentrate on learning Japanese; as European consumers warm to Japanese products, Japanese companies will continue to raise their presence in Europe significantly. For similar reasons, young Japanese managers should brush up on their English: foreign investment into Japan is likely to rise significantly as well. Envy the British and the Americans; when it comes to foreign tongues, the default status of English as the language of international business offers them a free ride.

6. Globalization is here to stay

A sentiment that is often part of the hype surrounding the "new economy" is that globalization, like a genie, is out of the bottle and cannot be pushed back in. Here again, there is some truth to the claim, but serious skepticism is also warranted. To see why, consider the key developments that have enabled globalization.

First and most familiar are technology changes. It would appear that these are unlikely to be reversed. Second is the phenomenon referred to as economic convergence. As per capita incomes converge across nations, demand patterns tend to converge (people in more and more nations want fast food, cars, and PCs), and capabilities converge as well (people in more and more nations can now write software, make new medicines, and build fancy products). This convergence process might suffer interruptions (witness the recent Asian crisis), but it appears unlikely to be arrested for long, let alone reversed.

The most important driver of globalization, though, is the spread of economic liberalism. The recent and widespread change in ideology – from state socialism to market capitalism – has unleashed much internal deregulation and external liberalization, from France to the former Soviet Union. The embrace of openness that took hold during the late 1980s and early 1990s trailed a half-century of economic growth and global peace. Take away either of the latter two conditions and liberalization might become a potential casualty. Globalization has been willed into existence due to the changed beliefs and acts of national governments. Bring serious war or sustained high unemployment into the picture and governments may start to act in ways that could reverse globalizing trends. Even at the end of 1999, with just

5 percent unemployment and a seemingly unstoppable economy, the US sometimes appeared to be ambiguous on globalization. What would the attitude be if it faced Europe's double-digit unemployment?

Implications: Economic growth is key if globalization is to continue apace. In a "winner takes all" economy, we are building a shaky enterprise and a fragile society if all cannot (sooner or later) be winners. Companies need to explore issues such as unemployment, employee retraining, and equality of opportunity, if not incomes. If business does not become more sensitive to this possibility, expect to see much more resistance to the structural adjustment that globalization tends to bring, and expect to see governments reasserting themselves.

7. Governments don't matter any more

Beneath a headline saying that 1998 sales by the world's 100 largest multinational enterprises were one-and-a-half times the gross domestic product (GDP) of France, a cartoon in *Le Monde* newspaper showed executives (atop skyscrapers) clasping their stomachs and roaring with laughter at a remark by Prime Minister Lionel Jospin, "L'état ne peut pas tout" (roughly, "the state cannot do everything"). The cartoon's implicit message: multinationals are the masters of today's world, governments are powerless. Move over Lionel Jospin, make way for Bill Gates.

Those who fail to treat this as an exaggerated claim are likely to be in for some unpleasant surprises. As long as people attach value to a collective national identity and as long as they value local representation in decision making, governments will continue to matter greatly. The reality is that people are not very mobile across national borders; we tend to become part of the local and national communities where we are born. In this kind of society, concepts such as local and national interests have real meaning, and local and national governments have evolved to be the key institutions that promise to advance those interests with any constancy. After all, companies come and companies go (take Digital Equipment in Massachusetts); their identities may change through acquisitions (as in DaimlerChrysler or Renault–Nissan). To the extent that corporate interests align with those of the local community this may be welcome, but it is no longer to be counted on (just ask the community living in Clermont-Ferrand, home town of the French tyre maker Michelin).

In a world where people no longer expect companies to give primacy to local interests, local and national governments will be viewed as a necessary counterweight. Governments know this and will willingly serve that function. Of course, to do so credibly, from time to time governments will push their weight around. They may break up large firms, prevent foreign investment in so-called culture industries, and tie up the hands of companies in other ways. All this is easier to do when the companies are foreign and the voters local. As Raymond Vernon warned in his book *In the Hurricane's Eye*, multinationals and governments – both legitimate entities – will confront one another again; when this happens, it will be seen that power has not slipped away from sovereign nations.

Equally importantly, a working global economy needs global rules. There are too many companies (with perhaps as many interests) and they can't all be invited to make those rules. Global rules are therefore still the prerogative of governments, and so long as rules matter (and, in the future, they are likely to matter more not less), governments will continue to matter.

Implications: Companies should resist the temptation to write off governments as ineffective anachronisms. Rather, they should recognize governments as important and legitimate institutions in the world economy. Indeed, if companies are to benefit from globalization and wish to encourage its spread, they should work with governments to establish how local and global can evolve in an acceptably balanced manner. Jobs and profits might be traded off in the short, but not the long run. Managers must recognize this. In the twentieth century, prime responsibility for jobs fell on governments, while that for profits fell on companies. If we are to retain the tremendous economic gains made in that century, this division of labor must work well. Without engagement and imaginative coordination among private enterprises and governments, neither the concept of the market nor that of democracy is likely to deliver its full promise. To avoid that outcome should be a goal of all economic entities.

Summary

Going global has drawbacks as well as attractions. In this article, **Subramanian Rangan** tables seven common myths associated with globalization and discusses their implications for companies large and small. A global strategy, he emphasizes, is no substitute for a sound business strategy. Successful cross-border operations are usually based on a unique service concept, proprietary knowledge or technology, lower costs, or a well-established brand name. Among other points, the author argues that services are no different from manufacturing in the international arena, that governments still matter, and that the best opportunities are still likely to be found in the developed countries.

Suggested further reading

McCallum, J. (1995) "National borders matter: Canada–US regional trade patterns," *American Economic Review*, 85: 615–23.

Rangan, S. and Lawrence, R.Z. (1999) *A Prism on Globalization*, Washington DC: Brookings Institution.

UNCTAD (1999) *The World Investment Report*.

Vernon, R. (1998) *In the Hurricane's Eye*, Cambridge, MA: Harvard University Press.

STRATEGY AND ORGANIZATIONAL STRUCTURES

Contributors

Randall Morck holds the Stephan A. Jarislowsky Distinguished Chair in Finance at the University of Alberta, Edmonton, Canada. He has published extensively on corporate ownership, corporate finance, and corporate governance. He is a visiting professor of economics at Harvard University.

Bernard Yeung is Abraham Krasnoff Professor in Global Business at New York University, Stern School of Business. Before joining this school in 1999, he was professor of international business and area research director of the William Davidson Institute at the University of Michigan Business School. His research focus is on international business, economics and finance.

Marc J. Knez is an associate professor of strategy at the University of Chicago Graduate School of Business. His research interests include managerial and strategic decision making, incentive systems, and organizational design.

Francine Lafontaine is associate professor of business economics and public policy at the University of Michigan Business School. Her research interests include franchising, vertical relations, and incentive contracting.

Robert Gertner is a professor of economics and strategy at the University of Chicago Graduate School of Business. He teaches courses in strategic investment decisions and advanced competitive strategy. He is also principal of Lexicon Inc., a Chicago-based consulting firm.

Richard Whittington is a university reader in strategy at Saïd Business School, Oxford, and a fellow of New College, Oxford. He is researching how managers learn to strategize as part of the Economic and Social Research Council's SKOPE (Skills, Knowledge and Organizational Performance) program.

Andrew Pettigrew is professor of strategy and organization at Warwick Business School, where between 1985 and 1995 he founded and directed the internationally renowned Centre for Corporate Strategy and Change.

Winfried Ruigrok is professor of international management at the University of St. Gallen, Switzerland. He focusses on organizational innovation, the integration of foreigners in top management teams and boards, and comparative corporate governance.

Karel Cool is BP Professor of European Competitiveness and professor of strategic management at INSEAD. His research, teaching and consulting focus on problems of industry and competitive analysis such as industry overcapacity, profit dynamics, product standards, critical mass races, value creation and building unique resources.

Contents

Introduction

Technology and hyper-competition are among the many new influences on organizational design. This module looks at the broader issues and at specific organizational forms like franchising. Executives often need to consider trade-offs – between, say, specialization and coordination, or reliability and flexibility – but the skillful manager tends to minimize these. A particular challenge is knowing when to outsource needs and when to integrate vertically – the choice often boils down to the relative values of market transactions and long-term relationships. Managers are also introduced here to the drivers of critical mass and how to triumph in "winner-takes-all" battles.

When synergy creates real value

by Randall Morck and Bernard Yeung

Large companies that do business in many places and in many industries are the archetypes of corporate success and power. So do sheer size, scale, and scope bestow an impregnable competitive advantage? The evidence is far from compelling. General Electric of the US is a large and highly diversified company consistently well liked by investors. Yet ITT Corporation, another highly diversified company, no longer exists. Before it was acquired, its market-to-book ratio was dismally low and it underperformed rivals across the broad range of industries into which it had diversified. Why the difference?

Academic studies by economists merely add to the confusion about the effects of diversification. Some find that it adds value. Others hold that it destroys value. The impact of diversification on company value rises and falls like hemlines. In the 1960s and 1970s, diversification was considered a boon. Companies were extolled to "spread the overhead" across operations in many industries. By the 1980s and 1990s, diversification had become a sign of poor corporate governance. Overgrown companies were prime targets for hostile break-ups.

Remarkably, this reversal was more than a new scholastic bandwagon. Serious empirical studies found that diversification really did seem to destroy value in the 1980s, although not in earlier decades. Credible evidence shows that diversification really was associated with higher value in the 1960s. What are we to make of this apparent hash?

The economic purpose of a company is to put a given set of activities and assets under the control of a specific team of managers. Diversification adds more activities to this set. Whether diversification adds to company value or not is therefore a question about where a company's boundary properly belongs. University of Chicago economist Ronald Coase won a Nobel prize in part for his 1937 theory that a company's boundary should be drawn at the point where the benefits of adding a set of activities just match the costs of including it.

The costs of adding more activities are obvious. Larger and more complex organizations are more difficult to manage. Corporate politics become worse, thereby hurting performance. Size and complexity make companies less transparent to investors. This can veil poor corporate governance until the company's problems have grown to near lethal proportion.

The benefits of adding activities are trickier to nail down. One purported benefit is that large diversified companies can pool the financial resources of their operations, allowing the head office to operate like an in-house bank. Highly profitable lines of business can bankroll new ventures or necessary expansions in cash-short divisions or subsidiaries. In theory, this internal financing might lead to better monitoring and better trust than external financing. If so, large and diversified companies might be able to respond to investment opportunities with more agility and precision than is possible for companies that depend on banks or public markets for capital. Large and diversified companies might also have more resources for training and more opportunities for career development. Diversification can spread risks and make companies more desirable employers, thus attracting better managers and workers. It might also make diversified companies more attractive as suppliers, customers, or joint venture partners. Any or all of these benefits could enable diversified companies to command an investor premium.

The clumsy conglomerate

A common feature of arguments about the possible benefits of diversification is that they are more convincing in economies with weaker institutions. As banks, capital markets, education, insurance, labor markets, and product markets become more efficient and sophisticated, alternatives to large, diversified companies become more attractive. (And, in a more efficient economic climate, the cost of being a clumsy conglomerate becomes more apparent.) This may explain the empirical findings by economists that diversification was associated with added value in earlier decades, but now seems to depress a company's share price.

Markets and economic institutions work better now than in the past, so corporate diversification is today a more equivocal strategy. Indeed, many consultants and strategists preach that diversification is always wrong, and corporations must ever strive to increase their focus on the core business. This is an oversimplification. A company should change its boundaries to capture "synergy." Indeed, synergy (or its absence) often figures prominently in corporate decisions about upsizing, downsizing, mergers, and divestitures. Unfortunately, the term is commonly applied very loosely along with the general proposition that $1 + 1 = 3$.

Daimler-Benz, the German car manufacturer, and Chrysler of the US saw synergies from a union of their operations. Adding a dominant European car maker to a thriving US car company would yield more than the sum of the two, despite limited overlaps in products and territorial strength. Citicorp and Traveler's Group also foresaw synergies from a marriage of their banking and insurance services. Adding Citicorp's activities and skills to Traveler's (non-overlapping) activities and skills reflected the same magical arithmetic. One plus one may not equal three, but the world might be better if it did. Fortunately, it sometimes can.

Some economic activities really do create value that did not formerly exist. Given that value is based on profits, and profits are the difference between revenues and cost, the magical arithmetic happens in at least two ways in a merger: shared costs (e.g., by sharing overhead) and enhanced revenue (e.g., by increasing sales without adding to costs). Cost sharing and revenue enhancement would seem more likely between activities in similar industries, such as in the aforementioned examples. Synergy should therefore be more evident in related than in unrelated mergers.

The difficulty here is in defining "related." Businesses that look distinctly unlinked to outside observers can turn out to be "related" in unexpected ways. Transportation and electronics are clearly different industries, but electronics is a large and rising component of the cost of an automobile. Entertainment and computer network technology looked unrelated until recently. Some of the most exciting advances in power transmission, for instance, involve new ceramic superconductors.

Whether or not two companies are in "related" businesses is a tricky question. Economically meaningful cross-fertilization can involve surprising bedfellows. US manufacturing conglomerate 3M, the maker of Scotch Tape®, has a wealth of knowledge about tapes, glues, and adhesives. It has found profitable uses for this knowledge in superficially unrelated businesses, such as stationery (Post-it® notes and adhesive tapes) and electronics supplies (sticking magnetic substances to plastic tapes for VCRs and cassette players). Accounting firms, with a wealth of business intelligence, have branched into consulting. Companies with brand capital have expanded into new lines of business where their name recognition carries weight. For example, Calvin Klein, one of America's best-known global brands, has moved from blue jeans into underwear and perfumes.

So companies diversify into businesses where they see a profitable use for their existing knowledge-based assets: technology, business intelligence, marketing knowledge, brand names, and the like. Such knowledge-based assets seem to underlie most examples of companies successfully leaping into new lines of business. Intangible and ephemeral knowledge-based assets underpin the real "synergy" that is measurable in the share values of successfully diversified companies. Small wonder that synergy is a difficult term to pin down.

Deeper investigation of a company's costs and revenues often explains why such assets can generate synergy. The trick is that developing knowledge-based assets usually requires huge up-front costs, but using knowledge-based assets on a large scale often costs little more than using them on a small scale. Once 3M had accumulated its hoard of knowledge about adhesives, jumping from Scotch Tape to VCR tape involved relatively little additional cost. Once Calvin Klein had developed a racy image for its jeans and T-shirts, selling underwear and perfume could be undertaken with high profit margins. The underwear and perfume businesses enhance the revenues produced by the Calvin Klein brand (revenue enhancement) without reinventing the wheel (cost sharing). Quite simply, knowledge-based assets are worth most when they are applied as widely and in as many lines of business as possible.

Keeping synergy in-house

Knowledge-based assets are difficult to sell, trade, or lease. Their value stems largely from their uniqueness. 3M's knowledge of adhesives is valuable for that reason and no one else has anything quite comparable. Understandably, the owners of knowledge-based assets want to preserve this uniqueness. That usually means that they want strong protection for their intellectual property rights.

Many governments have firmed up protection for intellectual property, but huge gaps remain. It is far from clear that any legislation can ever plug them. The best strategy that many companies see for protecting unique knowledge-based assets is simply to keep them secret.

The same goes for brands. Calvin Klein should strive to prevent cheap copies of its products from diluting the value of its name, and should be loath to license its name to unreliable joint-venture partners with low-quality products. Farming out can be impractical because knowledge-based skills, like designing and marketing, are hard to "explain and teach." Moreover, it is difficult to sell "knowledge," but easy to sell knowledge-based services. Thus, while it is difficult for Andersen, the consulting giant, to sell consulting knowledge, it is easy for it to sell consulting services. These sorts of considerations lead their owners to keep knowledge-based assets "in-house."

Juxtaposing the above arguments exposes the key problem of managing knowledge-based assets: such assets are most valuable when applied on the largest possible scale, but must often be kept "in-house" to preserve their value.

The solution, of course, is that a company with a valuable knowledge-based asset should grow as large as possible and as fast as possible. (In economists' jargon, this is called "internalizing" the market for the knowledge-based asset by expanding the company to encompass it.) This includes growth through diversification. The quickest way for a company to grow is through mergers or acquisitions.

The link between diversification and company value may therefore be very important indeed. The usefulness of corporate diversification as an end-run strategy around weak markets and dysfunctional economic institutions in general may have waned. But its importance as a strategy to broaden the application of knowledge-based assets shows no sign of fading.

This has practical significance. Our research (*see* Suggested further reading) shows that extensive cross-industry and geographic diversification add value to US companies that previously spent heavily on R&D or advertising, but destroy value in other companies.

These results have two considerable implications essentially delivering the same message. First, value-enhancing diversification is a consequence of a company's knowledge-based assets. Making diversification work boils down to creating, maintaining, and leveraging the return on knowledge. Second, when knowledge-based assets are absent, the costs associated with diversification (like opacity, bureaucracy, and corporate governance problems) are more likely to outweigh the traditional benefits (like overcoming ossified capital markets and institutions).

Why good governance matters

Valuable knowledge-based assets are much harder to create than narcissistic excuses for corporate empire building, although the two can often look alike in the short run. Good corporate governance becomes especially critical. How does a company establish and sustain responsible stewardship of shareholders' money in the creation, development, and profitable application of knowledge-based assets?

To answer this, it is useful to consider three differences between market economies and command economies. First, unlike in command economies, people in market economies see and have to accept the economic consequences of their decisions. Second, prices in a market economy reflect real economic costs rather than the accounting conventions of central planners. Third, a market economy creates and leverages a rapidly growing store of knowledge. By contrast, command economies stagnate behind rigid barriers to economic change and ultimately go bankrupt. The managers of state-owned enterprises saw innovation as a nuisance that upset five-year plans.

A poorly governed large company is often like a socialist economy. It is too large to be run on personal trust, so it imitates the command-and-control techniques of socialist economies. Its ponderous bureaucracy disconnects decisions from their consequences, hides true economic costs from decision makers, and stifles innovation by divorcing innovative effort from financial reward. Employees of such a company may possess the requisite technical knowledge, but it lies unused. They may have the potential to create innovative marketing plans, but they never really try hard.

Successful large companies try to mimic the efficiency of a free-market economy. They connect decisions to their economic consequences, use internal prices that reflect real costs, and employ value innovation. Just as innovators working in their garage vividly foresee reaping the economic value of their innovation, corporate employees need meaningful economic stakes in innovations that they conceive. Just as an innovator can raise money from venture capital funds, corporate employees with sound ideas must be confident of receiving financing and support. A large company can achieve this by letting innovative subunits borrow from headquarters, and by letting their employees share meaningfully in the returns that their innovations generate. The subunit should pay internal charges that reflect the cost of labor, capital, and other inputs. An internal price system, along with performance-based pay, makes the unit managers behave like owners/operators of a small business. (In economists' jargon, they "internalize" the economic consequence of their actions.) When unit managers behave like owners, a company has acquired the prerequisite to "create" and "leverage" knowledge.

Communicate, cooperate

While injecting the market mechanism into an organization is a useful idea, companies and economies are different beasts. Explicit communication or coordination of business efforts between companies in an economy is apt to arouse antitrust watchdogs. But similar communication and coordination between units within a company are perfectly acceptable, are expected, and may often be a prerequisite for the sorts of synergy we are talking about. A diversified company like 3M leverages its knowledge more effectively when its units communicate, coordinate, and cooperate effectively. The ability to make units communicate, coordinate, and cooperate is itself a valuable intangible asset for many large diversified companies. It enables them to outstrip smaller, one-industry rivals.

Does all this matter? Unquestionably! Our work shows that shareholders can distinguish justifiably diversified from excessively diversified companies. Diversified companies with knowledge-based assets have elevated share prices, while diversified companies without such assets have depressed share prices. Corporate raiders also appear to understand this difference.

Companies that diversify extensively despite having invested little in R&D or advertising (and so probably have few knowledge-based assets) are abnormally likely to become hostile takeover targets. Companies that possess knowledge-based assets, but have not diversified, are abnormally likely to become friendly takeover targets.

Overall, we find unwarranted diversification (diversification without supporting knowledge-based assets) to be ten times more common than value-enhancing diversification. Consultants who evangelize about focussing on core competences can therefore be forgiven. They are on track about 90 percent of the time.

Public policy implications

Economic growth is thought to arise primarily from innovation – from creating new knowledge-based assets and putting them to work in the economy.

Public policy must recognize the need to apply knowledge-based assets to very large scales of production very quickly. Mergers and acquisitions that bring this about are probably conducive to economic growth. But M&A that leaves companies with few knowledge-based assets operating at unsustainably large scales or in an unsustainable number of business lines is likely to be harmful.

Break-ups of these companies seem to happen spontaneously when their plights become obvious. Such takeovers are a clear public service. Public policies should encourage corporate takeovers to discipline poorly run companies.

Much M&A activity may well be economically pointless and driven by CEO egos, as critics of free market economics often claim. But M&A activity that realigns physical assets to mesh with new knowledge-based assets to create synergies is important to economic growth. We also need M&A that, while not wearing the clothes of "synergy," disciplines business empires.

Summary

Synergy, or the absence of it, tends to figure prominently in corporate decisions to get bigger or smaller, merge or divest. But according to **Randall Morck** and **Bernard Yeung**, synergy adds value only when linked to proprietary technological, marketing, or other knowledge assets. How a business handles knowledge depends on its governance and has profound implications for strategic management issues such as takeovers. The authors suggest that M&A plays an economically crucial role when it realigns physical and knowledge-based assets.

Suggested further reading

Acs, Z., Morck, R., Shaver, M. and Yeung, B. (1997) "The internationalization of small and medium size firms: a policy perspective," *Small Business Economics*, 9 (1, February): 7–20.

Coase, R.H. (1937) "The nature of the firm," *Economica*, 4 (Nov.): 386–405.

Jensen, M.C. (1989) "Eclipse of the public corporation," *Harvard Business Review*, 67 (5, Sept–Oct.): 61–74.

Jensen, M.C. and Meckling, W.H. (1995) "Specific and general knowledge, and organizational structure," *Journal of Applied Corporate Finance*, 8 (Summer): 4–18.

Morck, R. and Yeung, B. (1998) "Why firms diversify: internationalization vs. agency behavior," March.

Trade-offs in organizational design

by Marc J. Knez

The strategy of an organization defines both the way in which it intends to position itself in the market place so as to create value (its value proposition) and the set of necessary resources and capabilities required to generate and deliver this value to the market place.

More simply, the strategy determines what the organization needs to specialize in. The goal of its formal structure is to provide the means for implementing its strategy. This translates into a formal plan for grouping activities to achieve optimal levels of group specialization and between-group coordination. With this in mind, we can divide up the components of formal structure along two complementary dimensions.

Hierarchy of specialized units

Specialization occurs along three primary dimensions: function, product, and market segment, where each of these dimensions may come into play at different

The flexibility–reliability trade-off
Case 1 The reorganization of Hewlett-Packard's printer division

In the mid-1990s Hewlett-Packard, the company that pioneered laser printing, found its printer business subdivided by product line into the laser printer division and the inkjet printer division. Each type of printer was sold in both the consumer market and the corporate market, with the two divisions individually responsible for selling their particular type of printer to each of these markets. This hierarchy of specialization – product then market – placed the need for specialization and coordination within each product line above the needs for specialization and coordination within each market segment. Hence, any potential benefits to integrating the sales activities of both inkjet and laser printers within a market segment had to occur across these internal organizational boundaries. Under this structure, HP concluded that its inkjet printer business was underperforming in the corporate market (the focus of the laser division) and its laser printer business was underperforming in the consumer market (the focus of the inkjet business). As a result, it inverted the hierarchy of specialization. Now there is one division focussed on the corporate market and another focussed on the consumer market, where each division is now responsible for selling a portfolio of inkjet and laser printers to its respective market segments.

Note that HP's design problem exists because of the overlap between the product lines and their respective markets. This overlap is both good and bad. From an organizational perspective it creates an integration problem. However, the overlap also represents a synergy between the two product lines that can only be exploited through the effective integration of the two product lines.

levels of the organization. For example, an investment bank may divide itself up across functional lines: investment banking, sales and trading, and research. The investment banking function then may have an M&A product specialty, which itself is subdivided by market segments or product specialties. Each layer of the hierarchy defines an approach to specialization (e.g., market segment versus product specialties) and the structure of the specialization embedded in the formal structure should be tied to the strategy of the company.

Hierarchy of integration

The partitioning of specialized activities into groups promotes coordination and specialization within each group, but impedes coordination across groups. Organizational integration is the process of coordinating the activities of multiple, interdependent groups in the organization. Integration is difficult, because specialization within groups creates differentiation in the goals and behaviors of these groups, which hampers coordination between groups. This represents the first fundamental trade-off in organizational design – increasing the level of specialization and coordination within a group along a particular dimension (market, product, or function) invariably decreases between-group coordination on the remaining dimensions. (*See* Hewlett-Packard box above.)

Organizational integration occurs along two dimensions – vertical and horizontal. Integration via the vertical dimension occurs through the hierarchy of authority. In traditional structures, there is a one-to-one relationship between the hierarchy of specialized groups and the hierarchy of authority. Each group of specialized activities has a common boss who takes responsibility for the functioning and performance of the group. Coordination between the managers within the group occurs through the common boss. This common boss has control over the information that is shared between groups and he or she adjudicates conflicts that arise between the groups.

Integration via the horizontal (or lateral) dimension occurs via integrating mechanisms that generate communication and coordination directly between managers/specialists of different groups without the direct need to go through the chain of command (vertical hierarchy). The hierarchy of integrating mechanisms varies from low to high levels of formality, depending on the difficulty and importance of the coordination problem. At the low end of the hierarchy is the informal network of relationships; at the high end is the vertical hierarchy of authority. In the middle are three generic categories of integrating mechanisms increasing in levels of formality – liaison roles, cross-functional teams, and integrator roles.

The principal function of a liaison is to ensure that the requisite level of information is shared between interdependent groups. Liaisons have little or no authority to dictate actual decisions. Cross-functional teams are composed of members of different groups, and are typically charged with achieving coordination on one (or more) of the dimensions not used for partitioning the specialized units. Hence, they can take on many different forms, even within the same organization. A typical large consumer products organization may have product development teams, with representatives from several different R&D specialties charged with spreading basic research across several different product categories. It may also have client teams charged with coordinating the sale of a bundle of products to the same large customer. Note that no member of the team is accountable for its success, nor does any one member of the team have the authority to dictate the actions of any other members of the team. Rather, accountability and authority over each individual team member reside within each team member's specialized unit.

For particularly important and on-going coordination problems, integrator roles are created. An integrator is given formal responsibility for ensuring that the requisite level of cross-functional coordination occurs, and usually has responsibility for the performance of a set of cross-functional teams. Integrators are generalists. They possess the generalized knowledge necessary to determine what is optimal from a general management perspective with respect to a particular cross-functional coordination problem. Traditional examples of integrator roles include brand managers and account managers. While integrators have the formal responsibility for achieving cross-functional coordination, they do not have the formal authority to dictate the actions of any one functional area. It is in this sense that an integrator is not part of the formal hierarchy.

The critical distinction between the horizontal integrating mechanisms and the hierarchy of authority is authority itself. Each of these mechanisms is aimed at generating cross-functional coordination without allocating authority to anyone to guarantee that such coordination occurs. Such authority resides higher up in the hierarchy, in the hands of managers who are at least one step removed from the underlying details of the coordination problems. Put differently, these mechanisms are a substitute for managers higher up in the hierarchy acting as coordinating mechanisms through the formal authority they have over the groups they manage.

The end result is that the specialization/coordination trade-off does not go away. The coordination of activities within the specialized units will always take priority over the coordination of activities between units. However, in cases where the potential costs of giving one dimension of specialization priority over another are significant, companies implement structures aimed at putting two or more dimensions on an equal footing. The two most notable examples of multidimensional structures are matrix structures and team-based structures.

The flexibility–reliability trade-off
Case 2   GE's Retailer Financial Services division

The Retail Financial Services (RFS) division of GE Capital is one of the dominant providers of private-label credit-card services to large retail chains. RFS specializes in providing a complete portfolio of services to its private-label credit-card customers. Hence, it has grouped its activities directly around these customers, and much of its success is attributed to an effective team-based structure. These teams perform the credit card, customer service, and accounts receivable functions for each of the retail chains under their responsibility. Team members are given significant levels of authority in managing customer relationships and the teams themselves are self-managed. While a particular member of a team may have expertise in dealing with accounts receivable problems, the focus of this expertise is on the particular needs of a set of customers. Those activities and resources that are not specific to customers are handled centrally in order to maximize their efficient use.

A matrix structure is truly multidimensional in that it gives equal priority to two dimensions by having two lines of authority. One standard type of matrix structure groups activities by function along one dimension (R&D, engineering, manu-facturing, marketing) and projects (or products) along the other dimension. Functional experts involved in a project will have two bosses – a functional boss and a project boss. This two-boss structure is aimed at giving each dimension equal priority. Unfortunately, matrix structures create their own set of problems, most of which stem from the missed benefits of a single line of authority. In particular, it becomes the responsibility of the common subordinate to coordinate and resolve conflicts between his or her two bosses. Under a single line of authority, a common boss has the formal authority to coordinate and resolve conflicts between his or her subordinates.

Perhaps the most recent and notable approach to minimizing the trade-off between specialization and coordination has been the effort to organize around process rather than function. Organizations implementing this are often referred to as team based. The basic idea is to raise cross-functional teams to a status equal to their functional counterparts. These cross-functional teams are responsible for managing a complete cross-functional process. In the prototypical case, the process evolves around meeting the immediate and specific needs of large, important customers. (See GE retailer financial services division box above.)

What distinguishes team-based structures from the simple use of cross-functional teams is twofold. First, under team-based structures the organization is designed explicitly to support the cross-functional teams. Second, these teams are given significantly more responsibility and discretion relative to the traditional cross-functional team. That said, the functional units are still in place. However, their primary role is to manage processes and resources that are shared across the organization and to develop the functional specialists who are placed on the cross-functional teams. This sounds a bit magical.

How does the organization generate the required levels of functional specialization without allocating control over these specialized resources to the functional units, and thus facing the trade-off between specialization and coordination? Of course, the trade-off does not go away, but the extent to which it can be minimized depends on the informal structure of the organization.

The informal structure

The formal structure of the organization provides a formal plan for how work is supposed to get done in the organization. In the extreme, it provides well-defined roles and responsibilities governing how specialized activities are coordinated in some relatively standardized way. Surrounding the formal structure is an informal one that governs how employees actually go about doing their jobs and interacting with one another within the discretionary limits built into the formal structure. The informal structure is a combination of a network of employee relationships and a set of shared beliefs and norms that govern behavior within these relationships (organizational culture).

The formal and informal structures are tightly linked. Higher levels of formalization (standardization) imply lower levels of employee discretion within the informal structure. This includes lower levels of employee discretion over how their work is organized and with whom they have relationships inside and outside the organization. In a relatively static environment, where the attributes of the product or service provided by the organization change slowly, the reliability generated through higher levels of formalization can be optimal. For example, airlines require extreme levels of reliability to maximize safety, increasing the need for formalized procedures. Moreover, the process of "turning aircraft" efficiently to maximize on-time arrival rates can be almost completely standardized across airport locations. Hence, highly standardized work processes and well-defined roles and responsibilities of the various functional areas (flight crew, baggage handling, fueling, gate operations, etc.) characterize airline operations.

Of course, the reliability provided by the formal structure makes it difficult to alter organizational processes in order to be flexible in the goods or services that the company supplies to the market. The organization cannot alter its formal structure every time new market conditions imply that changes are required in the way specialized activities are coordinated. The ability of the organization to be flexible in dynamic environments can only come through the informal structure. These changes need to occur organically at the discretion of managers at low levels of the organization. But of course, relaxing the formal structure in order to increase the flexibility of the informal structure reduces reliability. This second fundamental trade-off in organizational design is characterized in Figure 1.

Minimizing organizational design trade-offs

Innovations in organizational design in the last couple of decades have been largely focussed on minimizing these two fundamental trade-offs. Two critical factors have

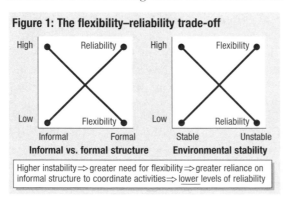

Figure 1: The flexibility–reliability trade-off

Higher instability ⇒ greater need for flexibility ⇒ greater reliance on informal structure to coordinate activities ⇒ lower levels of reliability

been the impetus for these innovations. First, there is the general increase in competition in many industries, requiring organizations to be much more capable of developing and deploying critical resources. The increased pressure to possess critical resources that distinguish a company from existing and potential competition places increased emphasis on specialized activities that both develop and coordinate these resources. At the same time, increased competition requires a company to be flexible in both responding to changes in the market place and satisfying the idiosyncratic needs of a more demanding customer base.

Second, the development of powerful information technology that reduces the costs of controlling and transmitting information and knowledge across the organization has made it technically feasible to reduce the need for the vertical hierarchy to control and disseminate information. With the costs of disseminating information decreasing dramatically, what remains is the development of the appropriate formal and informal mechanisms that ensure the information is used effectively to implement company strategy.

The management challenge can be summarized as follows: the organization should be structured so as to maximize the amount of cross-functional coordination of specialized activities occurring within the informal structure. At the same time, the organizational structure needs to formalize the processes that act as a platform for lateral coordination to occur reliably.

Meeting this challenge requires the effective implementation of a minimal set of formal integrating mechanisms that serve two roles. First, they have the direct effect of focussing attention on specific cross-functional coordination problems. Second, they have the indirect effect of both generating a network of personal relationships that cut across functional boundaries and fostering a shared understanding of cross-functional interdependencies. It is this shared understanding within the network of cross-functional relationships that serves as the foundation for spontaneous and reliable cross-functional coordination.

Summary

The term "organizational design" generally encompasses a company's formal structure, its planning, control, and human resource management systems, and its organizational culture. Discussion at a broad level tends to focus on the "fit" or "coherence" of these and other dimensions. In this brief overview of the issues, **Marc J. Knez** concentrates on two fundamental trade-offs, that between specialization and coordination, and that between reliability and flexibility. The management challenge – and the focus of much innovation in this area in recent years – is to find structures that minimize such trade-offs.

Suggested further reading

Ashkenas, R., Ulrich, D., Jick, T. and Kerr, S. (1995) *The Boundaryless Organization*, San Francisco, CA: Jossey-Bass.

Eccles, R.G. and Crane, D.D. (1988) *Doing Deals: Investment Banks at Work*, Boston, MA: Harvard Business School Press.

Fisher, M. (1996) "How Hewlett-Packard runs its printer division," *Strategy and Business*, 5.

For more information on team-based structures, *see* Mohrman, S.A., Cohen, S. and Mohrman, A., Jr. (1995) *Designing Team-Based Organizations*, San Francisco, CA: Jossey-Bass.

Myths and strengths of franchising

by Francine Lafontaine

Franchising is an integral part of the US economy and a growing phenomenon internationally. The reason lies in the combination of skills and incentives embedded in this type of organization.

Franchised chains benefit from the sort of brand recognition and economies of scale not available to independent entrepreneurs. Yet because units are managed by owners rather than employees, franchised chains also benefit from the drive and dedication that entrepreneurs bring to unit-level operations. In a real sense, these chains get the best of both worlds.

Franchising, however, is not a panacea. After defining franchising and establishing its importance in the world economy, this article examines a number of myths surrounding the topic. It shows that success is not guaranteed to franchisors or franchisees, that not all franchise systems are the type of established chains that most people associate with franchising, and that franchisees are not always small, single-unit owners. The goal, in highlighting and analyzing these and other facts, is to develop a more realistic understanding of franchising and of its strengths and weaknesses. This should allow potential franchisors and franchisees to approach franchising with the right expectations and thus reach more enlightened decisions.

A franchise is a contractual agreement between two legally independent companies whereby the franchisor grants the right to the franchisee to sell the franchisor's product or do business under its trademarks in a given location for a specified period of time. In return, the franchisee agrees to pay the franchisor a combination of fees, usually including an up-front franchise fee, royalties calculated as a percentage of the unit revenues, and an advertising contribution that is also usually a percentage of unit sales.

Although there are no really good recent data on the extent of franchising in the US, most analysts agree that 35 to 40 percent of retail sales there occur through franchised businesses. These sales represent about 15 percent of gross domestic product. These figures, however, include sales at petrol stations and car dealerships, as these are part of what is called "traditional franchising" in the US. This is a type of franchising where the franchisor is mostly a manufacturer selling its product through a franchised network. The other type of franchising, called "business-format franchising," is where the franchisor sells a way of doing business to its franchisees.

Business-format franchising includes companies involved in the fast-food and restaurant industry, hotels and motels, construction and maintenance, and non-food retailing. When data about the extent of both types of franchising were last collected by the US government, business-format franchising accounted for 27 percent of all franchising sales, 68 percent of all franchised establishments, and 74 percent of employees of franchised businesses. The discrepancy between these figures highlights the labor-intensive nature of business-format franchising and the lower sales of such outlets, especially compared to car dealerships.

Cross-country comparisons of the extent of franchising are rare, mostly because of lack of data. Also, in most countries beside the US, only business-format franchises are included in official franchising statistics. To get around some of these difficulties, a study by Arthur Andersen in 1995 focussed on the number of business-format franchisors and franchisees in 36 countries, as reported by franchise associations established in these countries.

The study revealed a wide range in the number of franchisors per country, from 0 (in Bulgaria) to 3,000 (in the US). The second and third largest numbers of franchisors were 1,000 for Canada and 932 in Brazil. At the other extreme were Israel, with 18, and the Czech Republic, with 35. On average, there were 333 franchisors per country, or 252 excluding the US.

As for the number of franchisees, Arthur Andersen found more than 250,000 in the US, followed by 140,000 in Japan, and 65,000 in Canada. On average, there were almost 25,000 franchisees per country, falling to 12,253 when the US was excluded. The data implies that there is about one franchisee per 500 people in Canada, one per 1,000 people in countries like the US, Japan, and Australia, and one for every 2,000 people in Britain, Brazil, and France. At the other extreme, countries like the Czech Republic and Columbia have one franchisee for every 100,000 inhabitants.

Finally, the study reported on the percentage of retailing volume represented by franchising. This showed the US at 40 percent, Britain at 32 percent and Australia and Brazil at 25 and 24 percent respectively. At the other extreme, several countries had franchising sectors accounting for only 1 or 2 percent of overall retailing. While such comparisons can be tricky, given definitional issues, they still show much variance in the extent of franchising worldwide.

The conclusions to be drawn from the above figures are that:

- the US continues to dominate franchising internationally through its sheer number of franchisors and franchisees;
- on a franchisee per capita basis, countries such as Canada, Japan, and Australia have franchising sectors that are as well if not more established than the US sector;
- the extent of franchising varies significantly across countries, with some markets still almost untapped.

Misconceptions

The figures above clearly show that franchising is often a useful, desirable, and efficient way to develop and organize business activities. However, a number of misconceptions about franchising need to be put in perspective. In the remainder of this article, I discuss and bring data to bear on four of these misconceptions: franchising is safe; franchising is growing exponentially in the US and elsewhere; all franchisors are large, established chains; all franchisees are owner-operators of a single unit.

1 Franchising is safe

For decades, the trade press, the International Franchise Association (the principal franchise association in the US), and individual franchisors, in their promotional materials, have made statements to the effect that investing in a franchise is much safer than starting a business independently. Over time, this has become a "well-known fact" about franchising.

When one examines the failure rates of units of blue-chip franchises, the probability of a unit going under is, in fact, relatively small (although not as small as the statements in the press often suggest). For example, a study by Frandata Inc., a Washington, DC research firm, found a yearly "failure" rate of 4.4 percent for the establishments of the 584 leading franchise systems in the US. Separately, however, Timothy Bates, a professor at Wayne State University, found that failure rates of franchised small businesses were greater than those of independent businesses (34.7 percent for franchises as opposed to 28.0 percent for independents over a six to seven-year period). The discrepancy comes in part from the samples, since the Frandata study focusses on leading franchisors whereas Bates's data is a representative sample of the population of franchised units of all chains. But the figures differ also because franchisors often fail in their first few years in operation, most often bringing their franchisees down with them. In producing its yearly directory, *The Franchise Annual*, Info Press Inc. has found that it has lost an average of 350 franchisors every year (details can be found in the December 1992 issue of *Info Press, The Info Franchise Newsletter*). A study by Scott Shane in 1996 showed that less than 25 percent of the 138 companies that started offering franchises in the US in 1983 were still franchising in 1993. Similar attrition rates have been documented in other studies, including studies of franchising in the UK.

Additional issues of measurement, definition, and the like have been raised by those attempting to put a number on franchising success and failure rates. The bottom line from the studies mentioned here, and others, is that franchising is not obviously "safe" for franchisors or for franchisees. For franchisors, the above figures show that companies fail despite franchising, while many others choose to stop franchising after trying it for a period of time. Obviously, these companies have decided that franchising is not for them.

On the franchisees' side, the studies imply that joining a new franchised chain is probably more risky than starting one's own business. This is because success now depends not only on one's own resourcefulness and dedication, but on the capacity of the franchisor and of the other few franchisees to pull things together as well. Of course, the upside of joining a new franchise also can be very high: those who joined McDonald's, the US fast-food group, when it was a fledgling new chain have profited handsomely. The probability of failure is lower, as are the likely returns, when one joins an established chain.

2 Franchising growth

The notion that franchising, or more specifically business-format franchising, is growing incredibly fast in the US and abroad is widely aired in the business press. Yet since 1988, when the Department of Commerce canceled its yearly publication of *Franchising in the Economy*, hard data on the extent and growth of franchising in the US have been very hard to come by. An example of the problem can be found in an April 1996 article in *The Franchise Times*, which began with the statement that: "Franchising growth should increase in 1996, with total unit expansion projected between 12 percent to 14 percent, up from 1995's 10 percent to 12 percent." The article went on to mention that this projection came from Franchise Recruiters Ltd's annual business development survey, which covers 100 of the projected highest-growth franchising corporations in the US. Naturally, though, this sample would show an especially large level of expected growth.

The idea that franchising is growing very fast also comes from reports that many new franchise opportunities are becoming available each year. For example, *Entrepreneur* magazine's annual survey of new franchises lists close to 200 companies each year. In 1996, the report notes: "Last year, hundreds of small businesses entered the franchise arena..." But the number of new franchisors is not in itself sufficient to assess growth in business-format franchising; it ignores the other side of the equation, namely the number of franchisor exits. As indicated earlier, this is a sizable number.

In reality, since the late 1980s, franchise directory listings suggest that the actual number of business-format franchisors in the US has grown at a rate that is at best commensurate with the rest of the economy. And since the number of business-format franchisors has been found to be a good indicator of the extent of franchising in the economy, one can conclude that franchising growth, while rapid in the 1960s and 1970s, has slowed significantly in the US in the last decade or so. At best, the growth in business-format franchising has been in line with that of the US economy over this period.

This slowdown is not purely an American phenomenon either; John Stanworth and colleagues at the International Franchise Research Centre at the University of Westminster in London found that franchising in the UK was going through a period of "consolidation" in the 1990–95 period, having grown by a modest 12 percent. If the figures are adjusted for inflation, British franchise turnover even modestly contracted during this period.

Finally, while many other international markets show sizable franchising growth, it is important to keep in mind that growth-rate statistics for small numbers can be misleading. For example, the hypothetical addition of only three new franchisors in Israel would imply a growth rate of 16.6 percent – this sizable growth rate would hardly be a sign that this form of business organization is making significant inroads in that country.

3 Franchisor size

Two of the most oft-quoted benefits for franchisees compared to independent business owners are access to a well-established and advertised brand name under which they operate; and a time-tested and standardized business system. The former is expected to translate into a higher level of demand for the product or service, while the latter largely reduces the franchisee's costs. Both of these benefits arise from belonging to a well-established franchised system. Yet many franchised systems are relatively new and small. In its recent study of 1,156 franchisors operating in the US, the International Franchise Association Educational Foundation found that more than half the franchisors had fewer than 50 domestic units. In its last yearly report, the US Department of Commerce found an even larger proportion of small systems, namely 1,503 of the population of 2,177 franchised systems in operation in 1986, had 50 units or fewer, with 739 of these having fewer than ten. These smaller systems tend to be regional in scope, and fairly unknown outside their market.

The counterpoint to the presence in the economy of many small and relatively unknown franchisors is that the vast majority of franchisees join large, established chains rather than small ones. The 1986 Department of Commerce data, for example, show that franchisors with 500 units or more accounted for 65 percent of all franchised establishments in operation. More recent data compiled by Roger

Blair, at the University of Florida Department of Economics, and myself imply that this proportion was very similar in 1997.

It remains the case that a significant number of franchisees join systems far less developed than those that most people have in mind when they think about franchising. This has a significant impact on what the franchisees can expect to gain from their franchisors, and on their likelihood of success. Thus the need for franchisees thoroughly to investigate a number of potential franchisors before making a final decision about franchising cannot be overemphasized. This process should also include a complete assessment of the franchisee's strengths and weaknesses, and of the expected benefits of franchising. Such an assessment will allow a potential franchisee to gauge whether different franchisors are likely to provide the benefits that the franchisee is seeking, and at what relative cost.

4 Franchisee size

One final misconception is the notion that all franchisees are owners of a single unit. In fact, multi-unit ownership is pervasive: for example, the average McDonald's franchisee in the US owns three such restaurants. A 1996 study by Patrick Kaufmann and Rajiv Dant, both at the Boston University School of Management, showed that the vast majority of fast-food systems have multi-unit owners. Recent work by Arturs Kalnins, at the University of Southern California Marshall School of Business, and myself showed that 88 percent of the restaurants in the six largest franchised fast-food chains in Texas in 1997 were operated by multi-unit owners. Ownership was most concentrated at Pizza Hut: on average, franchisees operated 24 units each in this chain in Texas.

What are the implications of this ownership profile for people contemplating franchising? From the franchisor's perspective, these figures imply that franchisees often want to grow their business within the chain, and that most franchisors find it beneficial to allow them to do so. But the type of franchisee that will perform well as an owner of a set of units may be different from the one that will do well with a single unit. Consequently, a company embarking on a franchise program would do well to develop a long-term strategy about how large it wants its franchisees to be, and adjust its recruiting accordingly. The size of franchisee holdings will also influence how the chain interacts with its owners – an owner of several units usually has more bargaining power and wants more say in its franchisor's decision making than single unit owners do. This different level of franchisee involvement also should affect the extent of multi-unit ownership that a company chooses to pursue in the development of its system.

Franchisees purchasing their first unit need to be aware of their franchisor's policy and practices with regard to multi-unit ownership and to make sure that these are suited to their own expansion plans. Those contemplating multi-unit ownership should also consider whether they want to pursue an area development agreement from the start, where the franchisor would grant them a territory and the right and obligation to develop many units within this territory, or whether they are content to grow their business one unit at a time, subject to franchisor approval. These are the two main ways in which one achieves multi-unit ownership in franchising.

Conclusion

While franchising is a successful method of doing business in many contexts, success is not guaranteed to franchisors or franchisees. Not all franchise systems are well-established chains of the type that most people associate with this form of organization.

Companies thinking of expanding in this way must take the time to develop their business system thoroughly and determine how franchising is likely to serve them in the long run. Although franchise contracting has not been discussed here, potential franchisors also need to develop a franchise agreement that allows both them and their franchisees to benefit from the partnership. Individuals considering becoming franchisees, meanwhile, must take the time to investigate a variety of opportunities before choosing one, and ask themselves whether franchising, given its costs, is really the best way for them to obtain the benefits they seek.

Summary

Franchising can be a useful and desirable way to develop and organize certain types of businesses – but it is by no means always a win–win proposition, says **Francine Lafontaine**. Not all franchise systems are well-established chains of the type that many associate with the concept; indeed, many are very much smaller than expected. The author explodes a number of other myths – notably that franchising is safe, that it is growing exponentially, and that franchisees are typically owners of a single unit – and offers advice for those contemplating this activity for the first time.

Suggested further reading

Arthur Andersen & Co. (1995) *Worldwide Franchising Statistics*, Arthur Andersen & Co.

Bates, T. (1998) "Survival patterns among newcomers to franchising," *Journal of Business Venturing*, 13: 113–30.

Bond, R.E. (1998) *Bond's Franchise Guide*, 11th edn, Oakland, CA: Source Book Publications.

IFA Educational Foundation Inc. (1998) *The Profile of Franchising*, Vol. 1, Washington, DC: International Franchise Association Educational Foundation.

Info Press (1992) *The Info Franchise Newsletter*, December.

Kaufmann, P.J. and Dant, R.P. (1996) "Multi-unit franchising: growth and management issues," *Journal of Business Venturing*, 11: 343–58.

Lafontaine, F. and Shaw, K.L. (1998) "Franchising growth and franchisor entry and exit in the US market: myth and reality," *Journal of Business Venturing*, 13: 95–112.

Shane, S.A. (1996) "Hybrid organizational arrangements and their implications for firm growth and survival: a study of new franchisors," *Academy of Management Journal*, 39: 216–34.

Stanworth, J., Purdy, D., Price, S. and Zafiris, N. (1998) "Franchise versus conventional small business failure rates in the US and UK: more similarities than differences," *International Small Business Journal*, 16 (56–69): 2–3.

This article is loosely adapted from Chapter 2 of the author's forthcoming book with Roger Blair, *Franchising: Economics and Public Policy*, to be published by Cambridge University Press.

Vertical integration: make or buy decisions

by Robert Gertner and Marc J. Knez

Vertical integration decisions are among the most difficult strategic decisions faced by management. They include decisions on whether to make or buy particular inputs, including services such as information technology, as well as how far to integrate down the vertical chain into distribution. Our experience is that MBA students come into strategy classes with a good intuitive and analytical grasp of most types of strategic decisions, with the exception of vertical integration. We also observe a great deal of soul-searching over make or buy decisions in practice, and significant differences in vertical integration among companies within an industry and between industries.

A company that makes a vertical integration decision determines whether or not to enter an industry – many of the considerations that are relevant to other entry decisions apply equally, therefore, to vertical integration. The distinction between a standard entry decision and a vertical integration decision is the difference between what happens if a company decides not to enter an industry and what happens if a company decides not to integrate vertically. In the standard entry decision, the alternative is just to continue in one's existing business. In a vertical integration decision, the alternative to integration is to purchase the input from an outsider. Thus, the decision depends on the relative costs of integration and using an outside supplier.

The alternatives to vertical integration are varied. At one extreme are anonymous spot-market transactions, such as a company buying petrol for its cars at the petrol station. However, in many situations when companies do not make their own inputs they have a long-term relationship with one or more suppliers. These usually involve a formal contract that sets prices, quantities, quality, delivery times, service and other features. The parties could have a strategic alliance that includes exclusivity provisions and significant joint efforts in designing or producing inputs. They may even have a joint venture that involves common ownership over a separate organization that produces the input. Therefore, when thinking about make or buy decisions it is important to focus carefully on what structure the "buy" choice would entail.

There are two basic approaches that focus on different aspects of what "buy" means. In what we refer to as the market approach, we analyze the choice between market transactions and long-term relationships. In the organizational approach, we take the long-term relationship as given and focus on whether the structure of the relationship should include vertical integration or not.

The market approach

The main advantage of market transactions is that markets do a great job of producing products efficiently, and competition among suppliers passes much of the benefits to the buyer. Competition also allows a buyer to take advantage of product or cost improvements from a competitor to an existing supplier. Imagine not being able to change department stores, restaurants, cereal brands, or camera suppliers as new products become available or selection and quality shift. A vertically integrated company relies on its own cost structure and product choice rather than the best from a set of competing suppliers.

Giving up the enormous benefits of the market should not be done lightly. The justification for vertical integration comes in one of two forms. Either there is some reason why a company's presence in one market gives it an advantage in a vertically linked market, or market competition does not work effectively in the vertically linked market. One interesting implication is that vertical integration by many companies in an industry may be a justification for the others to integrate vertically. When competitors vertically integrate by buying up independent distributors, it becomes more difficult for a non-vertically integrated company to garner the benefits of market competition in distribution. Hence, vertical integration may become more attractive. If movie studios own movie theaters, a new studio will not be able to distribute its films unless it also owns movie theaters. If no studios own exhibitors, then the market for exhibition should work well and a new studio will be able to distribute its films without vertically integrating.

Synergies from operating in vertically linked markets may reduce production, coordination, transportation, and related costs. These synergies are often small relative to the benefits of effective competition among many external suppliers, but in the cases where they are not, vertical integration may be justified. Harvard professor Michael Porter discusses an example of vertical synergies in steel production – the steel billet does not have to be reheated if the steelmaking and rolling operations are combined. Common ownership over the two stages of production can reduce costs. One possibly more subtle source of economies of scope is knowledge about the market, which is effectively a fixed cost. For example, many oil refiners are vertically integrated into oil tanker shipping. The refiners as purchasers of shipping services and as purchasers of crude oil must become informed about worldwide supply and demand conditions of oil and shipping services. Given the investment in this expertise, they may have a competitive advantage in shipping.

Another reason to integrate vertically is to affect bargaining power with suppliers. If the upstream market is perfectly competitive, this makes no sense, since price will equal marginal cost and bargaining power is irrelevant. However, if there is some upstream market power, the price for the input will depend on the downstream company's demand elasticity, which is in turn determined by its substitution possibilities. If the possibility to expand one's own production is credible, this increases demand elasticities and reduces price. A brewer who manufactures some of its own cans has a more credible threat to a can supplier that it will increase can production than a brewer who does not manufacture cans.

Economists have studied how vertical integration may benefit a company with market power. Among the potential benefits of vertical integration are more effective price discrimination, avoidance of double markups, foreclosure of competition, and avoidance of regulation and antitrust liability. Many of these issues have already been discussed. We do not discuss them here and focus instead on the organizational issues associated with vertical integration.

The organizational approach

Market transactions for vertically linked goods and services will not work well if buyers and sellers must make investments that tie each to the other. For example,

Boeing, the US aircraft manufacturer, must have a close relationship with its parts suppliers. A supplier must customize its plant to manufacture a particular model; details of quantity, quality, and turnaround times must be agreed. It will not do for Boeing to use the power of market competition once it has settled on a supplier – alternate suppliers become poor substitutes for chosen suppliers once the relationship has been established. The choice is no longer one between the market and a long-term relationship, but choices among different forms of long-term relationship, ranging from long-term contractual arrangements between the buyer and supplier (vertical alliance) to complete vertical integration.

We should first point out that an operational definition of vertical integration is surprisingly subtle. Think about restaurant franchising. The franchisor is not vertically integrated but has a very detailed long-term contract with its franchisees. Many aspects of the relationship could be achieved with company-owned restaurants and complex incentive contracts for the manager. In fact, many franchisors also own some outlets themselves. At first, it is not clear what the operational distinction between the two is. This, in and of itself, is an important point – the integration/contract decision is not the only important choice that governs the relationship and in many cases may not be the most significant one. Returning to the restaurant example, ownership means the residual rights of control over the restaurant's assets. An owner decides what to do with that which he or she owns. However, the owner can assign these rights to others via contract. Thus, the owner is not necessarily the party with greater control rights, but rather the party who makes decisions that are not explicitly contracted for. So in the restaurant example, the contract might not specify the hours of operation. If it is a franchise, the franchisee can choose – if the franchisor wants to extend the hours, it must negotiate with the franchisee. If the restaurant is company owned, then the parent company can command the restaurant manager to keep the store open longer hours. If hours of operation are in the contract as are all other relevant decisions, ownership does not matter.

However, in most cases ownership does matter because complete contracts cannot be written. It is the benefits of ownership in light of incomplete contracts that may lead a company to opt for vertical integration over a vertical alliance. There are two critical benefits that come with the ownership of critical assets. First, there is the ability to dictate how the assets are used. Such power eliminates bargaining costs and facilitates the coordination and control of interdependent activities. Second, ownership increases the incentives to make relationship-specific investments.

Lower bargaining costs

One of the main differences between contracting and integration is that renegotiation and coordination in a contractual relationship can be very costly, given that contracts are quite incomplete. In a 20-year contract between a bauxite mine and an aluminium refinery, it may be difficult to write the correct price-adjustment clause. (Although one might think that one would just use a market price, this can be difficult unless you specify the exact market price carefully. In the coal industry the relative prices of different types of coal have moved a great deal because new environmental regulation made alternative coals cheaper to burn.) Renegotiating the new price might be quite costly and might lead to disruptions. In a vertically integrated company, the parties know that the mine should trade with the refinery. It can use control to make sure it happens. The price may be an important number for accounting and incentives, but there is no danger of disruptions on either side.

Coordination and control

A key difference between a vertically integrated company and a vertical alliance is the way in which conflicts are managed. One of the authors (Knez) together with Duncan Simester of MIT's Sloan School studied the decisions to make or buy parts by a manufacturer of made-to-order, complex, high-technology products. Some types of parts are outsourced, others are manufactured internally, and some are procured both internally and externally. Conflicts and coordination problems occur both internally and externally. The internal or external buyer wants high-quality, timely production and effective responses to design changes, while the internal or external parts manufacturer wants to minimize cost and production complications.

The study documents how coordination between an outside parts supplier and the engineering staff at the company can be more difficult than the same coordination with the company. The key difference is that price and bargaining power play a more prominent role in the external relationship. A design change may lead to price renegotiation. The process of implementing a design change is thereby more complex. Internally, if the two divisions do not agree on what needs to be done, an internal chief technologist resolves the conflict. The incentives of the chief technologist are aligned with the integrated company as a whole. This, coupled with the appropriate expertise, should lead to correct decisions. The knowledge that conflicts will be resolved correctly may also lead each division to cooperate more with each other and limit the need for the chief technologist to intervene.

In an external relationship, a conflict such as this is likely to have implications for the profits of each of the two companies. If the contract does not specify exactly what will happen for every possible design change, as it almost surely will not, the resolution of the design choice will likely affect the profits that each company will make. More importantly, in the process of negotiating the design change each company may have an incentive to withhold relevant information to preserve its bargaining position. The result is that coordination becomes more difficult.

Organizationally, the company that Knez and Simester studied has procurement officers who mediate interactions with suppliers. The procurement officers act to protect bargaining power, but make it more difficult for the engineers to share information and coordinate effectively. The main trade-off they identify involves the lower bargaining costs and improved coordination and control through vertical integration, versus the loss of competition or the threat of competition among suppliers.

Hold-up risk and specific investments

Contracts are inherently imperfect and incomplete as well as costly to write and enforce. It is impossible (or at least prohibitively expensive) to anticipate all the relevant uncertainty that affects the relationship between buyer and supplier. It is even more costly to negotiate and draft a contract that specifies how the parties should respond to these uncertainties. This makes contractual relationships risky, especially contractual relationships that may allow a supplier to exercise some control over a buyer's core strategic assets.

Maintaining control through integration allows a company to avoid the risk that some unforeseen contingency will lead to hold-up from a contractually linked company.

One situation where this consideration arises is when a company has a strong brand name that could be valuable in a line of business where it has no expertise. It may correctly be reluctant to license the use of that brand name to another company. Walt Disney, the US entertainment company, has a strong brand name that it realized could be used effectively to sell clothes and other merchandise. It had to decide whether to own its retail outlets or enter into a licensing agreement. If it chose licensing, there would be some chance that the contractual protections might be insufficient to prevent the licensee from degrading the value of the brand or threatening to do so, thereby extracting money from Disney. On the other hand, blithely entering into a line of business where a company has no expertise makes vertical integration a problem. This trade-off may play out differently in different situations. Disney chose to develop its own stores, but it has a long-term promotional relationship with McDonald's. The choice not to integrate vertically here is simple – it is probably not too difficult to control McDonald's use of Disney's brand name and McDonald's has a significant interest in maintaining the relationship. Moreover, Disney has no business entering the fast-food market given the different set of skills, management, and other assets needed and the high entry barriers.

Finally, ownership of productive assets under vertical integration provides the company with residual control rights over those assets. These control rights affect incentives to make relation-specific investments. A party with more control rights over an asset will get more of the benefit of the specific investments that increase the value of the asset. An advantage of franchising is that it creates a better incentive for the store manager to invest in the long-term value of the franchise. If it is difficult to write these improvements into a contract, a store manager who is an employee may overinvest in today's profits relative to future improvements. But the franchisee will extract the benefits of the improvements when he or she sells the franchise.

Conclusion

There is no simple formula for determining the optimal vertical scope of a company. Obtaining a deep understanding of what can be achieved through contract and what the risks are requires a detailed analysis of the specific structure of uncertainty, investment, coordination, and bargaining costs. When the consumer electronics companies Sony and Matsushita vertically integrated into entertainment, the justification was that it would assure them of a supply of software for any new platforms they might develop. It is not difficult to see why such assurance of supply is valuable to these companies. The difficult issue is why they cannot achieve this through contract. Sony could sign a contract with CBS Records that requires CBS Records to release its top 100 albums on whatever new platform Sony develops. A justification for vertical integration has to explain why the contract is a less effective way to achieve this outcome than entering a market that requires different assets and management style. The decision cannot be made independently of the entire structure of the two alternative relationships and how they affect efficiency and coordination.

Summary

No simple formula is available to help a company decide whether to outsource its needs or to integrate vertically, note **Robert Gertner** and **Marc J. Knez**. Decision makers need to balance the contract benefits against the associated risk. The authors highlight the choice between market transactions and long-term relationships, as well as analyzing whether vertical integration is appropriate in situations where the long-term relationship is a given. The authors conclude by asking why two Japanese electronics giants integrated into the entertainment world when they might have achieved the same results through contracts.

Suggested further reading

Hart, O. (1995) *Firms, Contracts, and Financial Structure*, Oxford: Oxford University Press.

Putterman, L. and Kroszner, R. (eds) (1996) *The Economic Nature of the Firm: a Reader*, Cambridge: Cambridge University Press.

Williamson, O. (1987) *The Economic Institutions of Capitalism*, New York: The Free Press.

Williamson, O. and Winter, S. (eds) (1991) *The Nature of the Firm*, Oxford: Oxford University Press.

New notions of organizational "fit"

by Richard Whittington, Andrew Pettigrew, and Winfried Ruigrok

Increasing competition, new information technologies, the rise of the knowledge economy, and extended global scope are all forcing many large companies to experiment with new forms of organizing themselves. The concepts vary – they are seeking to become networked, virtual, horizontal or project based. But all these concepts express a need at the dawn of a new century to develop flatter, more flexible, and intelligent forms of organizing.

Many commentators compare the current period of organizational change to the birth of the divisional organization 80 years ago in the great American corporations like DuPont and General Motors. These companies had changed their strategies from focus to diversification. They discovered that as they did so they needed new structures to match. Diversification was followed by decentralization into distinct product divisions. As business throughout the world increasingly diversified during the middle years of the century, so did it increasingly adopt the divisional form of organization. As Alfred Chandler, the great business historian of this process, famously summed up: "Structure follows strategy."

The need to fit structure to strategy is now well accepted. But nearly a century after the innovations of DuPont and General Motors, we are discovering that just as the old divisional form needs extending, so do our old notions of fit. The new forms of organizing are radically challenging the traditional profiles of big business and demanding a more comprehensive and dynamic concept of fit.

Structure is no longer the simple dependent variable of strategy. They are equal partners. And it is more than just strategy and structure that must fit together; it is the corporation as a whole.

Fit involves not a static interlocking of variables, but rather a continuous co-evolution of a complex whole.

Figure 1: The virtuous circle of complementary change

This article will illustrate the importance of new notions of fit for organizational innovation using a survey of European firms and case examples from ABB, BP Amoco, and Unilever.

The new notion of fit is captured by the notion of complementarities, developed by economists Paul Milgrom and John Roberts. Complementarities refer to the potential for mutually reinforcing effects when one or more business practices are joined together. Practices are complementary when doing more of one increases the returns to doing more of another. In other words, the practices are synergistic: two plus two produces more than four.

But complementarities are not the same as synergies. In the first place, Milgrom and Roberts do not emphasize pair-wise synergies (for instance, between strategy and structure) but synergies between systems of many practices. Successful business models – Japanese manufacturing in the 1980s, the flexible specialization of Italian craft manufacturers, the high-tech ventures of Silicon Valley – all involve complete and coherent systems of practices. In these cases, it is not just strategy and structure, but process, culture, and context that contribute to performance. In our work, we have concentrated on the complementarities between strategy, structure, and processes. We shall show that, in line with complementarity theory, there can be a virtuous circle of high performance between strategy, structure, and process (*see* Figure 1).

This emphasis on coherent systems takes us to the second additional insight from the notion of complementarities – the potential for negative synergies. Synergy traditionally emphasizes the upside; the complementarities notion warns of the downside. Milgrom and Roberts' modeling suggests that a particular practice not only depends on its complements to yield its full benefits, but it may also have negative effects if those complements are absent. Thus, while just-in-time delivery works wonderfully as part of a coherent system, the result can be chaos without matching manufacturing, information, and human resource practices.

The importance of systems of synergistic relationships and the dangers of negative synergies produce some powerful predictions. Because the payoffs to change depend on a complete system of complementary practices:

■ Local experiments and piecemeal initiatives are unlikely to be successful; successful change is likely to require strong leadership from the top to achieve system-wide transformation.

■ Even system-wide transformations are likely to pass through a significant performance trough as old systems of complements are disrupted and the new are yet to be completed.

■ It is easy to get stuck in a suboptimal system of complements as any step outside the system toward a potentially better one is likely to be rewarded by initial performance decline.

■ The inertia of suboptimal systems and the initial penalties of change mean that whole-system change is likely to be rare.

■ However, achieving a new virtual circle of complementary practices will lead to high performance gains, which is hard for competitors to imitate as they are relying on complex and opaque whole systems.

■ The virtual circle of complementarities must stay in motion, as constant incremental shifts in strategy will need to be matched by equivalent shifts in structures and processes.

Innovative organizations

How well do these predictions stand up in practice? The notion of complementarities certainly explains key findings from the INNFORM research program (*see* Suggested further reading) on innovative forms of organizing around the world. This research program has involved a survey of large and medium-sized companies in Europe, Japan, and the United States, plus a series of 18 in-depth case studies of companies engaged in organizational innovation.

The results of the European part of the survey (which covered over 450 European businesses) confirm two of the key predictions arising out of complementarity theory. They are that whole-system change is indeed rare, and that there are penalties attached to partial change. Our survey focussed on three potentially complementary elements that are associated with new forms of organizing:

■ *Strategic change*: particularly moves toward less diversified strategies focussed on core competences; increased use of joint ventures and alliances to access resources; more reliance on outsourcing for non-strategic activities in the value chain.

■ *Structural change*: particularly management delayering to enhance organizational leanness; increased operational and strategic decentralization to improve organizational responsiveness; and increased use of project and team-based forms of organizing to increase horizontal knowledge and resource sharing.

■ *Process change*: particularly high investment in new forms of information technology; increased emphasis on vertical communications for accountability and horizontal communications for knowledge sharing; and soft investments in team building, mission building and training, to provide the skills and glue to make flatter and more horizontal structures work.

The survey found widespread initiatives on almost all these elements of the new forms of organizing in the period 1992–96. In terms of strategy, there was a general trend toward outsourcing and joint ventures, although limited reductions in diversification. In terms of structure, there was a widespread tendency across Europe to decentralize operational decisions (although less so strategic decisions), greater use of project structures, and significant management delayering. As for process change, there were substantial moves on all three dimensions, with remarkable investments in information technologies such as Lotus Notes and intranets, in support of internal networking.

There have been plenty of changes in European business. However, just as complementarity theory predicts, many of these changes have been piecemeal rather than systemwide. These piecemeal changes have often been associated with negative performance payoffs.

Piecemeal, not system-wide change

While most companies have been experimenting with at least some new initiatives, very few combine them into a comprehensive system of change. Half were making major changes across all the elements of strategic change; just over a quarter were making major changes across the elements of process change; and a fifth were high on the elements of structural change. However, only 5 percent had succeeded in making major initiatives on all three dimensions. Thus even of the few which were making major structural changes, three-quarters were not combining it into a full system including process and strategic change.

Payoffs to system-wide change

Our financial performance analysis found that system-wide change paid off best. The 5 percent of companies combining all three types of change (strategic, structural, and process) enjoyed an average performance premium of 60 percent. Despite the payoffs, very few seemed capable of imitating by changing across the whole set. The only change element to yield significant performance benefits on its own was investment in information technology. Otherwise, a partial combination of full system elements typically yielded negative performance consequences. There was a *J*-curve effect – described as the risk of performance decline as one system of complements is dismantled, while the next system is still expensively being put in place – with partial change leading to declining performance, and only comprehensive change yielding high payoffs (*see* Figure 2).

The main conclusion from the survey on new forms of organizing is that, while many companies are moving in the direction of flatter, more flexible and intelligent forms of organizing, very few are doing so coherently. But it is only those that do innovate coherently that get the rewards. Piecemeal initiatives typically cost more than they are worth.

Complementarities in action

Our survey evidence backs complementarity theory predictions that it is whole system change that delivers the significant payoffs, but that such comprehensive change is rare, hard to imitate, and entails initial performance penalties. Our case-study evidence from ABB, BP Amoco and Unilever confirms these insights, while giving greater understanding of the practical demands of managing complementarities.

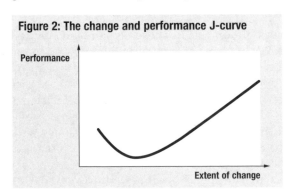

Figure 2: The change and performance J-curve

Performance

Extent of change

Closing the circle

Complementarity theory emphasizes the importance of completing the full set of strategic, structural, and process change. The Anglo-Dutch consumer goods giant Unilever has been engaged in a process of transformation for more than a decade. In terms of strategy, the company has been steadily building its areas of core competence since the 1980s, making key acquisitions such as Calvin Klein and Chesebrough-Pond's, while selling peripheral businesses such as Speciality Chemicals. From the early 1990s, the company has also been emphasizing new processes. New innovation processes based on decentralized innovation centers around the world and backed by international product networks have increased the pace of new product introduction. New strategy processes have been developed both at the center and in the businesses.

Unilever's main structural changes waited until 1996, with its "Restructuring for outstanding performance" program. The new structure gave a newly created executive committee responsibility for the strategic oversight of product areas globally, at the same time as decentralizing profit and operating responsibility to "business groups," organized typically on a regional basis. Responsibilities were clearer, layers were taken out, and decisions could be taken in an integrated fashion at the level of regional markets. Unilever now became a "multilocal multinational."

"Restructuring for outstanding performance" completed the circle of strategy, structure, and process. Since 1997, Unilever's performance has taken off, beating almost all its competitors on the main measures. It was not the structural changes by themselves that achieved this. The structural changes relied on better processes and a more focussed strategy to work. The Unilever story emphasizes that higher performance requires the full set of complements, but that putting them all together can take years of careful foundation building.

Strong leadership

The complementarities perspective values strong leaders with coherent visions of change. When Percy Barnevik created the engineering group ABB in 1988 by merging Brown Boveri of Switzerland with ASEA of Sweden, he had an opportunity for rapid, system-wide change rarely available to an established group such as Unilever. Barnevik acted quickly across all three dimensions – strategy, structure, and process.

Barnevik's strategy was to combine global scale with local presence. The new ABB began its life with a series of further joint ventures and acquisitions. Key were the acquisitions of Westinghouse's power businesses and Combustion Engineering, the power and automation group, together securing ABB's presence in North America, one-third of the world market. At the same time, Barnevik introduced his famous global matrix structure, with 1,100 highly decentralized front-line companies and a downsized head office. New processes were introduced underlining faster decision making and accountability, guaranteed by the standardized and transparent ABACUS reporting system.

Barnevik's high-profile leadership was critical in achieving radical and swift change across all three dimensions of strategy, structure, and process. He was famous for his constant face-to-face presentations to managers around the globe, traveling some 200 days a year. Barnevik became the most admired manager in the world, and ABB a model for international managers everywhere. However, we shall see that Barnevik's position was a very unusual one and that even at ABB his model could not be cast in stone.

The perils of the *J*-curve

Barnevik put his complementarities together fast; Unilever built them step by step. The transformation process at international oil company BP, now BP Amoco, illustrates the perils of going fast except in unusual conditions.

In 1990, Robert Horton became chairman and chief executive of BP and launched an aggressive transformation program entitled "Project 1990." In terms of strategy, the company set out to divest non-core businesses and outsource services. In terms of structure, head-office functions were radically cut and power decentralized to global business streams. Process changes were encapsulated in the slogan OPEN: Open thinking, Personal impact, Empowering, and Networking. Networked, empowered teams became the key management tool.

Hit by recession and distracted by change, BP's profits collapsed. In 1992, after 35 years with the company, Horton resigned. But although Project 1990 had been very much Horton's personal crusade, his successor David Simon substantially pursued it. Simon's slogan was PRT – Performance, Reputation, and Teams. Performance had to recover, but Horton's emphasis on teamwork stayed. Simon's own successor, John Browne, essentially still followed the same logic internally, while also launching a series of industry-changing acquisitions and joint ventures. Thus Browne continued the decentralization thrust while developing the network and team ideas through emphasis on peer-group problem solving. By 1997, profits were more than twice the level of the pre-Horton era, and eight times the Horton trough.

Horton's resignation was in part the result of style and bad luck. But his fate also illustrates the perils of the *J*-curve. After Horton's departure, the process at BP became more like Unilever's, a steady brick-by-brick construction that finally put the company in position to take over Amoco and become the third biggest oil company in the world.

Continuous co-evolution

Barnevik's success in fast-paced complementary change depended on the crisis conditions of a mega-merger. But even at ABB, his legacy was not unchanging. The virtual circle of complementarities must stay in motion: strategy, structure, and process co-evolve.

When Barnevik stood down in 1997, his successor Goran Lindahl took the strategy of global-scale strategy one step further by strengthening the product divisional leg of the matrix. The four main product divisions ("business segments") became seven and the regional coordinating layers were eliminated. The highly decentralized operating units remained, but processes of interunit networking and collaboration were re-emphasized.

The post-Barnevik changes built cumulatively on the past, rather as Simon's and Browne's did at BP. Lindahl emphasizes continuities in terms of combining globalization with decentralization and retention of the ABACUS reporting system. In other words, these changes illustrate the importance for established large companies of complementary co-evolution – continuous coherent change rather than disjointed radical change. Lindahl recognizes the imperative of such continuous change in defining a structural life cycle of just five years. Further change for ABB is already penciled in.

Summary

Companies are experimenting with new forms of organizing – virtual, horizontal, and project-based structures, for example. This burst of innovation recalls what happened in North America 80 years ago, when the likes of General Motors and DuPont discovered new structures and strategies that have lasted to today. The need to match structure with strategy is well accepted, but as **Richard Whittington, Andrew Pettigrew** and **Winfried Ruigrok** argue here, our old notions need to be re-examined. Structure and strategy should now be seen as more equal partners that fit together with other variables in the organization as a whole. Drawing on new research – and short case studies of ABB, BP Amoco, and Unilever – the authors show that in line with complementarity theory, there can be a virtuous circle of high performance if businesses act simultaneously in three key areas.

Suggested further reading

Pettigrew, A. and Fenton E. (eds) (2000) *Process and Practice in New Forms of Organising*, London: Sage.

Ruigrok, W., Pettigrew, A., Peck, S. and Whittington, R. (1999) "Corporate restructuring and new forms of organising in Europe," *Management International Review*, 39 (2).

Shaw, D. (1999) *Organising for the 21st Century*, London: PricewaterhouseCoopers.

Whittington, R., Pettigrew, A., Peck, S., Fenton, E. and Conyon, M. (1999) "Change and complementarities in the new competitive landscape," *Organization Science*, 10 (4).

The INNFORM project on which this article draws is led by Professor Andrew Pettigrew.

Critical mass and the winner-takes-all battle

by Karel Cool

Consider a situation in which most of the players in an industry are losing out completely, while just a handful of competitors, often with similar products, are winning all the spoils? These so-called critical mass races, where the "winner takes all," are happening with increasing frequency in a variety of settings: in smart cards, e-commerce, airline reservation systems, digital recording, and business school reputations, to name but a few. This article aims to address such issues as when you can expect a critical mass race to occur in your industry, what you should do to win, and what options you have if you are losing the battle.

While many companies want to achieve critical mass, notions are rather vague about what is "critical" about critical mass, what "mass" has got to do with it, and how to determine whether critical mass has been achieved. To most, critical mass has some connotation of size: it conveys the idea of the minimal scale in operations (e.g., salesforce, R&D) to be cost effective or innovative. While it has a similar ring to "economies of scale," critical mass is based on a completely different mechanism.

Economies of scale represent the potential to reach lower unit costs when a larger scale or capacity of operation is achieved. Once the investments toward the new scale have been made, the crux of the problem is to maximize throughput in any given period to achieve those economies. This is essentially a static concept concerned with cost optimization.

The "dying seminar"

Critical mass, by contrast, is dynamic in nature, and while there are important consequences for costs, they are not necessarily the driving factor. Consider the following example of the "dying seminar."

The appointment of a new business school dean is often accompanied by a surge of enthusiasm. With most members of staff keen to be involved, early participation in taskforces for this purpose is usually a high 60 to 70 percent. But some think that all staff members should have been there and had they known differently at the outset they also would have opted out. At the second round of meetings these ones fail to show, reducing participation to 50/60 percent. Others now proceed to have second thoughts. Some stay away at the third stage. Yet others begin finding excuses. Some months later, with meetings at the typical 20 to 30 percent attendance level, a decision is taken to renew the initiative at a later date. Meetings, meanwhile, are adjourned.

This is "bandwagon" or "herd" type behavior. Here, people do something because they see or expect others to behave similarly. People who are risk averse typically wait to join until a "sufficient" number of people show interest. This question of "sufficient" depends on the person. It is the interaction of people with a different notion of "sufficient" attendance that underlies "winner-takes-all/loser-loses-all" dynamics.

In the example above, nobody would attend the meetings if they expected that nobody else would go. If 5 to 10 percent of staff is expected, there is one person – the dean – who would find it worthwhile to attend.

This type of behavior has consequences for group dynamics.

As sequential groups of attendees at meetings become increasingly unhappy about the non-attendance of others they had expected to see there, those who are unhappiest begin to stay away from future meetings. This causes a downward spiral of declining presences, until the only stable attendance level becomes zero and the seminar dies.

At this point, it is sometimes concluded that an activity petered out because "there was no genuine interest." But this is most certainly not the case. In the seminar example above, a high percentage of staff members would like to participate. But they will only do so if they expect "enough others" to follow suit. So how to save the seminar from dying?

One good move is to appoint a fixed number of obligatory group members, eight in this example, who have to attend whatever the expected behavior of others. Their attendance is thus not a function of the number of people they expect to attend. As staff members now know there will always be eight people at the meetings, it becomes worthwhile for at least one other also to attend.

Figure 1 shows the effect on expected attendance of these eight "die-hards." At point I, nine people attended and expected nine others to attend, giving "equilibrium." The attendance curve in fact crosses the "equilibrium 45° line" on two other occasions: at 27 percent attendance (II) and at 67 percent (III). So because eight people were found to attend under all circumstances, it becomes possible to reach equilibrium at 67 percent. Without them, seminar attendance inescapably goes to zero.

Which equilibria will be achieved? This is a function of the "chain effect" inherent in critical mass processes. If, say, seminar attendance were to reach 35 people at a

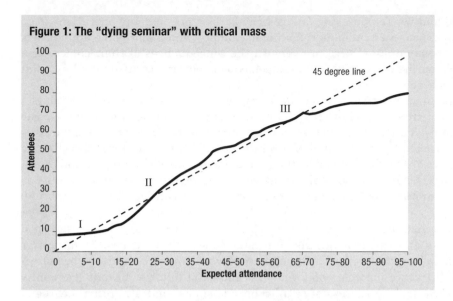

Figure 1: The "dying seminar" with critical mass

particular point, more people would show up than were expected. And this higher-than-expected attendance stimulates a further increase in attendance. Will everybody ultimately attend? The chain effect stops at II: beyond 67 percent, some attendees are disappointed and stay away because they expected higher participation. Similarly, if attendance falls below 27 percent, participation slides toward 9 percent. It does not slide toward zero because the eight die-hards pull in a ninth attendee.

Point II is called the point of critical mass. This point is critical because it is unstable: attendance beyond II triggers a chain effect toward III. Attendance below II causes a slide toward I. Points I and III are stable because attendance naturally gravitates toward these points. That is, it is impossible to have a steady 20 or 35 percent attendance. It either goes all the way up toward 67 percent or falls to 9 percent. Between these "market shares," there is no stable stopping point.

Business dynamics

Very often, rational considerations are at the basis of "success-breeds-success" dynamics in critical mass. The following criteria help to identify when one can expect competitive outcomes in markets to be driven by critical mass dynamics.

Evaluation of the product before purchase. Many products can be assessed only after they have been paid for. For example, the choice of a life insurance policy, restaurant, travel tour package, business school, consultant, investment banker, etc. can be judged only after the fact. Consumers with limited experience therefore tend to seek advice or rely on word-of-mouth information for the various options. Products and services that are first to build a large word-of-mouth reputation have a head start, which results in an increasing gap between them and the competition.

These experience effects are frequently found in the services sector. Since every "product" is made on the spot, affected by conditions at the time of consumption, and may need active customer involvement, there is potentially a high variance in the quality of outcomes.

Product durability. Experience effects are also found in markets where products are durable and where operating failure heavily disrupts on-going operations (e.g., aircraft, house construction, paper-making machinery, and major home appliances). Since the customers may have to live with the consequences of their choice for a considerable period of time, risk averse behavior is observed: customers buy what others say is best.

One of the biggest difficulties for the European Airbus consortium at the outset was its lack of credible proof that the aircraft had a long life and a healthy resale value in the used aircraft market. Similarly, entry into the aero-engine business is effectively blocked by the caution of aircraft manufacturers and airlines. Engine manufacturers are further helped by the need to have a worldwide repair and spare-parts network ready to service planes at very short notice. A similar stability is found in the market for paper-making equipment that can last for more than 40 years.

Trial costs also affect the degree to which customers are risk averse. Food products have an experience component, since they can be assessed only after purchase. However, the trial costs are often too low to protect established brands. A high price difference between well-known brands and follower brands frequently induces switching. The success of retailer brands shows that a minimal degree of reassurance can lead to significant switching by the customer. In contrast, reputation is very important for exclusive restaurants, because their trial cost is often considered substantial for many customers.

Network dependence. Critical mass dynamics are frequently observed when products have network characteristics, i.e., when the value that a customer derives from a product or service is dependent on the size of the network being accessed. For example, the value to a customer of paging services depends on how many people can be paged on the system. Similarly, the value of telephone or e-mail services depends on how many people can be accessed.

Transportation costs. Express delivery services such as UPS, Federal Express, and DHL can substantially reduce the delivery costs per customer in a given area if they can achieve a high market penetration. Similar economies are observed in soft drinks and cigarette distribution through vending machines. A high penetration of machines boosts sales and reduces distribution costs.

Impulse characteristics. Network effects may also be found in products or services with impulse characteristics (e.g., fast food, ice cream, video rental). Besides local availability, sales of these products are strongly determined by a customer's previous experience with the product, possibly in other locations. Fast-food chains like McDonald's and Burger King attempt to establish many locations in each area. Apart from transportation cost advantages, multiple locations allow them to capture a wandering customer who feels like a burger.

Host–complement interactions. When a "complementary" product is needed to add functionality to a "host" product, the company that succeeds in building a large base of either product is likely to stimulate the demand of the other. Initial success breeds further success and latecomers have to incur an increasingly larger cost to convince reluctant customers to join a smaller network. This has been observed in, among others, the computer industry (software and hardware), consumer electronics (cameras and lenses), and the automobile industry (sales network and service network), etc.

Reversing slides

What if you do not get critical mass? What are your options in such a slide toward extinction? The adoption curves express intentions to attend, buy, etc. as a function of expectations about others' behavior. Generally speaking, therefore, there are two main strategies to improve the odds of surviving and, possibly, achieving critical mass. First, try to engineer an upward shift of the adoption curve, and/or second, try to produce a shift along the adoption curve (provided that the curve crosses the 45° line at some point). The first strategy tries to change customers' willingness to buy at any given level of expected market share without changing customers' expectations. The second strategy aims to bring about a change in customers' expectations about the future market share of the product.

Changing customers' willingness to buy

If the product concerned has network characteristics, customers are reluctant to buy early since they are afraid to jump on the wrong bandwagon and – when complementary products are important – to miss out on these. Therefore, tactics must be devised to alleviate customers' fears that they will not bet on the wrong network and be stranded.

Various actions may be considered: invest heavily in complementary products and publicise the fact that contracts have been concluded with third parties that will provide complementary products. Provide discounts for early purchases. Supply upward compatibility with products that customers already use. Give customers a "two-way ticket" and make it possible for them to return to their original products if the network fails to develop. Provide a "gateway" or "conversion" technology to the winning standard so that customers can use the competing standard's complementary products while you focus on developing a superior "host product." If possible, radically improve functionality over the existing standard such that new customers reverse their preferences.

Changing customers' expectations

Once customers' expectations are publicly known, reversing a slide requires dramatic interventions, requiring credible signaling. There are a variety of tactics: claim adoption by very important customers (e.g., government support). Invest heavily in product promotion. Pre-announce new product introductions. Perhaps the most credible signal is to demonstrate to customers how much you will lose if the product does not take off. Unless your "hands are tied," customers may not believe that you are really serious about developing your network. Customers will not make a change if they see only a weak commitment by the manufacturer.

Consolidating a lead

While a loser in a critical mass race is making efforts to "move its critical mass curve up" and to "move up along the critical mass curve," the winner is in the comfortable position of doing just the opposite: pushing the rival's curve downward and producing a slide along the curve. A leader will undertake actions to draw new customers into its network to maximize the retention rate.

Maximizing network inflow

A frontrunner in a standards race can stay ahead by merely matching the actions of the follower. For example, simply matching rival product introductions or price cuts will pull in a wavering customer because of a preference for belonging to the bigger network. Moreover, the leader's larger scale makes such matching moves more economical for itself than for the follower. Since the gap between competing installed bases grows with time, these matching moves need to be maintained only as long as the rival network has critical mass potential.

Second, a leader may resort to signaling to maintain and build its network. Since adoption is driven by "expectations" about future adoption, signals may "freeze" current purchases and maintain the installed base gap. Hence Microsoft's well-known ploy of pre-announcing product introductions to stall competitors' sales when the latter introduce new lines.

Third, a leader may seek to reduce the functionality of the rival network product. Going beyond matching tactics and signaling, a frontrunner may resort to various "sabotage" ploys:

- *Product proliferation.* The open systems movement in the mainframe computer industry was initiated to create a common, open language that would "unlock" customers and make it easier to integrate different vendor hardware. A uniform software environment based on Unix System V, led by Unix International, promised to reduce customer confusion. International Business Machines and some other vendors responded by creating a rival open systems movement. Claiming that the Unix International environment was not completely open, they argued that they were "forced" to create an alternative. This was added to other already available Unix operating systems. In answer to customer inquiries, they could credibly state: "We can give you Unix, but which one?" Afraid of betting on the wrong environment, most customers were unwilling to adopt Unix V systems until enough others had done so. Meanwhile, the installed proprietary systems base continued to increase.

- *Insist on the perfect solution.* A frontrunner may join a movement to create a new standard, commit resources to it, and then withdraw saying: "It will not work." In the open systems battle, IBM in 1989 willed its own Unix version – AIX – on to OSF, the open systems grouping sponsored by IBM, DEC, and other IT companies. As it publicly demonstrated its intention and commitment to investigate the potential of Unix solutions, IBM could not later be accused of not seriously evaluating the Unix environment. In fact, it could credibly claim that its proprietary systems were, if not superior, definitely better supported than those of the "fickle" open systems group. IBM later withdrew from OSF.

- *Create a standard to which nobody will adhere.* Faced with a powerful and credible group of competitors, a leader may try to get consensus around a "white elephant." Knowing that nobody will adhere to the agreed standard, alternative standards will develop, creating customer confusion. This plays into the hands of the market leader. For example, the important 1984 Video Conference on 8mm technology was attended by all consumer electronics manufacturers to set a standard for 8mm video. While there are various theories on why the Japanese electronics giants Matsushita and JVC attended, one "conspiracy" view is that their intention was to derail the 8mm threat in the VCR market. The definition of the 8mm standard, especially concerning playing length, was so restrictive that many Betamax vendors decided to bring out their own 8mm version. While harmonized later, it was a success for the VHS camp: they had derailed the threat of pre-recorded tapes in 8mm and consolidated their VCR market stronghold.

- *Principled discussion.* Another ploy to stall the development of a rival network is to engage in a debate on "principles." Dragging the discussions away from an agenda of issues, possibilities, and compromises to a discussion of "elevated" principles is a "tried and tested" recipe for creating delays and confusion.

■ *A leader may open its proprietary network.* To discourage further investments in the rival network, the market leader may invite its competitors to join the system. This may take the form of licensing, or supplying critical components. For example, the fact that Sony was given the possibility to make and sell VHS machines provided a face-saving solution and shortened the period of rivalry between the networks.

Most airline reservation systems provide uniform access to all airline carriers to slow or stop the development of rival systems. Opening the system changes the nature of competition away from network competition to product competition. Having neutralized the superior network advantage, a market leader needs to excel at other competitive dimensions.

A leader may also try to strengthen its own base by reducing the "outflow" of existing customers. This may be done by offering special services to current customers, introducing frequent upgrades with discounts for current customers, proposing long-term service contracts, and organizing "frequent-buyer" or "club" advantages. The essence of these actions is to build in switching costs.

Conclusion

Critical mass battles are taking place in an increasing range of settings. The internet age has brought this reality home to many businesses. However, critical mass is not only relevant in electronics or telecommunications; the examples have illustrated that many other conventional businesses are driven by critical mass. Managers need to be aware of the critical mass drivers, how they may triumph in a "winner-takes-all" battle, and how they may reverse a losing situation.

Summary

Managers need to be aware of factors that drive critical mass, of how to triumph in a winner-takes-all battle, and, says **Karel Cool**, of how to reverse a losing situation. This article offers insights into the dynamics and perceptions of critical mass and outlines strategies to get there. Critical mass battles – where most competitors lose out completely – are taking place in an ever-increasing range of businesses.

Suggested further reading

Besanko, D., Dranove, D. and Shanley, M. (1996) *Economics of Strategy*, New York: Wiley.

Cool, K., Neven, D. and Walter, I. (eds) (1992) *European Industrial Restructuring in the 1990s*, London: Macmillan.

Day, G. (1990) *Market Driven Strategy Process for Creating Value*, New York: The Free Press.

Dixit, A. and Nalebuff, B. (1991) *Thinking Strategically: the Competitive Edge in Business, Politics and Everyday Life*, New York: Norton.

Ghernawat, P. (1991) *Commitment: the Dynamic Strategy*, New York: The Free Press.

Grant, R. (1995) *Contemporary Strategy Analysis*, Cambridge, MA: Blackwell.

Hamel, G. and Prahalad, C.K. (1994) *Competing for the Future*, Boston, MA: Harvard Business School Press.

Hax, A. and Nicholas, M. (1984) *Strategic Management*, Englewood-Cliffs, NJ: Prentice-Hall (contains an overview of most of the "techniques" and tools used in the strategy/marketing field).

Itami, H. (1987) *Mobilizing Invisible Assets*, Cambridge, MA: Harvard University Press (a very good book analyzing firms from a "resource"-based perspective).

STRATEGY AND TECHNOLOGY

6

Contributors

 **Allan Afuah** is assistant professor of corporate strategy at University of Michigan Business School and presently does research in the fields of competitive advantage, innovation, and entrepreneurial rents.

 **Ron Adner** is assistant professor of strategy and management at INSEAD. His research focusses on the influence of market demand on strategy and the challenge of managing emerging technologies.

Contents

Introduction

Technology issues were extensively discussed in an earlier *FT* series, *Mastering Information Management* – in this short module the focus is on the most appropriate technology product strategies for an information intensive age. Preventing others from imitating your technology is shown to be increasingly difficult, the result being that companies often have little choice but to cannibalize their own products before someone else produces something superior, or to form alliances (a topic discussed later in this book). A particular danger lies in failing to manage market expectations for technologically successful innovations.

Technology approaches for the Information Age

by Allan Afuah

A company that seeks to outperform the market today must offer customers better value than its rivals. Such value typically comes from some form of knowledge generation and exploitation, underpinned by technology. In the case of Intel, the world's biggest semiconductor manufacturer, this means some subset of R&D, design, fabrication, testing, marketing and sales, and field applications support. A company must make choices about which activities to perform, when to perform them, and how to do so. It must answer some basic questions: should it develop the technology in-house or depend on others for it; should it be the first to introduce new products using new technologies or wait for others to test the waters first; once it decides to adopt a new technology, should it adopt this straight off or gradually ease it in?

In answering such questions, a company chooses to perform certain activities at different times in different ways. A commitment to one set of such activities rather than another is its technology strategy.

A winning technology strategy should enable a company to gain and maintain a competitive advantage; it should allow the company to make more money than the average for its industry. An important technology strategy goal is to develop superior technologies. For three reasons, however, a superior technology does not always mean a competitive advantage. First, it often takes more than technology to deliver value to customers: it also takes what Professor David Teece of the University of California, Berkeley calls "complementary assets." These assets can be distribution channels, marketing capabilities, brand-name reputation, or manufacturing. These are elements that a company needs to leverage value from technology to customers. Thus, a company can have a great technology, but if it does not have the complementary assets, it will not be able to profit from the technology.

For example, the invention by EMI, the then UK electronics, research, and music company, of the Nobel prize-winning CAT scanner did not earn the company the kinds of profits that the product would later earn General Electric of the US, because EMI did not have the salesforce, manufacturing capabilities, distribution channels, and close relationships with hospitals that are critical to selling such expensive machines. Companies can obtain complementary assets by teaming up with someone who has them. A second reason why technology does not always mean a competitive advantage is that competitors will find some way to copy or get around the technology, and either catch up or leapfrog the inventor. Thus, a company that can protect its technology, or has the complementary assets, can make money from the technology.

The third reason why a superior technology does not always mean a competitive advantage is that, where two or more technologies compete, the superior technology does not always win.

The case of how the VHS system became the dominant video standard in spite of Betamax's superior quality is a popular example. According to Professor

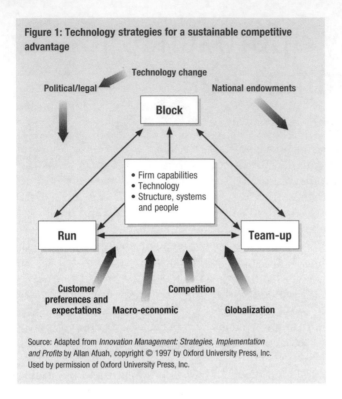

Figure 1: Technology strategies for a sustainable competitive advantage

Technology change

Political/legal   National endowments

Block

- Firm capabilities
- Technology
- Structure, systems and people

Run   **Team-up**

Customer preferences and expectations   Competition   Macro-economic   Globalization

Source: Adapted from *Innovation Management: Strategies, Implementation and Profits* by Allan Afuah, copyright © 1997 by Oxford University Press, Inc. Used by permission of Oxford University Press, Inc.

Brian Arthur of Stanford University, this can happen because of positive feedback effects, whereby an inferior technology that finds itself ahead (through chance events or strategic moves by its sponsor) moves even further ahead. Again, some form of teaming up with other companies can give a company's technology an early lead on which to build. It has been argued that Victor Company of Japan's (JVC) VHS system won out against rival Betamax because JVC teamed up with its parent, Matsushita Electric Industrial, and others to push this VHS technology.

Block, run and team-up strategies

In order to gain sustainable competitive advantage from technology, a company must undertake some subset of three generic strategies: block, run, and team-up (*see* Figure 1).

A company can block in two ways. First, if its capabilities at each stage of its value chain are unique and inimitable, it can limit access to these capabilities, thereby excluding competitors. One example is when a company has intellectual property that can be protected. Second, if all businesses are equally capable of performing these activities, incumbents may still prevent entry by signaling that post-entry prices will be low. This is achieved, for example, by establishing a reputation for retaliating against new entrants or by making heavy non-reversible investments. Such signals can prevent profit-motivated potential entrants from entry. Blocking, however, works only as long as a company's capabilities are unique and inimitable, or as long as industry barriers to entry last. But competitors can, for example, circumvent patents and copyrights or challenge them in court until they fall.

Moreover, such capabilities last only until discontinuities such as deregulation/regulation, changing customer preferences and expectations, or radical technological changes render them obsolete.

By contrast, the run strategy admits that blockades to entry, no matter how formidable, are often penetrable or eventually fall. Sitting behind these blockades only gives competitors time to catch up or leapfrog the innovator. The innovator must run. That is, it must be innovative enough to build new capabilities and introduce new products rapidly, well ahead of its competitors. It must be able to render its own capabilities obsolete or cannibalize its products before competitors do. Running can give a company many first-mover advantages, including the ability to control parts of its own environment.

The third strategy, team-up, is almost the opposite of block. Here the incumbent actually encourages entry. The question is: why would a company want to give away its technology? One reason is that teaming up, as the VHS example suggests, can give a technology a small lead that in turn can carry it toward imposing the technology as a standard. Several other reasons have been suggested by researchers: to win a standard (dominant design); to increase downstream demand; to build capabilities; to exploit the second source effect (so called to describe how companies, especially in semiconductors, will only buy from a supplier that can provide a compatible component if anything goes wrong with the primary supplier); and to access markets that would otherwise be inaccessible.

The success of a particular strategy is a function of the company's local environment. When the knowledge that underpins innovation is tacit – that which is acquired largely through personal experience like learning by doing or observing – a run strategy requires an environment with suppliers, customers, and related institutions such as universities and government laboratories in close proximity. This is because customers may not be able to articulate their preferences and expectations without repeated contact with manufacturers who can help flesh out their needs. Likewise, using components from suppliers may require repeated interaction, which only a local supplier can provide efficiently. Teaming up is easier when potential teammates are local, as it is also (just like "running") a function of local policies and affected by such policies. For example, until the mid-1980s, US antitrust laws did not allow certain types of R&D cooperation. However, the regulations were loosened in 1984 after many companies lobbied, making the formation of such alliances as Sematech, the US semiconductor research consortium, possible. Without local laws that protect intellectual capital, a block strategy is more difficult. These laws and their amendments are examples of how local policies can have an impact on both "teaming up" and "running" strategies.

Furthermore, the strategy that a company pursues is a function of its capabilities. For example, if a company is going to run, it must have the capabilities that allow it to innovate, turn new knowledge into new products or services. Not every company can waltz into the semiconductor industry and start manufacturing the type of microprocessors that Intel produces. A successful company must have the R&D prowess and money to fund new product development and fabrication. The company's structure, systems and type of people employed are also relevant. Finally, the type of technology being pursued matters. If the technology is radical, in that incumbent knowledge is largely useless in exploiting it, incumbents will have trouble running.

The information-intensive age

In an information-intensive age, blocking is more difficult and running becomes even more critical if a company is to have a sustainable competitive advantage. Teaming up also plays a greater role in a company's success. With information intensity, many of the factors on which successful blocking rests are challenged.

Take all the information available to companies via the internet. Learning about competitors' products, the technologies that underpin them, and methods to reverse engineer these products is considerably easier. A company that wants to reverse engineer a competitor's new product has several options. First, it can search through its own intranets for existing employees and internal experiences and knowledge on the product and technology. It is not unusual for groups in large companies to need expertise in an area and not to know that it already exists somewhere within the company. A second option is to obtain the rest of the information for the project from outside the company. As the project proceeds, the company can approach internet chat groups connected with itself and its professional societies with specific questions on its project.

In this information-rich context, a software developer that once depended on the scarcity of distribution channels to keep out competitors can no longer do so, since new entrants can now sell their products over the internet. A pharmaceutical company that depends on patent protection and loyalty of prescribing doctors to protect its profits from new cholesterol drugs finds its position threatened by the possibilities presented by better availability of information. The availability of information on disease mechanisms and drug safety and efficacy on the web means that patients can influence their physician's loyalty to a drug, challenging any advantages that a company may have had from its relationships with physicians. More information also means that imitators have a better chance of challenging and circumventing patents. With the available databases on patents in an age of information intensity, for example, an imitator can more quickly search through its own patents and those of its target competitor in order to challenge the patents more effectively or to determine what it needs to leapfrog the competitor. Special relations with customers that gave a company an advantage may no longer do so since such customers can solicit bids from other suppliers over the net.

For several reasons, the run strategy becomes extremely important in an information-intensive age. First, in a world where blocking is more difficult, a company must run even more if it is going to have a sustainable advantage. Once a company has an advantage, the best way to maintain it is to move on before others catch up or leapfrog it. Often, that can mean cannibalizing one's existing products before competitors do. Intel offers a good example of this approach. It usually introduces a new generation of microprocessors before unit sales of an existing one have peaked. If it does not, despite its microcode copyrights, other companies will find a way to catch up.

Additionally, more information means a proliferation of products that must work together. For many of these products, standards are needed. This means increased teaming up. Very often, running also entails teaming up. For example, developing some chips may require more resources than one company can afford, necessitating teaming up. For example, Toshiba, IBM, and Siemens had to team up to develop the 256M memory chip.

Implications for technology strategies

What the information-intensive age means for companies:

Pick the right races to run

If companies have to run to succeed in an information-intensive age, the chances are that a given company is not the only one that knows that it must run. Its competitors want to run too. Therefore it must pick its races carefully. A company must find out what it is not good at, to get rid of it and "trim down," making it more fit to run. Intel's great run in microprocessors is often linked to its decision to get out of dynamic random access memory (DRAM) chips and concentrate on the former.

Consider the local environment

Remember that a local environment of suppliers, customers, and related research institutions is critical to innovation. The question here is, given information intensity, do they still need their local environments to carry out their run strategies? After all, they can obtain information on customers and knowledge about components over the internet, no matter where customers and suppliers are located. If they hope to gain a competitive advantage, the answer is *yes*, more than ever. A lot of the knowledge that underpins innovation is tacit, and its transfer, combination, and recombination to develop new products require in-person learning-by-doing or observing. When it comes to the transfer of tacit knowledge, there is still no substitute for physical co-location of transferring and receiving parties. For example, a company developing a new airport security system that uses microchips that are themselves under development has an advantage if the suppliers of these chips are local. In this case, the company can interact with suppliers as the chips and the system jointly evolve. It also pays to have local airports that are extremely demanding about security, since once it identifies and satisfies their needs, it will be easier to satisfy the needs of less demanding airports.

Pay more attention to intangibles

It takes both technology and complementary assets to profit from an invention, and complementary assets include intangibles such as brands and reputation. While information intensity may make it easier to imitate technology, it reinforces complementary intangibles such as brands and reputation and their importance. More information about brands to more people – even from so-called high-technology companies – builds and reinforces the brands. Intel realized this when it started its "Intel Inside" campaign.

Pick the right teammates

If a company is not in the right environment or does not have a strong brand or reputation, it may want to pick a teammate to complement or reinforce its assets. In some cases, a company may want to reinforce what it has. In any case, if a company has to trim down to run, its teammates must be fit enough to run with it. Thus, it wants a teammate that brings something to the field that complements or reinforces but does not carry too much baggage. A potential partner with a history of not running well may be signaling something even if, on paper, it has the complementary capabilities that a team needs. When AMD, Intel's principal rival, decided to team up with NexGen, a California company that designed X86 Intel-compatible microprocessors, it looked like the dream team that would finally beat Intel. NexGen had the microprocessor design capabilities, while AMD had the complementary assets. But AMD had a history of not running well and the team has not lived up to its dream potential.

Summary

A company's technology strategy can be defined as a commitment to one set of technology activities over another, says **Allan Afuah**. In this article, he identifies three generic approaches that can be pursued in different combinations depending on a company's capabilities, and its competitive and local environment. The three are: block, where a company prevents others from imitating its technology; run, where a company frequently introduces new products even to the extent of cannibalizing its own before someone else does; and team-up, where a company allies with others. In an information-intensive age, blocking becomes difficult, but run and team-up strategies are likely to be desirable. Local environments and intangible complementary assets such as brands become critical.

Suggested further reading

Afuah, A. (1997) *Innovation Management Strategies, Implementation, and Profits*, New York: Oxford University Press, Inc.

Innovation beyond ideas: expectations in managing technology

by Ron Adner

The challenge for innovators and those managing them is to come up with ideas which, once developed, dominate existing markets and create new ones.

On the whole, there is no shortage of new ideas. Indeed, the many examples of companies turning down the opportunity to pursue innovations that subsequently proved critical in defining industries and markets suggest that the problem is choosing the best of the many options presented to them.

International Business Machines, for example, rebuffed xerography; Xerox, the copier manufacturer, rejected the Ethernet and the graphical user interface; and Digital, now owned by Compaq, disregarded the personal computer.

This article highlights one important aspect of the innovation selection process: the setting of management expectations. Expectations provide the impetus for the initial pursuit of an innovative initiative and influence the structure of benchmarks against which continued support is evaluated. Well-calibrated expectations are thus essential for both the process of initial selection as well as for providing an environment in which development and implementation can proceed successfully.

Expectations for innovation management must therefore distinguish between the expected level of technology performance and pace of improvement toward these levels; the expected size of the innovation market and the rate of market development; and the companies' expectation for profits and market position. This, in turn, will stem from the company's rate of market penetration and profit strategy. Some factors in the innovation-management process clearly lie beyond managerial control. But the setting of expectations is a venue in which strategic judgments and decisions come into play in a way that affects not just the immediate fate of proposed initiatives, but the environment in which these initiatives will function throughout their development.

Four issues must be considered when setting these expectations: the level of interdependence between the technology under development and other factors critical to successful deployment; the degree to which the innovation must be integrated along the value chain before it can make an impact on its critical market; the choice of initial markets for the innovation and their relation to the ultimate market at which the innovation is targetted; and the company's own system of incentives and controls that will guide managerial motivation and activity.

Technology interdependence

A primary component of setting expectations in innovation management is technology development. This means that the way in which the technology is implemented to add value in its application ultimately determines its success. While solving the pure technological challenge of an innovation is a prerequisite for success, a self-contained solution may be of little use if it depends on other developments. If an innovation is a component of a larger system that itself is under development, its accomplishment is tied to the successful development of all other components of the system. For this reason, calculating the probability of success for the initiative must include the probabilities of success of all the initiatives on which the innovation relies.

Take the example of Go! (not to be confused with the British Airways low-cost subsidiary of the same name). This early pioneer of pen-based computing, which successfully developed the requisite touch-screen technology and software interface for pen-based computing, failed because the expectations set for the handwriting-recognition technology proved overoptimistic. The same problem plagued Apple's Newton initiative.

The challenge of interdependence is even more critical when development efforts must be coordinated across separate companies or platforms. Lotus Corporation's decision to tailor its next-generation products to IBM's OS/2 operating system in the early 1990s set up a dependence that exposed it not only to the hazards involved with completing its own software projects, but also to any difficulties that IBM might face. Interdependence, of course, may also involve non-technical components. The enormous investments made in supersonic commercial aviation were dissipated not because of technical failure, but due to institutional difficulties in altering noise regulations on which overland flights depended.

When other pieces of the puzzle need to fall into place, the success of any one component is dependent on the success of all others. Thus, expectations for the success of any single component must incorporate the probabilities of success of all relevant components – the greater an innovation's interdependence with other developments, the smaller its influence over its own final success. Recognition of these implicit interdependencies is a critical component of setting expectations for the external difficulties to which a project will be exposed. It informs expectations for its overall chances for success and offers insight into the kind of support it may require throughout different stages of its development.

Value chain integration

The critical market for an innovation is not always the market into which it is sold. The further up the value chain an innovation resides, the larger the number of intermediaries that must adopt it before it can reach its "critical target market," the market that will ultimately determine its success. As the number of intermediaries increases, the uncertainty surrounding the rate and extent of market realization increases as well.

For example, in the pharmaceutical industry, the critical market for prescription drugs consists of the consumers who will ultimately use them for therapy. But before this ultimate market can be reached, the drug must be adopted by the prescribing doctor as the best treatment for the ailment in question, and possibly by the ultimate consumer's insurance plan. Thus, although success is determined by consumption at the final consumer stage of the value chain, its realization first requires adoption and integration of the drug into therapeutic routines at several earlier stages. So diffusion of the innovation needs to be seen as a multitiered adoption process, with the implication that the greater the number of intermediaries that must adopt the innovation before it reaches its final consumers, the greater the time to market realization.

When success in the critical market depends on the actual integration of the innovation into downstream products, beyond its simple adoption by downstream actors, the uncertainties surrounding market realization are even greater.

For example, in the industrial market for flat screen displays, applications range from car dashboard information systems to hospital room equipment displays to handheld video games. Before reaching consumers in any of these markets, the flat screen manufacturer first needs to go through a product-development cycle to manufacture the screen. The screen must then be integrated as a component into the equipment manufacturer's own product-development cycle. The final product must then be introduced into the consumer market and suffer the traditional difficulties involved with marketing and adoption. Setting expectations for such a project, as regards timing, funding, payback rates, and expected time to market realization, without taking into account the complications introduced by the requirements of downstream integration, will lead to missed targets and, potentially, premature cancelation of promising initiatives.

Initial and final markets

The degree of integration and interdependence (as discussed above) is intimately linked to the market context in which the innovation is to be applied. The choice of market context thus presents a powerful managerial lever in guiding development.

In most organizations, support for innovation initiatives is correlated with expected market impact; the natural course for eliciting support for an initiative is therefore to target large and important markets for its application. These markets, however, tend to be more difficult to penetrate because they often require a relatively high level of performance from both the core innovation and the complementary innovations on which it will depend.

An alternative to targeting mainstream markets as initial entry points for the innovation is to structure market entry as a sequential progression, which follows the development of the technology. By initially targeting niche markets that can value the benefits of the innovation independently of complementary developments, companies can gain market rewards as well as learn about both the market environment and the technology's characteristics in a direct and applied fashion.

Several early companies developed successful pen-based computers for industrial users whose image-recognition requirements (e.g., signature capture, recording tick marks for inventory control) were easier to satisfy than those of the mainstream computer users targetted by Apple and Go! As another example, the first xerographic copiers required operators to follow a 14-step manual to make a single copy. While ten years of development were necessary to achieve the level of automation required for the copiers to be relevant to corporate users, the early machines found a profitable home in the offset printing niche. By identifying market niches where the innovation could function more as a standalone product than as a component technology, the Haloid Corporation (which would later be renamed Xerox) was able to support its efforts in xerography to a point at which the mainstream office market became attainable.

Targetting more focussed markets may ease the burdens of both interdependence and integration, but at the price of initial market size. A development path that matches markets to the state of the technology may also lengthen the time required to achieve success in the ultimate target market. While decisions regarding these trade-offs are implicit in the market justifications used to support innovative projects, their explicit consideration will serve better to inform expectations.

Drawing boundaries

The methods by which a company sets expectations for innovative initiatives must be aligned with the incentive and control systems with which it sets expectations for its managers. While the uncertainty inherent in innovation *per se* is largely outside the company's control, the ways in which innovative activities are structured, and the degree of uncertainty to which the company exposes itself at any given time, form a strategic and organizational choice.

Decisions regarding how boundaries are drawn around innovative initiatives are critical to the way in which projects will adapt in response to the changes and discoveries that occur throughout their development. Flexibility in resource allocation and in their deployment – funding, but even more importantly the timing of budget cycles, and the availability of managerial attention, development, and production capabilities – must be matched with human resource policies that do not discourage managers from taking risks that may result in educational failures or changed project goals.

For example, at Florida-based Symbiosis, one of the few early success stories of the minimally invasive surgery equipment market, the critical factor in its ability to react quickly to new market opportunities was ready availability of small-scale production equipment for new initiatives. This allowed for fast manufacturing of prototypes and samples. Such flexibility in production was matched with the freedom to cross operational boundaries, so that developers of initiatives were able to market their product to customer groups outside of the company's existing marketing focus.

Because each project did not need to be separately justified and repackaged internally every time new capabilities were required, this structure allowed for fast and flexible development.

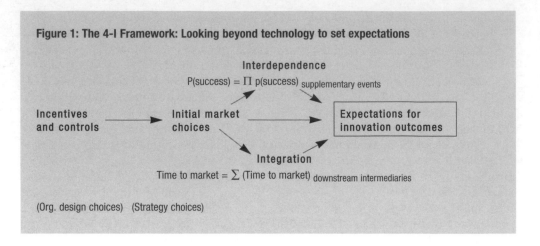

Figure 1: The 4-I Framework: Looking beyond technology to set expectations

If a company's culture is only to reward big successes, managers cannot be expected to commit wholeheartedly to risky ventures in emerging technologies likely to appeal, initially at least, to small market niches. If resource allocation is structured along rigid budget cycles and well defined activity constraints, it is unreasonable to expect managers to be able to adapt projects effectively in response to new ideas.

Conclusion

Innovations considered technologically successful may nonetheless be disappointing because they do not meet the market expectations that were set at their launch. By explicitly considering the interdependencies and integration requirements inherent to an initiative's success, expectations can be better informed regarding both ultimate performance levels and the rate at which these levels may be achieved.

Given these external factors, it becomes possible to consider the initiative within the context of the company itself, and to evaluate whether and how existing incentive and control systems can be used to support the innovation.

Summary

Choosing an innovative idea that will both dominate existing markets and open up new ones is one of the toughest decisions a company can face, writes **Ron Adner**. A key part of the process for managers is the setting of expectations. Four critical issues need to be considered: the level of interdependence between the technology under development and other success factors; the degree to which the innovation must be integrated along the value chain; the choice of initial markets; and the company's system of incentives and controls. Without realistic market expectations at the outset, the danger is that a technologically successful innovation will be considered a failure.

Suggested further reading
Adner, R. and Levinthal, D. (2000) "Technological speciation and the emergence of emerging technologies," in Day, G. and Schoemaker, P. (eds) *Wharton on Emerging Technologies,* New York: John Wiley and Sons.
Christensen, C. (1997) *The Innovator's Dilemma*, Cambridge, MA: Harvard Business School Press.
Moore, G. (1998) *Inside the Tornado,* New York: HarperBusiness.

MERGERS AND ACQUISITION STRATEGY

Contributors

Robert Gertner is a professor of economics and strategy at the University of Chicago Graduate School of Business. He teaches courses in strategic investment decisions and advanced competitive strategy. He is also principal of Lexecon Inc., a Chicago-based consulting firm.

Laurence Capron is assistant professor of strategy at INSEAD. Her research interests include mergers and acquisitions, foreign entry, modes of acquisition of new competences, and corporate development in the telecommunications industry.

Jay Anand is an assistant professor of corporate strategy and international business at the University of Michigan Business School. His interests include mergers and acquisitions, and strategies for multinational and multibusiness firms.

Maurizio Zollo is assistant professor of strategy at INSEAD. His work focusses on the mechanism underlying the creation and the evolution of organizational capabilities and their impact on the performance of complex, infrequent and heterogeneous processes, such as acquisitions and alliances.

Philippe Haspeslagh is Paul Desmarais Sr. Chaired Professor in Partnership and Private Enterprise at INSEAD. His interests are in the management of mergers and acquisitions, the implementation of value-based management, and in corporate governance policies.

Contents

Introduction

M&A is a key option for companies seeking new value creation, growth, and globalization. All the statistics show high levels of M&A activity continuing in the main industrial sectors and major territories – but getting M&A strategy leads inevitably to value destruction, management distractions and unnecessary job losses. Issues tackled in this module include the common mistakes made by acquirers, governance mechanisms to limit the risk of poor acquisition, rules of thumb for selecting appropriate targets (and identifying bad ones), the peculiar challenge of merging "equals," the contrast between pre-acquisition motives and post-acquisition behavior, and the subtle process of sound integration.

How boards can say nay to M&A

by Robert Gertner

Acquisitions are among the most important strategic decisions a company makes. Successful acquisitions can be an important source of value creation and growth. Unsuccessful acquisitions can destroy value rapidly, lead to enormous operating problems, and often result in top executives losing their jobs.

The vast academic literature on mergers and acquisitions suggests that the short-run stock market return to acquiring companies is approximately zero. This average zero return hides the large variation that exists in bidder returns – the market gives an obtrusive thumbs down to many acquisitions. Assessing the long-run performance of acquisitions is much more difficult. Separating out the effect of an acquisition from other factors that influence performance is difficult to do systematically. Nonetheless, we have all read anecdotal accounts of acquisition disasters that have caused us to shake our heads in wonder.

Mistakes

Why are there so many bad acquisitions?

There are three broad categories of explanation: 1) unpredictability; 2) agency problems; and 3) mistakes. There are undoubtedly elements of all of these, but I will argue that it is worth focussing attention on the mistake category.

- The first explanation for bad acquisitions is simply that it is *difficult to predict* which mergers will work and which will not. Many of the mergers that turn out to be mistakes were not really mistakes at the time they occurred because their lack of success could not be predicted. Although we may think we are able to explain why the merger failed, we are doing so with 20–20 hindsight. There is some evidence to suggest that this is not the entire explanation. In a 1990 study, Mark Mitchell and Kenneth Lehn find that acquisitions where the stock market reacts negatively to the merger announcements are more likely to be divested subsequently. This implies that the market has some ability to predict bad acquisitions when these are announced. Surprisingly, there is no systematic study that correlates broader measures of performance with the effects flowing from such announcements.

- The second category of explanations concerns *agency problems*. If management and shareholder incentives are not aligned, then acquisitions that are bad for shareholders may actually be good for managers. This explanation has received a great deal of attention in the academic literature. There are several reasons why such acquisition incentives diverge. Managers may prefer controlling larger enterprises either because they value size directly or because company size and compensation are related. Some economists have argued that managers may try to entrench themselves by going for acquisitions that make the managers difficult to replace. Recently, there has been a significant trend toward aligning executive compensation with stock market performance. Although this should mitigate the conflict of interest, it may not eliminate it completely. Some bad acquisitions can probably be explained by misaligned incentives, but I believe it quite unusual for a CEO to think: "While not in the interest of my company's shareholders, this merger is still in my interest, so I will go forward."

■ The third category of explanations for bad acquisitions is *managerial mistakes*. There are many reasons why individuals and organizations make mistakes. First, there is just plain lack of knowledge and errors of judgment. No individual is omniscient and managers must make decisions based on information provided by (at least) equally fallible subordinates. These employees may have incentives to tell the CEO what they think he or she wants to hear rather than what they think is right. Investment bankers, lawyers, and consultants have an incentive for the acquisition to occur because it generates higher fees, although the impact of this on the quality of advice is difficult to document and is therefore speculative. Another source of acquisition mistakes that has received attention is managerial hubris. The argument is that because of their position and history, some CEOs exhibit overconfidence in their decision-making abilities. One reason for this is that to become CEO one needs both skill and luck, but CEOs ascribe more of their success to skill than is justified.

Mistakes are also made because certain issues are too subtle and difficult to assess accurately before a merger. In particular, issues of merger implementation often involve tricky management and personnel issues. Salesforces must be integrated, management responsibilities redefined, facilities combined, and employees may be fired or relocated. There are reasons that these issues will not be sufficiently analyzed before a deal. For example, if they were made beforehand, individuals with relevant information who feared for their jobs could try to sabotage the deal. This makes it much more difficult to get the information before the merger than after it.

The line between mistakes and unpredictability may be a bit fuzzy, but the distinction is nonetheless useful. The mistakes category captures the idea that it is possible to make better decisions at a reasonable cost. This implies that reforms in governance may help companies avoid acquisitions.

We now explore the role of boards of directors in identifying and blocking adverse acquisitions.

Role of directors

Boards of directors have a fiduciary duty to oversee the corporation's business affairs. Among the board's responsibilities is to appoint the CEO, determine the CEO's compensation, nominate directors, oversee financial reporting, and approve important strategic and financial decisions. The board's role is both to monitor the performance of the company and its management as well as to employ individual and collective expertise and experience to advise management. Monitoring and advising are generally complementary activities, but they can conflict – for example, close outside associates of the CEO may be the most effective advisers but may not be the most effective monitors.

The role of the board in acquisitions is also to advise management about strategic direction and to monitor management decisions. If bad acquisition proposals arise because of agency problems or mistakes, the board can play an important role in evaluating a proposed acquisition.

Traditionally, however, the board does not possess sufficient information to exercise strong, independent judgment on a proposed acquisition.

Board procedures vary greatly across companies. A typical role in overseeing acquisitions is that the board has previously discussed and approved a basic strategic direction for acquisitions, such as seeking to expand into a specific type of market.

Once management has identified and researched a target, it will seek board approval to go forward. Top management and outside advisers will give the board a presentation that will include the strategic justification of the merger and financial projections. Outside directors usually will not have enough information or knowledge to challenge thoroughly the underlying bases of the presentation.

The board, therefore, is rarely in a position to identify mistakes in management's analysis or significant issues that have been missed. For example, many observers have explained the failure of the merger between Quaker Oats, the US cereals and sport drinks business, and Snapple, a US soft drinks company, on the difficulties of maintaining good relations with existing Snapple distributors while expanding distribution into supermarkets, a strong Quaker channel. It is unlikely that outside directors of Quaker would have had the information to identify this potential problem when they approved the acquisition.

The composition of the board of directors as well as management compensation, retention, and succession are all issues that have been tackled by corporate governance activists. Board independence, it is true, has been strengthened and the structure of managerial incentives improved. However, not much has been done to enhance the board's ability to be informed arbiters of major business decisions; boards have not turned into bodies that can identify and correct most management mistakes.

Enter the naysayer

What can a board do? It can try to get better, more detailed, and more objective information from the company directly. But this is a difficult challenge.

- First, it takes a great deal of time, a scarce resource for accomplished outside directors.
- Second, it is difficult to obtain appropriate information without relying on senior management. Such reliance may result in biassed information or fail to uncover any mistakes in management's analysis. One suggestion that has been made is to have a full-time agent of the board of directors participate in every aspect of senior management. This is fraught with problems – the agent may then be co-opted by, or just ignored by, management.

I suggest a simple institution that may go a long way toward allowing the board to play a more effective role in acquisitions. Once management decides that a potential acquisition is worth pursuing, the outside directors of the board will hire its own outside adviser to be a naysayer on the acquisition. This adviser, who may be an investment bank or a consulting company, will play devil's advocate and try to shoot down the proposed merger.

At the board meeting held to take the decision, the proponents and the professional naysayer will each make presentations. The naysayer would have been given access to the same information as management's outside advisers. The meeting will become more like an adversarial judicial hearing or arbitration proceeding, with the board acting as judge or arbitrator.

The adversarial system is a time-tested institution for efficient, impartial decision making. A good judge has many of the characteristics of outside board members: intelligence, judgment, but limited knowledge of the details before the hearing. The two existing judicial systems in modern democracies are the common law adversarial system and the civil law system, such as applies in France. In the latter, the judge is also chief investigator and devotes significant resources to establishing facts.

The analogy is clear: the current governance system is biassed; a civil law role for the outside directors is difficult to implement, while an adversarial system may have some potential. If the arbitrator is not going to be a fully informed expert, he should at least hear both sides of the argument.

The adversarial system certainly has its faults. The legal system in the United States and elsewhere is not the most efficient institution that humanity has developed. But it is important to remember that outside directors will be able to shape the rules by which the system operates. This makes the analogy to private arbitration more appropriate. Almost all private arbitration adopts some form of adversarial proceeding. The main difference with the legal system is that arbitration rules reduce the costs and delay, and the manipulation of the system.

The naysayer has both direct and indirect effects on the quality of information available to the board.

First, the direct. The naysayer will present the other side of the argument. For example, the institution will choose a set of comparable companies to the targetted one, indicating that the bidder is planning to pay too much. Management's advisers will choose a different set to show that the size of the bid is appropriate. This will allow the board a fuller set of comparisons.

Second, the indirect incentive effect. The presence of the naysayer will make management and its advisers present less biassed information. Extending the example, the choice of comparable companies that management's advisers will present is less likely to be biassed if these know that the naysayer will offer both a critique and alternatives. In addition, those issues that are problematical will surface and the proponents will have to analyze and defend these.

This indirect effect may be much more important than the direct one. Perhaps few proposed acquisitions will be shot down successfully by the naysayer, but fewer bad acquisitions will be brought to the board by management. If it works well, the naysayer will often have a weak case.

Implementation issues

The direct cost of this institution will not be trivial, since the naysayer will need to have valuable skills and devote significant time to the task. Given the size of many acquisitions and the potential losses from bad decisions, the benefits are likely to justify the costs in many circumstances.

If the causes of bad acquisitions are mistakes and difficulties in predicting the outcome of a merger, rather than agency problems, senior management should welcome the institution. If the worst acquisitions are weeded out, it may lengthen the CEO's tenure, since a large bad acquisition often leads to the CEO's removal or retirement.

Even if management does not want naysayers, if the institution develops and works well, shareholders and other market forces will likely pressure boards to make use of it. Mergers that are approved without recourse to the use of the naysayer may be more likely to be met by a negative stock reaction. This implies that there is no reason to make it mandatory by changing corporation or securities law.

An important issue is how to compensate the naysayer. The advisers on the other side of the aisle usually have an incentive for the deal to occur. It may be worthwhile for the naysayer to receive a bonus if the deal is squashed. Alternatively, long-run benefits from maintaining a reputation for quality work may be sufficient to create incentives for the naysayer to do the job effectively.

A criticism of having naysayer advisers to the board is that management may be less willing to propose good mergers, especially risky deals, for fear that they will be rejected and management replaced. There are many reasons to reject a deal. If the board feels simply that the price is too high, the impact on management may be small, while if the board rejects management's strategy, it may mean that management will be replaced. But this is exactly the role of the board. Debates need not be antagonistic, but if a company does not want to risk the congeniality of the boardroom and the relationship between outside directors and management, it might rightly choose not to require a naysayer.

The strongest criticism against the naysayer is one that views the role of outside directors a little differently. In this view, the board should delegate authority over virtually all business decisions, including acquisitions, to management so long as the company is performing well and the board has confidence in the company's leadership. It is only once a board loses confidence in management that the board should get involved in strategic decision making. The board only becomes active when performance deteriorates, and even then its focus is on whether or not to replace top management. However, if managerial mistakes are important, this kind of limitation on the board's role eliminates an important way that such mistakes can be identified and avoided.

The acquisition naysayer can be viewed in a broader governance context. The first stage of the governance revolution has been to create truly independent boards of directors acting in the interest of shareholders. The second stage is to make them more effective in doing their job.

This second stage is a real challenge, given the information and time limitations that are inherent in boards of directors dominated by outsiders with other important jobs. Effective boards will need to develop creative ways to deal with this challenge.

Summary

Successful acquisitions can create value and add growth. But the short-run stock market return for companies that opt to acquire others is approximately zero, says **Robert Gertner**. The market appears to give the thumbs down to many mergers and acquisitions. Failures broadly fall into three categories, among which managerial mistakes are perhaps the most significant. Sharpening the mechanisms of corporate governance could be helpful. The governance movement's current focus has succeeded in increasing board independence and improving the structure of managerial incentives. However, boards of directors are not yet able to identify and correct most management mistakes. The answer may be the naysayer. Such an adviser would play devil's advocate, earning a bonus on successfully shooting down a management-proposed M&A.

Suggested further reading

Jemison, D. and Sitkin, S. (1986) "Corporate acquisitions: a process perspective," *Academy of Management Review*, 11: 145–63.

Mitchell, M. and Lehn, K. (1990) "Do bad bidders become good targets?" *Journal of Political Economy*, 98: 372–98.

Monks, R. and Minow, N. (1996) *Watching the Watchers: Corporate Governance for the 21st Century*, Oxford: Blackwell.

How many matches are made in heaven?

by Jay Anand

Essayist H.L. Mencken once quipped: "For every complicated problem, there is a simple solution – and it is wrong." His observation can be applied to the current wave of mergers and acquisitions in North America and Europe. Hardly a week goes by without an announcement of another awe-inspiring deal between mega-companies (*see* Figure 1). As M&A fever continues unabated, one wonders if the performance of the latest transactions will be any better than those of the past. While managers justify their acquisitions by reference to the changing landscape of competition, technology and policy, plenty of lessons can be learned from the past.

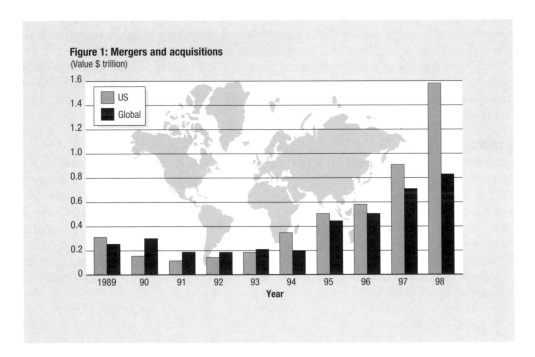

Figure 1: Mergers and acquisitions
(Value $ trillion)

This article outlines some general principles that should help companies avoid the more common pitfalls and enhance value creation in M&A.

Only time will tell how many of these individual transactions ultimately yield positive results for shareholders. But if past research is any guide, the number that are successful will be small. Results from academic research and studies by management consultants, along with managerial experience, consistently underline the low odds for success in these transactions. For example, a number of these studies have shown that "value creation" is often in the minds of chief executive officers, and is less obvious to the stock markets, which often punish the shares of acquirers.

When any value is created, it is usually completely appropriated by the shareholders of the acquired company in the form of a premium, leaving a negative or a small positive return for the acquirer shareholders. Of course, many would argue these studies are often based on immediate reactions to the news of an acquisition, and do not do justice to the long-term potential of corporate combinations.

But studies using long-term analyses of post-acquisition performance are even more unflattering to M&A, for they reveal a negative pattern of returns that lasts for years.

Further, the lack of success for many transactions is illustrated by the very large proportion of acquisitions that come apart within a few years. History shows that anywhere between one-third to more than half of all acquisitions are ultimately divested or spun off. This proportion does not include the regular sales of partial assets that follow many acquisitions. Some might argue that, since these transactions represent corporate experiments, some are bound to fail. While some of these divested acquisitions may represent experiments, they are very expensive experiments because most divestitures fetch sales prices below the acquisition price. Overall, it seems that a premium is often paid but seldom recovered.

Nonetheless, a few success stories can be found within the overwhelmingly negative statistical evidence for M&A. There is a lot to learn about the "what" and "how" of acquisition strategies from this select group. Interestingly, several regularities appear in the most successful cases. A small number of companies have been able to take these lessons to heart and have reaped rewards. The successful growth strategy of CISCO, the telecoms equipment company, comes to mind, as do the gentle integration processes of General Electric, the US conglomerate.

No pain, no gain

Some kinds of acquisition are particularly suspect even as they are announced. It is important to remember that, in today's developed financial markets, there is only one good justification for doing a deal. This is the unique ability of the acquirer to obtain higher economic value from the assets of the potential target company.

On the other hand, when the justification is based on the intrinsic attractiveness of the target, value is not likely to be created, because this attractiveness is already factored into the price of the company. So at most the acquirers get the equivalent of what they pay for, or less if they pay a high premium in their zeal to complete the deal. Consequently, a deal motivated by the target company's superior positioning, growth prospects, or profitability is unlikely to succeed on such grounds alone.

Another hazardous approach to M&A is vertical integration, which aims to appropriate a larger slice of the profits in an industry. Such a move can alienate other customers of the business. PepsiCo, the US soft drinks distributor, found this out to its cost after acquiring the KFC, Taco Bell, and Pizza Hut fast-food businesses. Archrival Coca-Cola was able subsequently to convince Wendy's and other fast-food chains that selling Pepsi would indirectly benefit their Pepsico-owned competitors.

Even when this is not a major issue, vertical integration seldom creates value because integration of businesses usually involves sacrificing one set of interests for another. A few years ago, Walt Disney, the entertainment company, vertically integrated by acquiring the ABC television network. Any money that changed hands between the two prior to the acquisition as licensing fees became an internal transaction, not a source of value creation by itself. If the idea was to show more Disney programs at ABC, it is important to think about the process of program selection that might have existed at ABC before the acquisition. Such a process would have sought to maximize revenues by maximizing the viewer potential of programs. Any change in such a process will tend to destroy, rather than create, value. Other sources of value may exist, but are likely to be minor and difficult to articulate.

When the proposed relationship between two companies is defined at an abstract level, there are further grounds for doubting the value-creation potential.

If a company cannot articulate where synergies are going to be found, chances are that there aren't any. This is analogous to what is taught in basic communication classes: "Convoluted writing stems from clouded thinking." Furthermore, if the strategy is unclear, how can implementation be decisive? Good implementation begins with clear strategy. If the goal is cost reduction, then managers can proceed with asset rationalization. This is no doubt difficult and painful, but it can be achieved as long as it has been defined as the destination. Similarly, if the goal is cross-selling, managers can proceed with creating a structure and a set of incentives that enable this result to be achieved. Otherwise, one is reminded of the interchange between Alice and the cat in Lewis Carroll's *Alice in Wonderland*:

"I don't much care where – so long as I get somewhere," Alice added as an explanation. "Oh, you're sure to do that," said the cat, "if you only walk long enough."

It is not a bad idea for managers to write a moot contract clearly expressing the goals and processes of the deal before completing it, to evaluate their clarity in thinking.

If the strategy needs to be clear before the deal is completed, integration needs to be prompt and decisive once the financial transaction is over. The longer the delay in integration, the greater the synergy needs to be to recover the premium. This is based on the simple principle of the time value of money. Premium is paid up-front, but is recovered over a long period of time, one that does not begin until the fruits of integration begin to show. The process needs to be set in motion right away, and the plan needs to be ready before the deal is completed. A marriage is more than a wedding, and it takes years of hard work to make it a success. There is no gain without pain.

Without integration, a company achieves little more than financial diversification, a goal that has long been discredited with the enhanced (and increasing) ability of shareholders to diversify their financial investments on their own. Financial interdependence must be supplemented with strategic and operating interdependence. This is particularly important for acquisitions motivated by "convergence" between industries. Even if acquisitions are undertaken as a means of buying "options," they need to be more than a passive financial bet. Outcomes of market and technological evolution are not independent of the endogenous processes within the company, and these processes need to be initiated with a clear vision.

Of course, this is possible only if the management of the acquiring company has a basic understanding of the business of the acquired company. Too many disparate businesses have attempted union without a grasp of the fundamentals of each other's business.

The 1990 acquisition of the Hollywood film studios Universal by Matsushita Electric, the world's leading consumer electronics maker, and that of its rival Columbia Pictures in 1989 by Japanese consumer electronics concern Sony, were heralded at the time as a breakthrough in the integration of hardware and software. But even beyond the length and breadth of the Pacific ocean that separates the companies, there are many differences between the prudent design, manufacture and marketing of VCRs, and the work of the arty Hollywood celebrities wanting their flamboyant lifestyles exposed in *Lifestyles of the Rich and Famous*, the US television series. Within a few years, Matsushita's investment in Universal had dwindled to 16 percent (the majority is now owned by the Seagram spirits and beverage empire), while Sony continues to hold on to its stake in Columbia.

One effective M&A strategy is to form joint ventures or alliances with potential targets. Some of the most successful mergers have been between companies with a history of interactions and relationships. This tends to mitigate the surprise factor, which is generally negative. Acquirers rarely report positive surprises. Even executives at DaimlerChrysler, the German-US group, had to revise downward the expectations from the merger once the complexity and vastness of the integration processes became clear.

In high-tech acquisitions, effective integration carries the added requirement of retaining key people. One ill-thought memo, and the employees may not return the following morning.

Furthermore, acquisitions made by otherwise failing companies should be viewed with cynicism. It is more likely that the source of failure in the acquiring company will infect the acquired company rather than the latter rejuvenating the former. For example, attempts by defense companies to convert into civilian outfits have rarely been successful since the end of the Cold War. Warren Buffett, the portfolio investor, once remarked that acquiring managers were "overexposed to the story of the princess and the toad in their impressionable childhoods . . . we have observed many kisses, but very few miracles."

Similarly, managers of cash-cow businesses need to be extra careful in buying growth-potential companies. Boredom in managing a mature business can make one look for easy growth opportunities outside, even when true strategic linkage is absent. Without the judicious oversight of a board, this risk is multiplied.

Hostile or contested takeovers are also less likely to provide adequate rewards. Without the buy-in of the acquired company management, integration is bound to be harder. In the case of high-tech acquisitions, there is also a risk of being trapped in a "scorched earth" game. When you finally make the acquisition, there is little of value left because key employees have sought employment elsewhere. Similarly, when managers pursue a target with a goal to acquiring it at any price, they are more

One-stop networking

CISCO's strategy has centered on creating a broad enough product line to become a one-stop shop for the networking industry. In choosing candidates that broaden its product line, it focusses on small and adjacent companies, which makes the task of integration less challenging once the deal is consummated. Its target screening involves a combination of the usual hard data as well as soft factors such as compatibility in vision and chemistry.

Consequently, its acquired companies bring complementary technology and products, but a shared emphasis on customer orientation. CISCO's frugality is illustrated by its reluctance to use external M&A advisers; instead, it chooses to do most such work internally. But its strongest point in the acquisition-management process is the smooth integration that has accompanied most of its transactions. In technology-oriented acquisitions, the key performance measure is the retention of the workforce. The turnover rate for employees in companies acquired by CISCO is much lower than the norm, and almost equal to the turnover rate in the company as a whole. Part of the reason for such a high retention rate is the lucrative, but performance-contingent, compensation that the company offers. Of course, no approach is risk free, and CISCO has made some errors in judgment leading to overestimation of potential and overpayment in price. Nevertheless, with dozens of successful acquisitions behind it, it has become the acquirer of choice for many start-ups – a reputation that further translates into value.

likely to overpay. Managers who pursue an acquisition without regard for the price are likely to be overcommitted, and end up like the auction winner who pays more than what anyone else thought the item was worth.

The winning habit

In the 1999 Cricket World Cup, commentators often mentioned the "winning habit." A team that has performed consistently is more likely to keep winning. There are many reasons why a single slip-up in the acquisition game can prove costly, not only in terms of financial results, but also in terms of reputation. Some of the most successful acquirers have been able to establish strict guidelines in the pursuit of other companies.

There are three stages to an acquisition:

- target selection;
- negotiation;
- integration.

Successful acquisitions involve a well-thought-out strategy in selecting the target, avoiding overpaying, and creating value in the integration process. Furthermore, successful acquirers do not consider these as sequential; rather, they think through the latter stages first. Like any other management challenge, a good acquisition strategy combines the analytical with the intuitive, and the linear with the iterative. CISCO's acquisition approach is a good illustration of one such successful approach (*see* box above).

Summary

There is only one good justification for doing a deal: the acquirer must obtain uniquely higher economic value from the assets of the potential target company, says **Jay Anand**. Too many businesses have attempted a union without a proper grasp of the fundamentals of each other's activities. In this article, the author develops a number of experience-based rules of thumb that may help in the selection and execution of good acquisition plans. In particular, he highlights types of acquisition that are generally suspect. These include situations where justification is based on the intrinsic value of the target, is defined at an abstract level, or involves vertical integration. One effective M&A strategy is to form an alliance first so that there is a history of interactions and relationships.

Suggested further reading

Bauman, R., Jackson, P. and Lawrence, J. (1997) *From Promise to Performance*, Boston, MA: Harvard Business School Press.

Sirower, M. (1997) *The Synergy Trap*, New York: The Free Press.

Managing the mating dance in equal mergers

by Philippe Haspeslagh

Consolidation fever is sweeping across industries as the competitive arena changes from the merely national to being regional and global. It is most visible in pharmaceuticals, automobiles, banking, telecommunications, and (most recently) electricity, but away from the public glare mergers are also taking place in smaller, diverse industries like furniture, trucking, and component distribution.

Key players in these industries are more likely to consolidate through acquisition. Second-tier companies, however, are increasingly turning to "mergers of equals" to leapfrog to the top of the league and jointly maintain control over their destiny. Many industries are still fragmented enough that a merger of two mid-size companies can produce a European or even global contender.

The idea of the "equal merger" gives rise to much cynicism – at least to the extent that equal means equal managerial influence over merger decisions and outcomes. Many companies would have been better off not giving their deals such a label, the automobile manufacturing giant DaimlerChrysler for one.

Yet other companies that have been the product of "equal" mergers – for example SmithKline Beecham, the pharmaceuticals giant, ABN-Amro, the international bank, Borealis, Europe's largest producer of polyolefin plastics, and many others since – illustrate how world beaters can be shaped out of also-rans, provided that the right commitment and leadership qualities are brought to the merger process.

This wave of equal mergers raises many questions. Industry after industry seems caught up in a mating dance. At some point every actor is seemingly talking to or eyeing up every other one, considering the risks and advantages of a cross-border marriage, or contemplating a less adventurous domestic solution.

What ultimately explains the deals that are finally sealed, given the large numbers that fall through even at an advanced stage of preparation? More importantly, how does the particular nature of equal mergers affect the overall process and the requisites for success?

When the mating dance leads to marriage

As insiders well know, for every merger that is announced many more fall by the wayside. In the author's experience, as a researcher and consultant in this area, the same few issues tend to determine if a merger will go ahead or not. They include the following.

Compatibility at the top

Who will be chairman and who will be CEO? The lack of a clear answer to this simple question has torpedoed many a done deal.

A leading US carmaker and a still independent European company would have married their European operations were it not for the assumption by both sides that they would hold the chief executive position.

More recently, a negotiated solution between the oil groups TotalFina and Elf Aquitaine was clearly held up more by the egos of its top managers than by differences over industrial logic. Although age differences, style differences, and differences in market credibility are obvious ingredients of a possible division of roles, it remains hard to predict the size or chemistry of egos.

The importance of rapport between the top two people goes much further than just agreeing their respective roles. It takes determination and guts to push a management team and board off the go-it-alone path. In doing so, the shortcomings in their present strategy are being acknowledged.

Trusting in the commitment of those involved to see the merger through the inevitable difficulties is essential. It is even more crucial that the two leaders speak with one voice in public. Whatever the style and personality differences, public unity becomes both a symbol and a testing ground for managers on both sides for many months thereafter. Any perceived differences in wavelengths will amplify any strain in merging the organizations.

A shared vision of the industry's future

Ultimately, the momentum behind any merger depends on a shared understanding of the future. A common view of industry trends is a key component here.

Why, for example, did the merger between two UK pharmaceutical makers SmithKline and Beecham transpire while the first engagement between SmithKline Beecham and Glaxo was broken off? Bob Bauman and Henry Wendt – respectively chief executive and chairman of SmithKline Beecham at the time of the merger – were clearly on the same wavelength in envisioning the pharmaceutical industry moving into healthcare. While the next chief executive Jan Leschly bet on integrated healthcare, Sir Richard Sykes, chief executive of Glaxo Wellcome, believed in the traditional success formula: innovative R&D to sell drugs.

Any merger between two complex organizations involves many early choices in terms of portfolio strategy, divestment, and development priorities. These in turn reflect different considerations about the industry future. They cannot be resolved if the parties do not hold the same view on this future.

A clear benefit case

Capital markets do not like mergers: there is no acquisition premium. For the deal to avoid coming under attack from analysts and fund managers, the case must be compelling. The benefits must also be clear to those inside the companies if discussion is to move beyond skirmishes over relative valuations.

In practice, the merger benefit case is often hastily put together by very small teams secretly meeting in hotel rooms accompanied by investment bankers doing the spreadsheets.

The perceived pressure to announce compelling cost reductions is huge. All too often this leads to a wide gap between the promises made and the management teams' ability to deliver acceptable synergies. Yet analysts use these rough-and-ready estimates as their yardsticks in judging the progress of a merger.

Sticking to a fair valuation

Financial valuation may seem to be the sticking point in many negotiations. This is certainly so in private deals. Every owner sees his or her own company as more valuable than the figure for which it is externally assessed. Where publicly listed companies are involved, the market price is obviously hard to ignore.

Whatever the profitability of Chrysler of the US when it was negotiating with DaimlerBenz, the latter's higher price–earnings ratio made it the more valuable partner. Reluctance to compromise between valuations advanced by investment bankers to both parties, or to break any deadlock through a third party, usually reflects a desire to break off over issues other than financial ones.

Nevertheless, financial aspects ultimately lead to the break-off of many merger discussions after a figure has been agreed. It may take many months to complete a deal, and as time goes by one side inevitably gains a different momentum from the other. After a while the temptation to start renegotiating is great, as happened in the British Telecommunications/MCI deal when MCI, the US telecoms company, started to flounder. Almost always, however, any attempt to renegotiate the agreement ends in failure, with the prize going to a third party, in this case Worldcom.

Handling symbolic issues

Two merger issues tend to drain more emotional energy than any other aspect: headquarters location and the new name. They are the core symbols of where power really lies. If the name of one company appears first, the other will insist on holding on to the headquarters. A better solution may therefore be to adopt a new name, thereby symbolizing the need to leave old baggage behind. A move to a new headquarters also helps, although few companies take this step.

A new board?

Have you ever seen a merger where the new board is not essentially just the old boards combined? Board members, indeed, have to approve the merger and recommend it to shareholders. Yet what sort of example are they offering when they first combine the boards and then ask middle management to make all the sacrifices?

Making equal mergers successful

If these issues largely explain the odds of a merger happening or not happening, they are not necessarily predictors of ultimate success. This, in the author's experience, depends heavily on the leadership of the merger planning and integration process.

There is no single best way to plan a merger. Much depends on culture and style.

Contrast, for example, the merger between two Dutch banks, ABN and Amro, and the parallel merger between two Spanish banks, Banco Bilbao and Banco Vizcaya to form BBV. The former moved rather slowly through successive layers of the hierarchy, each division and each level seeking consensus before moving on to announce appointments at the next level. The two Spanish banks, on the other hand, delegated the same process to a small team of people chosen from both sides, quickly proposing an overall new structure and staffing to the combined boards. It took ABN-Amro three times as long to pass similar milestones as it did at BBV. Yet to conclude that the latter's speed was better would be misleading. This became evident when, after the sudden death of BBV's first CEO, the sides almost split up in a succession battle.

In practice, the key is to find the right balance between speed in the formal integration and progress in the merging of minds. Shared ownership achieved at the merger planning stage usually yields dividends in the actual integration.

From equality in blood groups to equal chances

There are a few aspects that stand out in achieving the right atmosphere for an equal merger process. Insisting on equal representation for both sides – which many companies make a tenet for the equality of the merger – is not one of them. Granted, middle managers will initially look at the proportion of top appointments coming from their side, and the importance of the positions they hold. By the time consideration reaches their level, however, the principle of equality is actually grossly unfair: equal mergers are the sum of many unequal parts. A fair process and equal chances in appointment to positions are critical to re-enlisting people.

Increasingly, companies are paying heed to the need to achieve a fair process, and executive recruitment companies are glad to help, offering systematic appraisal and selection services. Nothing substitutes for top management's willingness also to spend their own time cross-interviewing candidates from both sides.

From best of both to new and better

Another myopic practice is the all-too-frequent emphasis on trying to select the best of both, a practice that is eagerly supported by consulting firms offering to benchmark the quality of both sides' IT systems, for example. Selling the principle of best of both only serves to focus on the differences and to argue for one's own side. Probably neither side is world class.

"New and Better," which became a slogan in Bob Bauman's integration of SmithKline Beecham, and was supported by the requirement to benchmark others outside the pharmaceutical industry, underlined the importance of creating a forward-looking rather than a comparative dynamic.

From merging to continuous change

Mergers require tremendous efforts and ask a lot of the key individuals who have to both plan and deliver integration while maintaining performance. The tendency to slow down or slip back after a while is natural. Leaders are not popular when they make their troops confront the harsh truth: merging by itself does not produce a world-class company, it merely opens the door to opportunity. Further change will be necessary, and indeed many of those first fielded in the management team may not be there for the next stage.

Experienced leaders seize the opportunity that a merger offers for restructuring benefits, which might be equally necessary but more difficult to achieve outside of the melting pot of a merger. But they must also not lull themselves and their staff into believing that a merger is the only solution.

As managers across the globe are now discovering, a merger provides a unique chance to break the mold and shape a new destiny.

The leadership and stamina required are daunting but rewarding for those who move beyond the deal and grab the chance to introduce qualities previously missing into the merged organization.

Summary

Big company consolidation may dominate the headlines, but many second-tier companies, particularly in Europe, are also placing their faith in "mergers of equals." Here **Philippe Haspeslagh** explores some of the factors determining whether merger negotiations lead to agreement, including the size of chief executive egos, the choice of corporate names and headquarters, valuation issues, and shared visions. Capital markets do not like mergers – there is no acquisition premium – so the benefits must be clearly articulated. The author concludes with a discussion of some of the issues influencing success. The planning process is critical and hearts and minds need to be won at the integration stage; appointments must be fair; and the emphasis should be on "new and better" rather than trying to select the best of both.

Suggested further reading

Haspeslagh, P.C. and Jemison, D.B. (1991) *Managing Acquisitions: Creating Value Through Corporate Renewal*, New York: Simon & Schuster.

Lawrence, J.T. and Bauman, R.P. (1997) *From Promise to Performance: a Journey of Transformation at SmithKline Beecham*, Boston, MA: Harvard Business School Press.

Horizontal acquisitions: the benefits and risk to long-term performance

by Laurence Capron

Horizontal mergers and acquisitions – that is to say, those acquisitions that involve companies operating in the same industry – are generally explained in one of two ways. Neo-classical economists and strategy scholars argue that M&A helps businesses improve their competitive position by exploiting synergies, for example through asset rationalization or the transfer of specific competences. The other main "school" (rooted in the industrial organization economy) views M&A as a means for companies merely to increase market power and capture higher profits at the consumer's expense.

Empire building, oversized egos, overconfidence, faddishness, and other emotional and political factors drive mergers too. But the purpose of this article – based on research into more than 250 companies in Europe and North America – is to explore the conditions under which horizontal acquisitions can result in greater efficiency and long-term performance. This subject has gained more attention in the wake of studies by academics and consulting firms suggesting that 50 to 70 percent of acquisitions end in failure. It has also been shown that stockholders of bidding companies gain little or nothing from the announcement of an acquisition, presumably because the market is skeptical of the ability of managers to recoup the control premium and post-merger integration costs.

It is true that acquirers are often overoptimistic about the scale of potential synergies, but the poor averages mask the fact that some businesses do manage to enhance performance and more than offset the implementation cost.

Cost and revenue synergies

Two types of synergy need to be distinguished: cost based and revenue based.

Cost-based synergies generally receive more attention since horizontal acquisitions are typically seen as a mechanism to reduce costs by acquiring overlapping businesses. Traditionally, such acquisitions have been considered an effective means of achieving economies of scale in manufacturing, as well as in R&D, administrative, logistics, and sales functions. For example, in a mature industry characterized by severe cost-reduction pressure, product standardization, and high advertising expenditures, an acquisition makes it possible to increase volume and standardization, and to spread fixed costs without adding substantial capacity to the industry.

Revenue-based synergy can be exploited if merging businesses develop new competences that allow them to command a price premium through higher innovation capabilities (product innovation, time-to-market, etc.) or to boost sales volume through increased market coverage (geographic market and product line extension).

An acquisition can be an effective means of getting access to skills or competences that are difficult or time consuming to develop in-house or that are not easily tradable through a market transaction. Successful technology acquisitions, indeed, can require command of the culture and processes behind that technology. An acquisition is a way of buying technical competences along with the corporate context, people, and mindset that have fostered their development.

For example, UK-based Getty Images, a provider of stock photos and film footage with 25 brick-and-mortar stores worldwide, wanted to make a quick technical and cultural transition to e-commerce. Thus in 1998, it acquired Seattle-based PhotoDisc, a distributor of royalty-free photos over the internet, which provided both technical expertise and a digital culture that Getty Images worked to infuse in to its other brands.

Although these two paths toward value creation have been identified as reasons behind the current wave of acquisitions, few empirical studies have investigated the extent to which merging companies exploit economies of scale and leverage their competences after acquisition.

Empirical setting

Method

To investigate post-acquisition consolidation practices (asset rationalization and competence transfer), we used data obtained through a large-scale international survey in Europe and North America. For this study, we identified more than 2,000 companies in the manufacturing sector that had acquired competing companies between 1988 and 1992. The 1988–92 period was chosen to exclude both recent deals where consolidation had not yet taken place and earlier acquisitions whose principal actors might have moved on. The companies represent a wide range of industries mainly in the UK, France, Germany, and the US.

The data are gathered from the responses of managers at 253 horizontally merged companies: 70 percent were cross-border, 30 percent domestic. Particularly well represented were chemicals (15 percent), foods (15 percent), and pharmaceuticals (12 percent).

Pre-acquisition features

Our data showed that acquisitions, in general, are undertaken by strong companies that target other strong companies. The acquirers' performance was in 58 percent of cases superior to and in 31 percent at least equivalent to the industry average. More than two-thirds of target businesses also performed as well as or better than their sector average, even if on the whole they were weaker in this area than their would-be parents. The same picture emerged when managers were asked about pre-acquisition resources. The targets were particularly strong *vis-à-vis* the competition in commercial and technical areas like R&D and manufacturing. The operational, managerial, and financial resources of the target businesses before acquisition, however, were significantly more limited than those of the acquirer.

Acquisition motives

Acquisitions were seen by sample respondents as an effective way for an acquirer to grow into new markets and to access complementary products, brands, and skills. Revenue-based synergies seem to drive many acquisitions. For example, 52 percent of the respondents recognized access to new brands or products as an important driver of the acquisition. The search for economies of scale seemed less important; 35 percent felt that this was a significant factor in functional areas (R&D, logistics, administrative). One-fifth of respondents also identified a defensive motive, namely pre-empting the target at the expense of a competitor, underlining the truth that strategic motives can be intertwined with tactical ones.

Post-acquisition behavior

Asset rationalization

Figure 1 shows the extent to which the merging company's assets (facilities and

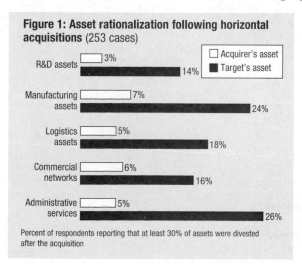

Figure 1: Asset rationalization following horizontal acquisitions (253 cases)

□ Acquirer's asset
■ Target's asset

R&D assets: 3% / 14%
Manufacturing assets: 7% / 24%
Logistics assets: 5% / 18%
Commercial networks: 6% / 16%
Administrative services: 5% / 26%

Percent of respondents reporting that at least 30% of assets were divested after the acquisition staff) in R&D, manufacturing, logistics, sales, and administration were significantly rationalized (divested) after acquisition.

Irrespective of function, significant rationalization measures affect only a small percentage of merged companies, suggesting that the search for cost-cutting and downsizing gains motivates only a limited number of horizontal acquisitions. This interpretation is consistent with the pre-acquisition objectives ranked by managers.

Furthermore, post-acquisition asset rationalization affects the acquiring and target businesses asymmetrically: the target's assets are three to five times more likely to be divested than the acquirer's assets. For example, 24 percent of the targets underwent rationalization of manufacturing assets that affected at least 30 percent of their staff or units, while only 7 percent of the acquiring companies faced an identical experience. Similarly, 26 percent of the targets underwent a rationalization of administrative services that affected at least 30 percent of staff or units, while only 5 percent of the acquirers underwent such rationalization. Manufacturing and administrative functions tend to be the most affected by post-acquisition asset divestiture, as their divestiture presents a lower risk of damaging innovative capabilities, commercial presence, or image.

The asymmetric rationalization of assets supports previous research findings of economic and behavioral motivations. From an economic standpoint, acquirers in the same industry as the target can recognize target inefficiencies due to their experience in managing similar lines of business. From a behavioral standpoint, acquiring managers are often more confident of their own capabilities than those of the target. Moreover, it is politically easier for the acquirer to impose divestiture measures on the target than on its own businesses.

Transfer of competences

Figure 2 shows the extent of competence transfer both to and from the target within nine competence categories.

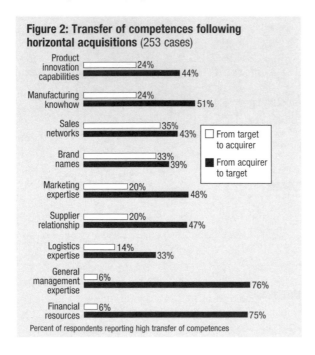

Figure 2: Transfer of competences following horizontal acquisitions (253 cases)

Product innovation capabilities — 24% / 44%
Manufacturing knowhow — 24% / 51%
Sales networks — 35% / 43%
Brand names — 33% / 39%
Marketing expertise — 20% / 48%
Supplier relationship — 20% / 47%
Logistics expertise — 14% / 33%
General management expertise — 6% / 76%
Financial resources — 6% / 75%

☐ From target to acquirer
■ From acquirer to target

Percent of respondents reporting high transfer of competences

A significant number of acquisitions are followed by a substantial transfer of competences, either from acquirer to target or target to acquirer. Acquirers transfer their competences into the target's businesses, or tap new competences from the target. This transfer occurs in technical (product innovation, manufacturing), commercial (sales networks, brand, marketing expertise), and operational areas (supplier relationship and logistics expertise). For example, 43 percent of respondents recognized that the acquirer's network was used to a great extent to distribute the target's products, and 35 percent of the respondents reported that the target's sales network was used to distribute the acquirer's products.

Although respondents ranked access to the target's competences as a more important motive than the transfer of their competences to the target, in reality the acquirer is more inclined to transfer its own competences than to use the target's competences. There may be several reasons for this: the need for the acquirer's competences to support the target's rationalization process; a stronger knowledge and control of the acquirer's competence transfer; difficulties in gaining access to the target's competences due to information asymmetry; the departure of key target people and other target disruptions; damaged competences in the post-acquisition process.

In sum, it seems that time, trust, credibility, and process skills are needed to gain valuable competences from the target. Only a few businesses, such as NationsBank (now merged with BankAmerica) or Cisco Systems, the US-based market leader in data networking, have developed the sophisticated post-acquisition management processes to retain and leverage the target's skills and people.

Drivers of performance

Figure 3 shows acquisition performance as assessed by respondents. Respondents were asked to assess the extent to which the acquisition improved the performance of both the target and the acquirer, using four performance measures: general performance; cost savings (cost-based synergies); innovation capabilities (revenue-based synergies); market coverage (revenue-based synergies).

More than half the respondents assessed the acquisition as either unsuccessful or moderately successful. Only 49 percent of respondents considered the acquisition as highly successful – consistent with those studies mentioned earlier suggesting that 50 to 70 percent of acquisitions fail to deliver expected benefits. In our research this result is even more striking as we focus on horizontal acquisitions, or those that should have higher potential for exploiting synergies due to business relatedness. This result suggests that, among horizontal acquisitions, there is a huge variation in acquisition performance. For example, 56 percent of respondents recognized that the acquisition increased the combined market share of the merging companies. However, 41 percent reported that the acquisition did not help in developing additional market share. Similarly, 53 percent of respondents recognized that the acquisition improved combined profitability, while 47 percent reported that the acquisition either did not improve, or even damaged, the profitability of the merging businesses.

From a cost-based synergy standpoint, acquisitions improved the cost position of the merging companies in fewer than half the cases. But from a capability and revenue-based synergies standpoint they provided key benefits, especially in market coverage. Acquisitions were reported to improve R&D capabilities in 49 percent of the cases, product quality in 47 percent of the cases, and time to market in 47

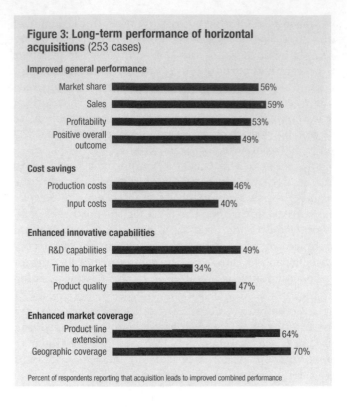

Figure 3: Long-term performance of horizontal acquisitions (253 cases)

Improved general performance

- Market share — 56%
- Sales — 59%
- Profitability — 53%
- Positive overall outcome — 49%

Cost savings

- Production costs — 46%
- Input costs — 40%

Enhanced innovative capabilities

- R&D capabilities — 49%
- Time to market — 34%
- Product quality — 47%

Enhanced market coverage

- Product line extension — 64%
- Geographic coverage — 70%

Percent of respondents reporting that acquisition leads to improved combined performance

percent of the cases. More importantly, 64 percent of respondents acknowledged that acquisitions broadened their product line, while 70 percent reported that they increased market coverage.

Performance implications

Several implications can be drawn from the above results.

Lesson 1. Managers should pay more attention to competence transfer and exploitation of revenue-based synergies.

Furthermore, rationalization measures send a clear signal to the market that the post-acquisition integration process is under way. However, the research shows that revenue-based synergies, which rest on a longer process of sharing or transferring competences into a new organizational context, also account for a significant part of acquisition performance.

Lesson 2. Rationalizing assets through an acquisition does not automatically lead to cost savings. There is some evidence that the acquirer is generally more effective in rationalizing its own assets than those of the target.

Interestingly, although acquisitions are rarely followed by a rationalization of the acquirer's assets, such a rationalization increases efficiency. This phenomenon may reflect several factors. It may be that the acquirer already understands and controls its own assets, while obtaining information on the target's assets is contingent on the willingness of the target's people to collaborate and share information. As a result, the acquirer may lack insight into the target's assets and force a rationalization that is not accepted by the target's people. Or it may be that the decision to divest acquirer assets is motivated by a strong economic rationale, while both economic and political motives may drive the divestiture of the target's assets (which would also explain why the target is three to five times more likely to be downsized than the acquirer).

Lesson 3. Excessive rationalization of the target's assets may damage the innovation and market capabilities of the merging businesses. As the target bears the brunt of rationalization measures, there is a risk of destroying valuable existing competences or impeding the development of new competences if the target is deprived of the organizational slack necessary to innovate and explore new markets.

The negative impact of excessive rationalization can be seen in mergers like those between Quaker Oats, the US cereals and sport drinks business, and Snapple, a US soft drinks company, or of two US banks, First Interstate/Wells Fargo. The acquisition of FI by Wells Fargo in 1996 led to a significant loss of FI clients. Wells Fargo chose to close FI's branch network (considered to be an overlap) and 75 percent of the top 500 FI executives left. In this example, not only were cost savings less than expected, but revenues declined as Wells Fargo tried to replace FI's "relational banking" with its own "transaction banking," switching FI clients from traditional branches to smaller mechanized branches in supermarkets. As a result, a significant proportion of FI clients moved to local competitors. FI was sold to Minneapolis-based Norwest in 1998.

Lesson 4. Cost savings can be achieved through transfer of competences, particularly to the target.

Thus, asset divestiture *per se* may not be the most effective way of reducing costs; transfer of competences can reduce costs by changing the way the target operates its businesses.

Lesson 5. Competence transfer both to and from targets improves the innovation and market capabilities of the merging businesses. Thus, acquisition can be an effective means to leverage competences.

The data indicate that the flow and effectiveness of competence transfer is bi-directional, suggesting that both target and acquirer competences can be exploited. For example, the merger of Nortel with Bay Networks in 1998 allows Nortel to share with Bay its competences in circuit technology, and gain access to the internet protocol (IP) technologies, routing technologies, and ins and outs of running IP networks that Bay possesses.

Lesson 6. The transfer of the target's competences into the acquirer's businesses is more challenging and less predictable than that of the acquirer's competences into the target's businesses.

Conclusion

A key result from our data is that the common practices of cost cutting and asset downsizing may not be the most effective way to increase acquisition performance. It is clear from the data that the target bears the brunt of rationalization measures, with a high risk of unrealized cost savings and competence destruction. Our data also show that acquisitions provide opportunities to leverage competences, as acquisitions are commonly followed by a transfer of competences both to and from the target. The transfer of competences is likely to enhance the capabilities of the merging companies, although the transfer from target to acquirer may not yield expected results.

Overall, our results show that both asset rationalization and competence transfer can improve acquisition performance. Managers should be mindful of the risk of damaging acquisition performance when rationalizing assets and transferring competences of the target company.

Summary

Two types of synergy – cost and revenue based – are typically used to justify takeovers. But to what extent do merging companies exploit economies of scale and leverage their competences after acquisition? In this article – based on a major study of more than 250 merged businesses – **Laurence Capron** compares pre-acquisition motives and post-acquisition behavior. Among the conclusions, she finds that cost cutting and asset downsizing may not be the most effective ways to increase performance; that managers need to understand the risks of damaging the takeover target; and that they should pay more attention to transferring competences and exploiting revenue synergies.

Suggested further reading

Capron, L. (1999) "The long-term performance of horizontal acquisitions," *Strategic Management Journal*, 20 (11, Nov.): 987–1018.

Capron, L. and Hulland, J. (1999) "Redeployment of brands, sales forces, and general marketing expertise following horizontal acquisitions: a resource-based view," *Journal of Marketing*, 63 (April): 41–54.

Haspeslagh, P. and Jemison, D. (1991) *Managing Acquisitions*, New York: The Free Press.

Learning to integrate

by Maurizio Zollo

Managerial practice and academic writings show that the post-acquisition integration phase is probably the single most important determinant of shareholder value creation (and equally of value destruction) in mergers and acquisitions. A recent Boston Consulting Group survey of CEOs of acquiring companies showed that poor performance in this regard was the leading reason for failure, followed by choosing the wrong acquisition candidate, then by overpaying for the target. Furthermore, part of the reason that acquirers fail to select the right candidates or pay a reasonable price lies in their lack of understanding of the complexities of the integration phase. Acquirers need to develop sufficient competence in managing the integration of the two organizational structures – conversion of information systems and retention and motivation of key employees, to name but two of the challenges – before they can, with reasonable confidence, start assessing how much value can be potentially extracted from the combined entities.

A specific ability to manage post-acquisition integration processes is therefore crucial to transforming the value-creation potential established during the search and screening phase (when the most attractive acquisition target is selected and pursued) into actual shareholder value. It also has important "retroactive" properties. It influences the success of practically all the earlier chapters of the acquisition process: preliminary screening, due diligence, financial evaluation and contractual negotiation. The contrary, however, does not hold true. While an expert integrator is likely to select better targets, do faster and more precise due diligence, and negotiate with better information, expertise in these prior phases does not necessarily translate into effective integration practices. On the contrary. Excessive pride in the sophistication of one's evaluation spreadsheets, or a strong conviction about success in a specific strategic move (e.g., entry into a specific country or industry segment), might actually undermine the level of attention required for design and execution of the integration phase.

But this begs the question: if the integration phase is so important for the success of the acquisition process, why is it that acquirers do not seem able to improve the odds of success by focussing on developing integration capabilities? On average, research shows that acquisitions do not create value for the acquirers' shareholders – a striking finding in itself, although less alarming when one remembers that alternative corporate growth strategies (joint ventures or internal solutions) have a similar or worse record of success. The puzzle is that most acquirers are not reporting improvements in the performance outcomes of acquisitions over time. A number of studies of acquisition performance, in a variety of industries, point toward the same result: the amount of acquisition experience does not seem to be a good performance predictor. In other words, the learning curve in M&A transactions seems to be pretty flat. Why is this? Are we talking about a collective learning disability? Or is it just a problem of identifying the right mechanisms to make learning happen?

Fortunately, empirical evidence suggests that the latter is the case. Selected acquirers seem to be able to develop effective integration practices and to produce consistent value enhancement with respect to their competitors.

Barriers to learning

GE Capital, a division of General Electric, NationsBank (now BankAmerica, the largest US retail bank), and Cisco Systems, a computer networking company, are excellent examples of companies that have delivered systematic value growth to their shareholders through the active pursuit of acquisitions. Other, equally experienced acquirers, however, did not have such fortune. Think of Hanson plc, the redesigned former conglomerate, or of soft drinks manufacturer PepsiCo's multiple acquisitions in the restaurant business, or of ICI and many of its chemical industry peers. Part of the difference lies in the inconsistencies between the value drivers in the type of acquisitions completed and the post-acquisition approaches selected. PepsiCo Restaurants, for example, kept on buying restaurant chains (Kentucky Fried Chicken, Pizza Hut, Taco Bell, and many minor ones) with huge potential cost savings from integration; but it failed to realize that value because its integration style prioritized accountability and autonomous decision making over coordination and collective improvements in overlapping functions.

However, adopting the wrong approach to post-acquisition integration with respect to value-creation drivers (cost efficiencies, revenue enhancements, standalone restructuring, innovation, and so on) need not be a disaster in itself. The problem is that acquirers typically have a hard time recognizing their mistakes as such, and then identifying and implementing the necessary changes. *Errare humanum est, perseverare diabolicum* (mistakes are human, the devil lies in persevering with them).

The root cause of this worrying phenomenon lies in a set of characteristics of the organizational task itself. Understanding the nature of these barriers to collective learning is the first step toward installing a continuous improvement system that would generate and help develop a post-acquisition integration capability. Compare acquisitions with most of the other administrative and production processes occurring on a more or less regular basis within any business organization (think of the manufacturing function, or the customer order-handling systems, the selection of new staff, the purchasing of raw materials, etc.). Some differences are obvious: acquisitions are much more infrequent events, and they typically come with a much higher degree of variety. "No acquisition is like another" seems to be a mantra that many managers, facing the complexity of the challenge, utter to themselves and to anyone else who asks them why the results fail to match expectations. Besides being true of any organizational process, these are not the only relevant dimensions. Acquisitions differ from other administrative and operational processes because they are fundamentally ambiguous in the causal links between decisions made to manage them, the actions taken to implement those decisions, and, most importantly, the performance outcomes that result from completion.

Complexity at its best

On the day that Intel, the world's biggest semiconductor manufacturer, kicked off the integration process of the semiconductors division of Digital, 6,000 different "deliverables" were due to be executed by hundreds of employees in dozens of different countries. And that was only the start! The integration process went on for about six months, involving every single staff and line function in each location where the two companies were doing business. Most of what had to be done by all these people was not part of their daily routines and had to be figured out more or less spontaneously. Now, how easy is it for Intel, in spite of massive preparation and detailed planning (computer supported decision making and project management, integration manuals for most functions, etc.), to distinguish correct decisions from bad ones, and identify those that were good but poorly implemented from those that were wrong to start with? The reason that it is extremely complex to understand the performance implications of post-acquisition processes goes beyond the sheer number and the simultaneity of subtasks that make up the integration phase. The biggest problem is that all these tasks are strongly interdependent on each other for their success. No matter how effective the IT people are in preparing for conversion of the information systems, all will go to waste if the human resources department fails to handle the training processes in an equally effective manner (and vice versa). No matter how well communication with the key customers of the acquired company has been handled, they will still run away *en masse* if the sales reps are not effectively retained and motivated (and vice versa).

Finally, add to the picture the fact that even the most sophisticated acquirers have a really hard time developing measures and tracking the performance of their integration processes, and you have a good sense of why acquirers not only often fail in managing acquisitions, but do not learn as well as one might expect. Note that standard accounting measures, even when available (typically they are not after a full integration of the acquired unit), do not suffice. The acquirer has to do much more in order to understand how well it did in its integration processes. It has to create metrics to assess the performance of the integration in each function of the value chain, from purchasing to marketing and sales, from the conversion of information systems to the integration of the supply and distribution chain, from the selection, retention, and motivation of human resources to the restructuring and reorganization of new product development as well as manufacturing or back-office processes. In a recent study of US bank acquirers, I found that only about 40 percent had developed specific performance measures for the systems-conversion process, in spite of the obvious importance of this task to the success of any bank merger.

Learning by doing?

So what to do to improve the chances that acquiring companies develop specific capabilities in the management of integration processes? For one thing, we should be clear that acquisition experience, in itself, is not enough. Not only that, but under certain conditions, it might even hurt! The results of two recent studies, including the largest one to date on post-acquisition integration and capability-building processes, show that experience curves are U-shaped; that is, that the performance declines for the first few acquisitions (eight or nine of them) before it starts improving. Furthermore, the more diverse acquisitions have been, the more serious the problem: acquirers tend to apply to the current acquisition lessons learned in contexts that appear superficially similar but are inherently different.

The second point is that the development of an organizational capability in such a complex learning environment requires a specific investment in learning activities. The acquiring company has to dedicate a significant amount of time, money, and managerial attention to the crucial task of extracting the appropriate lessons from earlier acquisition experiences. This means essentially two things: one is to articulate the knowledge that all the people involved in previous integration processes have gained by being exposed and involved in the decision and/or execution of all those tasks. Given their interdependence, only a collective effort to share individual experiences in debriefing sessions can achieve the expected result: understand what worked, what did not work and, most importantly, why. The second key learning practice consists in codifying the knowledge accumulated in people's minds about the integration processes completed and performance outcomes obtained by creating and constantly updating tools specific to the management of the acquisition process.

The most obvious tools, of course, are the performance-measurement systems, but this is not the entire story. Sophisticated acquirers develop a whole battery of support tools for each of the phases of the acquisition process, and specific to each of the key functions on which the success of the acquisition depends. In the search and screening phase, they develop databases of all the potential acquisition targets with preliminary evaluations and strategic assessments, which can be discussed with top management in order to clarify the strategic approach and speed up internal decision making if the acquisition opportunity materializes. In the deal-making phase, acquirers can go beyond the refinement of evaluation spreadsheets and due diligence checklists, and develop a strategically meaningful due diligence practice with dedicated coordinators, project-management software, and manuals for each of the key functional teams. It is worth noting that manuals are not just larger versions of checklists. They are qualitatively different in that, if well compiled and updated, they explain what should be done under different contingencies and offer the rationale for these guidelines and principles.

These tools play a role of crucial importance in the post-acquisition integration phase. GE Capital, NationsBank, Cisco Systems, Intel, and other acquirers that consistently create value in their acquisitive growth have in common a systematic approach to integration. Not only do they have people specialized in coordinating the integration phase, but they dedicate time and resources to developing tools specific to the value-creation logic they pursue. Specialization by function allows each team to be responsible not only for managing their portion of the integration process, but also for extracting the valuable lessons from each experience made.

A continual process

Finally, but importantly, one cannot over emphasize the role played by this knowledge-codification activity in the development of a post-acquisition integration practice. The advantage of investing in the creation and development of all these acquisition-specific tools goes well beyond the use that acquirers make of them in their decision making, coordination, and execution activities.

The process itself, through which these tools are created and updated, is a learning mechanism. In order to write a systems-conversion manual, the IT people responsible for this particular task will have to strive to understand what makes sense to do, under what conditions, and why. While they do that, they essentially clarify for themselves the nature of those linkages between decisions, actions, and performance outcomes, which, as we saw above, are typically blurred due to the complexity of the process itself and the lack of performance-monitoring systems. Often without realizing it, a collective competence in handling the integration phase emerges from the process of writing the manuals, developing the software, and updating them with the use of the new experiential evidence.

Learning to integrate is essentially a continual process through which acquirers first formulate rough hypotheses of what might work under what conditions, and then systematically use the lessons learned from each acquisition experience to test those hypotheses, reformulate them, and develop new, more fine-grained ones. This is neither a simple nor a cheap process. It requires significant investments in time, mental efforts, and technology. The returns on these learning investments, nevertheless, can be extremely high, and are likely to rise with the increasing bets being made on M&A-based corporate development and the accompanying levels of complexity in the post-acquisition phase.

The more you buy, and the more you intend to integrate, the harder you need to work in learning from the mistakes, as well as the successes, in your own shopping activity.

Summary

Learning to integrate two companies should be a continual process, says **Maurizio Zollo**, in which the acquirer works from a rough blueprint, then tests, reshapes, and fine-tunes it by applying lessons from earlier experience. The process is neither simple nor cheap, requiring significant investment in time, mental effort, and technology. The author argues that among other things success comes from understanding the interdependence of the many different integration tasks, setting appropriate performance metrics, and recognizing that post-acquisition integration is an organizational capability in itself. The good news is that the returns can be high, as long as the acquiring firm makes a serious effort to articulate and codify its own experience, and create and develop acquisition-specific tools.

Suggested further reading

Singh, H. and Zollo, M. (1998) "The impact of knowledge codification, experience trajectories and integration strategies on the performance of corporate acquisitions," *Academy of Management Best Papers Proceedings*.

Zollo, M. and Winter, S. (1999) "From organizational routines to dynamic capabilities," Working paper, R. Jones Center of the Wharton School, and INSEAD R&D (99/42/SM).

STRATEGY AND SHAREHOLDER VALUE/GOVERNANCE

8

Contributors

Colin Mayer is Peter Moores Professor of Management Studies at Oxford University's Saïd Business School and fellow of Wadham College. He focusses on corporate finance, corporate governance, corporate taxation, and the regulation of financial institutions.

Robert E. Quinn is Margaret Tracey Collegiate Professor of Organizational Behavior and Human Resource Management at University of Michigan Business School and a fellow of the World Business Academy. Among other issues he focusses on organizational change, organizational effectiveness, leadership paradox and intimacy.

Anjan V. Thakor is Edward J. Frey Professor of Banking and Finance at University of Michigan Business School.

Peter Johnson is a fellow of Exeter College, Oxford University and university lecturer in management studies (new business development). His focus is on development of a unified capital appraisal and resource allocation model; a framework for value-added measure and analysis.

Jeff DeGraff is a member of the faculty at University of Michigan Business School. Among other issues, he focusses on change and innovation leadership, creative problem solving and core competency development.

Contents

Introduction

Shareholder value and corporate governance are relatively recent "inventions" but no manager can afford to ignore either in strategy formulation. Three aspects are considered here. The first is the link between strategy and ownership systems – so-called "insider" models build commitment and trust, "outsider" models tend to be more flexible in the face of changing technologies and erratic markets. Second, the broad question of how managers discover the key drivers in a business that creates sustained shareholder value. Finally, the specific tools that managers can use from the familiar Economic Value Added (EVA) model to the Resource Margin Accounting alternative proposed here.

Corporate governance is relevant

by Colin Mayer

Corporate governance is "a question of performance accountability," according to a recent book in which the subject was defined. It is, in essence, about the protection of shareholders from self-interested managers.

A more recent view sees governance as concerned with conflicts between minority and majority shareholders – affording the former protection from the latter – rather than between shareholders and managers.

The performance accountability interpretation is particularly relevant to the UK and the US, where shareholders are dispersed and have little direct control over management. The shareholder protection debate is more relevant to Continental Europe or East Asia. In these economies there are large shareholders who can exert direct control over management, but potentially at the expense of minority shareholders.

In neither case does corporate governance appear to have anything to do with corporate strategy.

To many people, corporate governance conjures up images of schools – rules, monitors, detention, and punishment. It has no relevance to the things that matter: getting to the top of the class, winning games, and making friends. Consequently, some people regard it as largely irrelevant.

I will argue here that corporate governance is actually intimately related to strategy. It is therefore central to achieving good performance as well as avoiding the abuse of investors. Some of the recent mergers between companies from different corporate governance backgrounds illustrate this well – the merger of Chrysler of the US with Daimler-Benz of Germany into a powerful automobile manufacturing conglomerate and of Bankers Trust of the US with Deutsche Bank of Germany are two cases in point.

The relevance of governance for strategy is immediately evident when one compares the ownership of companies in different countries. The traditional view of the company as described in finance textbooks is that it is actively traded on stock markets by a large number of individual and institutional shareholders. Ownership is dispersed in the sense that there are few dominant shareholders in any one company. While this may be an accurate description of large companies in the UK and US, it is by no means the normal pattern. In many countries, ownership is quite different.

Beyond the UK and US, relatively few companies are traded on stock markets. Many of even the largest are private. Where companies are traded on stock markets, ownership is far more concentrated than it is in the UK and US.

Typically, around 80 percent of the largest listed companies in France and Germany have a single shareholder owning more than 25 percent of shares. In the UK, only 16 percent of companies have such large single shareholders.

The concentrated shareholdings in continental Europe are associated with two groups of investors: families and other companies. Large family holdings are much more prevalent on the Continent than they are in the UK and US.

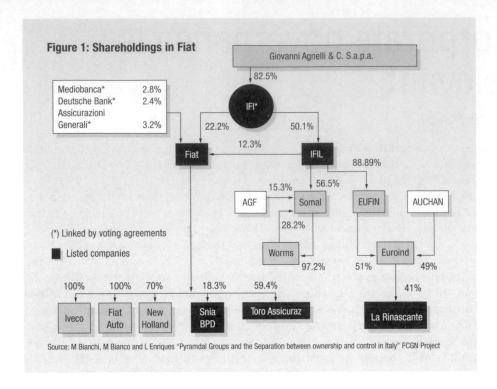

Figure 1: Shareholdings in Fiat

Source: M Bianchi, M Bianco and L Enriques "Pyramdal Groups and the Separation between ownership and control in Italy" FCGN Project

Holdings by companies are complex. They sometimes take the form of pyramids in which companies have controlling shareholdings of other companies lower down in pyramids. In other cases, there are cross-shareholdings or complex webs of holdings.

Continental complexities

The illustration of Fiat in Figure 1 exemplifies the complexities that are commonplace on the Continent. It shows:

- direct holdings of 22 percent by a listed company IFI, controlled by Giovanni Agnelli;
- indirect holdings of a further 12 percent via IFIL, an Agnelli family holding, which is in turn controlled by IFI;
- a further 8 percent held by financial institutions that have voting pacts with IFI;
- cross-shareholdings between companies controlled by IFIL;
- subsidiaries of Fiat that themselves are listed on the Italian stock exchange.

Inter-corporate holdings create a system of "insider ownership" by which companies and financial institutions have controlling shareholdings in each other (Figure 2). There are outside shareholders and, as the Fiat case illustrates, several companies in corporate groupings are frequently quoted. But outside shareholders are rarely able to exert control.

Several instruments are used to concentrate control among insiders. In some countries, dual-class shares are used. These involve different classes of shareholders having different voting rights. Insiders hold shares with a high ratio of voting to cash-flow rights. Outsiders hold shares with equal voting and cash-flow rights. In

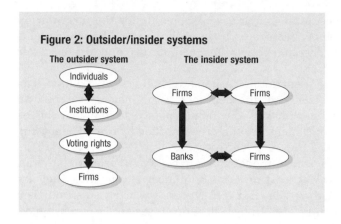

Figure 2: Outsider/insider systems

some countries (such as Germany and Italy), pyramid structures are commonplace. In these, owners at the top of pyramids can exert control at comparatively low cost over companies lower down in the pyramid.

In contrast, the UK and US are "outsider ownership" systems. Dual-class shares and pyramids are comparatively rare. There are few cross-shareholdings and control is dispersed among a large number of outside investors. In the US, until comparatively recently a high proportion of these outside investors were individuals.

But increasingly in both countries, shares are now held through financial institutions, pension funds, life assurance companies, and mutual funds. In total, these institutions hold a large proportion of corporate equity in both countries. Individually, no one institution in general holds a substantial fraction of the shares of a company. That is why, as noted above, ownership is much more dispersed in the UK and US than on the Continent.

The question that this raises is what is the significance of these differences in corporate ownership. Clearly, they are associated with the corporate governance issues described at the beginning. Insider systems have little difficulty in monitoring and controlling management. Large shareholders are well informed and in a position to exercise control where necessary. But minority investors are at risk of abuse from large shareholders. The corporate governance issue of insider systems is therefore protection of minority investors.

In outsider systems, dispersed owners have little incentive to engage in active monitoring and have little power to discipline bad management. The problem of corporate governance in outsider systems is performance accountability of management. Outsider systems emphasize transparency of information and protection of minority investors.

But the differences go beyond just corporate governance. They extend to relations between companies and between investors and companies. Insider systems promote close relations between companies and between investors and companies. There are large identifiable blocks of shares, attributable to particular investors. Responsibility for formulation and implementation of policy can be identified with the controlling shareholders.

Outsider and insider systems

In outsider systems, ownership and control are dispersed among a large number of anonymous shareholders. No one shareholder can be held accountable for the valuation of particular policies. Management is responsible for the formulation and implementation of strategies, but this is ultimately dictated by what yields greatest shareholder value. The market values companies and drives their strategies.

In insider systems, there are identifiable large shareholders with whom it is possible to establish relations. The large shareholders of the insider systems can offer commitments to other parties in a way in which dispersed shareholders of the outsider systems cannot. Insider systems are therefore marked by commitment and trust. Outsider systems are not.

Put in these terms, insider systems appear unequivocally superior to outsider systems. That might explain why at least in terms of number of countries, they are far more prevalent than outsider systems. But if they were so clearly superior, then one would expect to observe nothing else. In fact, in terms of economic performance, the outsider systems of the UK and US appear to be clearly dominating the insider systems of the Continent and the Far East. There must be an offsetting benefit to outsider systems.

Anonymity is the advantage as well as the deficiency of control by markets. The fact that one cannot have relations with the anonymous means that markets are not prone to the special interests and pleading of insider systems. Policy formulation and implementation are simply determined by shareholder value. This avoids all other considerations that may sway large shareholders, namely their private interests. Set against the commitment and trust of the insider systems is the flexibility of the outsider systems to implement value-maximizing policies.

Different systems therefore have different merits and deficiencies. Insider systems have advantages where sustaining relations with other parties through commitment and trust is important. Outsider systems dominate where flexibility to be able to implement the best strategy at any point in time is more significant.

Takeovers illustrate the difference between the two systems. Takeover activity is high in both the UK and US. In addition, hostile takeover activity is commonplace. Typically in the UK there are around 40 hostile takeovers each year. In Germany there were a total of three hostile takeovers in the whole of the post-Second World War period until the mid-1990s. There has been discussion about the emergence of hostile takeovers in Continental Europe and in Japan. In some countries, for example France, there has been a recent spate of activity.

In fact, there always has been an active market for corporate control on the Continent. However, it typically differs significantly in form from that in the UK and US. In the latter two countries, takeovers are associated with tender offers in which acquiring companies simply tender for the shares of targets. In the insider systems, it is frequently impossible simply to acquire through a tender offer. The reason is that a majority or large share block is held by a single investor.

Thus while there are markets in corporate control in both outsider and insider systems, there is an important distinction. In the insider system, changes in control occur only with the consent of an identifiable shareholder. In the outsider system, there is no single party who can be held accountable for the change in control. Value-enhancing changes in control in the outsider system can therefore take place behind the veil of the market in outsider but not insider systems.

This illustrates the merits and deficiencies of both systems. The problem with the insider system is that dominant investors determine the outcome of bids. They are prone to private interests, side payments, and so on. Changes may not therefore occur even where there are benefits to investors overall, simply because they are not in the interests of the dominant shareholders.

This is not a problem with the outsider systems, where outcomes are determined purely on shareholder value grounds. On the other hand, the interests of other stakeholders (employees, suppliers, purchasers) who do not hold equity in the company are not protected. In the insider system, the reputation of the large shareholder is at stake. In the outsider system, stakeholders do not have even this assurance.

The significance of trust and commitment in relation to flexibility differs across activities. In much of manufacturing, relations with networks of suppliers and purchasers are commonplace. Component suppliers frequently make investments that are dedicated to particular producers. They will not make these investments unless they have some assurance of continuity of a market for their products from the producers. But such assurances come at the expense of the ability of the producer to be able to innovate at low cost.

This suggests that different systems will be suited to different types of activity. Insider systems will be advantageous for the promotion of activities that rely on high levels of commitment and trust. Outsider systems will benefit activities requiring flexibility in the face of new technologies and markets.

The balance of advantage of different systems changes over time. Currently, we are going through technological advances that make the flexibility of the outsider system advantageous. We went through similar periods during the industrial revolution in the eighteenth and nineteenth centuries. Canals and railways in the UK and US were financed largely through the markets. At other times, there are benefits from developing long-term, stable relations that are characteristic of the insider systems. What are perceived to be the current advantages of the outsider system may not therefore persist indefinitely.

Even within particular systems there is considerable variety of structures. While most large companies in the UK are listed on the stock market, around one-third of the largest 1,000 companies are private. There have been more than 200 new companies coming to the UK stock market per annum over the last few years. But, at the same time, several prominent companies have opted to go private; for these companies, the drawbacks of control by outside investors outweigh the benefits of access to equity sources of funding. Large private companies tend to be concentrated in relatively low-technology sectors – retailing, wholesaling, food, drink, printing, publishing – and to grow significantly less through acquisition than their stock-market-listed counterparts. Ownership structures are therefore critically related to which markets companies operate in and how they choose to grow.

Summary

Corporate governance is central to achieving good performance and to avoiding the abuse of minority investors, says **Colin Mayer**. Its relevance to strategy is evident when one compares ownership patterns in different countries. The UK and US are characterized by "outsider ownership" systems where class shares and pyramids are comparatively rare. In much of continental Europe and Asia, by contrast, the system of "insider ownership" enables companies and financial institutions to have controlling shareholdings in each other. There are advantages and disadvantages to both. Insider systems are marked by commitment and trust. Outsider systems will benefit activities requiring flexibility in the face of new technologies and markets.

Suggested further reading

Allen, F. (1993) "Stock markets and resource allocation," in Mayer, C. and Vives, X. (eds) *Capital Markets Intermediation*, Cambridge: Cambridge University Press.

Carlin, W. and Mayer, C. (forthcoming) "How do financial systems affect economic performance?" in Vives, X. (ed.) *Corporate Governance: Theoretical and Empirical Perspectives*, Cambridge: Cambridge University Press.

Creating sustained shareholder value – and dispelling some myths

by Anjan V. Thakor, Jeff DeGraff and Robert Quinn

One of the most frequently used terms in business today is "shareholder value." The "equity culture" wildfire is spreading rapidly from the US to the rest of the world. There are many reasons that CEOs are worshiping at the altar of shareholder value – an important one is corporate control pressures.

During the 1980s and 1990s, corporate control contests in the US often resulted in removal of CEOs whose companies failed to deliver adequate shareholder value. One striking example was the replacement of Ron Miller by Michael Eisner as chairman of the Walt Disney Company in 1984. This was a consequence of the hostile takeover attempts provoked by Disney's relatively mediocre performance on shareholder value.

Interestingly, a year prior to these takeover attempts, Tom Peters and Robert Waterman, in their widely read book *In Search of Excellence*, had rated Walt Disney as one of their 14 "excellent companies."

A second important reason for the focus on shareholder value is executive compensation. Large institutional investors are increasingly influencing corporate policies. They are creating a heightened awareness of the role of compensation-based incentives in focussing executive efforts on creating shareholder value. Companies are rewarding senior executives with shares and with options on these shares. Thus, share price is now critical for most senior executives.

Share prices, of course, often show significant unanticipated volatility over time. They are driven by a host of factors, many of which are beyond the control of the company's management. Consequently, the "scorecard" of many companies focusses on the sustained creation of shareholder value. Such orientation provides a long-term view of shareholder value.

Measurements

There are various ways of measuring the long-term perspective. One is to look at total annual shareholder returns. This figure is calculated by taking share price appreciation, adding dividends paid during the year, divided by the share price at the beginning of the year. This process is done over many years. The goal of using total annual shareholder returns is to surpass the performance of a "benchmark portfolio." The benchmark portfolio can be the whole stock market, the industry to which the company belongs, or a subset of companies within the industry. Another approach to assessing long-term value is to look at the average Market Value Added (MVA) per year over a five- or ten-year time horizon. MVA is defined as the difference between the company's market and book values at a given point in time. If book value is the capital invested in the company by its shareholders and bondholders, and market value is the market's assessment of what this invested capital is truly worth, then MVA measures how much net value has been created for the owners of the company, the shareholders. Companies that have created the most MVA for their shareholders include retailer Wal-Mart, General Electric, Microsoft, and Coca-Cola. In fact, Coca-Cola had the highest MVA (almost $125bn) at the end of 1996.

How do companies achieve sustained creation of shareholder value? The answer lies in strategy. We believe that strategy is simply determining how the company will create shareholder value. This requires defining the scope of permissible activities and determining the allocation of resources to these activities. A security analyst once remarked: "To understand a company's strategy, I don't read what the CEO says. I look at where the company is allocating resources." If the right strategy is chosen, and then properly executed, sustained shareholder value should follow, as long as the strategy is adapted to changing environmental conditions.

The power of successful strategies is seen in companies that have created spectacular value for their shareholders. What helped turn the Walt Disney Company around was a new strategy. Michael Eisner, new chief executive of the giant entertainment enterprise, focussed the company on animated films. All of Disney's other business lines, such as theme parks, consumer products, real estate, etc., have since fed off the success of the company in creating new films.

In other companies, other strategies are necessary. Wal-Mart, for example, has focussed on size expansion and constant improvement in asset productivity. This focus has been driven by the nature of the retailing industry, where scale economies are significant and considerable assets are deployed, so that a small improvement in per-unit asset productivity can have a large overall effect on value.

How do companies develop winning strategies? The secret lies in discovering the key value drivers in the business, and then tying the strategy to those value drivers. Eisner recognized that the key value driver for Disney was its creative output. Making animated films was a tangible manifestation of that creative output. Sam Walton, founder of Wal-Mart, recognized that the key value driver in the retailing business was how fast you turned over your inventories, and not gross margins. In a brutally competitive industry, where competing companies exhibit little differentiation from each other in customer and vendor selection, it is difficult to outperform your rivals on gross margin. This is why Wal-Mart has focussed so much on its asset turnover. Its entire business design, including its management information system and its relationship with suppliers, is predicated on driving improvements in asset turnover. It is on this dimension that Wal-Mart has outperformed its rivals.

Simply put, to create sustained shareholder value, you need the right strategy, and to craft the right strategy, you need to discover the key value drivers in your business. This, of course, is not easy, as we tend to be blinded by a number of myths.

The myths of shareholder value creation

Numerous myths about shareholder value cloud people's thinking. Clouded thinking results in misallocation of resources and dissipation of value. What are some of the popular myths?

Myth number one

The way to create shareholder value is to have a single-minded focus on the "bottom line." This often means managing the company constantly to meet or exceed stock-market expectations about a company's earnings per share (EPS) or some other bottom-line measure of financial performance.

Myth number two

There are unavoidable tensions between the interests of stakeholders. Consequently, maximizing the value to shareholders will involve subordinating and sacrificing the interests of other stakeholders, like employees and customers.

Myth number three

Giving every employee a share of stock is a sure way to motivate employees to maximize shareholder value.

Myth number four

The stock market is myopic and cares only about short-term earnings.

In Table 1, we summarize how these myths can steer corporate behavior away from the sustained creation of shareholder value.

This table outlines how companies guided by myths make decisions that can destroy shareholder value. In short, strategies become misguided. For example, in the 1980s, virtually every major airline, guided by the fiercely competitive nature of the industry and the usual obsession with short-term financial performance, designed its strategy to become a low-cost provider of air transportation. The

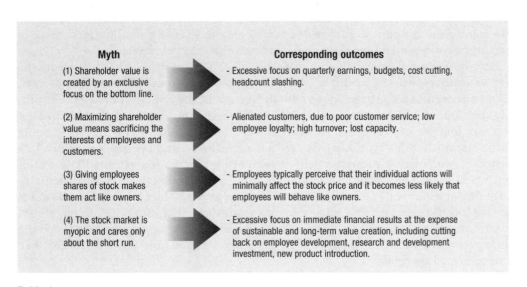

Table 1

resulting business design was driven by the fundamental assumption that most air travelers wanted just to get from point A to point B at the lowest possible cost. Customer service was cut to the bone.

By contrast, British Airways, under its then chief executive Sir Colin Marshall, crafted a strategy that focussed on providing the customer with a truly satisfying travel experience. Many dimensions of customer service, including the quality of the food and wine served on board, were enhanced, rather than sacrificed. British Airways' approach was truly product differentiation by strategic design at its best. It allowed the airline to create wider margins and outperform rivals financially. It is somewhat ironic that it has recently been criticized for its customer service while its share price has underperformed in the market, just as the Walt Disney Company has recently been criticized for lacking a clear strategy and having a weak board of directors.

Slow death

The question that should now be asked is why is it that a singular focus on the bottom line leads companies astray and fails to create sustained shareholder value? Perhaps the most intriguing of the many reasons is that companies monitor operational performance to determine whether they are creating value by keeping an eye on accounting measures of performance. Thus performance targets are typically set in accounting terms – EPS or operating project targets, sales growth targets, and revenue targets. The problem is that accounting has become a tool to disguise the slow death of a company. Because of the considerable flexibility that companies have in reporting accounting numbers, reported results are often not an accurate indicator of performance in that period.

Companies typically "smooth" reported numbers relative to actual results. This smoothing hides poor performance during hard times by adding to "reserves" during times of relative prosperity. A company that has accumulated substantial reserves due to past success, but is now in a slow death, can keep reporting relatively high earnings by drawing down on its reserves, even though actual profits are spiraling downward.

This disguising through accounting manipulations is possible to a greater extent in Europe than in the US. This was clearly seen in the substantial new information that was revealed about DaimlerBenz's financial condition when it decided to list on the New York Stock Exchange. However, the problem is increasing in the US as well. For example, Arthur Levitt, Jr., Chairman of the Securities and Exchange Commission (SEC), was quoted in the *CPA Journal* in December 1998 as saying:

Too many corporate managers, auditors, and analysts are participants in a game of nods and winks. In the zeal to satisfy consensus earnings estimates and project a smooth earnings path, wishful thinking may be winning the day over faithful representation.

A four-quadrant approach to value creation

To avoid the common myths of shareholder value and achieve sustained value creation, companies need to understand how value-driver analysis, strategy, leadership, and resource allocation can be integrated constructively, so that the truth behind the four myths can be extracted.

One way is to use the Four-Quadrant Value Propositions (FQVP) hypothesis

Figure 1: Value propositions across four quadrants

Collaborate	Create
Capability - Focusses on developing abilities - Creates a sustainable advantage	*Innovation* - Focusses on innovation in products, processes and services - Creates growth and industry leadership
Efficiency - Focusses on improving process efficiency - Creates better products more cheaply	*Market awareness* - Focusses on competitive advantage through agility and market awareness and speed - Creates asset productivity and shareholder value
Control	**Compete**

outlined in Figure 1. This is derived from the Wholonics Model, a total-value approach by the authors to developing integrated capabilities at all levels: strategic, organizational and individual. We focus on the FQVP aspect of the model here because it is the most relevant for the alignment between strategy and leadership that we want to explore.

The FQVP hypothesis asserts that there are four quadrants in which any organization creates value. Typically trade-offs are involved, so that an organization must choose its focus and resource allocation in each quadrant. Depending on its strategy, each organization will be positioned differently across these four quadrants. The central insight of the model is that this positioning will determine everything that has value-creation implications for the organization – resource allocation, performance metrics, organization culture, compensation contracts, and leadership style. This, in turn, means that all of these must be consistent with each other and with the overall strategy.

In using this model, one begins with an identification of the key value drivers in the business. These then help to define the strategy.

By way of illustration, consider two organizations: a power plant and an entertainment company like Walt Disney. The key value driver for the power plant is cost efficiency, which is driven by operating scale. Market awareness and innovation are relatively less important. Capability in employees is important, but can be readily purchased in the labor market. Thus, the strategy for the power company is to have large, efficient plants that focus on diminishing reliance on labor. By contrast, the entertainment company's success is driven by its product innovation, which means that its key value driver is its creativity. Therefore, the strategy for the entertainment company is to focus on hiring the most creative people in the industry and providing ample opportunities for their creative output to be manifested in the company's products and services. The resulting strategic value propositions for these two companies are as in Figure 2.

As the two figures show, efficiency is the principal focus for the power plant, although it cannot entirely ignore the other quadrants. By contrast, for the entertainment company, building individual capabilities and fostering innovation are just as important as the creative output of its employees, although this company cannot be oblivious to efficiency and market pressures.

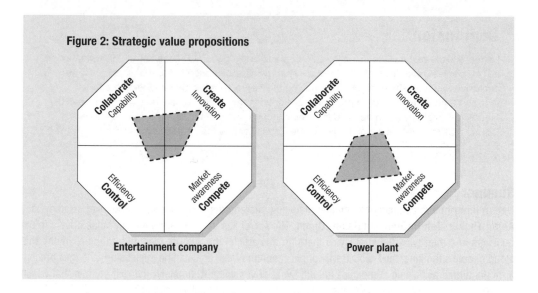

Figure 2: Strategic value propositions

Entertainment company

Power plant

These two organizations should look very different on a number of dimensions. First, the power plant performance measures will include cost productivity and power generation reliability. Conversely, the entertainment company metrics will include new product introductions, value of brand equity, employee turnover, revenue and margin growth, economic value added, etc. Second, the power plant will allocate most of its resources to projects that lower per-unit costs, via fuller capacity utilization, scale augmentation, equipment replacement, renegotiation of terms with vendors, etc. However, the entertainment company will allocate most of its resources to producing new shows or movies and leveraging the creative output of these shows or movies across other products.

These two companies will also differ in organization design and leadership style. The power plant, with its efficiency focus, will be hierarchical and will benefit from a command-and-control, top-down leadership style. The entertainment company will be flatter and more decentralized, with less of a command-and-control leadership style.

Each company, with the proper alignment between its value drivers, strategy, resource allocation, performance metrics, organization design, and culture, can create significant value for its shareholders. But each will do so in different ways.

Finally, in determining a strategy, companies should understand that what is a shareholder value myth for one company may be the appropriate guiding light for another.

For example, the power plant should focus on the bottom line and immediate results. That is, myth number one – "shareholder value is created by an exclusive focus on the bottom line" – and myth number four – "the stock market is myopic and cares only about the short run" – are not myths for the power plant.

But if the entertainment company were to use these myths as its guiding principles, and cut back on the resources it devoted to product innovation and people/capability development, it would be in serious trouble.

Conclusion

Ultimately, the real myth is that it is appropriate to apply generalizations about value creation to all companies, regardless of how they are strategically positioned in the four quadrants. An exclusive focus on shareholder value may be the key to creating shareholder value for a company like Wal-Mart that is primarily positioned in the Market Awareness quadrant seen in Figure 1. It might prove to be the death knell, though, for an internet start-up or one like Walt Disney that may be positioned largely in the Capability and Innovation quadrants of the same figure.

Summary

Determining how a company can create sustained shareholder value lies at the heart of strategy, say **Anjan Thakor**, **Jeff DeGraff** and **Robert Quinn**. The secret lies in discovering the key value drivers in the business and then tying the strategy to them. In this article, the authors identify a range of myths that cloud people's thinking; they explain why pure accounting measures can be misleading; and they present a model aimed at helping companies identify what drives value. Ultimately, the real myth is that which suggests one can generalize in the application of value creation to all companies.

Beyond EVA: Resource Margin Accounting

by Peter Johnson

Just before the market debut of Orange, the mobile phone company, an article appeared in the *Financial Times* telling investors to forget price–earnings ratios and to learn to love DCF (discounted cash flow) instead. The article brought a smile to my face, because I was busy telling my MBA students at the time to forget discounted cash flow and to embrace something that I then called VAPM (the Value-Added Pricing Model), and that is now described as Resource Margin Accounting (RMA).

The *FT* article about Orange demonstrated the difficulties with discounted cash flow valuation. A series of projections were made from 1995 to 2005 for profit and cash flow. The flows arising before 2005 were valued at £900m, and those arising after 2005 at £1800m using a 14 percent discount rate. In other words two-thirds of the value was associated with events more than ten years away in a business characterized by rapid development of technology and global restructuring. It is hard to place much confidence in such estimates.

It is easy to list some of the difficulties associated with any crystal ball view of valuation: predicting events that are far away; deciding over which time horizon to evaluate the performance of the business; choosing appropriate discount rates and terminal values. Besides these inherent difficulties, other subtler assumptions are often made. It is usually assumed, for example, that ownership of the company is constant, which may well not be the case. DCF analysis also often overlooks the strategic degrees of freedom created by good performance, and the constraints imposed by short-term disappointments.

More sophisticated modelers attempt to address some of these weaknesses by blitzing us with myriad scenarios. The trouble is that when a business is heading south at a fast pace, "management by auto-pilot" does nothing to correct the situation. Real options may be grafted on to other decision-making tools, but who in practice will do anything but cherry pick the options that are most expedient? If these difficulties were not enough, how are we to incorporate the long-term effects of government policy and other macro factors?

Eugene Fama and Kenneth French, two distinguished financial economists, summed up the current state of play as follows:

> Project valuation is central to the success of any company. Our message is that the task is beset with massive uncertainty. The question then is whether there is an approach that values projects with less error than its competitors. Is the net-present-value approach, advocated with zeal by textbooks, typically more accurate than a less complicated approach like payback? And how would one tell? Our guess is that whatever the formal approach, two of the most ubiquitous tools in capital budgeting are a wing and a prayer, and serendipity is an important force in outcomes.

If you are a corporate strategist, you might be inclined to say: "Does this matter?" Some strategists are apt to dismiss these problems, advocating a notion of strategy that is concerned primarily with positioning or outmaneuvering rivals. For them, the problems with discounted cash flow analysis merely serve to highlight the importance of strategy as a discipline distinct from finance or valuation.

In my view, that attitude is wrong-headed. Business is about making money, and any strategic decision must ultimately be described in terms of a set of likely financial consequences for the organization. Whether these consequences are oriented toward shareholders or employees is beside the point. Strategy without numbers is like flying without instruments.

A number of articles have appeared over the years aiming to diffuse the apparent conflict between finance and strategy. The titles of two recent examples – "CFOs and strategists: forging a common framework," by Alfred Rappaport; "Must finance and strategy clash?" by Patrick Barwise and others – give a flavor of the argument. For the practicing strategy consultant or corporate strategist, however, it is hard to understand how these two sets of considerations can ever be held to diverge. What is the purpose of strategy, after all, if not to make money?

From an academic perspective, the inseparability of finance from strategy is a clear consequence of the resource-based view of the company. Money is one of the most important resources a company has. As a director of a small technology start-up, I know from experience how much more soundly you sleep when your business is generating rather than draining cash. How this resource is applied and augmented is inevitably and necessarily a critical determinant of corporate success.

Each year the financial outturn increases or decreases the financial resources available to a company, directly affecting the degrees of strategic freedom that it enjoys in the following year. Articulating the financial consequences of resource-allocation decisions must therefore be a central and integral part of the formulation of strategy. Funds provide access to other resources: people, intellectual property distribution. There is a basic inconsistency between believing both in the resource-based view of the company and the separability of strategy and finance.

If we accept that the problems with discounted cash flow cannot be brushed under the carpet, what can be done to overcome them? In recent years, the use of value-based planning systems among large companies has increased significantly. Much of this growth is attributable to the success of companies like Alcar, Marakon, and CVA, which tailor the value-management concepts of American shareholder value pioneer Alfred Rappaport and others to meet the specific needs of client organizations. What Rappaport did was to give practical meaning to the notion of a value-creating spread. This is the threshold operating margin, after taking account of working capital and capital expenditures, which a company must beat if it is to create value.

This has proved to be a good way for looking at the critical drivers of value growth. It has also helped to devolve value-focussed thinking to operational managers. It also provides a tool to examine the spread implicit in the current share price and relate it to the likely level of operational returns in the business. The trouble is that the method requires projections of sales, margins, and investment over the period when a positive value-creating spread is earned. These projections confront the same problems as plain vanilla DCF analysis, resulting in a wide range of strategy values.

One possible response to the DCF problems is to collapse the time frame for strategic evaluation to a single period. This is what occurs with EVA (Economic Value Added) analysis, as promoted by the consultants Stern Stewart. This approach relies on an established accounting identity:

$$P_t = y_t + \sum_{\tau=1}^{\infty} E_t \left[x_{t+\tau}^a \, R^{-\tau} \right]$$

where P_t is the market value of a company at time t, y_t is the book value of the company at time t, x_t^a are residual earnings in period t (essentially the same as what Stern Stewart calls EVA), R is 1 plus the cost of capital r. $E_t[Q]$ represents the expected value at time t of variable Q. Residual earnings, i.e., earnings after taking into account investor expectations for returns r on existing capital, are given by:

$$x_t^a = x_t - (R-1)\, y_{t-1}$$

where x_t^a are residual earnings in period t, x_t are earnings in period t, R is 1 plus the cost of capital r, and y_{t-1} is the closing book value of the previous period.

In plain English, what are we saying? The first equation says that the market value of the company is equal to its book value plus a goodwill item, which Stern Stewart calls Market Value Added (MVA). This term is made up of the sum of earnings in excess of that which the market requires on the book value of capital in the business, discounted at the investors' cost of capital. Stern Stewart calls these residual earnings terms, which it calculates using its own accounting conventions, Economic Value Added. The second equation describes how these terms are defined.

This approach is intuitively appealing. It says that the value of a company consists of what is in the books, plus the goodwill that arises when we make more than investors require on the company's assets. John Kay of London Economics has described these residual earnings, more simply, as profits after a company has paid its keep. With his former colleagues at London Business School, Kay pioneered the development of comparative rankings of the goodwill (or MVA) created by companies.

Because Stern Stewart's approach makes managers account for capital in their business on a risk-adjusted basis, and because of its simplicity, it has won a large measure of acceptance as a single-period operating measure. Many companies now use EVA, or some equivalent, in their strategic planning. Nonetheless, this approach also has problems.

The first is that a single-period measure is not necessarily a reliable indicator of how best to maximize the value of a business. If a company always chooses the course of action that maximizes its residual return next year, this may lead to the rejection of a strategy that maximizes value over a longer period. Cutting your time horizon to a single year is too constricting a tool in strategic evaluation.

Second, there is no reason that a company's EVA in any given period, even theoretically, should equal the total return to shareholders in that period. And in fact, as Ken Peasnell and John O'Hanlon have shown, it is unlikely that it ever would. A company that sees potential for value creation in a particular strategic option, on the basis of EVA analysis, has no guarantee that this value will be seen or rewarded in the same way by the stock market.

A third problem is that, using this type of analysis, companies systematically generate too many positive residual returns to be credible. Investors are not stupid, so if nearly all companies are apparently earning positive residual returns, investor expectations will change and result in different required rates. Why, if residual returns are nearly always positive, do a large number of companies have a market value less than their book value?

One answer is that the values in the books may be unreliable. But even if the book numbers are right, conceptual problems still remain. How do we treat unrecorded intangibles? How do we treat fluctuating cycles of working capital? To what extent should we look at gross rather than net assets? How should we think about the returns that are made through the efficient financing of operations?

The latter point, in particular, is not a trivial one. The EVA approach conflates questions about economic efficiency with questions about funding efficiency. Part of the capital in the basic EVA equation (y_t) is required to fund working capital because of the operating cycle of the business. This need for capital has nothing to do with the efficiency of the use of resources by the company in competitive markets. Sensible strategists will want to distinguish clearly between the two.

In the same way that EVA mixes up resources and funding, it might be argued that it also illogically mixes up past and present economic performance. The approach combines assets and balance sheet items (stocks) with profit and loss items (flows) in order to create a single return measure of economic performance. This can be misleading. For instance, the book value of equity includes not only money spent in the past buying assets, but also earnings from the past that have not been paid out as dividends.

EVA tries in effect to convey whether a business is using resources efficiently now by reference to the resources that it has consumed in the past. Some managers will rightly protest that they do not care how the business performed in the past. What they want to understand is whether the business is making good economic use of the resources it is consuming today. Is there an alternative?

These difficulties mean that the search for a coherent and pragmatic tool of strategic evaluation continues. The outlines of what is required are clear. What is required is a robust valuation model that directly links economic performance and market value; that incorporates reasonably accurate financial projections; and that focusses on a shorter and more relevant time frame than most current approaches. An appropriate time frame might be three to five years. This coincides well with typical management tenure of a business position, and avoids the pitfalls of looking at either too short or too long a period.

The ideal model will also cut across finance, accounting, micro-economics, and strategy. It will draw together information that can be captured effectively by accounting systems; that describes the economic use of resources in terms familiar to those who study industrial organization and consistent with modern financial theory; and that also embraces the established concepts of competitive strategy.

This is where Resource Margin Accounting comes into the frame. This approach aims to provide an account of how well resources in a business are being put to work, using a framework that is compatible with the strategist's resource-based view of the company. The fundamental measure is resource margin. This is defined as:

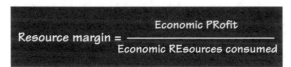

$$\text{Resource margin} = \frac{\text{Economic PRofit}}{\text{Economic REsources consumed}}$$

It is essentially a single-period internal rate of return that links unambiguously to value creation. The numerator, economic profit, is accounting profit computed on a "clean surplus" (or "comprehensive income") basis. This measure of profit incorporates all changes in book value during the period in question.

Although there may be a difference between economic depreciation of the assets and the depreciation recorded in the accounts for any given period, the accounting will eventually catch up with the economics. Since we will be looking at resource margins over a number of years, the effects of this distortion will be mitigated.

The denominator in the equation, economic resources consumed, is a measure known to economists as "net output," and to the taxman as "value added." The aim is to measure the resources that the business has under its control and from which it molds the distinctive competences on which competitive advantage is based. This means excluding the undifferentiated inputs that the business purchases as raw materials or services it has bought in from other companies.

This measure, clean surplus divided by net output, has distinguished antecedents dating back to the nineteenth-century economist Ricardo. Industrial economists in particular have done much research into the consequences of monopolies and oligopolies by looking at the relationships between concentration in an industry and a profitability measure called the "price–cost margin" (PCM), which is probably best seen as a cousin of RMA.

The price-cost-margin is defined as
$$\frac{\text{Net output} - \text{employee compensation}}{\text{Net output}}$$

If employee compensation represents a large majority of value-added costs, then the numerator in the above expression will be approximately equal to profit and the two measures will give broadly similar results.

Price–cost margin already has an established place in strategy literature. Research by economists at an industry level highlights the impact of concentration and barriers to entry on profitability (an approach made familiar to business people by Michael Porter's five forces model). A focus on average profit levels within an industry is also consistent with the structure–conduct–performance model elucidated by Bain (1959) and others. What Resource Margin Accounting aims to do is to apply the same kind of strategic thinking at the level of individual companies.

High levels of resource margin will typically arise where businesses are protected by competitive barriers to entry – what academics also call mobility barriers. Within a business segment, the returns earned by individual companies will vary as a function of their ability to sustain a highly efficient use of resources and their relative competitive advantage. Valuing strategies then becomes a question of calculating and evaluating resource margins.

It is possible to incorporate resource margins rigorously into a valuation framework that draws on accounting information and is entirely consistent with financial theory. Results similar to those for EVA are obtainable for RMA:

$$\frac{\text{Market value}}{\text{Book value}} = 1 + \frac{r-g}{r} \sum_{\tau=1}^{\infty} \gamma^{-\tau}(RMA_{\tau}-r)$$

where g is the rate of growth of resources (i.e., net output, value added), γ is a discounting factor and RMA_{τ} are the resource margins in successive years. In the case of $g=0$, this simplifies to:

$$\frac{\text{Market value}}{\text{Book value}} = 1 + \sum_{\tau=1}^{\infty} \Upsilon^{-\tau}(RMA_{\tau}-r)$$

Formally, the equation states that for an idealized company, the ratio of market to book value is given by one plus the sum of the discounted spread of the resource margin over the rate of return required by investors. The magnitude of this ratio – and hence the value-creation potential of a company – is determined by the size of the spread. The formula therefore makes explicit the importance of excess resource margins and the growth in resources in the creation of shareholder wealth through competitive advantage.

While Resource Margin Accounting is consistent with EVA, it avoids some of the conceptual confusion associated with that approach. In particular, it provides a means of separating the capital tied up in funding a business from the resources used to pursue business strategy. The UK and US data that have been analyzed to date suggest that RMA does not suffer from the credibility problem of generating a disproportionate number of positive returns. Many of the accounting revisions needed to compensate for divergences between book and replacement values of assets in the EVA approach are avoided by focussing entirely on profit and loss measures. RMA also avoids mixing up past and current elements of performance through the retention of historic spreads in the book value of the company.

In a nutshell, it would be fairly accurate to say that RMA takes the spread concepts of Rappaport and makes them consistent with clean surplus accounting. Early evidence suggests that it does, as one would hope, also provide a closer and more direct link between the value perceived by strategic analysis and the value that is rewarded by the market – which is ultimately the litmus test for any corporate strategist. For example, statistical analysis of companies in the UK has shown that resource margins are significantly correlated to market to book ratios.

Research under way at Oxford is extending these investigations to the US. The research also examines whether it is possible to discern particular patterns in the way that spreads of companies evolve over time. If clear patterns do prove to exist, it should be possible to demonstrate that each pattern is rewarded by a predictable appreciation of the market to book ratio – and hence opens a clear and direct line to the value placed on a business by the markets.

As a result, if we can obtain empirical confirmation of how investors reward performance, we will be able to predict with some confidence how we would expect share prices to evolve over a few years in response to the economic performance of a business as it executes a given strategy. If so, many of the difficulties associated with traditional DCF analysis would be overcome. Valuation could then be framed within horizons that are spanned by current management, and based on fairly robust forecasts of near-term performance grounded in models that reflect the way investors actually behave.

It is hard not to believe that this would be a significant development in applied corporate strategy making, as well as having important implications for investment bankers, securities analysts, and others for whom valuation is part of their day-to-day work. The truth is that the armory of valuation techniques open to corporate strategists has matured rapidly over the past 30 years, but there is still some way to go before the concept and processes can be said to have been taken as far as they can go. We may at last, however, be approaching a glimpse of the summit.

Summary

Strategy without numbers is like flying without instruments, says **Peter Johnson**. If business is about making money, any strategic decision must ultimately be described in terms of a set of likely financial consequences for the organization. In this article, he considers the limitations of discounted cash flow analysis and Economic Value Added, and argues that Resource Margin Accounting may prove to be a more useful alternative.

STRATEGY AND
RISK MANAGEMENT

9

Contributors

Keith J. Crocker is Waldo O. Hildebrand Professor of Risk Management and Insurance at the University of Michigan Business School.

Andrew Rosenfield is chief executive officer of UNEXT.com, a provider of online business education. He is also chairman of Lexecon, Inc., an economic consulting firm, and a trustee of the University of Chicago.

Robert Gertner is a professor of economics and strategy at the University of Chicago Graduate School of Business. He teaches courses in strategic investment decisions and advanced competitive strategy. He is also principal of Lexecon Inc., a Chicago-based consulting firm.

Marc J. Knez is an associate professor of strategy at the University of Chicago Graduate School of Business. His research interests include managerial and strategic decision making, incentive systems, and organizational design.

Contents

Introduction

Risk – a topic which will be more fully explored in the series following *Mastering Strategy* – lurks in the shadows of all key management decisions. In an increasingly uncertain world, however, the challenge for companies is increasingly to take a pro-active approach and to understand better the odds of the game. Identifying risk, avoiding or at least mitigating it, insuring against it and learning to cope with crises are among the key steps. Besides a general summary of the issues, this module specifically considers the attractions of real options, demonstrates how game theory concentrates attention on a company's competitors, and explains why scenario analysis through effective story telling can be a powerful strategic tool. Combining game theory and scenario analysis can be even more effective.

Managing risk before it manages you

by Keith J. Crocker

"This has got to be the worst day of my life," observed William Clay Ford Jr., Ford Motor Company chairman, as he contemplated the February 1999 natural gas explosion in boiler number six that had just leveled part of the River Rouge powerhouse in Detroit, Michigan.

The disaster cut off power to the 1,100-acre facility and ultimately resulted in the loss of six lives, with 14 people seriously injured.

While his remarks were directed toward the human dimension of the tragedy, from a corporate standpoint the prognosis must have appeared equally sobering. The Rouge complex powerhouse – the centerpiece of Henry Ford's dream of building entire cars in a single location – had supplied electricity, compressed air, mill water, and steam to six assembly and parts plants employing 10,000 workers, and also to the independently owned Rouge Steel plant.

Although an engineering marvel of its time, the concentration of production at River Rouge had precipitated a risk manager's worst nightmare, as the effects of the integrated plant's shutdown rippled through Ford's internal supply network.

First hit was Rouge's own Mustang assembly plant, which had been working overtime with two ten-hour shifts daily cranking out the popular sports compact. Next came Rouge's metal-stamping plant, supplying metal parts – fenders and similar products – to 16 of Ford's 20 North American plants. Results were predictable. Shifts were cut from eight hours to four hours at the Wayne County plant producing Ford Escorts and Mercury Tracers, at the Wixom, Michigan factory assembling luxury Lincolns, as well as at the Lorain, Ohio, facility making Ford Econoline vans. Also affected was the Rouge's frame plant, where lost production resulted in the elimination of scheduled overtime at truck plants in Kansas City, Missouri; Norfolk, Virginia; and Oakville, Ontario.

Even at these reduced levels, production was supported only by the buffers of existing inventories and supplies in transit that, once exhausted, would necessitate plant shutdowns. The implications of the powerhouse loss were even more serious for Rouge Steel, a much smaller company than Ford. And a previously planned $240m replacement powerhouse would not be completed for at least a year.

Operational risks, a corporate drama

While the economic effects of high-profile financial dislocations – like the default on Russian debt or the Asian crises currency devaluations – tend to attract most popular press attention, seemingly mundane hazards associated with day-to-day business operation – the company's operational risks – rarely make the front page unless accompanied by some headline-grabbing catastrophe.

But for most companies, management of operational risk is where the action is. This landscape is both broad and in continual flux, with risk exposures that include product and environmental liabilities, property and business interruption losses, workers' compensation, and concerns about employee health and pension benefits.

For example, a recent change in liability law limiting manufacturer liability to 18 years has resulted in the production of single-engine light planes by Cessna, part of US conglomerate Textron, for the first time in more than 15 years. In Albuquerque, New Mexico, a jury awarded Stella Liebeck $2.9m in a dispute with McDonald's, the US fast-food group, over spilled hot coffee. The US Occupational Safety and Health Administration recently considered limitations on the exposure of workers to cadmium, which have been estimated to cost industry more than $160m a year. The Supreme Court upheld a New York Court decision that makes all manufacturers of the antimiscarriage drug DES, or diethylstilbestrol, jointly liable for the effects of a drug last prescribed in 1971. In another legal decision, the highest court in Texas ruled that a convenience store chain could be required to pay damages to the family of a murdered clerk, even though the crime was not witnessed and has not been solved. And, finally, employers are finding it difficult to provide affordable health insurance to their workers, as health insurers are becoming more selective in the policies they write.

As these examples show, the effective management of operational risks has become an increasingly important concern for businesses, particularly since a single event can involve multiple risk exposures. In practice, managing risks involves four distinct stages: risk identification, risk mitigation and avoidance, risk financing, and, finally, crisis management.

Identifying business risks

Many potential workplace hazards are easily identified, as with cases of exposed machinery or electrical wiring in a factory setting, or slippery floors in an office or retail establishment. Other types of risk exposures may be apparent only to those formally trained, or with experience in a particular area of risk analysis. Much as standing under a tree during a thunderstorm might seem to be a reasonable move to those uninitiated in the hazards of lightning, many perils involve risk exposures that are not apparent to an untrained eye.

In the case of the Rouge power plant, for example, there were certainly engineering economies involved from consolidating production of the electricity, steam, and high-pressure air required by the various Ford Rouge manufacturing plants and by Rouge Steel. And this approach is by no means unique to Ford's US operations. For example, the Ford Dagenham complex located outside London is similar in design and in susceptibility to a Rouge-like debilitation.

But the operational risks of this approach have also turned out to be substantial. In addition to the costs of business interruption, Rouge Steel faces legal action by injured Ford employees as a consequence of its shared ownership of the powerhouse.

As in most states, Michigan law stipulates that workers' compensation is the sole remedy for employees injured in the workplace, which limits employer liability for injuries sustained on the job. That makes it difficult for Ford employees to sue and collect from Ford, but the same protection apparently does not extend to similar suits filed by Ford employees against Rouge Steel.

Perhaps the most insidious, however, are the latent risks resulting from evolving legal rules or standards of care. A particularly topical case is that of the notion of contingent environmental liability. This encompasses unforeseen environmental risks in which the dollar amount of the exposure is unknown and changing, depending on events that have yet to occur.

The precedent for such actions has already been established by CERCLA, the

1980 Superfund hazardous substance clean-up legislation, which introduced strict as well as joint and several liability for cleaning up hazardous waste sites.

As a result of CERCLA, a business could have been in compliance with all applicable laws at the time of the waste disposal, or simply be the current owner of an existing site, yet still be strictly liable for the costs of clean-up, as well as the associated damages to natural resources. And, since the liability is joint and several, even partial contributors to the harm are fully liable for the entire amount, leading to the predictable tort search for "deep pockets." These liabilities are transferred to any successor corporation resulting from a merger or acquisition, and there has also been discussion about contingent liability transferring to a company's lenders, although this latter issue remains largely unsettled.

Daniel S. Sobczynski, Ford's director of corporate insurance, is a strong proponent of proactive risk assessment. "The highest potential risks are those that are unidentified and unmanaged. It is critical to evaluate your risks and to learn from the lessons of others," he says. "The problem of learning from personal experience is that it gives you the lesson after the test has been administered."

Reducing exposure to operational risks

Once the nature of a business risk is identified, the next step is to craft a cost-effective strategy to mitigate the company's exposure to the peril. Generally, this requires identifying tactics to reduce the probability of hazard occurrence, and timely actions that if adopted would reduce the extent of any ultimate loss from an adverse event. Installing sprinklers in a warehouse, for example, reduces the damage that might result from fire. The regular inspection of electrical wiring would serve to lower the risk of such a fire starting. Whether a particular risk-mitigation strategy makes business sense from a profitability perspective depends on whether it passes the cost–benefit analysis, i.e., whether the cost of implementation exceeds the expected reduction in loss exposure.

While such decisions may seem relatively straightforward from a business perspective, the real world is somewhat more complicated. In cases ranging from Ford Pinto's alleged susceptibility to fires in rear-end collisions, through a later debate on the safety of the "side-saddle" gas tank design in General Motors' pickups, to the recent decision awarding $4.9bn to six people burned in an accident involving a 1979 Chevrolet Malibu, jurors have demonstrated a deep-seated prejudice against the use of cost–benefit techniques in situations involving a potential loss of human lives.

Indeed, in the Malibu case, the mere existence of a cost–benefit analysis by a GM engineer (the now-infamous 1973 "Ivey" memorandum suggesting that fuel-tank fires were costing GM only $2.40 per vehicle, while a redesign would cost $8.59) was viewed by jurors to be evidence of a callous corporate disregard for customer safety – even though no evidence was presented that the analysis was requested by management, nor that they ever saw it.

Clearly, a business that implements a formal economic analysis of the costs and benefits of (theoretically) preventable fatalities does so at its own peril, at least in the current legal climate.

Financing the costs of resulting losses

Even with reasonable precautions to reduce identifiable operational risks, companies will still be faced with residual risk exposures, along with the decisions of how best to finance the costs of any resulting losses.

Traditionally, businesses would retain risks involving small or fairly predictable losses, either treating them as a current business expense (a strategy adopted by retail establishments faced with shoplifting or employee pilferage), or by using a line of credit to cover the loss (as when a business borrows to replace a critical piece of machinery lost to failure).

Larger, or more uncertain losses would generally be shifted to an independent insurer with established expertise in the specific claim line. In turn, the insurer would reduce its cost of bearing the risks assumed either by risk pooling (combining risks from numerous companies and using premiums paid by those who do not suffer the loss to indemnify those who do; known in statistical circles as the "law of large numbers"), or by risk spreading (reselling portions of assumed risk portfolios in the reinsurance market). In many settings, particularly involving smaller business, this approach is still the norm.

However, larger businesses have adopted an increasingly aggressive approach to financing operational risks. Many have opted to perform functions internally that had previously been farmed out to independent insurers. Increased retention of risks allows the company to avoid the substantial frictional (such as insurance taxes and underwriting fees) costs associated with insurance purchases.

Larger businesses often have sufficient risk exposures to enable them to establish an internal self-insurance pool. Generally, this strategy is coupled with purchase of explicit catastrophic insurance protection to absorb any losses exceeding the company's target retention limit. Of course, risk retention makes an effective risk-management strategy all the more important to the company, since it ultimately bears the costs. One disadvantage of the retention approach is lack of an insurer's expertise in establishing reserves to cover losses and servicing of claims, but these can generally be purchased from insurers as standalone services. This option is often utilized by businesses that self-insure the costs of medical benefits for their employees, yet hire a traditional insurer to handle the administrative tasks involved in processing claims.

Many businesses prefer the control that risk retention provides in the claims litigation process. Such decisions would otherwise be solely at the discretion of the indemnifying insurer, whose interests in settling are not always aligned with those of the insured.

Some businesses with extensive operational risk exposures have opted to bypass the primary insurance market entirely, and place their risks directly with the international reinsurance market. The development of a new class of tools for risk securitization means that such companies may ultimately be able to circumvent even the traditional reinsurance markets. One such device is the catastrophic bond, which, depending on the particulars of the offering, places either the interest or the principal at risk, in the event of a stipulated catastrophe.

Although these tools have been used primarily by insurers as an alternative to reinsurance in shedding their hurricane or earthquake risk exposures, as the market matures it will likely become increasingly attractive to businesses wishing directly to shift their own operational risks.

Reducing post-catastrophe losses

In spite of the most diligent pre-catastrophe risk identification, mitigation, and financing programs, accidents will happen. When they do, actions taken immediately following the event may have a critical impact – either advantageously or adversely – on the magnitude of the ultimate loss.

In the turmoil immediately following the River Rouge disaster, Mr. Clay Ford Jr. gave his personal credit card to an aide, with instructions to find the families of the victims at the hospital and provide for meals, hotels, or anything else they required. Close behind were Ford's human resource professionals, coordinating humanitarian assistance in conjunction with the United Auto Workers, the employees' union.

Ford's suppliers set aside their production schedules, working overtime to produce electrical switching equipment and to procure portable boilers for steam, while the Detroit Fire Department used one of its boats to refill the Rouge water mains and tanks, and Detroit Edison, the local power supplier, built an outdoor substation in a week – a task some say would normally take more than a month. Within a week of the powerhouse explosion, all of Ford's River Rouge operations were back up and running, a triumph of effective crisis management.

Part of this success was undoubtedly attributable to the close relationship that had long been established between Ford, its suppliers, and the community. Indeed, in southeastern Michigan, people often speak of working at "Ford's" (as in "Henry's"), so familial feelings run deep. But management's actions after the tragedy also counted for a lot.

Other businesses have also learned this lesson, sometimes the hard way. In 1986, when product tampering resulted in a death from Tylenol painkiller capsules that had been laced with cyanide poison, response from Johnson & Johnson, the health-care group that makes the capsules, was immediate. It publicly recalled all capsules and designed the generation of tamper-proof containers still in use to this day.

In stark contrast was the reaction of US insulation and building products manufacturer Johns-Manville, once the world's biggest producer of asbestos, which collapsed under the weight of asbestosis claims in 1982. Johns-Manville's decision to ignore the risks of asbestos exposure to its workers, long after management may have suspected a problem, resulted in untold lives ruined by asbestosis and, ultimately, corporate bankruptcy.

Mr. Sobczynski puts it best: "Either manage the risk, or it will manage you," he says, "and, when it does, the loss will happen when you are least prepared."

Summary

A disaster on the scale of the natural gas explosion at Ford's River Rouge plant in Michigan in 1999 represents a risk manager's worst nightmare, says **Keith J. Crocker**. Yet the management of day-to-day or operational risk – covering everything from product and environmental liability to staff health and pension benefits – rarely hits the headlines. There are four stages to risk management: identification, mitigation and avoidance, financing, and crisis management. In this article, the author highlights the rapidly changing legal landscape, spells out lessons for the non-professional risk manager, and considers some of the issues and new instruments when it comes to financing operational risk.

How real options lead to better decisions

by Robert Gertner and Andrew Rosenfield

A newspaper publisher has to decide whether to give free access to its internet site or to try to continue to levy a subscriber fee; an integrated oil company has to decide whether to build a new refinery; a successful retailer has to decide how rapidly to expand; a chemical manufacturer that is losing money has to decide whether to shut down a plant or keep it operating; an aircraft manufacturer has to decide whether to expand its product line before its rivals. All these strategic decisions involve large costs and are fraught with uncertainty.

Traditionally, the way to evaluate investment projects and other similar strategic initiatives is to use discounted cash flow (DCF) analysis. Finance executives, strategy personnel, or line staff develop a model of the "project" and predict its costs and revenues. These are then discounted using the appropriate interest rate. The value of the project is summarized by a net present value (NPV) internal rate of return (IRR) or payback period. Sensitivity analysis may be incorporated by varying demand, cost, or other parameters. If the company is choosing among several mutually exclusive alternatives, the returns from the competing projects are compared.

In addition to financial modeling, a company will usually engage in strategic analysis that tries conceptually to capture some of the ambiguous, dynamic industry and competitive effects that may be difficult to incorporate in financial projections. Adjustments for the "strategic" effects not included in the model are usually done intuitively or heuristically. A difficult challenge is to incorporate some of the ambiguous parameters directly into the financial projections.

There has been a great deal of debate over the past 20 years among finance professionals and academics about how best to implement DCF analysis. There is controversy both about the choice of the appropriate interest rate at which to discount the future and even the different rules to apply to discounted flows.

More recently, academics, consultants, and a growing number of corporate decision makers have realized that there often can be fundamental problems in the use of simple DCF analyses to assess complex investment projects, especially those that are not inherently and completely "binary."

The problem is that DCF typically ignores that dynamic flexibility present in almost any investment project. Since there often is huge uncertainty in long-term projections, rarely do *ex ante* projected cash flows turn out to be precisely identical to actual *ex post* cash flows.

When things don't work out exactly as expected, the company will often adjust its investment strategy or operation to take account of new information and the resolution of uncertainty.

It may expand more rapidly, enter a new, related market, abandon a project entirely, delay further investment, lay off workers, or divest some assets. A simple static DCF analysis does not incorporate the cash flow implications from responding in these and other ways, as uncertainty is resolved. Not only will valuations fail to reflect the value of flexibility; a company may make the incorrect choice among projects if they differ in the flexibility they allow.

For example, the choice between two technologies, one that involves large sunk costs and one that does not, may be incorrect if the analysis does not also value the different costs of shutdown should the project fail.

Real options defined

Real options is the term used to denote the explicit valuation of the opportunities associated with changing decisions in response to the resolution of relevant uncertainty. The term derives from the link between methods to value real operating flexibility and methods to value financial options.

A financial option allows its owner to purchase or sell a specified security at a specified price and time. For example, a call option may allow its owner to buy one share of Exxon at $110 on or before January 15, 2000. The decision to exercise that particular option or not depends on whether the Exxon share price exceeds $110 on the exercise date. This in turn depends on resolution of uncertainty about the Exxon stock price. Over the past 30 years, financial economists have developed sophisticated methods to value these and other more complex options.

Like financial option valuation, real option valuation involves incorporating into the valuation process today the opportunity that the company will enjoy later to take actions in response to new knowledge and the resolution of uncertainty.

Take the example of a company pondering whether it should build a new $50m chemical plant. Suppose that of the total expected $50m in cost, there are initial expenditures of about $500,000 associated with plant planning and environmental permits. The company can analyze the entire project today in a static sense (performing a simple DCF) as if its only choice is to go forward and commit the entire $50m or not to proceed at all. But it is far better to incorporate directly and expressly the fact that the company does not face an "all or nothing" choice. Instead, it can invest the $500,000 now and then see about environmental approval. If so, it can go forward and invest $49.5m. If not, it can abandon the project without spending the $49.5m in "hard costs." Quite obviously, it can make a much better decision regarding its large investment once environmental risk has been resolved. Combining these risks in a simple DCF leads to below-optimal decision making.

Decisions where real options may play an important role include all investments that can be delayed, sequential investments such as R&D stages, investments that may be abandoned, investments that may be expanded, and investments that may lead to new market opportunities.

Numerous books and articles have suggested applying the valuation methods used with financial options to real options. Although a full treatment of option valuation is beyond the scope of this article, we can demonstrate the basic ideas and the power of using this way of thinking about decision making under uncertainty. We will develop the concept sufficiently so that the reader can easily understand the trade-offs between simple decision-tree valuation and financial option valuation.

Consider again the call option on a share of stock in Exxon. Suppose that the current price of a share of Exxon stock is $100 and that the risk-free interest rate (between now and January 15, 2001) is 10 percent. Assume (don't ask why) that somehow we know that the price of Exxon on January 15, 2001 will be either $125 or $80. And to make the example even more structured, we also know that the probability that Exxon will be worth $125 is 0.8 and the probability that Exxon will be worth $80 is 0.2. (These probabilities are actually irrelevant to the option valuation.) On January 15, 2000 the option will be worth $25 if Exxon is at $125 and $0 if Exxon is at $80. The question is how much it is worth today.

One might start by saying that the expected value of the option is .8(25) = 20. The problem is we do not know at what rate to discount this. A key insight of option pricing is that we can construct a portfolio that consists of the stock and a bond bearing no risk, which exactly replicates the payoffs from the option. Since two portfolios with the same payoffs must trade at the same price to avoid arbitrage, and since we know how to value each component of the portfolio, we can value the option.

In this example, a portfolio consisting of 5/9 shares of Exxon stock and borrowing $40.40 will give the same payoff as the option. If Exxon stock is $125, this portfolio is worth (5/9)*125 − 40.4*1.1 = 25, and if Exxon stock is $80, this portfolio is worth (5/9)*80 − 40.4*1.1 = 0. The cost of this is simply 5/9*100 − 40.4 = $15.15. This must also be the price of the option, since the option and the security give identical returns. (The implied discount rate for the option is 32 percent. The reason this discount rate is so high is that $1 invested in the call option is a good deal riskier than $1 invested in a share of Exxon. An option fluctuates in value by $25 while the stock fluctuates by $45; so the option is 5/9 as variable, but the option costs 15 percent of what a share costs, so the risk per dollar is greater.)

Option pricing theory extends this method to derive pricing formulas when the uncertainty in the stock price is more complex than in this example. The Black-Scholes option pricing model formula gives the price of an American call option for a non-dividend paying stock whose returns satisfy a specific distributional assumption. The formula gives the option value as a function of the risk-free interest rate, the current stock price, the exercise price of the option, and the variability of the stock price.

Developing an oil field

Some types of real options are closely analogous to simple financial options. An example is the decision of an oil company to develop an oil field. If the company does not develop the field today, it can do so in the future. The return from development depends on the price of oil, while the cost of developing the field does not. The flexibility in timing is analogous to a call option to buy the returns from the oil field, with the exercise price equaling the cost of development. So just like a financial call option, there is a fixed exercise price and a payoff on exercise that depends on the price of a traded asset – the price of oil. Thus, it is possible to use option pricing techniques to value the option and thereby determine the value of acquiring the oil field as well as determine if and when to exercise the option. A simple DCF analysis would ignore the possibility of delay; it would simply tell a decision maker if it were better to develop today than to abandon development; it would undervalue the oil field if the option to delay were valuable.

In most settings, the analogy to financial options is less direct, because the underlying uncertainty that drives the value of flexibility is not a traded asset and its distribution is neither known nor simple to estimate. It is only in rare circumstances where the decision to expand, contract, enter, or abandon depends on the value of a traded security or a variable with a known dynamic distribution.

Decision trees are an alternative to financial option pricing for modeling flexibility of strategic decisions. Decision trees have been around much longer than financial option analysis and allow for more general specifications of uncertainty than options pricing. A decision tree is a representation of decision making under uncertainty in which decisions and outcomes of uncertainty are represented by branches. By attaching payoffs to end nodes and discounting optimal decisions back to the branch of the tree, one can value flexible strategic alternatives.

The main advantages of decision trees over option pricing methods derive from their greater transparency. The process of building a tree usually must involve communication among analysts and decision makers that can result in a better model. The ability of a decision tree to incorporate different forms of uncertainty is created around statements such as "within one year we will know if the product is a flop, is OK, or a hit."

The results of the analysis can be presented in a way that makes the individual ultimately responsible for the decision, comfortable with the underlying assumptions and their implications. The black box of option pricing makes it seem easy, but if the CEO doesn't understand how the model works and why it generates particular results, that person is unlikely to use it to make a decision.

Vast and unwieldy decision trees

If a decision is complex, with many different sources of uncertainty, decision trees can become vast and unwieldy. A number of techniques have been developed to simplify the process or its expositions. Influence diagrams are a way to describe the structure of complex decision problems in a more compact way than a tree. Scenario analysis helps hone the modeling of uncertainty to its most essential elements.

The main advantage of the option pricing approach is that it simplifies the process by using the market values of existing securities to substitute for assumptions about the environment and by using a parameterization of uncertainty that is amenable to formulaic valuation. In particular, if there is a comparable traded security, the modeler does not have to worry about determining the appropriate risky discount rate and how it should vary at different points of time and for different realizations of uncertainty.

However, if there is no closely traded security, the relevant parameters must be estimated in any case and the information advantage of option pricing models evaporates. Simple option pricing models can give a quick estimate of the value of embedded real options that can be used to determine if more detailed analysis is justified.

The art of valuing real options comes from effective modeling of the relevant uncertainty and adopting appropriate tools to estimate value. Much of the existing literature uses stylized examples. In these settings, option pricing models may have an advantage because the stylization tends to allow for a simple structure for the underlying uncertainty. Rather than focus on such a stylized example – where the link to financial options is strong – we will use an example of a typical investment decision that involves significant strategic flexibility in order to highlight the trade-offs in various methods to incorporate the value of flexibility into the analysis.

Urban entertainment destination

Sony, the consumer electronics and entertainment giant, recently opened Metreon, an innovative entertainment and retail complex in San Francisco. Sony calls it an "urban entertainment destination."

Metreon has interactive children's exhibits. These are based on Maurice Sendak's book *Where the Wild Things Are* and David Macaulay's *The Way Things Work*, a multiplex complex with a 3-D IMAX theatre, a state-of-the-art video arcade with interactive games unavailable elsewhere, stylish restaurants including outposts of several popular local restaurants, numerous stores, many selling Sony products, and several one-of-a-kind stores.

Sony faced what is in many ways a typical strategic investment decision when it had to decide whether and when to move forward with Metreon, and how many centers to build initially.

A standard DCF analysis would include projections for revenues and costs for different possible locations. It would probably provide little guidance on how many locations to go forward with initially; it might have individual projections for different locations, so locations can be ranked.

This is not sufficient. Strategically, the decision of how many Metreons to build initially cannot be analyzed effectively without considering the way in which different decisions affect the company as time passes and uncertainty is resolved.

Sony ought to have addressed the following questions (and it may well have done). What is the shutdown cost if the concept proves unsuccessful in the marketplace? How much will be learned from the first locations that will help decide how aggressively to expand? Where to expand? How should later Metreons differ from the initial ones? What are the costs of delay, given that consumer tastes may shift and competitors may beat it to market with a substitute in some target cities? (The authors have no knowledge of what processes Sony used in making these decisions.)

All of these questions involve issues of how initial strategic choices affect future decisions as uncertainty about the market, demand and costs of Sony's offering, and competitive responses play out. This is exactly the domain of real option analysis.

Modeling the dynamic process

Advocates of the financial option pricing approach to real option analysis would have their hands full with this problem. A key step in the analysis is modeling the dynamic process for the relevant uncertainty in a way that is consistent with the assumptions of option pricing models.

The sources of uncertainty here are complex. They include uncertainty about demand, competitive responses, movements in real-estate prices, stock-market valuations, interest rates, and macro-economic conditions.

A decision-tree analysis of Sony's decision is also not simple. However, it does allow a decision maker to focus on the main sources of uncertainty and key drivers in the decision of the number of companies.

The benefit of building more Metreons initially is that it increases the first-mover advantage over potential rivals, may deter competitive entry, and provides more information about demand. The cost of building more Metreons initially is that if the entire concept fails, the costs to Sony are greater. And if Sony learns that the optimal Metreon design is different from the initial design, it will be more costly to make the others conform to the optimal design than it would have been if more had been built only after Sony found out which worked best. The decision tree should incorporate all the elements of this trade-off.

Key model choices include how long it takes to learn about demand; the likelihood of different demand realizations; how the likelihood and costs to Sony of competitive entry vary depending on the number of initial Metreons; and cost of abandonment or restructuring. Adding these features into a tree that incorporates the basic financial modeling will allow Sony to value the embedded flexibility in different choices.

In some cases, uncertainty may be too complex and the problem too ambiguous for formal modeling to add much value. Nonetheless, real option thinking can play an important role in strategic decision making even when analytical attempts to value these choices or options expressly are absent. If analysts and decision makers adopt a real options approach, that mode of thinking often will uncover the embedded flexibility in strategic investments. And that will greatly improve strategic analysis and lead to better decision making.

Summary

Managers frequently have to make decisions that involve high costs and are fraught with uncertainty. According to **Robert Gertner** and **Andrew Rosenfield**, they should consider real options. This denotes the explicit valuation of opportunities associated with altering a decision in response to changing circumstances. The authors show how techniques for valuing financial options are relevant and offer practical examples. They also explain why decision trees are sometimes a more transparent alternative. Real options help decide on investments that might be delayed, abandoned, or expanded – employed well, they will expose the flexibility embedded in a strategic investment, improve analysis, and lead to better decision making.

Scenario analysis: telling a good story

by Robert Gertner

Strategic decisions require a company to commit to a course of action that precludes significant alternatives and influences performance over a long time horizon. Typically, these decisions must be made without the ability to predict the implications of the alternatives with any degree of uncertainty. Strategic decisions are almost always fraught with ambiguity and uncertainty.

This creates complexity for decision makers. A fully rational approach to decision making under uncertainty involves careful consideration of how company performance varies with possible outcomes under different choices.

This is not easy. Human beings are subject to biases and imperfect reasoning about uncertainty. Psychologists have been studying this problem for a long time and have uncovered numerous ways in which people fail to make effective decisions in risky environments. People tend to misperceive events that are quite unlikely. Depending on the circumstances, we tend either to ignore or to put too much weight on unlikely but significant possibilities. Sometimes we repress consideration of outcomes that are especially unpleasant to us. People make different decisions when the same problem is framed in different ways.

The problems of individual decision making under uncertainty may be exacerbated within organizations. Agency problems create conflicts of interest between analysts and decision makers as well as between decision makers and shareholders. Group decision making may magnify individual biasses as each member's biasses are passed along to the group.

Companies can benefit by adopting processes and tools designed to overcome these imperfections that incorporate more objective and detailed analysis of uncertainty into strategic decision making. The most common tools that companies use to analyze risky strategic decisions involve some form of cash-flow projections coupled with sensitivity analysis. The cash-flow projections are made by estimating the most likely realizations of cash flows for the alternative decisions. These estimates, in turn, are derived from estimates for the most likely outcomes for the most significant uncertainty, such as demand growth, cost reductions, and price changes. The company may then perform sensitivity analyses by varying the assumptions for each of the sources of uncertainty and checking their effects on the return from different strategies.

There are limitations to this approach. The sensitivity analysis is overly simplistic and can be misleading. By varying one parameter at a time, it fails to incorporate any links or correlations among them. For example, if demand growth is much greater than expected, this may have implications for competition, pricing, and costs that, in turn, are other parameters of the model but do not vary in the demand-growth sensitivity analysis. In addition, the process of deriving the "most likely" outcomes may ignore the full range of relevant uncertainty and does nothing to overcome the biasses in thinking about uncertainty.

The idea of scenario analysis

Scenario analysis is an approach to decision making under uncertainty that overcomes many of the shortcomings of traditional methods. A scenario is simply an internally consistent view of the future. Scenario analysis is the process of generating and analyzing a small set of scenarios that are relevant to a particular decision or a company's long-run performance. Rather than varying a single parameter from a detailed model of the most likely outcome, scenarios allow decision makers to vary many parameters in unison. Although there are several different approaches to generating scenarios, they are all designed to overcome the biasses evident in human decision making under uncertainty. Scenario analysis can be adapted to either qualitative understanding of a strategic environment or quantitative measurement of the value of alternative decisions.

Many companies have used scenario analysis as a planning and decision-making tool for years. Scenario planning began as a military planning tool and was first applied to business planning in the 1960s. Perhaps the company most closely associated with scenario analysis is Royal Dutch/Shell. Kees Van Der Heijden, a former Shell planner, lists the benefits obtained by Shell from scenario planning in his book *Scenarios: the Art of Strategic Conversation*. They are: 1) more robust decisions and projects; 2) better thinking about the future by "stretching mental models"; 3) enhancing corporate perception and recognizing events as a part of a pattern and realizing their implications; 4) improving communication by using scenarios to provide a context for decisions throughout the company; and 5) a way to provide leadership to the organization. Van Der Heijden also describes how Shell was able to respond more quickly and effectively to the 1973 oil crisis because it had analyzed such a scenario.

US wireless telecoms

I will use an extended example of the wireless telecommunications industry in the United States to demonstrate the basics of scenario analysis. In 1994, notwithstanding the rapid growth of cellular telecommunications, government regulation restricted competition to two competitors throughout the country; the identity of the license holders varied across geographic markets. Entry was prohibited, although a company called Nextel had figured out a way to use licenses for mobile radio services to provide wireless telephony and was in the process of implementing that technology. The cellular business was very profitable – price competition was limited by the small number of competitors, the restrictions on entry, and the scarcity of allocated spectrum.

The Federal Communications Commission (FCC) had allocated an additional 120 MHz of spectrum for Personal Communication Services (PCS) licenses. PCS is a form of digital wireless service that can compete directly with existing cellular providers. Existing cellular providers had been allocated 25 MHz of spectrum each; total spectrum was to increase by over 200 percent. In addition, digital technology multiplies the capacity of a unit of spectrum many times. The FCC planned to auction six licenses in each geographic region (three 30-MHz licenses and three 10-MHz licenses).

A company considering bidding in an auction for a license to enter this market should be willing to pay any amount less than the present value of its expected profits from entry into this market. Determining this amount is a problem full of uncertainty. In addition to uncertainty about market demand, there was significant competitive, regulatory, and technological uncertainty.

Investment analysts calculated estimates of the value of PCS licenses. These estimates were typically based on a discounted cash flow analysis. The analyst would make a variety of assumptions including market growth, PCS share evolution, price declines, and costs to generate a "most likely" outcome that could be used to calculate the value of a PCS license. Scenario analysis provides an alternative way to value licenses and develop a strategy for bidding in the auctions.

Three distinct steps

Scenario analysis consists of three distinct steps: scenario creation, scenario elaboration, and integration of the scenarios into explicit decision-making processes.

Scenario creation is the process of analyzing the uncertainty in the strategic environment and structuring it into a small number of internally consistent scenarios. There are many different approaches to this process, as I will explain in my analysis of the PCS market below. Once the scenarios have been set, it is necessary to analyze the structure of competition and company performance in each scenario. This scenario elaboration may be qualitative or quantitative or both. The result is a rich understanding of industry and company performance in each scenario. The last step is to integrate the analysis of each scenario into the company's strategic choices. This process involves understanding how particular strategies perform in each scenario as well as how strategic choices affect the likelihood of different scenarios.

The crux of scenario analysis is developing a small set of distinct scenarios that cover the most significant uncertainty a company faces. One way to accomplish this is to build scenarios from a systematic description and analysis of the key uncertainties. I call this the "bottom-up" approach. An alternative approach is for decision makers to think collectively and creatively to develop scenarios directly, and then refine them by analyzing the uncertainty that distinguishes the scenarios from each other. I call this the "top-down" approach.

I begin with the top-down approach. Start by thinking about competition and profitability in the long run. Profits in this market will arise from three possible conditions. First, spectrum may be scarce. If there is insufficient spectrum to meet the market demand at competitive prices, then prices will exceed competitive levels and all companies in the market should be able to make money based on their ownership of a scarce asset. Further entry will be foreclosed by the limited spectrum made available by the FCC for wireless telecommunications. A second way in which profits could arise is by limited rivalry. If the number of competitors is small and none has an incentive to engage in aggressive price competition, profits would result. Finally, there may be differences among wireless providers such that some have a competitive advantage that allows them to make money.

This simple analysis allows us to begin to develop relevant scenarios. For example, it suggests a scenario where none of the three sources of profits is present. In this scenario, demand growth is moderate so spectrum is not scarce, there is little differentiation among providers that matters to consumers, and there are many competitors leading to significant rivalry. We could call this scenario "Wireless becomes a commodity." The basis for a second scenario is where there is enormous demand growth, perhaps driven by wireless replacing wireline telephones or large demand for wireless data communications. Spectrum scarcity results and limits price reductions. Additional scenarios can be developed where there is significant differentiation among competitors. Different sources of differentiation could be part of the same scenarios or could define different scenarios. It is always useful to think of a worst-case scenario and it easy to imagine many reasons why PCS demand would not materialize – problems with digital technology, leapfrogging by a new technology, or health problems from use of cellular phones. The next step would be to go from these basic descriptions of scenarios to a more fully specified description of the uncertainty that underlies them.

An alternative approach to developing scenarios is from the bottom up. We begin by listing the critical uncertainties that a PCS licensee faces. These include overall demand for wireless telecommunications, preferences of consumers across different providers, the effects of entry on industry rivalry, the response of regulators to industry developments, and uncertainties about different technologies. The next step of scenario building is to dig deeper into the underlying drivers of each of the critical uncertainties. In particular, some of the uncertainties may depend on the realizations of other, more fundamental uncertainties. For example, the extent of industry rivalry may depend on the level of demand and the importance to consumers of product differentiation.

We refer to the small number of fundamental independent uncertainties as scenario variables. Once the scenario variables are identified, we must determine the minimum number of states for each scenario variable to capture its essential variation. This will depend on the economic stories that go along with a particular uncertainty. For example, the level of demand for wireless communications could not be captured with just two states: high and low. Instead, we probably need at least three states to capture slow growth, significant increases in demand but use remaining mainly for mobile telephony, and explosive growth with wireline replacement and significant data-transmission demand. The different states for each of the scenarios create other potential scenarios. If our three scenario variables are demand, degree of differentiation, and technology, and we have three states of demand and two states for the other scenario variables, then there are 12 possible scenarios. So a possible scenario will involve explosive demand growth, significant product differentiation, and successful technological innovation. Some of the 12 potential scenarios may not be logically inconsistent. For example, any scenario with explosive demand and unsuccessful technology innovation may not be possible.

Once the scenarios are created, the next step is scenario elaboration. In this stage, each scenario is analyzed independently. We study the effect of different, earlier strategic choices on company performance given the scenario as well as how competition is likely to evolve in the scenario. Depending on the goals of the scenario analysis and the amount of information the company has, the scenario elaboration can either be qualitative or quantitative. It may be valuable to develop financial models of performance in each scenario in some situations and not in others. The scenario elaboration allows one to think carefully about different ways the market may evolve. For example, in the elaboration of the PCS scenario where demand growth is explosive, we would consider the possibility that the FCC would try to reduce the capacity constraints by increasing the spectrum available to wireless services. This may reduce the projected profits in this best-case scenario. Sometimes the scenario elaboration may lead us to redefine our scenarios. In the elaboration of a scenario with a high degree of product differentiation, we may realize that we need to treat differently differentiation advantages created by national scope and the ability to offer other services from differentiation due to existing customers with high switching costs.

The final stage of scenario analysis is to integrate the analysis of individual scenarios into the broader strategic decision-making process. If the analysis is quantitative, this is straightforward in concept if not always easy to execute. Since each scenario elaboration tells us how the company does with different strategic choices, all we need to do is determine the probabilities of each scenario and how these probabilities are affected by the company's strategic choices. Valuing different options is then a simple matter of multiplying outcomes by probabilities. If the scenario analysis is qualitative, then the challenge is to integrate the information from the scenario elaborations into thinking about strategic options. Among the questions to consider is how robust strategies are across scenarios and the extent to which strategies allow the company to change direction if it finds itself in a scenario where the strategy performs poorly. Even in the absence of quantitative data, the scenario analysis can inform decision makers of key trade-offs and where more information and detailed analysis are in order.

Conclusion

Scenario analysis can be a powerful strategic decision-making tool. Although there are certain specific elements to any good scenario analysis, its effective use is as much an art as a science. The development and elaboration of scenarios in a way that an entire organization understands and absorbs involves creativity and effective storytelling. A company cannot rely exclusively on consultants to do this for them; senior management must be involved in all steps of the process.

Summary

Scenario analysis is an approach to decision making that overcomes many of the shortcomings of traditional methods, argues **Robert Gertner**. Using the US wireless telecommunications industry as an example, he shows how scenarios can be created, elaborated, and integrated into company processes. The key challenge is to develop a small set of distinct scenarios covering the main areas of uncertainty, either through a top-down or bottom-up approach. Creativity and storytelling are required and senior managers need to be involved at all stages.

Suggested further reading

Fahey, L. and Randall, R.M. (eds) (1998) *Learning from the Future*, New York: Wiley.

Porter, M. (1985) "Industry scenarios and competitive strategy under uncertainty," Chapter 13 in *Competitive Advantage*, New York: Free Press, pp 445–80.

Schoemaker, P. (1995) "Scenario planning: a tool for strategic thinking," *Sloan Management Review*, 25–40.

Van Der Heijden, K. (1996) *Scenarios: the Art of Strategic Conversation*, New York: Wiley.

Game theory in the real world

by Robert Gertner and Marc Knez

Companies face two forms of uncertainty – structural and strategic. Structural uncertainty arises from economy-wide factors (macro-economic, demographic, technological, and regulatory) and industry-specific factors (demand structure and growth, input markets, concentration levels, channel structure, substitute products, and so on). The critical feature of structural uncertainty is that no one company can directly affect the outcome. Instead, a decision maker must bet on how particular uncertainties will be resolved.

Scenario analysis (discussed in the previous article) is a method for generating a small set of possible scenarios that are relevant to a particular strategic decision. Each scenario is an internally consistent set of outcomes associated with a set of critical structural uncertainties. Using decision theory, these scenarios can be incorporated into analytical models (decision trees) and various alternatives can be evaluated mathematically.

A limitation of scenario analysis is that it does not incorporate strategic uncertainty. Strategic uncertainty derives from a company's inability to predict the actions of rivals, suppliers, large buyers, and potential entrants. In such circumstances, the strategic planner's optimal action depends directly on the actions taken by one or more of these players. The theory that is used to model decisions – and to predict outcomes – under conditions of strategic uncertainty is called game theory. For the time being, we can describe game theory through a simple example, but a more in-depth treatment can be found in "Game theory: how to make it pay" on p 32.

Figure 1 describes a simple entry game between an entrant and an incumbent. The entrant must decide whether to stay out of or enter the incumbent's market. If

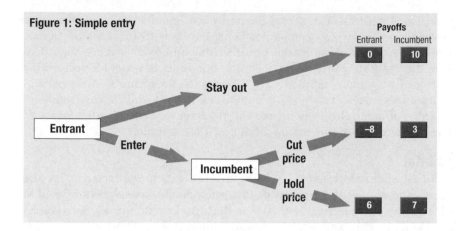

Figure 1: Simple entry

the entrant enters, the incumbent must decide whether to cut its price or to hold the price at its current level. This dynamic game, like all others, is defined by four dimensions: identification of the players, the actions available to each player, the timing of these actions, and the payoffs attached to each possible outcome of the game.

From the entrant's perspective, the incumbent's decision to cut or hold price represents strategic uncertainty. To see the value of game theory, suppose the entrant ignores the information it has on the incumbent's payoffs and simply assumes that there is a 50–50 chance that the incumbent will cut price. Then the expected value of entry is simply $(0.5 \times 6) - (0.5 \times 8)$ = minus 1. So the entrant should stay out of the incumbent's market. Game theory, however, makes the opposite recommendation. Taking the incumbent's payoffs into consideration and assuming that the incumbent will maximize these payoffs, the entrant should infer that the incumbent will do better to hold than to cut price (7>3) if it enters. The entrant should therefore enter in the expectation that the incumbent will hold price.

This simple example highlights the value of game theory in two ways. First, the rules for constructing games (identification of players, actions, timing of actions, payoffs) provide a way to apply analytical structure to complex strategic settings. Second, assumptions about how players will behave given their payoffs provide a method for predicting how the uncertainty will be resolved. In standard game theory, each player is assumed to maximize his or her payoffs (as described in the game), and each player assumes that the other players will also maximize their respective payoffs. In more practical terms, when the entrant takes the incumbent's perspective, it is able to resolve the strategic uncertainty by determining what it would do if it were the incumbent.

Of course, real-life entry decisions are more complicated: there may well be many incumbents and potential entrants whose payoffs are seldom obvious (especially when the game is repeated again and again). Structural uncertainty – regarding demand for an entrant's product, say – also muddies the waters. However, formal models can incorporate these complications; what is important for our purposes is to recognize that this simple game is at the core of just about any complicated entry decision where there are large and potentially threatened incumbents.

Critics of game theory as a tool for strategic analysis argue that it relies on excessively artificial descriptions of complicated strategic decisions and involves erroneous assumptions about how companies behave. It is certainly true that game theory can be misapplied: complicated equilibrium analysis is more useful in understanding the basic structure of a type of decision than as a tool for prescribing courses of action. But when combined with a tool such as scenario analysis that explicitly incorporates uncertainty about competitors' actions and the environment, the practical value of game theory is its capacity to structure complicated strategic decisions. The best way to see this is through a real-life example.

AMD versus Intel

In 1997, Advanced Micro Devices (AMD) introduced its K6 microprocessor. Its aim was to capture leadership of the market for fast microprocessors, a position held at the time by Intel. The primary risk to AMD was that Intel would quickly introduce a comparable or superior chip and, with its brand equity, drive AMD out of the high-end chip segment.

This risk was dampened by the emerging cheap PC market. While the K6 chip was aimed at the high-end market, alternative versions (made in the same plant) could be sold in the low-end market. However, this low-end "hedge" depended on Intel's staying out of the low-end segment. Our strategic scenario analysis will focus on the uncertainty surrounding Intel's decision to enter the low-end segment or not.

The key to strategic reasoning in general, and the application of strategic scenario analysis in particular, is for the decision maker to take the perspective of other players in an effort to predict how they will behave. In this case, decision makers at AMD needed to take Intel's perspective. So in what follows we develop a simple scenario game to capture the trade-offs that Intel had to make when deciding whether to enter the low-end segment. The results of that analysis in turn provide a foundation for the judgments that AMD had to make about the likelihood of gaining significant low-end market share.

In our game, Intel has to decide whether to bide its time in the low-end segment, with the option of introducing its Celeron chip at some later time, or to introduce the Celeron without delay. Besides Intel, there are two other sets of players: the competition – AMD and National Semiconductor (NS), which will surely introduce low-end chips immediately – and the major PC manufacturers – NEC, Compaq, IBM, Toshiba, DEC, and others.

Intel faces many critical uncertainties in making its "wait/introduce" decision. The most important are: 1) the demand for cheap PCs; 2) the quality of its competitors' low-end chips; and 3) whether its brand equity is strong enough to overcome its second-mover disadvantage if it waits.

Intel's uncertainties are linked to those faced by the PC manufacturers and the competition. The PC manufacturers will have to decide whether to buy the AMD/NS chips or Intel's. AMD and NS face capacity and pricing decisions that will depend on whether Intel has entered the low-end market.

For simplicity, we focus on a single structural uncertainty – cheap PC demand – and a single strategic uncertainty – PC makers' purchase decisions. The next step in any scenario analysis is to determine the minimum number of states that each scenario variable can assume. The idea is to choose as many states as will lead to qualitatively different outcomes. In many situations two or three states will suffice: "average," "more successful than expected," and "failure" may capture the essence of the uncertainty.

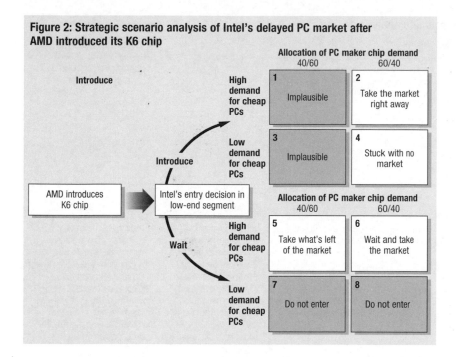

Figure 2: Strategic scenario analysis of Intel's delayed PC market after AMD introduced its K6 chip

So while there is a continuum of alternative demand outcomes, we assume that there are only two: "high" or "low." Similarly, for the PC makers we assume a 60/40 versus a 40/60 split, where Intel retains either 60 percent or 40 percent of the market. Note that the PC makers have mixed motives in their purchase decisions. The demand for their product is likely to be higher if they use an Intel chip, but the price of competitors' chips is likely to be lower. The decision will come down to the price/performance trade-offs and the strength of Intel's brand equity.

The simplified description of the game generates eight initial scenarios, four under each of the possible Intel actions (*see* Figure 2). The next step is to eliminate scenarios that are either implausible or internally inconsistent.

Beginning with those that arise under "introduce," 1 and 3 are relatively implausible. If Intel enters with a low-end chip that is comparable to the competition's low-end chip, its competitors should be able to capture at least 60 percent of the market, whether demand is high or low. Hence, we are left with two scenarios under "introduce," whereby Intel gets 60 percent of either a large or small market for cheap PCs.

Under the "wait" decision, all four scenarios are plausible, conditional on Intel's actually introducing its low-end chip after observing the level of demand for cheap PCs. However, it will not be optimal for Intel to introduce its low-end chips if demand for cheap PCs turns out to be low. Hence, scenarios 7 and 8 are not internally consistent from a game theoretical perspective. This leaves us with two scenarios to consider under "wait," whereby Intel gets either 40 percent or 60 percent of the cheap PC market under conditions of high demand.

From this simple scenario analysis, we see that Intel's downside risk from introducing is simply that the market for cheap PCs does not materialize – the "stuck with no market" scenario. Of course, the upside is that the market does

Table 1: Ten steps to strategic scenario analysis

1. Identify key players.

3. Under each strategic decision determine actions that are both feasible and the most relevant. Examples include entry: yes or no, pricing: high, medium, or low.

5. Identify the timing of actions. Timing is either predetermined or strategic. If it is strategic, then it should be treated as an action in step 3.

7. From steps 1–6, construct the game tree.

9. Where necessary, make judgments about each player's beliefs about the independent uncertainties as well as the strategic uncertainty.

| 1 | 3 | 5 | 7 | 9 |
| 2 | 4 | 6 | 8 | 10 |

2. Identify critical strategic decisions for each player. Each decision represents a potential scenario variable. Examples include: entry or exit decisions, investment decisions, and pricing or capacity decisions

4. Identify critical structural uncertainties – apply standard scenario analysis.

6. Identify the information structure. Three categories of information: 1) information about past decisions, 2) information about payoffs, and 3) information about independent uncertainties and when they are likely to be resolved.

8. Estimate payoffs under each of the possible outcomes in the game. An outcome of the game is a "strategic scenario." Payoff estimation should incorporate both short-run outcomes and judgments about the long-run objectives of each player in the game.

10. Using 8 and 9, examine the plausibility and internal consistency of each strategic scenario. There are two parts to the internal consistency analysis: 1) internal consistency of structural uncertainties, and 2) internal consistency of players' actions – within a particular strategic scenario, are players selecting optimal actions?

---

materialize – the "capture the market right away" scenario. If Intel waits, the risk is that demand will be high and the PC makers will commit to buying from the competition, which will give Intel a second-mover disadvantage – the "take what's left" scenario. Alternatively, many PC makers may switch to Intel as soon as it enters because of its brand equity – the "wait and take the market" scenario.

As in most entry decisions, the benefit of waiting is the option value of observing whether demand is high or low before committing assets to enter. The value of this option depends on the degree of second-mover disadvantage. In Intel's case, that disadvantage is relatively low. It knows that it will be able to capture significant market share with its brand equity (provided it has a competitive chip). The question is to what extent profits will be dissipated through price competition.

The next step is to take the model beyond its role of explaining the strategic structure of the competitive environment and to use it to provide insights into the decision itself. The way to do this is to analyze each scenario in detail and determine payoffs for each player. This can then be used, like our simple entry game example, to predict competitors' behavior and to determine which course of action is most profitable.

In 1997, Intel decided not to introduce a low-end chip for the emerging cheap PC market. Subsequently, the demand for cheap PCs grew rapidly. Intel was forced to introduce an underperforming chip in early 1998, leaving 80 percent of the low-end chip market to its competitors (mostly AMD). Andy Grove, Intel's chairman, commented that the cheap PC boom was "broader and more profound" than he had anticipated the previous autumn.

From AMD's perspective, Intel's delayed entry opened a critical window of opportunity. AMD had time to establish a strong position in the low-end market that could support its attempts to enter the more lucrative high end – Intel's dominant market. Ignoring the obvious criticism of hindsight bias, our simple strategic scenario analysis suggests that AMD had good reason to bet that Intel would delay, increasing AMD's expected payoffs from the K6 chip.

The Intel example is an abbreviated description of a complete strategic scenario analysis. In Table 1 we list the ten steps required for a complete analysis.

Summary

The field of strategy is long on conceptual frameworks and relatively short on formal tools that support strategic decision making. Game theory and scenario analysis, for example, provide valuable techniques for modeling the business environment, but each fails to capture all the relevant variables. Thus game theory focusses on competitors' strategies at the expense of the big picture; scenario analysis, on the other hand, sketches the big picture but misses the strategic details. But when the two are combined – in what **Robert Gertner** and **Marc Knez** call strategic scenario analysis – strategists can add structure to even the most complex competitive situations. To show how this tool works, the authors present a case study of the competition between AMD and Intel in the microchip market.

LEADERSHIP
AND STRATEGY

10

Contributors

B. Joseph White is Dean and Wilber K. Pierpont Collegiate Professor of Business Administration at the University of Michigan Business School.

F. Brian Talbot is Associate Dean of Executive Education and Keith E. and Valerie J. Alessi Professor of Business Administration at the University of Michigan Business School.

Noel M. Tichy is a professor at the University of Michigan Business School and a worldwide consultant specializing in leadership and organizational transformation.

Ram Charan has advised CEOs and worked with boards of directors. He was named in *Business Week*'s top ten educators for in-house corporate education.

Richard Whittington is a university reader in strategy at Saïd Business School, Oxford, and a fellow of New College, Oxford. He is researching how managers learn to strategize as part of the Economic and Social Research Council's SKOPE (Skills, Knowledge and Organizational Performance) program.

Ronald S. Burt is the Hobart W. Williams Professor of Sociology and Strategy at the University of Chicago Graduate School of Business, and the Shell Professor of Human Resources at INSEAD. His work describes the social structure of competition: network mechanisms that order careers, organizations and markets.

Yves Doz is the Timken Chaired Professor of Global Technology and Innovation at INSEAD. His research on the strategy of multinational companies has led to numerous publications, including four books.

Heinz Thanheiser is professor of strategy and management, INSEAD, where he also served as dean from 1980 to 1985. The focus of his current work is on competitive revitalization and corporate renewal, mostly in multinational corporations, where he conducts "action-learning" programs and projects with various layers of management.

Contents

Introduction

The virtues of strong leadership has been a consistent theme in recent managerial literature – the link with effective strategic implementation is perhaps obvious. Authors in this module urge leaders to embrace management education in the battle to align front-line employees with corporate goals, to develop a "teachable" point of view in their quest for growth, and to add "know-how" and "know-who" abilities to the conceptual skills freely available on the market. The controversial topic of corporate culture is addressed and advice offered as to when this should be nurtured and when it can be ignored. The nature of corporate renewal and how leaders are changing their approach to it is also discussed.

Winning hearts and minds with education

by B. Joseph White and F. Brian Talbot

A well-designed management education program helps a CEO execute corporate strategy through aligning the company's leaders and his or her vision of the future. Once a company chooses a strategy – whether it is to focus, diversify, become the quality leader, become the low-cost producer, or be the most innovative competitor – the challenge is to implement the strategy as quickly and fully as possible. This requires that leaders at every level of the company get it: that they and their people are "marching in the same direction," "reading off the same page," "singing from the same hymn book," to quote some of the phrases popular with business leaders. To put it succinctly, everyone in the company needs to align with the company's new strategy.

A CEO has limited means for achieving this critical alignment. Among these are: placing leaders who enthusiastically embrace the new strategy into key positions; communicating the need for change in every possible way; establishing measures and rewards that reflect and reinforce the new strategy; and using management education as a tool to create understanding and deepen the commitment to the new strategy throughout the organization.

When revolutionaries take over a country, among the first things they grab are the media and the education system. The reason is obvious: when you want to lead change you have to engage people's hearts and minds, which invariably means changing their knowledge, their beliefs, and their values. In modern business, successful CEOs are like revolutionaries, dedicated to achieving fast and vast change in strategy and tactics, to responding quickly to change in their competitive environments, and to leading those changes. But even the most insightful and dynamic CEO still faces the age-old problem: how to get these desires enacted through others. Worse, in large global companies, these "others" number in the tens or hundreds of thousands and are separated by distance, language, and culture. In the face of this massive challenge, management education is essential.

The numbers suggest that in the 1990s many CEOs recognized the power of management education. Consider, for example, the tenfold increase in the 1990s from a few hundred to more than 2,000 in the number of "corporate universities," within-company organizations dedicated to training employees. Consider also that among top business schools in the US and western Europe, the fastest growing part of their executive education business in the 1990s was "custom programs": management education sessions designed for and delivered by the school's faculty to the management team of a single company. The dominant theme of custom programs is, invariably, strategy implementation.

The executive education operation at the University of Michigan Business School is a good example. Custom programs doubled in the 1990s to 20 percent of the school's business. A typical program design begins with consultation with senior management on the messages they seek to convey and their goals for the program in terms of strategic, operational, cultural, and individual change. The program itself is a blend of contemporary business topics from finance (e.g., EVA – return on net capital employed), strategy (strategic intent, core competence), marketing (customer satisfaction), operations (management of technology, supply chain management), and human resources (high-performance organizations) with the company's own competitive situation, strategic direction, and change objectives. It is common for senior management to join the course periodically as teachers and for the CEO to handle a wrap-up session with several hours of presentation and give-and-take.

Do such programs effectively help a company execute its strategy? Growth in the volume of custom programs and the frequency of repeat business suggest that CEOs think they do. Moreover, evaluations at the end of custom programs at Michigan and elsewhere suggest that participants value them highly.

An adjunct to corporate strategy

Management education as an adjunct to corporate strategy is, of course, a well-established idea. General Electric, the US industrial giant that has perhaps the world's best reputation for management development, has used its Crotonville, New York facility – the grandparent of corporate education centers – for just this purpose for half a century. Few CEOs have ever tied strategy and education together more tightly and effectively than Jack Welch, the renowned head of GE for the last 19 years. Welch set GE's goals and direction firmly in the 1980s: aggressive growth in shareholder value, number one or number two in an industry or get out, no security for anyone except that based on performance, intense focus on cost, quality, and innovation, and development of the "boundaryless" organization. Educational programs were designed to hammer home these themes to GE's leadership. A promotion or new assignment was deemed to create "a teachable moment" and Crotonville provided an appropriate education experience to a chosen leader. Welch involved himself in these courses, reportedly spending hundreds of hours over the years in "the pit" (the amphitheater-shaped classrooms) at Crotonville, educating his management team on the new strategies and their role in leading successful execution. Like all good teachers, Welch described, explained, persuaded, challenged, listened, clarified, cajoled, and repeated key messages. GE's results, for the past decade and a half, speak for themselves.

There can be little doubt that all this education helped Welch achieve alignment throughout the company. Anyone who has listened to GE graduates like Larry Bossidy of AlliedSignal (the diversified US manufacturing group), or Glen Hiner of Owens Corning (the US fiberglass manufacturer) – men who left GE to become CEOs of their own companies – knows that they are still aligned with GE's basic strategy and values. They are like missionaries who have absorbed the true faith, and are now bringing salvation to other companies and their people.

Perhaps the most vivid illustration of the tight connection between strategy and education is the global quality movement of the last 20 years. Quality excellence has made its way into the strategic objectives of every successful company in every industry during the past two decades. Senior management has deemed excellent quality to be essential. It may be as an offensive weapon (quality so much better than the competition's that it creates product/service differentiation and supports price premiums) or as a defensive weapon (quality at least as good as the competition's as a necessary but not sufficient condition for competitive success). In either case, the question facing senior management has not been "Is quality excellence a strategic objective?" but rather "How do we execute our quality strategy effectively?" How to align the organization in pursuit of this goal, from the CEO through front-line employees, and, indeed, to external partners such as suppliers and distributors, has been a key question. And management education has been an important part of the answer.

The experience of Cummins Engine Company, the world's largest independent manufacturer of diesel engines, is illustrative. In the 1980s, threats from foreign competition and rising customer expectations, of both original equipment manufacturers and end users, made it clear that much higher engine quality, especially in terms of reliability and durability, was essential for the company's survival. One of the earliest actions taken by Henry Schacht, the CEO, and Jim Henderson, the chief operating officer, was to invite Kaoru Ishikawa, the late Japanese quality guru, to do a three-day seminar for the company's top hundred people. In other words, management education was the very first action to follow establishment of drastically improved quality as a strategic objective. In the years since, a vast amount of additional education, for senior management, middle management, and front-line supervision, has been integral to achieving Cummins' strategic quality objectives. People throughout the organization had much to learn: quality concepts, analytical techniques, and methodologies for improvement. Topics ranged from the mathematical to the managerial and cultural. People needed to learn strategic quality management, quality function deployment, statistical process control, group problem solving, and other new knowledge, attitude, and skills from top to bottom. Most importantly, Cummins' experience is typical of companies that have excelled over the past 20 years.

More than a million and a half copies of the Criteria for Performance Excellence, commonly known as the Baldrige guidelines, have been distributed over the last ten years by the US government office that manages the Malcolm Baldrige National Quality Award. The Baldrige criteria may well be the most widely used conceptual framework in management education courses in corporate history. And the results of quality improvement and increased competitiveness in thousands of companies have been nothing short of spectacular. Quality improvement as a strategic objective, with strong management education as a vital underpinning of the execution process, has been a winning combination in the US and around the world.

Education – a powerful success tool

What advice can be offered to senior executives who want to use management education to support successful strategy implementation?

First, it is a powerful tool, use it.

Second, begin by focussing on key leaders, the people we call the "gateways" to your organization. In every company, no matter the size, there are no more than 100 senior people who direct the key operations and support functions, who absolutely must understand the company's strategy and lead its execution enthusiastically. This is the target audience for the first wave of management education. Ultimately, this education must cascade beyond this group, but without their support and leadership, the strategy cannot be implemented successfully.

Third, have the highest standards when it comes to selecting faculty to teach your key people. Several years ago, a Japanese executive was asked what he saw as the main difference between a particular US-headquartered company and his own Japanese operation. He responded: "We only permit the most admired, most capable people to teach others. Your teachers are not highly respected." That insight is as valid and provocative today as it was then.

Fourth, use your own leaders as part of the teaching staff, in addition to using consultants, business school faculty, and other professional instructors. Teaching in-company management education programs provides a powerful platform for leadership by company executives. Our faculty colleague at the University of Michigan Business School, Noel Tichy, says that leaders need to have a "teachable point of view." What better way to develop and disseminate it than as a teacher, in the classroom? Rarely does anyone understand and believe in the subject more than the teacher, so seize the opportunity to engage senior people, including the CEO, as faculty members in the program. Senior executives as teachers add credibility and importance to a program. Smart executives will embrace the opportunity to listen to and learn about their people and their views in this unique setting.

Finally, only start the management education process if there is a commitment to following it through. Powerful forces are unleashed when corporate leaders are invited to learn about, discuss, and challenge the company's strategy and the execution hurdles it presents. Concerns need to be aired, doubts answered, problems addressed, expectations met.

Invariably, educating one group of managers gives rise to the need to educate others, and this need cannot be ignored. Not long ago, the University of Michigan Business School delivered a management education program for upper-middle management at a large Korean company. Successful achievement of the company's global ambitions and strategy was a driving force behind the program. Before it was half over, the bosses of the participants decided that it was essential for them to undertake an accelerated version of their subordinates' course, quickly. The leaders discovered that they needed to keep up with and understand the new ideas and points of view they heard coming from their people.

Conclusion

The familiar forces of globalization, competition, new technologies, and people's heightened expectations of involvement and participation in the work place have made obsolete the traditional hierarchical command-and-control organization. This has happened far faster than any of us dreamed possible. Corporate leaders are left with this vital question: How do we execute strategy successfully when the effectiveness of giving orders and telling people what to do is at an all-time low? There are many responses to the question. One of the key answers is that a vibrant, relevant, well-led management education experience is an effective way of engaging and winning people's hearts and minds.

Summary

Top business people can learn from revolutionaries, suggest **B. Joseph White** and **F. Brian Talbot**. Just as rebels often seize the education system when taking over a country, so CEOs dedicated to leading and achieving change must find an effective way of winning hearts and minds. A well-designed management education program – aimed at aligning front-line employees with corporate goals – is an important adjunct to corporate strategy. The authors urge companies to focus carefully on the human "gateways" inside their organizations, to pick high-quality teachers, to use their own senior managers to educate others, and only to start the process if there is a will to follow it through.

Suggested further reading

Ashkenas, R., Ulrich, D., Jick, T. and Kerr, S. (1995) *The Boundaryless Organization*, San Francisco, CA: Jossey-Bass.

Prahalad, C.K. and Hamel, G. (1994) *Competing for the Future*, Boston, MA: Harvard Business School Press.

Quinn, R. (1996) *Deep Change*, San Francisco, CA: Jossey-Bass.

Tichy, N. (1997) *The Leadership Engine*, London: HarperCollins.

Do you have a teachable point of view on balanced growth?

by Noel M. Tichy and Ram Charan

Although the bull market in US equities continues, underperformers are harshly dealt with: Eckhard Pfeiffer lost his job as Compaq Computer CEO, as did Sven-Christer Nilsson at mobile phone giant Ericsson of Sweden. Howard Schultz, chairman and CEO of Seattle-based Starbucks Coffee, oversaw a 28 percent decline in his company's stock value overnight after a profits warning.

A failure to deliver balanced growth was the reason in all cases. The bottom line is not enough. Capital markets demand solid top-line growth. This balanced growth challenge has stalled such corporate stalwarts as the US manufacturing conglomerate 3M, Emerson Electric, the US industrial products and electrical components maker, and Eastman Kodak, the US photographic products company.

Exhortation by the CEO will not turn these companies around. What is required is what we call a teachable point of view. Senior leadership must have a very distinct set of business ideas that translates into growth products. Leaders need divisions that are clear about distribution channels, customer segments, and how the company can create a new growth trajectory. Their ideas should be coupled with a clear statement of core values to guide behavior in the organization and support the business ideas. The teachable point of view involves being clear about how to create positive emotional energy: how to excite and energize all the workforce around these ideas and values. Finally, there is edge, a clear position on the courageous yes or no decisions needed in terms of investment, product, and people.

This teachable point of view on balanced growth is the core building block of the company's "genetic code." Leaders at all levels must personally teach it and mobilize the organization to implement it (*see* Figure 1).

The "outside in" company

Growth is a creative game. It requires curiosity, imagination, and emotional energy – qualities that we believe exist and even abound among people working in most companies today. The qualities may not be immediately visible, but enormous amounts of dormant creative potential tend to blossom in companies once leadership frees up employee ideas.

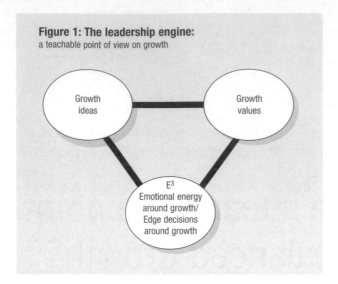

Figure 1: The leadership engine:
a teachable point of view on growth

A sustainable growth strategy starts with understanding the difference between what you make and what people need – which often turns out not to be the same thing.

Such a strategy requires you to tap your sources of energy and imagination, look at your company from the perspective of your once and future customers, ask endless questions about what is going on in the real world and what is happening in the market place. It means discovering how needs are changing, what is behind the changes, and where resulting opportunities lie.

Having stepped outside of your business, you work backwards to ask such questions as: What needs do we satisfy now? What needs could we satisfy now, and how do we bridge the gap? What advantages do we have? What advantages do we need to create? What old competences do we need to de-emphasize?

This is called looking from the outside in. Sound simple and obvious? Then your company is probably doing it already. The fact is, it is human nature to look from the inside out.

Astonishingly few companies ever try to see themselves as others see them. In what we call an inside-out company, people typically look at their business environment through the lens of their internal products and processes. They look at what they make, and try to figure out how they can sell more.

These companies and their people are trapped in their own past and experience. Looking from the inside out, they see mainly that they are stuck in industries and core competences with limited prospects. If your business has no top-line growth prospects, you are likely to find:

- *Your markets are at risk.* No matter how good you are, your market place is not safe any more. Powerful, growth-hungry companies – companies you may not even identify as competitors today – are moving in on it. When they arrive, they will meet your customers' needs better than you can. Do nothing until they attack, and you will be starting too late to catch up.
- *Your market valuation is at risk.* Investors – whether a public company's stockholders or a private company's bankers – will not settle only for cost-cutting gains; they will want to see increased earnings from growth as well.

- *Your human capital is at risk.* If you are not growing, you cannot attract and keep the people you need – the ones with confidence, enthusiasm, ambition, imagination, and ideas. They are looking for companies with expanding horizons.

Broadening the pond not market share

Looking from the outside in, successful growth companies' leaders think expansively and ask what related market places they can serve.

They are, in a phrase we use regularly, seeking to enlarge or broaden the pond they fish in. Broadening the pond is the antithesis of going for market share. The goal, in fact, is to put your current market share in its proper perspective by restating it as your share of your potential market.

For example, a company with 40 percent of a $10 billion market needs to look for the much larger pond of which its share is perhaps 4 percent. That's literally what Jack Welch tells his business leaders at General Electric, the US power generation equipment company: redefine your market to one in which your current share is no more than 10 percent.

For example, in 1995, Bob Nardelli, president of GE Power Systems, a subsidiary of General Electric, drew scant comfort from the company's 50 percent share of the $20 billion market for power generation equipment.

He saw that the market was stagnant and deregulation was creating opportunities for new competitors. Nardelli used the acquisition of Italy's Nuovo Pignone, the gas turbine manufacturer, not only to expand GE's presence in Europe but also to enter new market segments in the oil and gas industry. Today, he has totally redefined his pond and now fishes in a $700 billion pool, encompassing the whole value chain of power generation and delivery, from wellhead to end user.

He has unleashed incredible double-digit growth in a once slow and stodgy, mature business. He has created a new growth trajectory and an expansive set of possibilities. These require shifting perspectives and widening horizons.

Other similar examples

- Federal Express, the US freight carrier, created a growth trajectory when it began overnight delivery of components to companies that need to fill orders fast without carrying high inventories. In so doing, FedEx took itself well beyond overnight package delivery and into floating, fast-track warehousing.
- When Bill Gates concluded that the future of his business lay with the internet and not just with producing software, he put Microsoft, the US software giant, on a new growth trajectory.
- GE Medical Systems, a division of General Electric, created new trajectories twice, first with globalization and, later, by moving into services.
- Each of GE Capital's 28 businesses started as a new growth trajectory.
- Dave Holmes defined a new trajectory for Reynolds and Reynolds Co., which provides integrated information-management systems and services. He expanded his pond from selling forms and computer systems to helping his customers become more profitable, and added everything from database marketing to managerial expertise to his offerings.

Balancing growth is important

Not all growth is good growth. "The curse of all curses is the revenue line," the late Roberto Goizueta once told *Fortune* magazine. Revenue growth at US soft drinks maker Coca-Cola has been anything but shabby, but the point that Goizueta, its CEO, was making was that creating value for shareholders comes first. To do that, growth must be profitable and capital efficient.

Far too often, people think of growth as a panacea that will, in and of itself, cure a bottom-line problem. They pour resources into a new venture without first doing the hard work of ensuring productivity and profitability. It's the *Field of Dreams* approach: grow it, and the money will come. But the money will come only if there is a competitive advantage.

We maintain that the only growth worth having is sustainable, balanced, top-line and bottom-line growth. Olympic revenue goals must be accompanied by continuing cost and productivity improvements, restructuring as required, and intelligent reinvestment of capital.

Jorma Ollila has led Nokia, the Finnish telecommunications group, to be the premier balanced growth company in Europe. In 1992, Ollila as the 41-year-old CEO took Nokia from a faltering hodgepodge of a conglomerate to a very focussed mobile phone producer, doubling revenues in that period. Three years of stunning success left the company's young managers overconfident, even arrogant. Ollila faced a severe setback in 1997. The company share price shed 38 percent after he warned that profits were under pressure due to misjudgment of demand. He mobilized "commando teams" of leaders at Nokia to fix the company. By the end of 1997, Nokia was back on track. Ollila learned a painful lesson and developed a teachable point of view about balanced growth.

One lesson was that operational excellence is critical: without it a company can die. Another was that a workable set of corporate values must include humility, healthy paranoia, and a strong belief in energizing people by stretching them and sticking with them through rough times. (Ollila didn't fire any of his senior people, although some spent time on the sidelines as a result of the 1997 problems.) Finally, he learned the toughest part of leadership, how to teach what edge is all about, making difficult decisions about cost, savings, and investments.

A leader's challenge is to articulate the teachable point of view on balanced growth and then pass it to everyone in the organization. Develop leader/teachers at all levels of the organization so that the "genetic code" drives the growth trajectory.

Conclusion

Growth is a mindset – great business leaders have demonstrated this time and again. In an era of virtually unlimited opportunity, no business is mature; no markets are fully penetrated. The road to change starts with a grasp of basic business thinking: the common sense underlying strong financial performance. This is surprisingly uncommon.

Summary

The bottom line is no longer enough: balanced growth is today's challenge, say **Noel M. Tichy** and **Ram Charan**. Leaders need a teachable point of view tinged with "edge" if they hope to secure growth. Used properly, such techniques unlock the creativity and drive of staff and can help ward off classic traps that have occasionally caught some leading US and European companies. Growth is a mindset as well as a creative game. To succeed, a growth company needs to stand back and start looking at itself from the outside in. It also needs to broaden the pond in which it goes fishing. In an era of virtually unlimited opportunity, no business is mature, no market fully penetrated. To get on track, leaders should pay heed to the basic business common sense that underlies a strong financial performance.

Suggested further reading

Charan, R. (1998) *Boards at Work: How Corporate Boards Create Competitive Advantage*, San Francisco, CA: Jossey-Bass.

Tichy, N.M. with Cohen, E. (1997) *The Leadership Engine: How Winning Companies Build Leaders at Every Level*, New York: HarperBusiness.

Tichy, N.M. and Charan, R. (1999) *Every Business is a Growth Business: How Your Company Can Prosper Year After Year*, Times Business Random House.

Tichy, N.M. and Sherman, S. (1993) *Control Your Destiny or Someone Else Will*, New York: Doubleday.

The "how" is more important than the "where"

by Richard Whittington

Consider the following two managerial predicaments. The regional units of a large UK government agency badly need to develop local strategies for operating in a new quasi-market environment. But the agency's strategic planning director knows that his business unit managers have no experience of strategy. How can he help them create strategies for the first time?

Second, the general managers in a conglomerate that is moving toward a more focussed business portfolio are asked to think about their business's long-term strategy, rather than just squeezing out extra margin in line with next quarter's budget. Instead of competing with their sister businesses for capital, they are now supposed to work with them to create synergy. How are they and their management teams to set about this new kind of strategizing?

These are essentially questions about the "practice" of strategy, which is concerned with how to make strategy and how to learn to do it well. Such matters have only recently moved on to the agenda of those who study strategic management. But in a competitive and dynamic environment, good strategy practice is more likely to be a source of enduring value than clever strategic positioning.

Evolving perspectives

The evolution of strategic management thinking since the 1960s is described in Figure 1 according to two main criteria: target focus and main issue.

The vertical axis contrasts a large body of work that is essentially directional – concerned about where strategies should go – with the stream of work that focusses on how to get there. The horizontal axis divides attention between work that concentrates on organizations as wholes and that more concerned with

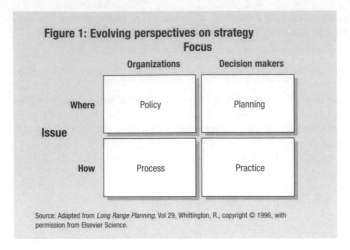

Figure 1: Evolving perspectives on strategy

Source: Adapted from *Long Range Planning*, Vol 29, Whittington, R., copyright © 1996, with permission from Elsevier Science.

particular decision makers – the managers and consultants who make the strategies.

The two axes in Figure 1 combine to define four basic strategy perspectives:

Planning

From the outset of formal strategy in the 1960s, the "planning" approach has focussed on tools and techniques to help managers with decisions about business direction. Key decision-making aids include the portfolio matrices produced by consultants like McKinsey and the Boston Consulting Group, and Harvard professor Michael Porter's industry structure analysis.

Policy

From the 1970s onward, "policy" researchers have developed a more macro focus, comparing the organizational payoffs to be achieved by pursuing different strategic directions. The policy options compared include various kinds of diversification strategy, internationalization, and innovation.

Process

The challenges of the 1980s led large organizations for the first time to consider the problems of transformation. "Process" issues – how businesses come to recognize the need for change and how they manage the change process – have become increasingly prominent. Giants have been downsized, "downscoped," and even been taught to dance!

Practice

Today's "practice" approach to strategy draws on many of the insights of the process school, but returns to the decision-maker level. It is concerned with how strategists "strategize." Privatization, deregulation and constant innovation are forcing many businesses to consider the effectiveness of their present strategy practices and to learn new ones. Decentralization and "delayering" mean that ever more managers must take up the challenge of strategizing.

Learning to strategize

Strategic positions are permanently precarious, always liable to being imitated by competitors or undermined by innovation. But a business whose focus is on good strategizing practice is perpetually in a position to grasp opportunities and respond to competitors. The "how" of strategizing becomes more important than the "where" of strategy.

Strategizing involves both inspiration and perspiration. The inspiration entails obtaining ideas, spotting opportunities, and grasping new situations. Success here implies high conceptualizing – or reconceptualizing – skills. The perspiration is in the annual budgetting and planning, the meetings in the corridors, the production of formal documents, number crunching, and presentations.

This kind of nitty-gritty hard work demands craft skills. Without the craft skills of procedure and persuasion, even the greatest concepts are likely to go unheard.

Conceptualizing skills and craft skills are learned differently. The skills of conceptualizing and reconceptualizing businesses come typically from outside:

■ from highly developed intellectual capabilities, involving a repertoire of techniques and frames for imagining and re-imagining a business and its industry;
■ from wide experience of different businesses and industries, providing a variety of practical, portable models that can be applied in new contexts.

These conceptualizing skills help the strategist to know what to do.

The craft skills of strategizing draw heavily on internally acquired expertise:

■ from proficiency in the internal procedures of strategy making within an organization and among stakeholders, so that the effective strategist never puts a foot wrong;
■ from mastery of the politics and culture of the organization, so that the effective strategist never steps on anybody's toes.

These craft skills involve knowhow and know-who.

The conceptualizing skills of know-what can be learned through MBA training or through experience as a strategy consultant. Such managers are equipped with a wide range of techniques and are exposed to many situations. The craft skills of knowhow and know-who, however, typically require in-depth organizational experience. Acquiring such skills may literally require a "strategy apprenticeship" within a company likely to last a good many years.

Necessary balance

The necessary balance between conceptualizing skill and craft skill will vary from context to context. Effective strategists, however, are unlikely to have conceptualizing skills alone. Conceptualizing skills are pretty generally available on the market. To get their strategic projects accepted, strategists need to fit their proposals to company procedures and match them to company politics. It is for this reason that businesses typically draw their senior managers and many of their corporate development specialists from inside the company. It takes internally acquired craft skills to be truly effective as a strategist.

Typically, companies only bring in outsiders for strategic positions when complete reconceptualization is required, and old procedures and politics are redundant. International Business Machines hired Louis Gerstner from RJR Nabisco, the big US food group, as chief executive at a time of crisis. Avon Products, the world's largest door-to-door cosmetics group, brought in Charles Perrin as chairman and CEO from Duracell, the US battery company, when seeking major strategic change. In more normal times, however, it is local knowhow and know-who that are important for effectiveness. Even external consultants advising on "what to do" often draw on long-standing relationships. Strategy consultants McKinsey & Co. have been involved with the BBC and Unilever, for example, for 30 to 40 years.

We can now return to the predicaments of the government agency and the conglomerate bent on refocussing with which we started. Both face times of discontinuity, when setting a new direction is very important. One immediate route forward is to seek a good deal of advice, whether from the central strategic planning unit or from external consultants.

However, ultimately both should invest in the business managers themselves. Give these business managers the skills and confidence to reconceptualize their businesses, and they will then add their existing knowhow and know-who to create an unbeatable combination. Consultants and the center should not hold hands, but hand over. For business managers learning to strategize, there is no substitute for their own practice.

Summary

Questions about the "practice" of strategy – how to make strategy and how to learn to do it well – have only recently moved up the management agenda. Good strategizing, says **Richard Whittington**, involves both inspiration and perspiration. The former requires conceptual skills, typically found outside the organization, which enable managers to know what to do. The latter requires craft skills, generally internally acquired, which are more about knowhow and know-who. Conceptualizing skills are pretty generally available on the market – only those with internally acquired craft skills, however, are likely to be truly effective strategists. In a competitive environment, good strategy practice is likely to offer better enduring value than clever strategic positioning, which is often precarious, subject to imitation, and threatened by innovation.

Suggested further reading

Eden, C. and Ackerman, F. (1999) *Making Strategy*, London: Sage.

Hamel, G. (1998) "Strategy innovation and the quest for value," *Sloan Management Review*, Winter.

Roos, J. and Victor, B. (1999) "Towards a new model of strategy-making as serious play," *European Management Journal*, August.

Whittington, R. (1996) "Strategy as practice," *Long Range Planning*, 29.

When is corporate culture a competitive asset?

by Ronald S. Burt

Culture is to a corporation what it is to any other social system, a selection of beliefs, myths, and practices shared by people such that they feel invested in, and part of, one another. Putting aside the specific beliefs that employees share, the culture of an organization is strong to the extent that employees are strongly held together by their shared belief in the culture. Culture is weak to the extent that employees hold widely different, even contradictory, beliefs so as to feel distinct from one another.

Culture effect in theory

In theory, a strong corporate culture can enhance corporate economic performance by reducing costs. There are lower monitoring costs. Shared beliefs, myths, and practices defining a corporate culture are an informal control mechanism that coordinates employee effort. Employees deviating from accepted practice can be detected and admonished faster and less visibly by friends than by the boss. The company's goals and practices are clearer, which lessens employee uncertainty about the risk of taking inappropriate action so that they can respond more quickly to events. New employees are more effectively brought into coordination with established employees because they are less likely to hear conflicting accounts of the company's goals and practices. Moreover, corporate culture is less imposed on employees than it is socially constructed by them, so employee motivation and morale should be higher than when control is exercised by a superior through bureaucratic lines of authority.

There are lower labor costs. Peer pressures – the attraction of pursuing a transcendental goal larger than the day-to-day demands of a job or the exclusion of employees who do not feel comfortable with the corporate culture – mean that employees may work harder and for longer hours where an organization has a strong corporate culture.

In other words, a strong corporate culture extracts unpaid labor from employees.

These savings mean that companies with a stronger corporate culture can expect to enjoy higher economic performance – a phenomenon known as the "culture effect."

The most authoritative evidence of the culture effect comes from a study by Harvard Business School professors John Kotter and James Heskett, based on data published in the appendix of their 1992 book *Corporate Culture and Performance*. Measures of performance and strong culture are listed for a large sample of companies in a variety of broad industries analogous to the industry categories in *Fortune* magazine.

To measure relative strength of culture, Kotter and Heskett mailed questionnaires in the early 1980s to the top six officers in each sample company, asking them to rate (on a scale of 1 to 5) the strength of culture in other companies selected for study in their industry.

Three indicators of strong culture were listed: 1) managers in the company

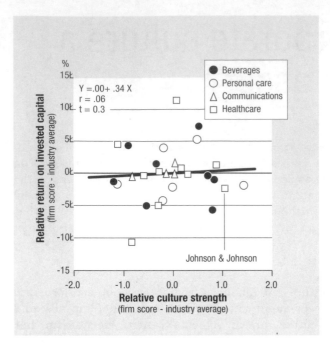

Figure 1

commonly speak of their company's style or way of doing things; 2) the company has made its values known through a creed or credo and has made a serious attempt to encourage managers to follow these; and 3) the company has been managed according to long-standing policies and practices other than those of just the incumbent CEO. Ratings were averaged to define the strength of a company's corporate culture, which can be adjusted for the industry average to make comparisons across industries.

For example, Johnson & Johnson, the healthcare group, is cited as benefitting from its strong culture in the rapid recall of Tylenol painkiller capsules when poisoned ones were discovered on shelves. In the Kotter and Heskett study, Johnson & Johnson received an average rating of 4.61, the highest given to a healthcare company in the study, 1.07 points above the 3.51 average for healthcare companies. The company is shown to the far right of Figure 1.

Relative economic performance is plotted on the vertical axis of the figure. Kotter and Heskett list three measures reported to yield similar conclusions about the culture effect: net income growth from 1977 to 1988, average return on invested capital from 1977 to 1988, and average yearly increases in stock prices from 1977 to 1988. For illustration here, I use average return on invested capital.

For example, Johnson & Johnson enjoyed a 17.89 percent rate of return over the decade, but pharmaceuticals is a high-return industry in which 17.89 percent was slightly below average, so you see Johnson & Johnson below zero on the vertical axis of the figure (17.89 minus 20.21 equals the Johnson & Johnson score of –2.32).

The point is the lack of association between economic performance and corporate culture. Figure 1 contains healthcare companies, along with sample companies from beverages, personal care, and communications – a total of 30 companies. No extreme cases obscure an association. There is simply no association. The correlation of .06 is almost the .00 you would get if performance were perfectly independent of culture. Kotter and Heskett report a slightly higher .31 correlation across all of their

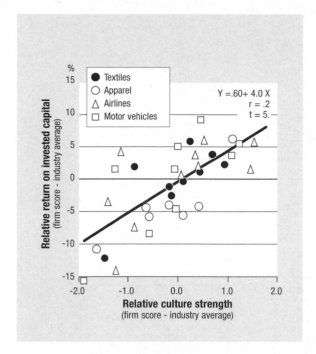

Figure 2

companies, but the correlation was still sufficiently weak for them to conclude in their book that: "The statement 'strong cultures create excellent performance' appears to be just plain wrong."

Contingent value of culture

There is a powerful culture effect in fact, but it occurs elsewhere in the economy. Figure 2 has the same axes as Figure 1 but plots data on sample companies from other industries – airlines, apparel, motor vehicles, and textiles. The 36 sample companies from these industries show a close association between performance and culture; the stronger the corporate culture, the higher the return on invested capital.

The key point is illustrated in Figure 3, which shows a predictable shift from culture being economically irrelevant (Figure 1) to its being a competitive asset (Figure 2). Nineteen industries from the Kotter and Heskett study are ordered on the vertical axis of Figure 3 by the correlation between performance and culture. Apparel is at the top of the figure with its .76 correlation between culture and performance. Communications is at the bottom with its negligible –.15 correlation.

The horizontal axis of Figure 3 is a measure of market competition in each industry. Using data in the public domain (primarily the benchmark input–output tables published by the US Department of Commerce; similar data are available for aggregate industries in most advanced economies), market competition is derived from the network effect on industry profit margins of industry buying and selling with suppliers and customers (thus the "effective" level of competition). The effective level of market competition is high in an industry to the extent that producers show lower profit margins than expected from the network of their transactions with suppliers and customers (for measurement details, *see* the author's 1999 paper on competition and contingency in Suggested further reading).

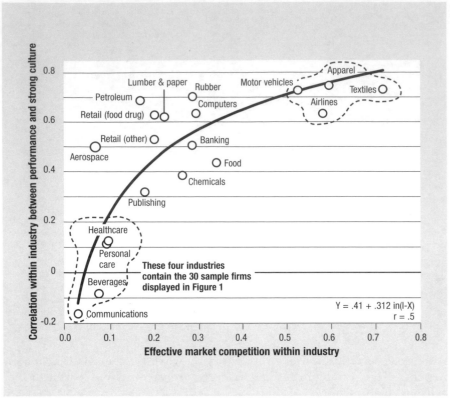

Figure 3

Figure 3 shows that market and culture are complements. To the left, where producers face an effectively low level of market competition, culture is not a competitive asset. These are the 30 sample companies in Figure 1 taken from the four industries enclosed by a dotted line in the lower left of Figure 3. These are complex, dynamic markets such as the communications and healthcare industries, in which profit margins are good, but companies have to stay nimble to take advantage of the next shift in the market. There is competition to be sure (*see* Suggested further reading for the 1999 paper), but the point here is that a strong corporate culture is not associated with economic performance. (The author's colleague at the University of Chicago, Jesper Sørensen, has studied these companies over time, and describes in his 1998 paper on reliable performance how the culture effect is weak in industries subject to market change.)

At the other extreme, to the right in Figure 3, where producers face an effectively high level of market competition, culture is closely associated with economic performance. These are the 36 sample companies in Figure 2 taken from the four industries enclosed by a dotted line in the upper right of Figure 3. In these industries of effectively high market competition, producers are easily substituted for one another, suppliers or customers are strong, and margins are low.

Contingency function

Between the two market extremes, the performance effect of a strong corporate culture increases with market competition. The non-linear regression line in Figure

3 (the solid bold line) can be used as a contingency function describing how the culture effect varies with market competition. For any specific level of market competition on the horizontal axis, the contingency function defines an expected correlation on the vertical axis between culture strength and economic performance.

Since industry scores on the horizontal axis are computed from data publicly available on all industries, the expected value of a strong corporate culture in any industry can be extrapolated from the contingency function. Results for a selection of industries are given in Figure 3.

The high correlation for the contingency function shows that the function is an accurate description of culture's effect in the diverse markets (r = .85; for details on deriving, and extrapolating from, the contingency function *see* Suggested further reading for the author's 1994 article).

At the level of individual companies, 44 percent of the variance in company returns to invested capital can be predicted by the industry in which they primarily operate, and their relative strength of corporate culture accounts for another 23 percent of the variance. Culture accounts for half again of the performance variance described by industry differences!

Thinking strategically

Contingent value is the main point here. A strong corporate culture is neither always valuable, nor always irrelevant. Value is contingent on market. A strong corporate culture can be a powerful competitive asset in a commodity market. In a complex, dynamic market, on the other hand, culture is irrelevant to economic performance.

The contingent value of culture can be a guide to thinking strategically about culture. The more a company's industry resembles a commodity market, the more economic return one can expect from investing in a strong corporate culture. When merging with a new company, one should ask about the industry in which it operates. If the industry looks like a commodity market and there is no corporate culture in the company, then performance would be higher if a strong culture could be instilled in the company. If the company's industry looks like a commodity market, and the company has a strong corporate culture, take pains to preserve the culture because the company's performance in some part is a function of its culture. On the other hand, if the company operates in a complex, dynamic market, one is free to integrate the company into one's own without concern for whatever culture existed before. Culture is irrelevant to performance in such markets.

Finally, beware of any consultant's report on corporate culture and performance that is based on a narrow sample. Consider, for example, what would be the outcome if one consultant selected ten telecommunication companies for case analysis – he or she had worked in the industry, has good personal contacts there – while another selected ten textile companies.

These are two reasonable and interesting projects, with a relatively large number of companies for case analysis.

There is no need to read their reports. The first consultant selected an industry with a low effective level of market competition (the communications industry is to the far left in Figure 3). A strong corporate culture is not a competitive asset in such complex, dynamic industries. This consultant will find no evidence of higher performance in strong culture companies, will generalize the results to conclude that the culture effect does not exist, then earnestly (since the consultant has research to support the conclusion) advise client companies against wasting resources on institutionalizing a strong corporate culture.

The second consultant selected an industry at the other extreme of the contingency function. Textile producers face an effectively high level of market competition (they appear at the far right of Figure 3). A strong corporate culture is a competitive asset in such industries. This second consultant will find evidence of higher performance in strong-culture companies, will generalize the results to conclude that performance depends on developing a strong corporate culture, and then earnestly (since this consultant also has research to support the conclusion) advise client companies to concentrate on institutionalizing a strong corporate culture.

If these consultants were to approach the same clients, those clients would hear equally earnest, but quite contradictory, results. They would conclude that the jury is still out on corporate culture. All of these people are drawing reasonable conclusions within the limits of their experience.

Nevertheless, all are wrong; simplistic in their ignorance of the contingent value of a strong corporate culture.

Summary

Those who talk of corporate culture affecting the bottom line tend to cite anecdotal, and therefore not very convincing, evidence. So why worry about it, not least when some companies without any obvious set of shared beliefs seem to do perfectly well? According to **Ron Burt**, much depends on the industry. In some sectors corporate culture has, indeed, no bearing on performance; but in others it can represent a powerful advantage over competitors. Knowing its contingent value can help in deciding when to invest in the culture of your own organization, when to protect the culture of an organization merged into your own, and when not to bother about it at all.

Suggested further reading

Burt, R.S., Gabbay, S.M., Holt, G. and Moran, P. (1994) "Contingent organization as a network theory: the culture-performance contingency function," *Acta Sociologica*, 37: 345–70.

Burt, R.S., Guilarte, M., Raider, H.J. and Yasuda, Y. (1999) "Competition, contingency, and the external structure of markets," www.gsb.uchicago.edu/fac/ronald.burt/research.

Kotter, J.P. and Heskett, J.L. (1992) *Corporate Culture and Performance*, New York: The Free Press.

Sørensen, J.B. (1998) "The strength of corporate culture and the reliability of firm performance," www.gsbuchicago.edu/fac/jesper.sorensen/research.

The art and science of corporate renewal

by Yves Doz and Heinz Thanheiser

"The trouble with corporate renewal is that it all depends on a powerful leader!" So concluded a frustrated executive at one of our recent seminars on corporate renewal. It is hard to disagree with him. Success in major corporate renewals tends to be closely identified with chief executives: Jack Welch at General Electric; the late Roberto Goizueta at Coca-Cola; Percy Barnevik at ABB; Jurgen Schrempp at Daimler. The same applies to corporate failures like Al Dunlap of Sunbeam, Edzard Reuter at Daimler, and John Sculley of Apple.

This article considers the nature of corporate renewal and how leaders are changing their approach to it. From close observation of corporate transformation at companies with which we have been involved, and at others documented in various publications, we have arrived at certain generalizations concerning the ingredients for successful transformation. However, inventing a creative recipe and cooking a perfect dish still require much talent from leaders. It is more art than science.

When we last summarized our insights into efforts at corporate renewal in large multinationals in the early 1990s (*see* Suggested further reading), we found that the development of organizational capabilities for mobilizing people and that of cumulative learning continued to elude many top managements. We concluded that orthodox management principles were a hurdle. We stated that the main challenge was to shed old ideas about how an organization should work and develop and institutionalize a new mindset. The trouble among established leaders was that change initiatives were typically too little and too late. This was true in the case of John Akers at International Business Machines, Robert Stempel at General Motors, Paul Lego at Westinghouse, Heinz Ruhnau at Lufthansa, and Cor van der Klugt at Philips, to name but a few.

Throughout the 1990s, transformation efforts increased in number, sparing hardly any large corporation in the developed world. Other articles in this book deal with the why, highlighting global competition, deregulation, privatization, the internet revolution, more influential and impatient shareholders, and so forth. We will focus on the dimensions – the what – and the dynamics – the how – of renewal.

The most common cause of problems flowed from liberalization (e.g., airlines, telecoms, banking, or utilities) where companies suffered from severe cost disadvantages, slow innovation, inward-looking management, and arrogance. On the other hand, companies that were used to working in competitive environments typically had to deal with shortening product life cycles, technological changes, or new competition from upstarts in other rich countries, or from emerging economies, or both.

Two distinct patterns emerge from a look at corporate changes over time. In the 1980s, the responses in virtually all situations included portfolio restructuring and – in more severe crisis situations – financial restructuring, along with mergers and demergers, acquisitions, alliances, and partnerships. Operations were "downsized" and headcounts reduced. Non-core activities were outsourced; reengineering or process-improvement projects were launched, together with quality improvement and waste-reduction efforts like TQM or kaizen. All, essentially, were geared to cost reduction. And this remains the standard response to performance pressures even today.

The 1990s produced some different stories signaling an interesting change in CEO thinking. Top managers initiated mobilization activities, real-time learning, solution-discovery workshops, value innovation teams, taskforces, empowerment programs and the like. The search began for behavior changes: for breaking inertia; forcing better local problem solving and learning; coordinating better by removing safety cushions; weakening functional silos in favour of horizontal cooperation; encouraging greater initiative and entrepreneurship in smaller, more market-oriented units.

More CEOs today are willing to entertain and experiment with a concept of organization and management behavior different from that of their predecessors. But this is not to say that all are succeeding. Despite the impressive array of recipes from academics and consultants, a CEO facing a performance crisis is still left with little guidance on what lasting renewal looks like or how to achieve it. In this article we propose a framework that offers some guidance on managing such processes.

The dimensions of change

In successful transformations, change encompasses three key dimensions (*see* Figure 1):

■ redefining corporate focus and ambition;
■ changing the "rules of the game" inside the organization;
■ energizing people for new efforts.

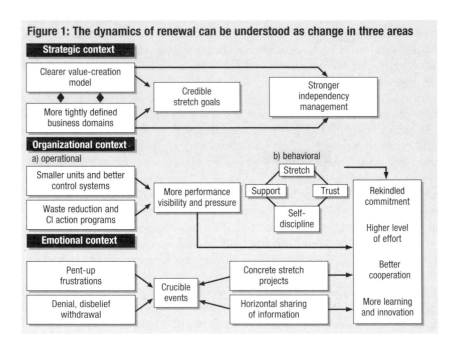

Figure 1: The dynamics of renewal can be understood as change in three areas

Strategic context

In the successful transformation cases we studied, the CEO – often a new appointment and working with other "fresh blood" from outside – developed a different value-creation theory for the company. This typically specified relationships between three aspects: domain, ambition, and integration.

A starting point is often to redefine how the company will create value for its various stakeholders. Sometimes this involves broadening the scope of activities, sometimes tightening it.

At PepsiCo Craig Weatherup, the new CEO, expanded the domain of the company to include a whole range of beverages beyond traditional colas. Conversely, at Nokia of Finland, Jorma Ollila focussed on mobile telecom businesses, narrowing the old corporate "conglomerate" domain. A clearer value-creation theory – typically focussing on areas where the company's various activities intersect to create the most value – allows management to decide which businesses and activities would be "core" and which would not. The latter could be outsourced, if part of an overall process like logistics at Philips, or divested, like all non-telecom-related activities at Nokia.

Redefining the business focus in this way allows a CEO credibly to set ambitious stretch goals, in terms of competitive breakthrough rather than as incremental financial targets. The stretch is usually not only quantitative but also intellectual – not just "(much) more of the same," but "something different." For instance, the ambition of EDS, the US information technology group, to take a leaf out of the books of Microsoft, Sony, and IBM and become a consumer brand – and hence to participate actively in educational markets worldwide – was based on a reconceptualization of the company's logic. It was a real intellectual stretch for one so steeped in "business-to-business" marketing.

A third facet of the change in strategic logic is the reflection of the new value-creation theory in a set of principles for managing interdependencies between businesses.

Kodak's concentration on imaging opportunities was decided by George Fischer, a new CEO hired from Motorola. It aimed at combining the forces of various Kodak units to create new businesses where photography and new digital technologies intersected. This created a much higher level of interdependencies and called for greater cooperation between divisions. Of course, this is not always easy, as business units usually resist what their managers initially see as encroaching on their turf.

In another example of a new strategic logic, Hewlett-Packard's E=MC^2 (Energy for growth from combining knowhow in Measurement, Communications, and Computers) had to be abandoned after a few years. The company then split into two independent entities, separating the computer business from instrumentation and other equipment businesses. Very different cost structures, the demands of fast-paced changes in computer businesses, the internet explosion, and the desire not to tinker with business unit performance measurement may all have played a role.

Organizational context

The "rules of the game" on how resources are obtained and work is to be performed have a powerful influence on a company's ability to change. A very simple example was Intel's rule that wafer-growing capacity was allocated to the most profitable end-product opportunity. Strict adherence to this rule over time led to the redeployment in the 1980s of Intel activities from memories to microprocessors. This was before top management – deeply committed to the "core" memories business – made this the explicit new strategy. Thus, the rule caused Intel to exit memories early and accelerate the building of its leading position in microprocessors. By contrast with what happened at Intel, many companies undergoing transformation rather than on-going adaptation develop performance problems due to wrong or obsolete decision-making rules and need to rejig their organizational context.

A first rule change is to make performance more visible, as a way to separate managerial performance more effectively from business performance and thus instill discipline in the goal-setting and budgetting processes. Mostly, this requires 1) the break-up of large, heterogeneous, hard-to-measure organizational entities into smaller units; and 2) the development of more accurate measurement and control. The former eliminates or limits hidden cross-subsidization between activities, and the latter establishes measurements more useful for decision making. (Clearly, this in turn will make value creation from synergies between units harder to achieve.) An excellent, if somewhat extreme, example of break-up for performance visibility is the creation by ABB, the Swiss-Swedish engineering group, of over 5,000 profit centers, made transparent and controllable by the "Abacus" measurement tool.

A second rule change, obvious in principle but hard in practice, is to make waste more visible and to eliminate as much of it as possible. GE's "Six Sigma" drive provides one of today's most prominent examples of strong dedication to this. Launched in 1995, it was aimed at becoming "the biggest opportunity for growth, increased profitability and individual employee satisfaction in the history of our company." By 1998, GE had achieved net savings of over $750m attributable to the Six Sigma drive and expected $1,500m in 1999.

The third rule change is to reduce the "command-and-control" approach (autocratic behavior) in favor of "empowerment" (coaching behavior) to mobilize the intelligence, creativity, and energy of large numbers of staff. This is probably the most difficult change for bureaucratic-style companies, but also the most important.

Emotional context

What differentiates transformation from mere strategic redirection or reorganization is the emotional context; that is, the rekindling of commitment and emotional loyalty to the organization and to its leadership. After years of downsizing, it may be difficult to rebuild trust and initiative. The extensive use of "Work Out" meetings at GE, aimed at simplifying work, eliminating stifling bureaucracy, and soliciting problem-solving participation by employees, is a well-known example of a very effective approach to improve the emotional context. SmithKline Beecham, the UK-based drugs company, avoided many of the usual post-merger traumas by involving all employees in a "grassroots" business process redesign exercise. Harvey Golub, at American Express, systematically used Socratic approaches to solicit involvement.

The wide sharing of information, good or bad, about the company's performance, including management problems, can also play a determining role in rebuilding trust. Percy Barnevik and his senior managers defined and adhered to "principles of fairness, openness, and respect" at ABB during the years of plant closings and layoffs to try to keep and rebuild trust. Lufthansa CEO Jürgen Weber used "town meetings" around the world to get the message personally to 20,000 employees that their company was in trouble and there would be no more subsidies from Bonn, only hard work ahead.

Fluctuations in the intensity of transformation activities are commonplace. Typically, they receive little attention. After all, ups and downs are to be expected in situations of crisis. Closer examination, however, reveals a clear pattern starting with a build-up of energy followed by a diffusion process.

An incoming CEO typically faces a high degree of inertia or momentum in the wrong direction. Breaking momentum or shifting direction requires a concentration of energy.

We have seen transformation efforts getting off to a slow start or stalling prematurely because energy concentration did not happen. Stalemated top management teams, a lack of leadership skills, or limitations on the CEO's power led to several false starts at Philips over the years, and delayed transformation substantially at both Rank Xerox and Siemens.

In more successful transformations, energy peaks were triggered by various kinds of "turning points," such as top management retreats. For example, at Lufthansa, a senior management training event in June 1992, originally entitled "New Thinking," was repositioned by Jürgen Weber as a "Crisis Staff Meeting." This event ended up triggering dramatic change on three fronts: a mindshift on strategy, a commitment to change in the way of operating and organizing, and a strong emotional experience, re-energizing management.

Such dramatic "crucible" events call for a special blend of leadership approaches. The ability to tell a story that resonates among members of the organization and draws out new meanings is one skill; it is also important to be able to persuade managers to transcend and abandon their starting positions as they work on the collective change agenda.

Energy dissipation

Crucible events have a short half-life and the energy levels need to be rekindled. Improvement initiatives, cost-cutting programs and the like require widespread involvement and run over extended periods of time – up to several years. Energy can quickly dissipate in conflicts, infighting or simply reverting to "business as usual" if no attention is given to follow-up events, celebrations of successes, and other reinforcing mechanisms.

An outstanding example of follow-up is Bob Baumann's merger and post-merger process at SmithKline Beecham. When there were signs of discouragement, declining motivation, or of managers getting tired, the management team went on a benchmarking trip together. Then a celebration known as the Simply Better Way was organized at Disney World for hundreds of managers. This event created an emotional high point.

But even if a leader applies all the ingredients described above, a final challenge remains: to "let go." The initial inertia-breaking process is usually strongly driven from the top and does not typically involve extensive consultation, empowerment, or incentives for risk taking; quite the reverse. This clearly was the nature of the Piech/Lopez process at Volkswagen. As an industry insider described it, "They took this paralyzed Wolfsburg giant by the neck and shook it." Similarly, at GE in the 1980s Jack Welch's nickname, "Neutron Jack," was not inspired by his participative style.

Yet the same Welch then launched this huge organization into "Work Out" activities to achieve employee involvement and "boundaryless" management behavior. It was a massive effort to change behavior, to establish trust, and to generate a sense of excitement. By 1997 the annual report proclaimed: "It became unthinkable for any of us to tolerate – much less hire or promote – the tyrant, the autocrat, the big shot. They were simply 'yesterday.'" The difficulty of "unlearning" the old culture at GE should not be underestimated. How will Volkswagen (and many others) move from top-down imposed solutions to emergent action? As we see it, the key challenge for CEOs in search of self-renewal for their organizations is to launch into the relative chaos of decentralized emergent initiatives. This requires both self-confidence and confidence in others; a capacity to create a shared context and common meanings within their own teams in order to "let go."

Today's wisdom of the desirable end-state for organizations is that they be learning and entrepreneurial.

To achieve this, companies need leaders at all levels taking initiatives and mobilizing their people. The CEO's role in this is even more difficult than before: to lead with as much courage and clarity as ever but as the "first servant" of the organization, not as the "autocratic boss." Steve Miller, member of Royal Dutch/Shell's Committee of Managing Directors, calls it "grassroots leadership." His theme, according to one account, was:

> Change how you define leadership and you change how you run the company. Once the folks at the grassroots find that they own the problem they find that they also own the answer – and they improve things much more quickly, aggressively, and creatively than old-style leaders based at headquarters.

Summary

Leaders in the 1990s moved away from portfolio and financial restructuring that typified the previous decade – but the ingredients for a successful transformation still elude many businesses. According to **Yves Doz** and **Heinz Thanheiser**, leaders need to set new ambitions and to redefine their organization's focus; to establish clear operational and organizational rules; and to rekindle the commitment and emotional loyalty of employees. An initial surge of energy should be followed by a carefully managed diffusion process. Current wisdom says that companies should adopt a learning culture and be entrepreneurial, while the CEO needs to be the "first servant" rather than the "autocratic boss."

Suggested further reading

Burgelman, R.A. and Grove, A. (1996) "Strategic dissonance," *California Management Review*, 38 (2; Winter): 8–26.

Doz, Y. and Thanheiser, H. (1993) "Regaining competitiveness: a process of organisational renewal" in Hendry, J. and Johnson, G. with Newton, J., *Strategic Thinking: Leadership and the Management of Change*, Chichester: John Wiley & Sons.

Kets de Vries, M. (1994) "Percy Barnevik and ABB," INSEAD video and case.

"SmithKline Beecham: the Making of the Simply Better Healthcare Company, (A) and (B)," (1995) INSEAD case study, as quoted in Pascale, R., "Grassroots leadership – Royal Dutch/Shell," *Fast Company*, 14: 100.

Welch, J.F. Jr. (1996) speech at the General Electric Company 1996 Annual Meeting, Charlottesville, Virginia, April 24.

STRATEGY AND PEOPLE

Contributors

James P. Walsh is the Gerald and Esther Carey Professor of Business Administration at the University of Michigan Business School. In collaboration with Joshua Margolis and the Aspen Institute, he is currently examining the substance and symbolism of corporate social responsibility initiatives in the US.

Canice Prendergast is a professor of economics at the University of Chicago Graduate School of Business. He teaches courses in managing the work place and international comparative organizations.

Wayne E. Baker is professor of organizational behavior and human resource management, and faculty director of the executive education program on building social capital, at the University of Michigan Business School. He is director of research at Humax Corporation.

Quy Nguyen Huy is professor of strategy and management at INSEAD. He trained as an electrical engineer, is a chartered financial analyst and worked in the information technology industry. His current research focusses on large-scale corporate transformations and quantum change in strategic capabilities.

Contents

Introduction

The phrases "human capital" and "our people are our most important assets" remain some of the most popular in company reports. This module considers the latest thinking on familiar management issues – such as incentive schemes – as well as more unusual reaches of this key topic. It includes a stimulating – and at times controversial – discussion of the social role of business, which poses a direct challenge to those unwilling to divert corporate resources for social purposes. It also contains a fascinating description of the role of "social" capital (which combines business and personal networks) and of how to harness emotional energy during periods of organizational change.

Business must talk about its social role

by James P. Walsh

Waxing eloquent about stakeholder management and corporate social responsibility is in some circles the surest way to stifle a business conversation, if not a business career. Corporate philanthropy brings satisfaction to those who give and receive, the argument goes, but let us not get carried away by talk of give-aways. Global competition is relentless and exacting. Comments such as "The purpose of the company is to make money for its owners" or "Any talk that distracts from this goal is tantamount to corporate treason" are not untypical.

This kind of corporate thought control may be street-smart, but it violates the basic tenets of freedom of inquiry and action that are essential to creating wealth. So, let us exercise our right to talk about a social role for business. What, if anything, should the company do to ameliorate the ills that beset society? And why is it seemingly an act of career suicide to talk seriously about these issues in our offices and boardrooms?

Social ills

We have just witnessed a period of unprecedented wealth creation. For example, the rise in US GDP and the wealth created by companies on the New York Stock Exchange in the twentieth century is amazing (*see* Figure 1). Senior managers have benefitted from this accomplishment. Tracking 800 of the highest-paid US chief executives, *Forbes* magazine discovered that, as a group, they earned $5.2bn in salary and performance-contingent compensation in 1998. The value of their common stockholdings was even more stunning. These 800 individuals hold stock

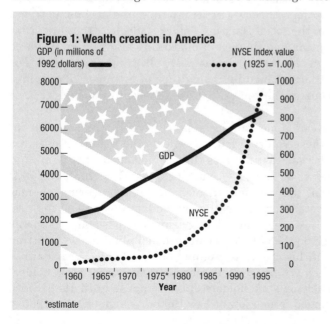

Figure 1: Wealth creation in America

GDP (in millions of 1992 dollars) ━━━

NYSE Index value (1925 = 1.00) •••••

*estimate

worth more than $241bn, which compares with South Africa's GDP in 1997 of $270bn.

Such corporate prosperity masks surprising social ills. Louis Harris and Associates, a US polling company, has been tracking feelings of alienation in the US since 1966. In its survey, the percentage of people who answered "yes" to such statements as "the rich get richer and the poor get poorer" or "most people with power try to take advantage of people like yourself" has risen from 29 percent in 1966 to 62 percent in 1997. Is this perception accurate? Chinhui Juhn, Kevin Murphy, and Brooks Pierce tracked real wages in the US population from 1963 to 1989 (see Suggested further reading). They found that the earnings of those in the 90th percentile, as compared to those in the 10th percentile, began to diverge in the early 1970s (interestingly, just when the New York Stock Exchange started to take off). Those at the bottom ended up earning nearly 10 percent less than they did 26 years earlier, while those at the top saw their wages increase by almost 40 percent. Lawrence Katz revealed in 1999 (see Suggested further reading) that this trend has continued – those in the 90th percentile in 1996 earned nearly five times as much as those in the 10th percentile. It seems that popular opinion is right: the rich are getting richer and the poor are getting poorer. Moreover, the US Bureau of the Census tells us that the percentage of children in the US living below the poverty level has increased from about 15 percent in 1970 to nearly 21 percent in 1995. Despite this documented disparity between corporate wealth and social wellbeing, companies rarely talk about their role in either creating this problem or solving it.

Control is subtle

I began with the provocative assertion that corporate "thought control" often inhibits serious conversations about a social role for business. The control is subtle; it resides in the unspoken assumptions about the purposes of the company. You see this both in what people do and say, and in what they fail to do and say. As a business school professor, I see it in the classes that our students embrace and those that they shun (a course on options theory will trump a course on business and society any day). I also hear it in the social Darwinist market ideology that underlies case conversations from accounting and finance to marketing and human resource management. I think I see it in the business press as well. Newspapers like *The Wall Street Journal* shape and are shaped by the culture of business. The values revealed in these newspapers mirror the values that are inherent in business. What are these values?

I did a keyword search of the Dow Jones online version of *The Wall Street Journal* from 1984 to 1998 to identify these values. Figure 2 reflects the results of a search for the number of articles each year that address the themes of "beat," "win," and "advantage," as well as the themes of "caring," "compassion," and "virtue." *The Wall Street Journal* search shows that the "beating" themes far outstrip "caring" themes over time. Moreover, articles about winning, beating, and advantage are on the rise. There does not seem to be much room for talk about caring, compassion, and virtue in business these days. A search on the phrase "social responsibility" shows it sitting squarely in the bottom range of this chart, averaging 136 articles per year (with a low of 109 in 1989 and a high of 176 in 1993). A search on the word "stakeholder" fared even worse. The first article on stakeholders did not appear until 1988. Since then, the number of articles ranged from a low of 1 in 1990 to a high of 11 in 1995.

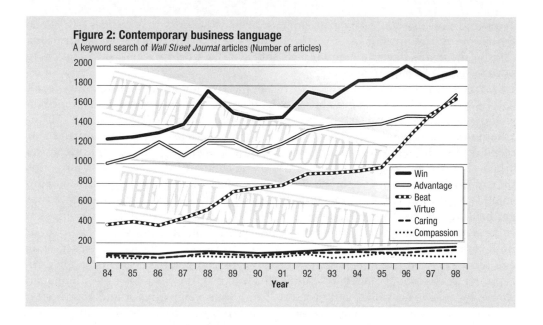

Figure 2: Contemporary business language
A keyword search of *Wall Street Journal* articles (Number of articles)

Legend: Win, Advantage, Beat, Virtue, Caring, Compassion

While I am unable to point to the mechanism that restricts conversation about these matters, I can point out that such conversations are rare indeed. What to do?

Corporate solutions

There are three views about the responsibilities of the corporation. All are associated with varying degrees of controversy. The first is the least controversial. If a company creates a social problem, then it is the company's responsibility to fix it. So when the *Exxon Valdez* dumped 232,000 barrels of oil in Alaska's waters ten years ago, everyone agreed that Exxon should clean up its mess (even if it cost it $3bn to do it).

Controversy arises, however, when there are questions about whether or not the company actually created the problem that others would have it fix. Advocates of a "living wage," for example, might argue that companies conspire to depress wages and so it is their responsibility to raise them. Others would vehemently disagree with this conspiracy premise. The stark differences of opinion on social responsibility in this view turn on the diagnosis of the problem's origin.

A second school of thought is less concerned with who caused society's problems and is much more focussed on who can solve them. This is the era of global competition. With national sovereignty compromised by international flows of capital, labor, and products, the multinational corporation is seen as the only powerful transnational institution on the world's stage. Only the multinational corporation can muster the resources to fight poverty, illiteracy, malnutrition, illness, and the like. This school of communitarian thought dates at least to 1919 and Henry Ford's comments at the time of the landmark *Dodge v. Ford* trial. Ford argued that there is more to running a company than making a profit. "I do not believe that we should make such an awful profit on our cars," he said famously. "A reasonable profit is right, but not too much. So it has been my policy to force the price of the car down as fast as production would permit, and give the benefits to the users and the laborers, with surprisingly enormous benefits to ourselves." In Henry Ford's mind, the pursuit of profit needs to be tempered by other considerations. Communitarians ask the company to address the world's social problems as it pursues its profit objectives.

Contractarians, who adhere to a third perspective on social responsibility, could not disagree more. They do not object to the idea that companies should enhance the welfare of society; they just anticipate a very different means to this end. Milton Friedman's renowned 1970 *New York Times* article, "The corporate social responsibility of the firm is to increase its profits," is emblematic of thinking in this school. Simply put, we can thank God that the companies created the wealth that they did. Without such wealth, we would all be mired in social misery. The company should pay its fair taxes to the state to support society's collective needs and then get back to the business of creating wealth. Diverting the company's resources to solve society's problems represents a double tax on the company and, worse, undermines our motivation to get up and go to work every day. Contractarians explain that even if managers were tempted to try to solve social problems, the capital markets would quickly discipline this waste of free cash flow. Such managers would soon find themselves out of a job. If not, their companies would be targetted for a takeover by others who would offer themselves to the company's abused shareholders as better able to manage its assets. This last view holds the greatest currency in management circles today.

Practical politics

The common wisdom has it that even if managers choose to invest (or some might say divert) some of their company's resources to solving social problems, they will be punished for squandering the owners' money. Boards of directors and the takeover market would discipline this perceived incompetence. This is not just a US story. The number of mergers and acquisitions (M&A) in the European Union increased dramatically in the 1990s, from 2,643 between 1981 and 1989 to 33,687 between 1990 and 1998. Managers who spend a corporation's money to address social problems, so the argument goes, do so at their personal peril. This seems to make sense. But is it true?

Interestingly, we do not yet know what happens to the careers of managers who lead socially responsible corporations. However, we know a good deal about just how exacting the control system is. The evidence from studies (listed in Suggestions for further reading) is surprising. Jerold Warner, Ross Watts, and Karen Wruck, for example, examined the relationship between company performance and CEO dismissal in a sample of 269 companies between 1963 and 1978. Ranking these companies in terms of mean annual stock returns, they found that companies in the top 10 percent exhibited a CEO turnover rate of 8.3 percent. This low number (no doubt reflecting normal retirements, illness, and the like) should not surprise anyone; these people are presumably doing great work. However, the results for those in the bottom 10 percent are surprising. These companies revealed only a 13.8 percent CEO turnover rate. Stuart Gilson went even further and looked at extraordinarily poor-performing companies. He looked at the dismissal patterns for the CEOs who led 381 companies in the bottom 5 percent of the NYSE and American Stock Exchange companies for three consecutive years (in the 1979–84 period), as well as those in this same performance group who also defaulted on their debt obligations, restructured their debt outside of bankruptcy, or went into bankruptcy. He found that such CEOs are not necessarily destined to lose their jobs. Only 19 percent of companies in the first group changed their CEO, while 52 percent of the companies in the second group of catastrophically distressed companies did so. Thus, contrary to popular belief, CEOs do not face high odds of losing their jobs if their companies do not perform well in the stock market. In the absolute worst case, they face only a 50–50 chance of job loss.

Well, you might say, if the company's directors will not dismiss a poorly performing CEO, then the takeover market for corporate control works to this effect. John Ellwood and I examined the relationship between pre-M&A company performance and post-M&A top management turnover in a sample of 102 target companies in the 1975–79 period. We found no evidence that M&As were capable of pruning "managerial deadwood." Indeed, the post-M&A turnover rate was tied to positive pre-M&A stock-market performance. It seemed that those best able to sell their services in the managerial labor market after a merger or acquisition did so. In a follow-up study, Rita Kosnik and I examined a more extreme case – when eight notorious corporate raiders in the 1979–83 period took equity stakes in a company. Similarly, we found no evidence that such raider activity was associated with abnormal levels of CEO or director turnover. These results are hardly unique to the US. Julian Franks and Colin Mayer examined the relationship between hostile tender offers and both inside and outside director turnover for 80 hostile bids in the UK in 1985 and 1986. They concluded that hostile takeovers do not appear to play much of a disciplinary role in the UK either. Despite the persuasive rhetoric of corporate control and management discipline, there is little evidence that CEOs face much of a career risk if their companies do not perform well. Thus, from the manager's perspective, there seems to be plenty of room to take a risk and invest in worthy causes that might fall outside the scope of normal business practices. If the investment does not pay off, managers are unlikely to lose their jobs.

The extraordinary amount of corporate wealth and power today suggests that executives could use some of this leverage to address the world's problems. Such a suggestion rekindles old debates about just what a company owes the society that sustains it. While there might be compelling reasons to act, the common view remains that managers cannot act because disciplinary pressures will not allow them to do so. My purpose in this article is to suggest that talk of exacting discipline is just that – talk. Let me be clear. I am not celebrating mismanagement or the destruction of company value. Rather, my point is that if a company's performance dips, its leaders are less likely to face grave disciplinary sanctions than they imagine. So why can managers not talk seriously about a social role for business? Why are managers afraid to experiment with social initiatives? Why can managers not reach for the possible benefits that might even accrue to those who act to solve social problems? I do not know why, but these are important questions.

Next moves

My ambition here has been quite modest: to stimulate debate about the role business might play in solving our social problems. The fact that we face serious social problems is unquestioned. The question is whether wealthy and powerful corporations can, or should, do anything about them. For those executives who reply that the capital markets tie their hands, the evidence shows that the vaunted discipline borne of this market pressure is much less exacting than we imagine. Executives have plenty of room to innovate in this domain. The more difficult problem may be to find a way to develop a strategy and a set of tactics to address these problems. The current language of business does not seem to allow for talk rooted in notions of compassion and caring. How can we develop such a strategy if we cannot even talk about it? It is going to take some courage to lead these conversations.

Just what will we talk about when we do talk? This will be like any other pragmatic business conversation. First, we need to decide which of the many social problems to address. We will certainly ask whether it is possible to solve society's problems and bring benefits to the company. Once we have picked our domain, we will need to decide how to deploy our resources to make a difference. We will face a "make or buy" decision. That is, do we have the capabilities to address problems that might range from illiteracy to youth violence to malnutrition? If not, can we find other resources to help?

Finally, there is the question of effectiveness. We will need to monitor and appraise the success of our efforts in meeting the needs of the targetted groups – as well as the needs of the company. The returns on these investments, however defined, must be calculated. The first step, though, is to have the conversation itself. Nothing will happen until we can talk frankly at work about a social role for business. With luck, this article will help us do just that.

Summary

Corporate "thought control" is stifling debate on the social role of business, argues **James P. Walsh**. In this article, the author reviews three schools of thought that focus on the wider responsibilities of a company, and challenges the views of those who refuse to contemplate any diversion of corporate resources for social purposes. Studies show that the risks managers run – i.e., dismissal for poor performance or in the event of hostile takeover – are exaggerated. Social commitment needs to be tied to strategy and have measurable returns – but first, managers must be encouraged to talk about it.

Suggested further reading

Bradley, M., Schipani, C.A., Sundaram, A.K. and Walsh, J.P. (1999) "The purposes and accountability of the corporation in contemporary society: corporate governance at a cross-roads," *Law and Contemporary Problems*, 62: 9–85.

Franks, J. and Mayer, C. (1996) "Hostile takeovers and the correction of managerial failure," *Journal of Financial Economics*, 40: 163–81.

Friedman, M. (1970) "The social responsibility of business is to increase profits," *New York Times Magazine*, September 13: 32–126.

Gilson, S.C. (1989) "Management turnover and financial distress," *Journal of Financial Economics*, 25: 241–62.

Jensen, M.C. and Murphy, K.J. (1990) "Performance pay and top management incentives," *Journal of Political Economy*, 98: 225–64.

Juhn, C., Murphy, K.M. and Pierce, B. (1993) "Wage inequality and the rise in returns to skill," *Journal of Political Economy*, 101: 410–42.

Nevins, A. and Hill, F. (1957) *Ford: Expansion and Challenge, 1915–1933*.

Katz, L.F. (1999) "Technological change, computerization, and the wage structure," Working paper, Harvard University and the National Bureau of Research.

Walsh, J.P. and Ellwood, J.W. (1991) "Mergers, acquisitions and the pruning of managerial deadwood," *Strategic Management Journal*, 12: 210–17.

Walsh, J.P. and Kosnik, R.D. (1993) "Corporate raiders and their disciplinary role in the market for corporate control," *Academy of Management Journal*, 36: 671–700.

Warner, J.B., Watts, R. and Wruck, K.H. "Stock prices and top management changes," *Journal of Financial Economics*, 20: 461–92.

Building social capital as an organizational competence

by Wayne E. Baker

Soon after Robert Rubin announced his intention to step down as Secretary of the US Treasury by July 1999, pundits were commenting on the differences between his style and that of his successor, then Deputy Secretary Lawrence Summers. In short, while Mr. Summers wanted to *be* the smartest person in the room, Mr. Rubin wanted to *hire* the smartest person in the room. Their different styles represent the two fundamental approaches to personal and organizational competence: achieving success through human capital and achieving success through social capital.

Both are essential, of course, but social capital (the resources in personal and business networks) is more important than ever for personal and organizational success. Massive organizational changes – notably, the widespread shift toward flat and fluid organizational designs, growing information and learning needs, continuous improvement, and closer integration of customers, suppliers, and competitors – require organizations to build social capital as a distinctive competence. Physical capital, financial capital, and human capital are no longer enough.

Over the past 15 years, sociologists, economists, organizational researchers, and political scientists have learned a lot about the nature, uses, and applications of social capital. Social capital, for instance, influences the acquisition of venture capital. Various surveys sponsored by the US Small Business Administration show that most start-ups find and secure financing through the "informal investing grapevine" (the social networks of capital seekers and investors). Similarly, polls of stock purchasers taken in the late 1980s and 1990s by Robert Shiller of Yale University reveal that most institutional and individual investors made their decisions to buy based on information from a friend or business associate, or because they knew someone who bought the stock.

Social capital influences the use and success of strategic alliances. Good alliance partners find each other through their social and business contacts. The more strategic alliances a company creates, the more it will create in the future, according to research by Ranjay Gulati of the Kellogg Graduate School of Management at Northwestern University. Corning, a US glassmaker, for example, has evolved into what it calls a "network of alliances." Companies like Corning have mastered how to create and manage alliances, making themselves excellent partners and thus attracting new alliance candidates.

Social capital reduces the chances of a successful hostile takeover. A company with a board of isolated directors is more likely to fall victim to a hostile takeover attempt, as Richard D'Aveni of the Tuck School of Business at Dartmouth found in his studies. Well-connected directors, in contrast, fend off hostile takeovers by finding white knights or learning about effective takeover defenses via their social networks. Good takeover defenses, such as the poison pill, spread or "diffuse" through the director network, according to studies by Gerald Davis of the University of Michigan Business School.

Social capital supports democracy. The regions of Italy with rich social capital (networks of cooperation, norms of civic engagement, and a spirit of trust) enjoy responsive regional governments and strong economic development. But the regions with poor social capital suffer from unresponsive governments, distrust, and social isolation, according to Robert Putnam of Harvard University in his 25-year study of democracy in Italy. Recently, Putnam charted the decline of civic engagement in American society, coining the phrase "bowling alone" (i.e., solo versus team bowling, in the game of tenpin bowling) to describe the fall-off of Americans willing to join voluntary groups and associations of all kinds.

Resources and structures

A social network does not translate automatically into social capital. Ben Van Shaik, CEO of the now-defunct Dutch aircraft maker Fokker, made the mistake of equating network size with social capital, as Roger Leenders of the University of Groningen and Shaul Gabbay of Israel's Technion University explain in their edited volume on social capital (*see* Suggested further reading). Mr. Van Shaik boasted in a February 1996 presentation to potential alliance partners that Fokker was "the second largest aircraft builder in the world." His claim was true (based on sheer number of customers). But Fokker's customers were small, resource-poor companies. Each leased (rather than bought) only one or two planes, and often failed to pay bills. Fokker declared bankruptcy just months later.

Social capital depends on the resources of the people and organizations in the network (as Mr. Van Shaik learned to his cost), the configuration or structure of the social network, and the strategies used to tap these resources. One of the best-documented findings in research on personal and organizational success is that social capital is positively correlated with the number of "structural holes" or gaps in a personal or interorganizational network.

A "hole" exists when two people (or two groups) are connected to a common third party, but are not directly connected themselves. Ron Burt of the University of Chicago Graduate School of Business shows that managers who connect many otherwise unconnected persons or groups are paid better and promoted faster, compared to peers who lack such "holes" in their networks. These managers reap rewards because they create value. Problems seek solutions; solutions seek problems. A manager who bridges disparate parts of the organization can link a problem in one group with a solution from another. A manager with lots of structural holes gets information quickly. And a manager with rich social capital knows where to find financial, political, and social support for projects.

The same is true for organizations. Profitability is positively correlated with the number of structural holes in a company's network of ties with customers, suppliers, and alliance partners.

A structural hole presents a person or organization with two choices, what doctoral candidate David Obstfeld and I call the "disunion" and "union" strategies (for details, *see* our chapter in the Leenders and Gabbay volume, listed in Suggested further reading). The disunion strategist exploits structural holes by keeping people or organizations apart. Management consulting firms, for example, often suffer because consultants hoard information, refusing to share ideas or best practices. A consultant who gets ideas from two unconnected peers is more likely to save the knowledge for private gain than to introduce the peers to each other and lose the advantage.

Computer-generated diagram of CEO Thomas Caprel's core network

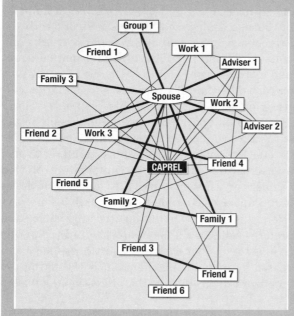

Each line represents a relationship between two people. Thickness indicates strength. Names are deleted for confidentiality. Roles are indicated as follows: Spouse, Family (family member or relative), Work (co-worker), Friend, Adviser (professional adviser, such as a consultant), Group (fellow member of a group, such as a professional or trade association, church, or a charitable/philanthropic organization). Numbers do not indicate order or sequence; they are used to distinguish different people who play the same role (e.g., Friend 1, Friend 2). Men are rectangles; women are ovals.

Source: Courtesy of Humax Corporation and Mr. Caprel.

Figure 1

In many firms, this is the only sensible choice, because the incentive system does not give credit to or reward those who share ideas or information. Still, a union strategist can find ways to create value (and get credit) by bringing people or organizations together. A firm can encourage the union strategy by implementing various practices. For example, a few years ago AT&T Global Information Solutions encouraged the formation of ties among 125 alliance partners by bringing them together in its first Global Alliance Conference.

Either strategy can be appropriate. The union strategy, however, is the prescription for long-term success. Devoted disunion strategists are eventually discovered and dismissed as unabashed opportunists. Conversely, those who use the union strategy as their *modus operandi* build a productive culture of cooperation, trust, and mutual aid, continuously creating value for themselves, co-workers, their organizations, and clients.

Profiling social capital

The first step to building social capital is to evaluate it. Most people have a distorted, incomplete "mental map" of their personal or organizational networks. The few who have a good mental map, as David Krackhardt of Carnegie-Mellon University shows, are influential and effective. Over the years, sociologists have developed various methods for measuring social capital. Early efforts include the 1985 Topical Module on Social Networks in the US General Social Survey, and Ron Burt's pioneering studies of social capital in large organizations. These, and other studies, show that it isn't necessary to measure a complete network (which is so large that measuring it is impractical). Rather, an evaluation of the configuration and composition of a "core network" represents the patterns and tendencies in the complete network revealing the essential nature of social capital.

It is possible to profile a person's or an organization's social capital. For simplicity of illustration, consider a personal profile, that of Thomas Caprel, a successful entrepreneur, venture capitalist, and founder of Caprel Consulting, Inc., a mid-size computer services firm in suburban Chicago. I analyzed his core network with the Humax Assessment, a web-administered survey for evaluating social networks and social capital. His profile includes a network map (*see* Figure 1), information about three dimensions of social capital, and a profile type.

Dimension 1 – Effective size of network. Mr. Caprel's network isn't as large as it could be, but its structure indicates rich social capital. In his responses to the survey, he named 17 people, just more than half of the 30 maximum possible in the Humax Assessment. If most of the 17 were connected to each other, his network would lack structural holes, and its "effective" size would be quite small. But most are unconnected, indicating many structural holes. The components of this dimension of social capital tell the same story. For example, the "density" of ties is low (only 16 percent of the maximum number of possible links actually exists). All indicators point to the same conclusion: this network is rich in structural holes and entrepreneurial opportunities. Therefore, value could be created by linking people (the union strategy). A helpful exercise is to consider each and every possible pair in the network map and the value created by introducing them (such as linking the friends located in the "south" of the network diagram with the professional advisers in the "northeast").

Dimension 2 – Composition of network. Similarity is the enemy of networking, because similar people (or organizations) tend to have similar networks. Diversity provides networking reach. The people in Mr. Caprel's network are quite diverse in most respects. For example, there is a considerable span of ages and levels of formal education, with some variation in gender. But his network is racially homogeneous (typical of the core networks of most Americans, according to the US General Social Surveys). Therefore, the overall composition of Mr. Caprel's network falls in the middle of the diversity scale. Value could be created by diversifying contacts.

Dimension 3 – Focus of network. Many networks either focus solely on work or show a sharp separation of personal and work life. Mr. Caprel's network, however, shows a mix of activities and bridges across the personal/work divide. For example, 24 percent of the people in his network are family; only 18 percent are work related (unusually low); two are professional advisers, a consultant and a business coach/mentor. Over 40 percent have lived and worked in other countries, giving his network an above-average global focus. Mr. Caprel is involved in a healthy number and range of outside groups and organizations. On average, Americans are involved with two outside groups, according to the 1995–1997 World Values Surveys. Mr. Caprel is a member of six: two professional associations, an industry group, a cultural organization, a sports club, and a personal development group.

My research with Humax reveals 27 different social capital profile types. At one extreme is a small, homogenous, internally focussed network. The profile represents social capital in the form of trust and cooperation among a tight network of very similar people. It is good for building group loyalty, identity, and a sense of common purpose. It is not good, however, for getting information or other resources, or for influencing people outside the network; it is subject to "groupthink" and the development of a we-versus-them view of the world. At the other extreme is a large, diverse, externally focussed network. This profile represents social capital in the form of entrepreneurial opportunities. There are many "holes" between people, so value can be created by introducing unconnected people (union strategy). This profile type is good for getting lots of new information, learning about new opportunities, and finding resources. It is not so good, however, for building consensus or developing a sense of mission; sometimes it causes conflicts and tensions.

Mr. Caprel's profile type falls between these two extremes. It is a medium-sized network, composed of a somewhat diverse set of people, with a combined internal–external focus. As such, it is a balance of the strengths and weaknesses of the two forms of social capital. It is a typical entrepreneur's core network.

Common practices

Companies use any number of practices to build social capital. These practices include both internal and external social capital, because one tends to reinforce the other. Corning, for example, discovered that building a network of strategic alliances put pressure on internal structure and culture, forcing the company to knock down internal barriers, cut layers, and adopt a more fluid, team-based network organizational design.

Reward and incentive systems

Many companies ask for behaviors they don't reward. For example, many financial services companies I know exhort their sales people to "cross-market," but don't implement this union strategy by financially rewarding people who share leads and make sales as a team. Team-based or collective rewards encourage building and using social capital; individual rewards are barriers to social capital.

Skills training

Social capital is a learnable skill. Building social capital as an organizational competence means providing significant, regular opportunities for training on relationship building and networking. Inside training is important, but outside is even more important because it provides natural opportunities to build external ties and create structural holes. Training budgets and schedules must be established. Participation should be a part of everyone's annual plan and commitments, and no one should be exempt (even the CEO should join outside associations and participate regularly in executive leadership programs). For example, CEO Thomas Caprel includes two professional advisers in his core network, along with active affiliations with key outside associations, to promote his continuing education and development. The range and number of educational opportunities are enormous, including executive education and training programs. Many associations sponsor training programs, as well as providing opportunities for informal coaching, mentoring, and peer support. Examples include the Young Presidents' Organization (over 60 chapters worldwide), the Club of Rome (26 associations worldwide), the International Bureau of Chambers of Commerce (headquartered in Paris), and the National Association for Female Executives (over 200 networks in the US, with others in the Netherlands, Israel, South Africa, and elsewhere).

Rotation programs

Simple, time-honored practices such as regular job rotations and temporary assignments naturally increase network size and add structural holes as a byproduct of daily routines. A related practice is to create formal liaisons that connect different groups, departments, offices, or locations. The classic is the "production engineer" who has one foot in manufacturing, the other in engineering. This is just one of many possible dual roles.

Co-location

Bringing different people or groups together in a single location creates natural opportunities for sharing information and building social capital. Capital Partners, a commercial real-estate development company, co-locates leasing agents, partners, senior partners, and accountants. The principle of co-location should not be limited to internal people or groups. People from all levels should have the opportunity to spend time with customers, suppliers, vendors, and alliance partners. For example, Hadady Corp., an Illinois-based diversified manufacturer, cut its product development and prototyping time by a factor of three by using concurrent engineering and networking with a core group of engineers at its customer Caterpillar. Whenever Hadady experiences a quality problem with its own suppliers, it sends one of its operators (not managers) to resolve the issue. The principle of co-location also includes the practice of "alliance fests," where a company's strategic partners are encouraged to form their own ties.

Communities of practice

Many manufacturers have discovered the benefits of communities of practice, such as informal groups of engineers from around a company who come together to share ideas, identify best practices, and brainstorm. Some communities of practice, such as scientific networks at chemical giant Rohm and Haas, extend far beyond the organization's boundaries. Communities of practice are vehicles for building and using social capital.

Managers encourage the development of these communities by providing facility space, time off for meetings, office support, and electronic tools such as web pages.

Overall, the biggest barrier to building social capital is denial (the ingrained attitude that going it alone is the key to success). If one can get past that, social capital is a competence that can be acquired. Chance favors the prepared organization, to paraphrase Louis Pasteur. Those organizations that are best prepared to face the uncertainties of the future are those that build social capital as a competence.

Summary

Social capital – the combination of personal and business networks – is a much under-rated asset these days, says **Wayne E. Baker**. It influences the outcome of takeovers, the direction of strategic alliances, and the acquisition of venture capital. Social capital is positively correlated with the number of structural "holes" or gaps in a network – these exist where two people or groups are linked to a common third party but not directly to each other. Managers who make these connections explicit are more likely to prosper in the long run. The author outlines a range of social capital profiles and illustrates his arguments with the case study of a successful US entrepreneur.

Suggested further reading

Baker, W.E. (1994) *Networking Smart: How to Build Relationships for Personal and Organizational Success*, New York: McGraw-Hill.

Baker, W.E. (2000) *Achieving Success Through Social Capital*, Jossey-Bass.

Burt, R. (1992) *Structural Holes: the Social Structure of Competition*, Cambridge, MA: Harvard University Press.

Leenders, R.Th.A.J. and Gabbay, S.M. (eds) (1999) *Corporate Social Capital and Liability*, Kluwer Academic Publishers.

Putnam, R. (1993) *Making Democracy Work*, Princeton, NJ: Princeton University Press.

Paying for performance

by Canice Prendergast

Traditionally, employees were paid by fixed salaries, and were only rewarded for improved performance when they were promoted or when salaries were revised at the end of the year. Yet in the past two decades there has been a huge change in compensation schemes, and more and more employees now see their pay vary with reference to some measure of individual or company performance.

Companies have tried all sorts of methods for providing incentives, such as piece rates, commissions, stock options, bonuses, stock grants, profit sharing, team bonuses, deferred compensation, and so on. The growing interest in such pay-for-performance plans has come from the realization that often the interests of employee and employer are not aligned, and that sometimes contracts can be designed to induce employees to work more closely in the company's interest. In essence, people work harder (or better) when their pay is affected by their actions. To take a simple example, a salesperson who is paid on commission will be likely to work harder than one who receives a straight salary, as his or her pay is more directly related to performance.

Many people are skeptical of this assumption, particularly outside the US, and instead believe that most employees are guided by "an honest day's work for an honest day's pay." However, one of the more surprising conclusions of research on incentives over the past decade has been that employees in many walks of life are quick to respond to measures that they can control. Many of these studies arise from changes in compensation in US companies. A well-publicised recent example involved a US company called Safelite, which installs car windscreens. When its managers switched compensation from fixed salaries to piece rates, productivity rose by approximately 35 percent in the space of 18 months.

Yet there is similar evidence throughout the world. Jockeys in the UK are typically rewarded in one of two ways: either they receive a retainer with little or no prize for winning a race, or they receive a prize for winning, typically 20 percent of the prize money. Recent research illustrates that those jockeys who are on the 20 percent commission significantly outperform those who are on retainers. Similarly, golfers on the European Tour achieve better scores when their prize money depends more on their finishing position. Perhaps the most convincing case for linking pay with performance comes from China in the 1970s. Deng Xiaoping allowed Chinese farmers to keep a fraction of the output that they produced and to sell it at market prices. Recent evidence suggests that 75 percent of the enormous increase in Chinese agricultural output during the 1980s was attributable to that change in compensation practice.

These examples are representative of a host of work illustrating how people generally respond when they are paid to do something they would otherwise not enjoy. These studies point to the benefit of offering pay for performance: people work harder, at least on the dimensions on which they are paid. This has provoked many commentators to emphasize the benefits of tying pay more closely to measures such as company profits, performance ratings, customer satisfaction surveys, and so on. Many of these commentators feel that productivity can be significantly increased by making employees more accountable for their actions.

There is little doubt that the productivity responses to incentive contracts in the examples above are impressive and point to potential benefits that can arise from pay for performance. Yet one should be careful about this conclusion, despite the evidence marshaled above. One warning signal is the fact that most employees do not have contracts that relate pay to performance. In other words, most employees still get straight salaries, with the best estimates suggesting that only about 20 to 25 percent of employees have some form of incentive pay.

In my view, this is not because companies have not thought about it or are behind the times. Instead, it suggests that they have reasonably decided that the benefits outlined above are outweighed by a variety of costs that make incentive pay less than desirable.

When incentives fail

Job complexity

There are three important drawbacks to pay-for-performance plans. First, incentive contracting can cause employees to carry out actions that are beneficial to them but harmful to their company's interests. The jobs that many people carry out are complex, and contracts typically cannot completely specify all relevant aspects of worker behavior. As a result, contracts offering incentives can give rise to dysfunctional responses, where agents emphasize only those aspects of performance that are rewarded. For example, a professional basketball player in the US, Tim Hardaway, was given a contract in 1998 offering him an $850,000 bonus based on the number of "assists" he made (an assist is where a player passes to a teammate who then scores). Hardaway realized toward the end of the season that there was a chance that he would not make enough assists to get his bonus. He admitted to not taking legitimate shots but instead passing to other players to increase his chance of the bonus. In other words, he changed his behavior in response to the incentive contract in ways beneficial to himself but harmful to the team. For other such examples, *see* the box on misguided motives.

In the examples given, employees carry out complex jobs in the sense that they can change their behavior along many dimensions when offered an incentive contract. This problem, referred to in economics literature as "multitasking," suggests that in many occupations the last thing that an employer should consider is an incentive pay scheme based on some subset of the activities carried out by the worker.

Specifically, it is worth bearing in mind that in the examples in which performance pay worked (jockeys, Chinese farmers, and windscreen installers), it is easy to identify a measure that represents the performance of the worker. Thus, winning a race is a good measure for a jockey, output is a good measure for a farmer, and so on. Having a good overall measure of performance is critical to implementing efficient pay-for-performance schemes. Yet in truth, most employees do not have jobs like this and most measures of performance are an inadequate representation of the employee's contribution. When pay-for-performance contracts are offered to employees, there is a real danger that they will focus too much on certain aspects of the contract to the detriment of all the other things that they should be doing.

Costs exceed benefits

The second problem with incentive pay is that it causes compensation costs to rise, which must be compared to the increases in productivity. In many cases, the

Misguided motives

There are many examples of dysfunctional responses by employees to incentive contracts:

- Salespeople are generally paid on end-of-year sales quotas. If they have reached their quota in November, they tend to stop selling in December, preferring to wait until the new year to make more sales. Their private interests conflict with the interests of their employer.
- At AT&T, computer programmers were rewarded for the number of lines of code that they produced in their programs. Not surprisingly, programs became much longer than necessary.
- US teachers were offered incentive contracts that promised them bonuses if their students achieved good test scores. Two responses occurred. First, the teachers would only teach "for the test," ignoring all other kinds of teaching that the students required. Second, some teachers dissuaded the worst students from sitting the test (or in some cases even coming to class) so they would not count against the teacher's score. In one case, a teacher obtained a copy of the test beforehand and gave it to his students.
- Finally, consider the response of US surgeons to incentives. In New York, surgeons are penalized if their mortality rates exceed a threshold. Despite having taken the Hippocratic oath, some have been found to respond by refusing risky surgical cases as they approach that mortality threshold – hardly the response that hospital managers had in mind.

increase in pay may exceed any productivity gains. This issue has become especially contentious in the literature on executive pay.

Executives are typically offered contracts in which their pay varies with the performance of their company, through the ownership of stocks and options. Some experts believe that these contracts are a necessary means of providing executives with incentives, although truthfully there is little convincing evidence one way or the other. Others feel that this system of incentive pay is doing little more than handing over shareholders' money to an executive. Yet the costs of such plans are not limited to executives, and many companies in the US and Europe now offer employees contracts that include options.

Identifying whether these contracts are efficient is extremely difficult. Recent work in economics illustrates that employees should indeed receive additional compensation on incentive contracts, both because their jobs are likely to be more arduous and because the contract imposes more risk on them. (From the studies that have been collected so far on incentive contracting, a reasonable estimate for the effect on total compensation of the successful cases of incentive pay described above is that it will increase by about one-third to a half of the value of increased productivity.) Many companies now offer options to all workers in the company – worth perhaps three years' salary. These are attractive to companies because they may provide incentives for employees to improve the stock price.

Yet they have one very unattractive feature, namely that when the stock market in general increases, everyone who holds options may make large sums of money for doing nothing. In other words, companies are handing over money to employees for reasons that have nothing to do with their performance. Thus, while the companies may believe that options provide incentives, the evidence over the past decade or so would suggest that this has come at an enormous cost. Do these companies truly believe that the effects of options on incentives are worth the equivalent of three years' salary? I have my doubts.

Contracts of this form also violate one of the fundamental principles of effective incentive contracting. Any effective pay-for-performance plan should make compensation depend only on things that the employee can control. If the worker has no control over some particular measure, what is the point of making his or her pay vary with reference to it? This may seem like an obvious point, but in fact it is violated in many incentive contracts, notably the option contracts just described. A huge increase in the stock market – such as we saw over the 1990s – increases the value of options for reasons that have nothing to do with the actions of the workforce. And why should workers and executives benefit just because the stock market has increased?

A revision of contracts could overcome this problem. Instead of offering options where the exercise price depends on the stock price of the company, the company could index the option contracts to how well the stock market is doing. Here, the exercise price of the option could depend on the company's performance relative to the market (or some competitor's performance). The payouts then depend not on the stock price of the company (as options currently do), but instead on how the company does relative to the stock market in general. This would considerably reduce the costs of incentive contracting.

Individual v. team compensation

The final problem with incentive pay schemes is that it is difficult to find a good measure on which to base the compensation. For instance, should one use an individual measure of performance or something more aggregate, such as a team bonus or a company profit-sharing scheme? Companies often prefer more aggregate schemes because many employees are employed in settings where output is not the result of the inputs of a single individual, but rather derives from the joint contributions of many individuals.

This logic has resulted in a huge increase in the use of company-wide profit-sharing pay schemes, where at the end of the financial year employees share in the profitability of the company either through wages or pensions.

This type of scheme has one significant problem, namely that it tends to encourage "free-riding." Suppose that I work for General Motors along with a million other people, and am part of a profit-sharing scheme. Any increased effort on my part is going to be shared with all the other employees, so from a rational perspective why should I work harder? For example, if I come up with an idea that increases profits by $100,000, I get 10 cents. Rationally, I should shirk and free-ride on the efforts of my fellow workers.

For this reason, there is considerable skepticism about the effectiveness of compensation schemes based on the outputs of many employees. In fact, there is clear evidence that in occupations where team-based compensation is prevalent, such as the legal and medical professions, individuals tend to work less hard when the benefits of their efforts are shared by many. For example, one study showed that when a medical practice used contracts whereby all doctors would share the revenues from all their patients, the doctors reduced the number of hours that they worked relative to doctors who retained more of their own revenues.

Despite this, company-wide profit-sharing schemes in large companies are growing in popularity. Why is this? A large part of the reason is that large companies that use them are about 4 to 5 percent more productive and profitable than those that do not. It is natural to infer that profit-sharing plans increase productivity. However, while the statistic is true, it may not be true to say that profit sharing itself caused these companies to become more profitable.

Instead, the causality appears to go in the opposite direction: namely, only profitable companies use these schemes. Put simply, companies that are going broke do not use profit-sharing schemes, because they do not have any profits. This explains the better performance of companies with profit-sharing plans.

Unfortunately, the data have been misinterpreted to imply that profit sharing is good for companies' bottom lines. When these selection factors are taken care of, it appears (at least to my reading) that there is no evidence that introducing profit-sharing schemes in companies actually changes productivity. Such schemes increase pay, so employees are very content to participate, but there is little evidence that they cause people to work harder.

Conclusion

These observations illustrate some of the trade-offs that companies face with incentive pay. Paying employees on individual measures of performance generally causes them to exert more effort on those things for which they get paid. In some cases this is exactly what is needed, such as in the case of Safelite or Chinese agriculture. But having employees respond to incentive contracts is not necessarily a good thing – employees can focus too narrowly on the things for which they get rewarded and ignore everything else. Few would argue that a sick patient being refused treatment by a surgeon because she was too risky a case to take on (see "Misguided motives" box) is a beneficial response to the contracts offered to surgeons in New York.

In response to these and similar concerns, companies often prefer to make contracts depend on a more aggregate measure of performance, such as company-wide profits. But these have another drawback, namely that if employees do not perceive that the measure is affected by their own performance, they will see little reason to exert that extra effort. It is hardly surprising that most employees are still simply paid salaries.

Summary

Companies are increasingly adopting incentive schemes to encourage their employees to be more productive and efficient. However, the popularity of such schemes does not guarantee their effectiveness, says **Canice Prendergast**. Incentive contracting, for example, can cause employees to carry out actions that are beneficial to them but harmful to company interests. There is also a real danger that workers will focus too much on certain aspects of a contract to the detriment of all the other things they should be doing.

Emotional capability and corporate change

by Quy Nguyen Huy

In the past decade there has been a growing awareness that internal organizational capabilities constitute the real source of sustainable competitive advantage. Nevertheless, many organizations have to go through endless "turnarounds" without being able to revitalize themselves by their own internal energy. In this article, I argue that part of the problem lies in the failure of organizations to understand how to deal with emotions.

This issue was recognized by Jack Welch, chief executive of US conglomerate General Electric, and his advisers after many years of transformation effort. Welch learned from painful experience how profoundly emotions could influence whole organizations. Fearful employees in the early 1980s fought him to a standstill through covert guerrilla warfare. The problem, as Welch later acknowledged, was not that he believed emotions were less important than rational calculations. The real issue was that he did not know how to deal with emotions at an organizational level. Most companies conveniently ignore them; at worst, they ban negative emotions as irrational and detrimental to the business.

Work, however, is inherently an emotional experience. Emotions are intrinsic to our human essence and cannot be artificially segregated between our personal lives (where feelings are allowed) and our professional activities (where cold logic is preferred). Neurologists recently located emotional processing in certain pre-frontal areas of the brain called the amygdala and the anterior cingulate. Individuals who suffer damage to these areas have great difficulty maintaining a sense of responsibility for themselves and for others, or planning their future as social beings. They know but cannot feel. Their logical reasoning skills and memory, which holds their knowledge base, are intact and performing well – some even have above-average IQs. This enables them to analyze various alternatives with great lucidity and detail, but they can neither select one option nor act on it. They have lost their ability to prioritize and make decisions on personal and social matters where choices involve incomplete data or incommensurable consequences. As a result, their adaptability skills in complex social environments have been severely diminished.

Separately, research on emotional intelligence suggests that beyond a certain functional IQ threshold of 110 to 120, emotional competence is a much better predictor of future business leaders and superior performance in society than is intellectual ability.

Emotional intelligence is defined as the subset of social intelligence that involves the ability to monitor one's own and others' emotions, to discriminate between them, and to use such information to guide one's thinking and actions. Emotionally intelligent individuals are able to recognize and use their own and others' emotional states to solve problems and regulate behaviors. This does not mean that they are always "nice" or constantly emotionally expressive. Emotionally intelligent individuals are more adept at influencing other people and accessing leadership positions in domains where social skills make a difference.

Emotion is thus an integral part of adaptation and change. How emotion affects corporate transformation can be better understood if the change process is divided into individual components. Based on my own research as well as a synthesis of previous research on emotion and change, I will now explain how various attributes of emotional intelligence affect various dynamics constituting a major change process. The three attributes are receptivity, mobilization, and learning.

Receptivity describes individuals' willingness to consider a proposed change. Resistance to change represents the opposite to receptivity and can range from moral outrage to quiet cynicism and withdrawal. Some degree of receptivity to change is necessary for mobilization and learning to occur.

Mobilization is the process of rallying different segments of the organization to undertake joint action and realize common goals. The ability to mobilize hinges on the availability of adequate resources (e.g., finance, time, and staff), support structures and systems, but most importantly the necessary commitment and skill sets to cooperate during the change process. Mobilization during corporate transformation requires significant emotional energy. Strategic change that alters core perspectives and values tends to arouse strong anxiety and skepticism. During such periods, too much analysis may breed increasing doubt and paralysis; warm emotionality has to supersede cold rationality to enable coherent collective action.

Beyond receptivity leading to mobilization, individuals and organizations can learn from the outcomes of the changes they enact. A person learns by thinking, then acting. Emotion provides the primary feedback mechanism that alerts the person that various goals are not being achieved, and this in turn motivates behavior. Emotion arouses dissatisfaction with the current state of affairs when a person compares the newly perceived reality unfavorably with his or her prior expectations. This stimulates learning and change.

Radical change in organizational beliefs and values often starts with the challenging of deep-rooted assumptions. The most prevalent form of learning in organizations is incremental problem solving, called single-loop learning. Members seek to adjust surface behaviors to achieve their desired objective. In contrast, double-loop learning operates at a more abstract level and refers to identification, then modification, of the underlying faulty assumptions (beliefs or values) that drive particular actions. This deep investigative and transformational process activates strong emotions. Organizational learning and change can therefore be facilitated by judicious attention to emotions.

When people mobilize, they may find that the outcomes of their actions are not as they had hoped. Ideally, under these circumstances, people: 1) appraise and learn from such outcomes; 2) grow receptive to alternative courses of action; and 3) re-mobilize, taking action along a more promising course. Continuous balancing is necessary because secondary effects of present actions often induce future imbalances. Effective learning processes capture early mistakes and rectify them before they become insurmountable.

What actions should organizations take to arouse appropriate emotions during corporate transformation? An organization's degree of ability to execute such actions effectively determines its level of emotional capability and likelihood of realizing major change.

The four organizational skills discussed below have a bearing on emotions. An emotionally capable organization does not necessarily require most of its members to be emotionally intelligent, or in influential positions.

1 Developing empathy and experiencing skills

Empathy is a central attribute of emotional intelligence. It represents an individual's ability to understand someone else's feelings and re-experience them. Empathy determines the success of social support and is a motivator for altruistic behavior.

Change agents are more effective if they can experience first-hand what it feels like to be in the shoes of those they seek to change. Trained change agents or those who have experienced emotional pain are better able to understand other people's psychological and social defenses and deal with them appropriately. Martin Luther King and Gandhi went through the painful personal transformation process and developed a deep sense of empathy and care for others that permeated their rhetoric and behavior.

Organizations should ensure that change agents experience appropriate emotions in response to others' feelings so that they can communicate and act on this experience. For example, Ford's CEO Jacques Nasser deliberately encouraged change agents in training openly to air "brutal" emotions about change and act them out in video clips. Demonstrating concern for one another constitutes an emotional basis for trust and has been found to lead to better work performance.

Acting on this emotional experience implies that a sense of honesty, fairness, justice, and respect for those affected by change will be projected. The organization can establish anxiety-reduction mechanisms such as informal communication structures during a threatening period. Emotional support structures such as psychological counseling services, self-help groups, team building aimed at both task accomplishments and satisfying member needs, interventions by process consultants to facilitate single- and double-loop learning, may help organization members cope with the new reality.

2 Developing sympathy and reconciling skills

Sympathy is a less demanding emotional process than empathy, but still represents a core attribute of emotional intelligence. The sympathetic are able to feel for the general suffering of others without directly sharing that person's experience. Unlike empathy, the person can retain his or her private feelings while understanding those of someone else. Sympathy is partly demonstrated by reconciling behaviors.

Any proposed major change could be usefully understood as a juxtaposition of additions and deletions. Corporate transformation sometimes requires bringing together two seemingly opposing values – for instance job security and shareholder interest, or cost efficiency and customer service.

The more a proposed change is framed and accepted by the recipients as an addition to existing values – e.g., streamlining to improve efficiency, delayering to improve customer service – the easier it is to accept. The more continuity is perceived to exist between the past and the future, the less the change is perceived as radical. Change agents and recipients can attempt to build a bridge by jointly developing metaphors that contain both familiar and unfamiliar experiences, or through cultural grafts that incorporate some positive elements of the old culture with the new directions. Emotional conversations to build new meanings gradually increase understanding and sympathy between various groups.

Apart from additions, change may require loss of certain cherished values. Mourning of these values should be organized. An adequate grieving process is essential in emotional reconciliation. Change agents should be mindful about this transition period, marked as it is by the recipients' frightful disorientation. The past is no longer appropriate while the future direction is neither clear nor fully accepted. People will need time to come to terms with what went wrong and why it needs changing now, as well as to figure out their own steps to renewal. This grieving should be monitored with attention and sensitivity. Wide inclusion should be encouraged, and change agents should openly acknowledge mistakes and losses. Research suggests that change agents who rush the organization through this mourning phase create an organization paralyzed by survivor sickness and devoid of creative energy.

Archie McGill, CEO of AT&T, rushed employees through the traumatic post-divestiture period and created a "psychologically damaged" organization. A higher degree of hostility was directed toward insiders than at competitors, and a lot of suppressed anger and depression was reported. After failing to come to terms with their past, AT&T employees were deprived of their full energy to attend to the future.

3 Developing encouragement skills

Christian Blanc, CEO of state-owned Air France, listened first to a vast number of people at all levels of the organization before designing his transformation program. Through open-ended questions and surveys led by neutral academic researchers, Blanc discovered that employees had resorted to extreme and violent actions in peaks of desperation where they felt they had no other way of being heard seriously. Previous change agents had been instilling a permanent climate of insecurity and fear without imparting any feeling of hope.

Hope is another attribute of emotional intelligence and implies a belief that one has both the will and the means to accomplish one's goals. It buffers people against apathy and depression and strengthens their capacity to withstand defeat and persist in adversity.

Research shows that most people are motivated by the psychology of hope: the expectation and wish that our future work situation will be better (or at least as good) as the present one. It has been shown that hope distinguishes the academic achievements of people with equivalent intellectual aptitudes. Leaders can engender hope by establishing change goals that are meaningful. Meaningful goals have three characteristics: they are 1) ambitious, which attends to aspirations for personal growth and development; 2) achievable, which increases propensity for action; and 3) beneficial to employees' welfare, which attends to safety and comfort needs. All these characteristics depend largely on people's perceptions, and so change agents can provide alternative ways of framing the same issue. A threat may also be perceived as an opportunity if the phenomenon is seen from a different angle.

Organizations should develop encouragement skills among change agents during traumatic transformation periods. Beyond establishing meaningful change goals (content), change agents can also improve the process of delivery. One can convey goals with the use of vivid images and emotional metaphors that captivate people. Martin Luther King Jr.'s "I have a dream" speech used relatively down-to-earth language that inspired people across many races. Simplicity is the essence of elegance and arouses emotion because it suggests authenticity and forthrightness. Other encouragement activities include frequent dialog – and not one-way information sessions – between change agents and recipients, allocation of quality time and resources, rousing speeches, and ceremonies to celebrate partial successes. The challenge for top managers is less strategy making than ideology setting. They can shape an ideological climate that encourages enthusiasm, nurtures courage, and reveals opportunities to bring new hope and life to their organizations. When people believe that their actions will lead to positive results, they will be more likely to initiate difficult and uncertain tasks.

4 Displaying emotions

Emotional authenticity describes a person's ability to acknowledge, express, and be sincere about his or her feelings. It is an attribute of emotional intelligence. Alexithymia refers to a psychiatric disorder whereby patients are unable to appraise and express their emotions. Individuals who lose this ability bury their real selves under false images.

Corporate transformations engender major upheavals in people's wellbeing and beliefs, and this arouses intense emotions. Denying and suppressing these emotions in work settings only drives their effects underground. Treating a display of negative emotions as cynicism or detachment with punitive consequences only means that resentful change recipients improve emotional acting skills and fake cooperation. The transformation process becomes more chaotic and unpredictable as covert resisters are indistinguishable from friends or the loyal opposition. Risk aversion, reduced knowledge sharing, and covert resistance to change intensify during a period where creativity and contextual knowledge are most needed to realize ambitious changes.

Individuals obliged continually to enact a narrow range of prescribed emotions are likely to experience emotional dissonance. This reflects the internal conflict generated between genuinely felt emotions and those required to be displayed. This can result in emotional exhaustion and burnout. Consequent emotional numbness alleviates stress by reducing access to feelings – the central means of interpreting the world around us – and leads to low sensitivity to new ideas and experimentation. This can degenerate into a vicious cycle. As the workload pressure increases because of burnout and downsizing, more and more employees will become tired from trying to compensate for work not done. This further reduces the self-reflection time needed for deep learning. This frustrating state is in turn interpreted as a failure in change, which exacerbates cynicism and depresses further efforts at collective learning and change.

Research by Arie Hoschschild on Delta Airlines' flight attendants and by David Noer on employees of a large organization shows the deep psychological damage caused by organizations' attempts to control and suppress what they believed were undesirable emotional expressions. The successful renewal of British Airways in the 1980s was attributed in part to the top management team's explicit recognition of employees' "emotional labor" and the development of both formal and informal emotional support systems to attenuate emotional exhaustion.

Jack Welch, chairman of General Electric of the US, explicitly stated that one of the key goals of his "Work Out" change initiative was to expose business unit leaders to "the vibrations of their business – opinions, feelings, emotions, resentments, not abstract theories of organization and management." During traumatic transformation periods, organizations should acknowledge full emotionality in the work place. How leaders of change deal with emotion is more important than the content itself (positive versus negative emotions). People should be encouraged to express their full range of emotions, without fear of reprisal. As the recipients' capacity to make sense breaks down under the stress of transformation, disenchantment and hurt should be allowed expression, and leadership should deal with it in an open, honest, and caring fashion.

Summary

Many organizations go through endless turnarounds but fail to revive themselves by using their own internal energy. In this article, **Quy Nguyen Huy** argues that part of the problem is a failure to understand emotions. These can profoundly influence whole organizations, so managers and change agents should be finely tuned to their impact. Emotions are intrinsic to human nature and cannot be artificially segregated between personal lives and professional activities. The author discusses four organizational skills that help harness emotions during corporate change.

Suggested further reading

Bennis, W. (1998) *On Becoming a Leader*, London: Arrow.

Goleman, D. (1998) *Working with Emotional Intelligence*, London: Bloomsbury.

Hamel, G. and Prahalad, C.K. (1994) *Competing for the Future*, Boston, MA: Harvard Business School Press.

Huy, Q.N. (1999) "Emotional capability, emotional intelligence, and radical change," *Academy of Management Review*, 24: 325–45.

Noer, D. (1993) *Healing the Wounds*, San Francisco: Jossey-Bass.

Salovey, P. and Mayer, J.D. (1990) "Emotional intelligence," *Imagination, Cognition and Personality*, 9 (3): 185–211.

Tichy, N. and Sherman, S. (1994) *Control Your Destiny or Someone Else Will*, New York: HarperBusiness.

SECTOR
STRATEGIES

Contributors

John Kay is a director and founder of London Economics, a UK consultancy. He was the first director of the Saïd Business School, Oxford. His research interests include economics and business, business strategy and the social context of markets.

Fiona Murray is a university lecturer in management technology at the Saïd Business School, Oxford, and is currently visiting assistant professor at the Sloan School of Management, MIT. She focusses, among other subjects, on the organization of R&D and the impact of science and technology on industry evolution.

Richard Whittington is a university reader in strategy at Saïd Business School, Oxford, and a fellow of New College, Oxford. He is researching how managers learn to strategize as part of the Economic and Social Research Council's SKOPE (Skills, Knowledge and Organizational Performance) program.

Laura Empson is a fellow of St Anne's College and lecturer in management studies at the Saïd Business School, Oxford. She has previously worked as a strategy consultant and an investment banker.

Contents

Introduction

This book concentrates mainly on the general principles of strategy – but different industries and sectors often require a specific approach and set of skills. Regulated industries, for instance, may confront most of conventional issues facing normal companies but they have a set of their own to contend with as well. Strategies for science-based businesses – a notoriously difficult area for extracting value – and the particular model used by professional services firms like McKinsey and Andersen Consulting are also explored. The module ends with a look at conglomerates and the proposition that rumours of their demise have been exaggerated.

Challenges of running a regulated business

by John Kay

Even in market economies, the state is deeply involved in economic activity. Some businesses are mainly undertaken by government – education, defense, policing. Others sell to the government – defense contracting. Still others are undertaken in a framework in which many ordinary commercial decisions such as pricing, investment, and product design are wholly or largely fixed by the state. Regulated industries, with which this article is concerned, are in the last group.

The normal rationale for regulatory intervention is the existence of some market failure, which means either that a competitive industry structure is not possible or, if it is, it is likely to have an outcome that is inefficient or undesirable. The existence of inevitable market power is one such kind of market failure, as with electricity transmission or water distribution, where a proliferation of suppliers is hopelessly uneconomic.

Markets fail through externalities, as with environmental or health and safety issues, where actions have consequences that do not immediately fall on those who engage in them. And an increasingly common source of market failure is information asymmetry: the seller knows far more about the product than the buyer does.

Typically, the main regulated industries are ones in which several of these market failures arise. These include gas, electricity, and water utilities, telecommunications and media industries, transportation, professional and financial services, and pharmaceuticals. All of these have been regulated in most countries for a century or more. Yet there have been important recent changes in the style of regulation.

The existence of some market failure was often used in the past as a springboard for wide-ranging supervision of the management and operations of the businesses affected. Airline regulation was clearly needed to secure the safety of passengers and the public at large. Yet around the world such regulation rapidly extended to control of fares, frequencies, and the financial stability of carriers. In many industries, including airlines, regulation took the form of nationalization and there was political accountability for specific management decisions.

Over the last two decades the focus of regulation has been narrowed. Most regulation is now targetted on specific market failures. Control over airfares, for example, is fast disappearing. Privatization has limited the involvement of government in utilities to specific issues of the control of pricing and the appraisal of investment programs. At the same time, however, competition and globalization have meant that much of what was formerly tacit regulation has become formalized, creating the apparent paradox of simultaneous deregulation and reregulation. Financial services display this tension most clearly.

Many of the strategic issues faced by regulated industries are similar to those faced by ordinary businesses. Those that are not fall into two main groups. First, the management of government and regulatory relations – a significant issue for all companies – takes on an overriding importance for a regulated company. Second, many of the ordinary rules of competitive interaction and influences on market and industry structure are suppressed in regulated companies. I consider each of these issues in turn.

Management of regulation

Regulation is culturally specific. An increasing number of regulated companies operate across national boundaries. Globalization, however, is less developed in many regulated industries than in business generally, partly for this reason. Still, there are few internationally transferable skills in regulation management and considerable sensitivity to the local environment is required. Around the world and across industries there is a broad spectrum from specific, rule-based structures to regulation based largely on individual political negotiation. There is no ideal system either for the companies affected or for the public interest: these differences are the product of broader differences in the business and political environmental and specific characteristics of the industries concerned.

In the US, regulation is characteristically formal and rule based. This frequently leads to litigious and adversarial regulatory processes, and specific forensic and technical skills are required in the management of regulation. British regulation is more discretionary. As a result, technical argument is equally significant but adversarial approaches are usually counter-productive: establishing a relationship of trust with the regulator acquires central importance. France is still further along the spectrum. The concept of independent regulation, mediating between company and state, is barely familiar there and regulation is integrated into conventional political processes.

At both extremes these forms of regulation collapse. Rule-based regulation can become so cumbersome that subverting or bypassing it becomes the main skill of the regulatory manager; discretionary regulation can degenerate into cronyism or corruption. As so often, the extremes of a spectrum differ little from each other.

Whatever the formal process, all mechanisms of regulation are managed in the context of the same underlying regulatory game. The regulated company is concerned to maximize its own returns. Its managers have superior knowledge of what costs are necessary, of what efficiency gains are available, of what investments are appropriate. The regulator is of necessity less well informed than the companies he regulates. He thus seeks to impose objectives which differ from the company's own. In a rule-based system, these objectives may simply be to interpret a set of statutory obligations; in a more discretionary system, to pursue broader public interest objects; in a political framework, to balance the concerns of a range of different constituencies.

The regulatory purpose is to find a structure that will make it advantageous – ideally, directly profitable – for the company to pursue the regulatory objective. Considerable ingenuity has been deployed in constructing formulas – incentive-based regulation – that are aimed at that result: the objective is to minimize direct control by regulators of individual management decisions. But the formulas themselves, and the information needed to apply them, are inescapably the subject of political negotiation. The regulatee's purpose is to manage the presentation of the information used in developing the regulatory structure and to make operational decisions that will maximize profits within it. All this is subject to the constraint – which rises in importance as the degree of regulatory discretion mounts – that behavior that undermines trust in the regulatory relationship will, in the long run, prove counter-productive.

The most effective strategy of regulatory management is regulatory capture, in which the regulatory agency increasingly adopts the objectives of the regulatory companies as its own. In the airline industry, for example, regulators came to operate a cartel on behalf of established carriers, in the belief that there was an overriding public interest in the financial stability of the industry. The same outcome can often be seen in financial and professional services industries.

More generally, regulation normally operates to the advantage of incumbent companies relative to entrants. The very complexity of regulation acts as a barrier to entry. Requirements for regulatory approval are routinely obstacles to product innovation and the use of new delivery mechanisms, two of the most common entry strategies. Many regulatory requirements demand a negligible share of the turnover of large companies, while identical obligations may be burdensome for small companies.

The profession of regulation, and of the management of regulation, is still in its infancy. There are some textbooks on how to regulate but, so far, no serious text on how to *be* regulated. Yet the returns from skills in regulatory management can be very large. It is common for managers simply to berate regulation, or to seek diversification into unregulated activities. However, many of the most persistently profitable companies, from Merck to Microsoft, have achieved this result precisely because of effective exploitation of the regulatory framework within which they operate. It is no accident that established companies in many industries resist the introduction of regulation – and also oppose its removal.

Regulation and competition

Industrial structures in regulated industries have been established in conditions where competition was restricted, or even eliminated altogether. In most markets, dominant companies are those that have developed and exploited their competitive advantages. In many regulated industries, dominant companies have emerged as a result of national protection or statutory monopoly. Within the last few years, privatization and deregulation have made many of these market structures contestable. This raises some of the most intriguing issues in strategic management today.

There is one general rule about how these liberalized structures will evolve. It is that in future, market shares will reflect not historic strength, but competitive advantage. The US airline industry illustrates this transition well. At the time of deregulation in the 1970s, the structure of the industry had been ossified for almost 50 years. A wave of new entry and innovation followed. Most of these entrants failed. So did some older companies with great names and histories. Eventually, the industry regrouped around a smaller number of carriers. The survivors included both entrants and members of the former cartel. All were companies that had developed real competitive advantages – strong hubs, powerful brands, lightly managed operations – and deployed them effectively.

As competition reaches many more regulated industries, these developments will repeat themselves. Outside regulated industries, we rarely encounter companies with large market share and resources but no competitive advantage. It is these companies that will go the way of Eastern or Pan American – once household names in the airline industry – which have either disappeared or become shadows of their former selves. We can expect this to happen to several large banks, telecom, energy, and media companies.

In the main, competition in regulated industries requires artificial stimulus. The hopes of those involved in early liberalizing were that merely removing statutory restrictions on competition would lead to competitive outcomes. Such hopes were repeatedly frustrated. Only where governments have insisted on access to established networks and other essential facilities, restructured the incumbents, or tilted the playing field in favor of entrants, has competition emerged. That raises issues for both incumbents and entrants.

In general, the rational strategy for an incumbent is to resist liberalization, and this is normally what is done; yet experience suggests that the issues are not so clear cut. If competition is inevitable, the early experience of it may be valuable both in a domestic market and internationally. At first sight, it seemed that British Gas – which maintained its effective monopoly – had won a battle that the dismembered UK electricity industry had lost; yet with hindsight the electricity companies won more managerial autonomy and a more competitive market positioning. Incumbents find it difficult, politically and organizationally, to be monopolists at home and competitors abroad.

Entrants may choose organic or inorganic approaches. Purchases of assets in liberalizing markets have repeatedly suffered from the "winner's curse" – the successful bidder is the one who overpays, given the intense competition. Greenfield entry naturally focusses on areas where regulatory distortion is greatest.

Almost all competition in telecommunications, for example, has focussed on areas – such as long-distance business traffic – where the gap between prices and costs is highest, rather than on those where the incumbent is least efficient. This strategy offers short-run benefits, but may not prove sustainable. Mercury Communications' strategy as a duopolist sheltering under the tariff structure of British Telecommunications failed when the government instituted full liberalization.

Conclusion

There is a canard that the management of regulated businesses is easy; this their managers justly resent. It is true that many such companies come to competitive markets with a historic legacy of assets and a scale of resources that others envy. It is also true that it is hard for a regulated company to go broke – although it is certain that over the next few years some will. But regulated businesses face almost all of the strategy issues confronting conventional companies, and some additional ones that are specific to their own environment. As deregulation spreads across Europe, the gap between those companies that handle these specific issues effectively and those that respond to regulation and regulatory changes with hostility, complacency, or defeatism will widen rapidly.

Summary

Regulated businesses face most of the strategy issues that confront conventional companies, says **John Kay**. But they also have to cope with others that are specific to their environment. Handling regulators effectively, for example, requires sensitivity to local conditions; as deregulation and privatization spread across Europe the gap between companies that are effective in this regard and those that respond with hostility, complacency, or defeatism will widen. The same forces are also changing industry structures established in conditions where competition was restricted or even eliminated. In future, market shares will reflect competitive advantage rather than historic strength. The author discusses the implications of liberalization for new entrants and incumbents: it might seem rational for the latter to resist, but experience shows it is not always that clear cut.

Strategies for science-based business

by Fiona Murray

The British government planned to spend over $2.4bn on scientific research in 1999/2000. The Wellcome Trust will contribute at least an additional £400m to basic science research in the UK. Many are anxious to capitalize on the economic benefits of these investments. Indeed, over the next three years, the government's stated goal is to increase by 50 percent the number of companies spun out of the UK science base. However, scientists and business leaders alike have little to guide their thinking on when and how science is successfully commercialized.

Unfortunately, a good scientific idea does not necessarily translate into a good business idea. Successful companies will require a blend of science, business, and finance. And without the right strategy, financing will not be attracted or will soon dwindle.

Sustainable strategies for science-based businesses are difficult to craft because the business value embedded within a scientific idea can be hard to capture. This article poses the following questions:

- Can you separate the scientists from their ideas?
- Can you contract for the exchange of a scientific idea?

The answers to these two questions provide clues to building generic science-based strategies. From them we can identify four types of scientific knowledge and four possible strategies for science-based businesses: selling scientific ideas; selling a scientific service; selling a science-based product (the most traditional); and seeking to be acquired.

Unique characteristics

These questions arise because of some of the special characteristics of scientific knowledge, as they relate to economic action. They have much in common with the characteristics of knowledge more broadly, and so we can draw on our insights from knowledge management to outline the nature of scientific ideas:

- Unlike many technologies that can be observed when they are being utilized, scientific ideas are often non-observable in use – their use cannot be readily monitored.
- Scientific ideas can often be used by more than one group simultaneously – they are non-rival in use. For physical assets such as land, alternative uses lead to rivalry.
- Scientific knowledge typically builds on a vast array of previous knowledge – it is therefore generally cumulative rather than isolated in both its nature and use.
- Scientific knowledge can be difficult to replicate. In fact, many early experiments are extremely difficult to repeat successfully.
- Problems with replicability often flow from the difficulty of separating an individual from his or her idea. Inalienability – lack of separability – often characterizes new scientific ideas.

■ Scientific knowledge can have a range of specificity. It can be general – useful for solving a range of problems. But it can also be quite specific.

Strategies for creating a successful science-based business recognize and leverage these unique characteristics. They will help us better understand why the questions of separability and contracting come about, and formulate strategies for overcoming and leveraging those characteristics.

People and ideas

The question of separating ideas and the people who generate them arises because science is cumulative, hard to replicate, and therefore often inalienable. The concept of alienability had an important place in Roman law and later in debates over land rights in the Middle Ages. However, it is typically thought of as granting an owner the power to separate (or sell) a right (which may be an idea). What is often more crucial with scientific knowledge is the ability to separate the idea and its initiator.

The strategic importance of understanding how easily a scientific idea can be separated from its creators can be illustrated with an imaginary but typical scenario. A small biotech company is working with a university on a joint research project. The university discovers a new method for protein purification that has widespread potential. The small company buys the "recipe" for the method from the university. However, on returning to their laboratory, its staff repeat the recipe again and again but simply cannot get it to work. Frustrated, they telephone the scientists at the university, who talk them through the process. Still it does not work. Finally, a post-doctoral researcher visits the company and gets the process to work in an afternoon.

This story is not unique to the life sciences. Indeed, there is considerable evidence that manufacturing skills can be hard to transfer, especially between multinational plants. However, in the scientific domain the close link between the scientific idea and the inventor can be puzzling to those outside the laboratory. Our common conception of scientific ideas is that they are very explicit, and indeed, to be scientific must be replicable by others. In reality, repetition can often be fraught with difficulty, and may take time to accomplish. During this time, the scientific idea can still be the basis for a good business even though it might not be considered to be "good science."

The idea of gradually separating ideas from individuals comes through clearly in the story told by anthropologist Paul Rabinow about Nobel prize winner Cary Mullis's discovery of polymerase chain reaction (PCR) and its subsequent commercialization by Cetus Corporation of California. In an interview with Rabinow, one of the scientists at Cetus Corporation recounts:

> When you work on a particular technique, it is sort of like a craftsman who develops an ability to do something . . . what was happening with PCR was that I was playing with it in many respects . . . and as a result . . . you do it better and better . . . It becomes rigorous in your hands. It works the way you would scientifically think it would work when you plan an experiment.

What, then, are the strategic implications of these observations? If you can separate the ideas and the people, then it is possible to build a business either based on a product created from the idea, or based on selling the idea directly. If not, it is crucial to keep the scientists engaged, but to sell a service based around the idea. Or to make investments in trying to render the idea alienable.

Whether alienable or not, businesses based on scientific ideas must be engaged in the economic market place in some way or another. Determining in what form to create a market for scientific knowledge is the second important question.

The contracts conundrum

It can be extremely difficult to write satisfactory contracts for the exchange of scientific ideas. Nobel prize winner Kenneth Arrow offered the insight that it is difficult to buy and sell information. If you want to buy information, you will not do so unless you have seen it; but once I have shown it to you, you no longer need to buy it from me. Scientific knowledge has similar characteristics to information.

To illustrate this, consider a small medical instruments company interested in a breakthrough in materials technology. The company scientists go for advice to a group of material science specialists. They enter into negotiations and insist on being shown the material and its chemical formula in detail – just to be certain the science makes sense. The materials specialists negotiate hard and the chief scientist at the medical instruments business decides that their ideas are too costly. The following week in the laboratory of the instrument business there is much excitement over some breakthrough new materials that are very similar to those under discussion.

We might overcome this problem by building reputations on both sides for good science on the one hand and fair exchange of ideas on the other. However, contracts for scientific ideas can still be problematic, because the rights to use scientific ideas can be hard to enforce. It is not always possible to observe the use of scientific knowledge – it may be too complex, or its language may be unknown to all but the scientist involved. Even when a company can observe use of its science by another party, they may not be able to do anything about it in a court of law. Strong intellectual property rights overcome part of this difficulty – intellectual property rights are legal rights. The combination of the idea and the legal right to the idea greatly improves the contracting problem by providing a means of verification and therefore increases the strategic opportunities available for capturing the value of science.

A four-pronged approach

In answering the two questions posed above, a series of possible science-based strategies emerge (*see* Figure 1).

A strategy based on capturing the value of *scientific ideas* is feasible when those ideas are reasonably separable from their developers. The alienability of the ideas, together with the ability to contract for their sale, can be used to build a business that creates value either by selling scientific ideas or by selling the rights to use the ideas. Universities engage in a scientific ideas strategy when they repeatedly license intellectual property. Indeed, the license for recombinant DNA won Stanford University enormous revenues. Companies such as ARM Holdings, the Cambridge-based semiconductor group in the UK, have also developed considerable revenue streams from selling their ideas for chip designs.

In instances where scientific ideas are hard to separate from their developers, the traditional response was for an individual with his or her ideas to join a company as an employee. More recently, businesses have been created that in turn are rapidly

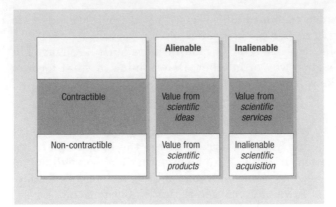

Figure 1

acquired by large R&D-driven companies such as the pharmaceutical makers Pfizer, chipmaker Intel, or even Microsoft. Through this route a company acquires a bundle of people and ideas, and indeed some start-ups follow this *scientific acquisition* path quite actively.

An alternative route to be followed when it is possible to contract for the use of the bundle of ideas and people is to base a business around providing *scientific services*. A business like Oxford Asymmetry International – a highly successful chemical services spinout from the University of Oxford – provides what it calls the "Complete Chemical Solution." Its strategy is to use the chemical knowledge of the people in the company to solve the difficult problems that pharmaceutical companies confront. Their chemists can solve these problems rapidly and build up a wealth of general knowledge because of their repeated problem-solving experience. The customers pay for the scientific services, but the general scientific knowledge (and the scientists themselves) remains with the company.

A more traditional approach, when ideas are alienable, is to create a *scientific product*. Rather than endeavoring to trade scientific knowledge, a company will use its knowledge to create a product – it could be a drug, an operating system, or perhaps a scientific instrument such as the CT, computerized axial tomography scanner. While this strategy can be effective (and is certainly more amenable to traditional strategic analysis), it poses several problems. Products, for example, often require not only scientific knowledge but also complementary manufacturing and marketing knowledge. This can be scarce or costly to acquire. Certainly, in the life sciences, the scientific product strategy is increasingly unpopular with investors in biotechnology, with scientific service companies outperforming the overall sector.

Making a choice

The translation of PCR from scientific idea into a business illustrates the choices available to science entrepreneurs. At first, even within Cetus, the PCR technique was quite inalienable. No one could repeat Mullis's experiments. It would have been difficult to use a scientific acquisition strategy, because the company would have lost the PCR team and would have simply transferred the strategy problem to another company. Cetus considered keeping PCR a trade secret and simply providing a scientific service to customers. However, the team at the company was eventually able to write down a "blueprint" for DNA amplification. Cetus was able to patent this idea. By writing a patent and disclosing the idea in return for legal protection, Cetus tried to improve its ability to contract for the science of PCR. The

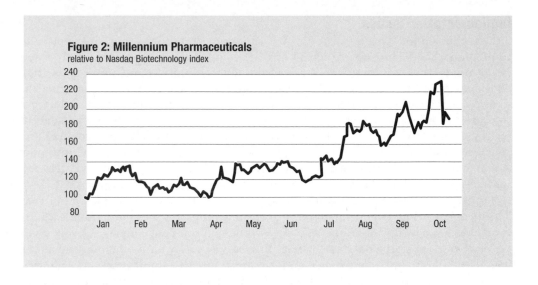

Figure 2: Millennium Pharmaceuticals
relative to Nasdaq Biotechnology index

question became whether to sell the idea or a product. The idea had widespread applicability and so a single sale may not have been appropriate. The licensing alternative – a scientific ideas strategy – was a challenge, because it would have been hard to observe people engaged in using the technique; non-contractability in this case arising from a lack of observability. With a piece of equipment – a scientific product strategy – it was easier to sell the scientific idea. In the end, Cetus licensed the idea to Hoffman-La Roche, which then created the product.

Mixing strategies

While Cetus chose a single strategy (for PCR at least), the different science-based strategies are not necessarily mutually exclusive. This is illustrated by the emerging genomics sector. Genomics, which includes the study of gene expression, provides information as to which genes may be activated or inactivated in certain disease or physiological processes.

Millennium Pharmaceuticals, the US gene-hunting company (*see* Figure 2), employs a combination of the strategies described above. In its initial public offering (IPO) documents Millennium described a two-pronged strategy that incorporated selling scientific services to a range of partners as well as the internal development of scientific products (in this case lead molecules with therapeutic value). These two elements both build on their general scientific knowledge of understanding of genes, their role in disease and their function.

Incyte, another genomics company, is selling access to the scientific ideas in its databases. According to Incyte, "The databases contain more information than any single company can exploit, and we believe our pharmaceutical partners will differentiate themselves from competitors by how effectively they use this data."

It is therefore exploiting alienable and contractable scientific knowledge, but taking this process a step further by recognizing that scientific knowledge can be non-rival in use. More than one person or company can use the scientific knowledge simultaneously, unlike land for example, when my use precludes yours. This multiple use allows both sides to benefit from the exchange.

Implementation issues

No discussion of strategy would be complete without some discussion of implementation. The science-based strategies outlined here, particularly those involving selling a scientific service, do involve significant implementation challenges. Again, these arise because of the unique characteristics of scientific knowledge. Implementation must address the need not only to protect ideas but also to protect scientists – meaning to keep them within the business. It must also focus on the cumulative nature of the science and the need to generate general and specific knowledge. Like our insights into scientific knowledge, implementation of science-based strategies can also be understood in the light of our growing understanding of knowledge management.

Scientific service businesses must consider the fact that scientists play a key role. The business is highly dependent on the continued input of these individuals. Share options are a positive inducement to stay, while non-compete clauses actively try to limit a scientist's alternatives. In scientific services as well as businesses selling scientific ideas, the continued maintenance and accumulation of scientific knowledge are also crucial to successful implementation. Knowledge can be accumulated using well-organized knowledge-management programs that seek to capture the knowledge of individuals in a range of different ways. Oxford Asymmetry International has undertaken an extensive knowledge-management program using consultants Cap Gemini with these goals in mind. However, like other companies it also recognizes that the continued engagement of scientists in its academic networks has a positive effect on research and development. In the life sciences, research has shown that successful companies are often actively engaged in industry–academia collaborations, typically on an informal basis. While this may lead to some leakage of scientific ideas, it also keeps the scientists within the business both interested in research and actively engaged in scientific progress.

The call to increase university spin-outs and to build on the small but growing group of science-based businesses in the UK is getting louder. However, these businesses will only find long-term success if they make the right strategic choices.

Summary

How best to commercialize the findings of science is an issue that concerns company strategists, venture capitalists, and government policy makers in many countries. There is widespread recognition that especially difficult challenges are involved. Nevertheless the UK government, for one, has set a target of increasing by 50 percent the number of companies that are spun out of the science base over the next three years. In this article, which draws mainly on UK experience, **Fiona Murray** outlines four possible strategies for science-based businesses: selling scientific ideas, selling scientific services, selling scientific products, and seeking to be acquired.

In praise of the evergreen conglomerate

by Richard Whittington

Rumors of the death of the conglomerate are much exaggerated. There have been some great conglomerate break-ups in recent years, such as those at ITT and Hanson Trust. But there is an upside to the conglomerate too. *Fortune* magazine's most admired industrial company is General Electric, whose businesses range from aircraft engines to television. Warren Buffett, the most successful US investor, is building a new conglomerate around insurance, executive jets, fast food, and home furnishings. Britain's most conspicuous entrepreneur, Richard Branson, chairman of the Virgin Group, presides over businesses stretching from trains to cosmetics.

The case against the conglomerate, however, seems strong. Since the 1980s, business leaders have been warned to "stick to their knitting" and focus on "core competence." The conglomerate, it is said, appears to offer no synergy gains and little scope for sharing operating resources between unrelated businesses. Conglomerate headquarters add extra costs and bureaucratic muddle to businesses that might otherwise be freestanding. And if investors wish to spread their risks over a range of unrelated businesses, they can do so directly themselves. They do not need a conglomerate as their vehicle.

In short, conventional wisdom has it that the conglomerate was just an aberration of the growth-happy 1960s and early 1970s. The restructuring, "downscoping," buyouts and spin-outs of the 1980s and 1990s are supposed to have brought about a long overdue correction. By rights, the conglomerate should by now be dead.

In fact, the conglomerate is alive and pretty healthy. To the examples of GE, Virgin, and Warren Buffett with which we started, we might add the acquisitive engineering conglomerate Tyco International of the US or Thermo Electron, a maker of high-tech analytical instruments. Citigroup of the US, the diversified financial group that operates in nearly every financial service from investment banking to personal insurance, is a further candidate for conglomerate status. So too is the emerging British services company Centrica, operating in gas supply, credit cards, and roadside breakdown services for motorists. For every broken-up former empire, it is not hard to find an example of a pushy new conglomerate player.

More systematic research backs this up. A study of diversification trends among Fortune 500 companies during the 1980s by Costas Markides (*see* Suggested further reading) found only a small decline in the proportion of conglomerates. Yes, poorly performing overdiversified companies did refocus, but by and large new conglomerates emerged to replace them. The majority of conglomerates continued to perform respectably.

The outlook for the conglomerate in Europe is even rosier. Taking the long view, my own research, along with that of a number of colleagues, suggests that there is a powerful post-war trend toward the building of more conglomerates among the top 100 domestically owned French, German, and British industrial companies. In Britain and Germany, at least, the restructuring of the 1980s and the early 1990s made no difference to the trend, so that by 1993 about a quarter of large industrial

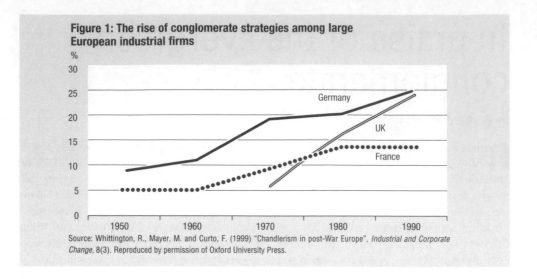

Figure 1: The rise of conglomerate strategies among large European industrial firms

Source: Whittington, R., Mayer, M. and Curto, F. (1999) "Chandlerism in post-War Europe", *Industrial and Corporate Change*, 8(3). Reproduced by permission of Oxford University Press.

companies were conglomerates (*see* Figure 1). More recent research, reported by Winfried Ruigrok and others (*see* Suggested further reading), examines western Europe as a whole between 1993 and 1996, and again finds no evidence for any significant trend away from conglomerates.

Hidden strengths

If, as the evidence suggests, conglomerates are here to stay, it is clearly important to understand their strengths and how best to manage them.

Critics of the conglomerate have focussed too much on the absence of synergistic relationships at an operating level. Rob Grant (*see* Suggested further reading) has distinguished two ways in which businesses can relate to each other. One is operating relatedness, where the sharing of operating resources (manufacturing facilities, distribution channels, and the like) is important. The other is corporate relatedness, where the kinds of decisions top managers have to make across a range of businesses are very similar (similar-sized investment projects, similar time spans, similar risk profiles, similar key success factors, and so on).

Aptitude for certain kinds of corporate decisions can be as much a source of value as synergies at the operating level. Where top management is able to take advantage of the strong corporate similarities between different business units, strategic decisions are likely to be both faster and better. Without corporate relationships of this kind, managers may lack the confidence and competence to take decisions as quickly and as effectively.

Some of the important corporate similarities that conglomerates can exploit across otherwise unrelated businesses include:

- *marketing skills*, as for instance Virgin exhibits across its diverse travel, cosmetics, music, drinks, and retail businesses;
- *investment skills*, the capacity to spot and back undervalued investment opportunities, as Warren Buffett does at his Berkshire Hathaway investment fund;
- *skill in dealing with government*, often important in the developing world, but also exemplified by French utilities and communications conglomerate Vivendi in its water, pay TV and telephone markets;

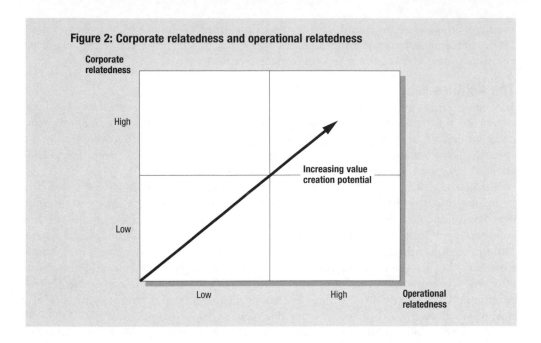

Figure 2: Corporate relatedness and operational relatedness

- *entrepreneurial skills*, as Thermo Electron has employed in its string of new ventures;
- *turnaround skills*, as applied by the fast-growing manufacturing conglomerate Tyco to its acquisitions around the world.

We can combine the notions of operating relatedness and corporate relatedness to distinguish those conglomerates with the greatest likelihood of adding value.

In Figure 2, the two left-hand boxes contain companies with low operating relatedness – conglomerates, in other words. In the two right-hand boxes are companies with high corporate relatedness. If we consider also the degree of corporate relatedness, it is not evident that conglomerates will always be outperformed by operationally related companies.

Compare the Virgin conglomerate with, for instance, an oil company that is vertically integrated with its own petrol stations. The oil company will be related operationally through petrol supply, but its top management may be poorly qualified to understand the retail marketing and location decisions entailed in managing many small station forecourt shops. Virgin, on the other hand, may have very few operational relationships between its diverse businesses, but all can benefit from the group's corporate flair at brand marketing and entrepreneurial decision making. Virgin's corporate relationships could be worth more than the oil company's operating relationships.

Of course, conglomerates that have neither corporate relationships nor operating relationships are unlikely to do well over the long term. The US conglomerate ITT, spread over manufacturing, hotels, and insurance, was operating in the bottom left-hand box of Figure 2. The company was finally split up three ways. Equally, however, the superiority of companies with both high operational relationships and high corporate relationships is by no means assured. As operating relationships increase, so do coordination costs. If they are overburdened with bureaucracy and managerial expense, companies in the top right-hand corner of Figure 2 can easily be outperformed by lean conglomerates that are skilled at exploiting corporate relationships and have few or no coordination costs.

The Achilles heel

If conglomerates are still doing well, it is in large part due to their skill at exploiting corporate relationships. But a closer look behind the aggregate trends shows that conglomerates also have an Achilles heel. Conglomerate strategies may be increasingly common among large European companies, but the evidence is that these strategies are hard to sustain over the long term.

European research reveals that while many companies with strong operating relationships are able to maintain their rankings and their corporate strategies essentially unchanged over long periods, conglomerates are much less stable. Thus a number of well-known operationally related companies, such as Unilever, the Anglo-Dutch consumer products group, Siemens, the German industrial giant, and Rhône Poulenc, the life sciences business now merged with Hoechst into Aventis, have succeeded in pursuing broadly consistent strategies over many decades. No British conglomerate and only a handful of French and German conglomerates successfully managed to stick to their conglomeratization strategies for the whole 1970–93 period. The growing numbers of conglomerates in Europe depend on a constant stream of new players to replace the exits and refocussers. The relatively short life cycle of the conglomerate is due to various factors. Essentially, the value potential of many of the sources of corporate relatedness are harder to perpetuate than the sources of operating relatedness. For example:

- Entrepreneurial, investment and turnaround skills are often highly personalized. Thus the Hanson group was broken up after the retirement of Lord Hanson and the death of Lord White, the conglomerate's two founders.
- Opportunities for the exercise of many corporate skills appear to be finite. British engineering conglomerate GEC simply ran out of companies to buy by the beginning of the 1980s, and effectively sat on its cash mountain for 15 years.
- Corporate formulas often have sell-by dates. After two decades of squeezing cash and raising prices in its industrial markets, BTR, the industrial controls group and star conglomerate of the 1980s, had nowhere else to go except into a humiliating merger with Siebe, a more focussed controls group.

Managing the life span

The challenge of the conglomerate lies in dealing with the limits of corporate relatedness. Conglomerate managers need to be continually focussed both on how these limits constrain them and how they can sometimes be beaten.

Three factors are potentially important in managing the conglomerate life span:

- *Sticking to your corporate relationships.* It can take just one ill-judged move to unravel the whole company. For instance, a question mark has hung over former industrial conglomerate star Tomkins ever since it bought foods business Ranks Hovis McDougall in 1992. Managing fast-moving, consumer branded products was not seen as this industrial company's corporate strength. After years of poor share price performance, Tomkins was forced to announce a break-up in 1999. The same fate may await the Virgin group, currently struggling with a rail business to which its brand marketing skills seem ill fitted.

- *Simplifying complexity*. After years of growth through acquisitions, conglomerates often build up ragbags of diverse businesses across which it is hard to apply common corporate strategy skills. Many manufacturing conglomerates, like Britain's TI, an engineering company formerly known as Tube Investments, and Germany's AGIV, once a diverse engineering conglomerate, have renewed themselves by radically simplifying their portfolios, retaining wide diversity but tending to concentrate on a few sectors with common corporate characteristics. Both TI and AGIV are now specialized in niches where technological leadership can give them global dominance.
- *Perpetuating corporate skills*. For nearly two decades, the GE empire has centered on the extraordinary talents of its CEO Jack Welch. However, Welch has worked hard to reduce GE's reliance on just himself and a narrow top management team. GE's years of steady investment in management training, exemplified by the world-famous Crotonville training facility, have built up an in-depth cadre of managers committed and skilled in GE management practice. GE, now more than a century old, ought to outlast the retirement of Welch, who is just the latest in a line of outstanding managers.

Conglomerate euthanasia

Sometimes it is best simply to abandon the conglomerate strategy altogether. Research shows typically enthusiastic stock market responses to refocussing or break-up announcements. When management succession plainly became an issue, Lord Hanson quickly did the decent thing by splitting out the US, chemicals, tobacco, and energy businesses, leaving a more manageable building materials core. At ITT, built up by the legendary Harold Geneen in the 1960s and 1970s, it took Rand Araskog 16 years before he finally bowed to the demerger logic. A good deal of shareholder value was destroyed in the meantime.

In short, conglomerate diversification is still a viable and widely practiced strategy. The trick is to know its limits and when finally to switch to something more sustainable over the long term.

Summary

Rumors of the death of the conglomerate are much exaggerated, says **Richard Whittington**. Poorly performing overdiversified businesses may indeed have refocussed – but new conglomerates have emerged to replace them, particularly in Europe. In this article, the author describes conglomerate strengths – which typically are rooted in the quality of their corporate rather than operating relationships – but explains that they are also likely to have a relatively short life cycle. The trick is to know their limits and when to switch into something more sustainable over the long term.

Suggested further reading

Grant, R. (1988) "On 'dominant logic,' relatedness and the link between diversity and performance," *Strategic Management Journal*, 9 (6).

Markides, C. (1996) *Diversification, Refocussing and Economic Performance*, Cambridge, MA: MIT Press.

Ruigrok, W., Pettigrew, A., Peck, S. and Whittington, R. (1999) "Corporate restructuring and new forms of organizing in Europe," *Management International Review*, 39 (2).

Whittington, R., Mayer, M. and Curto, F. (1999) "Chandlerism in post-war Europe: strategic and structural change in post-war Europe, 1950–1993," *Industrial and Corporate Change*, 8 (3).

Lessons from professional services firms

by Laura Empson

In his book, *The Intellect Industry* (1998), Mark Scott boldly states: "The professional services firm is the model of the firm of the future."

Whereas the "excellent" companies of the early 1980s were usually drawn from manufacturing and retailing, professional services firms like McKinsey and Andersen Consulting are regularly cited as models of best practice by current management writers. This raises a number of questions. What exactly are professional services firms? How do they work? What can we really learn from them? Is it correct to think of them as role models for best practice now or in the future?

One term, many meanings

Before we can accept that the professional services firm presents a model for all companies in the future, we need a clear definition of what a professional services firm is.

This is no simple task. Surprisingly, there is no consensus about the meaning of the terms "profession" and "professional."

While many people like to refer to themselves as professionals (after all, the term does imply high status and high rewards), the number of individuals who qualify according to the formal definition of the term is relatively small. Strictly speaking, a professional is someone who has won the right to membership of a professional association by completing an accredited program of training and examinations. This definition represents a very narrow group of organizations – accounting, law, architecture, and engineering practices.

But Mark Scott does not mean to imply that all companies should model themselves on legal practices. In common with other important writers in this field, such as David Maister, Mats Alvesson, and Bente Lowendahl, he uses the term more broadly to include organizations like consulting firms, advertising agencies, and investment banks.

According to this broader perspective, a professional services firm is any firm that uses the specialist technical knowledge of its personnel to create customized solutions to clients' problems.

What distinguishes these kinds of companies from the broader concept of the knowledge-intensive firm, or knowledge-based organization, is the emphasis on customization.

Thus, pharmaceutical companies and software companies can justifiably claim to be knowledge-based organizations, but they are clearly not professional services firms.

The difference is that once a drug or software company has created a physical product to resolve a specific problem, it can exploit the innovation by selling it to multiple consumers.

Professional services firms, however, tailor each solution to the unique requirements of the individual client – or so at least they would have us believe.

Core management activities

The core management activities within a professional services firm are:

- To create and disseminate knowledge within the firm.
- To recruit and motivate workers who embody that knowledge.
- To develop close and potentially collaborative relationships with clients.

These activities tend to take place within a working environment where individuals require considerable autonomy to respond flexibly to client needs.

At the same time, the authority of top management is constrained by the need to win approval from senior colleagues for major decisions, and by the fact that staff at all levels tend to be resistant to formal administrative controls.

Management writers are now encouraging companies of all kinds to become more flexible and innovative; these writers hold up professional services firms as relevant examples. But in many important respects, professional services firms are fundamentally different from other kinds of companies.

Money-making model

A professional services firm makes money by charging clients for hours worked.

The total potential output of a professional services firm is a simple function of the fee-earning staff in the firm, multiplied by the number of working hours. Total billable hours will be less than total potential output, because professionals must also devote time to non-billable activities such as sales, administration, and training. Actual hours billed depend on the firm's ability to win sufficient client work at appropriately attractive fee rates.

The profitability of a professional services firm is determined by the relationship between hourly fee rates charged and hourly salary rates paid.

Salaries are by far the biggest cost in a professional services firm. Plant and equipment are relatively limited and most project-related expenses are passed on to the client. Clients may not be aware of the actual number of hours worked and the fee rate charged by each professional employed. It is often in the interest of the professional services firm to bury this calculation in lump-sum billings. But clearly, the economic viability of all professional services firms depends on both maximizing hours billed and maximizing the margin between fee rates charged to clients and staff salaries.

Fee rates and salary rates are determined by an individual's position within the organizational hierarchy.

Unlike companies in most other industries, the economic and organizational structures of professional services firms can be seen as opposite sides of the same coin, because the staff are also the primary means of production.

Organizational structure

The basic economic structure described above applies equally to a small start-up operation with, say, three partners and a major global corporation of 150,000 professionals. In larger companies the organizational structure is inevitably more complex.

In their recruitment literature, professional services firms like to present themselves as "flat" and non-hierarchical organizations. In reality, professional services firms are structured around a hierarchy that is every bit as precisely defined as that of a conventional bureaucracy.

It is true that junior staff may be able to progress through the hierarchy relatively rapidly, compared to their counterparts in other companies. However, the key tasks they are required to perform, their cost to the client, and their remuneration are precisely defined at each level in the organization.

The typical professional services firm is organized by three generic levels of professional staff (*see* Figure 1).

As David Maister (*see* Suggested further reading) explains, this basic hierarchy is a fundamental condition for the efficient functioning of "leverage." This is one of the defining differences between the most and least successful businesses operating in the professional services sector.

The concept of leverage

Professional services firms seek to persuade clients that they possess distinctive and valuable expertise derived from years of solving complex problems for clients. How, then, can they justify charging a substantial fee for the services of a recent university graduate? Leverage is one way in which they seek to resolve this conundrum.

According to the concept of leverage, junior staff work alongside more experienced staff in close-knit project teams and learn the trade through an informal apprenticeship process. This enables senior professionals to communicate the highly personalized tacit knowledge that they have acquired through years of experience.

Not only is leverage an effective knowledge-management strategy, it is also an efficient means of making money for the firm. A skeptic might argue that such leverage enables professional services firms to make money by underpaying juniors and overcharging clients.

Professional services firms make profits by maximizing their margin – the gap between fee rates charged and salaries paid. The daily fee rates of senior professionals may be no more than two or three times that of junior colleagues, but their total earnings will often differ by much larger multiples.

Junior professionals accept relatively low salaries because these are still considerably higher than those available in alternative graduate-entry occupations.

Clients will pay high fees because they accept that juniors are leveraging the

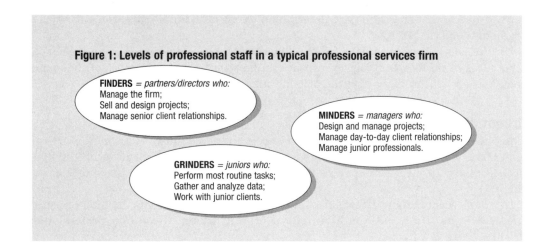

Figure 1: Levels of professional staff in a typical professional services firm

FINDERS = *partners/directors who:*
Manage the firm;
Sell and design projects;
Manage senior client relationships.

MINDERS = *managers who:*
Design and manage projects;
Manage day-to-day client relationships;
Manage junior professionals.

GRINDERS = *juniors who:*
Perform most routine tasks;
Gather and analyze data;
Work with junior clients.

expertise of senior professionals, and because they cannot afford to pay for large amounts of senior professionals' time.

Making the most of markets

Professional services firms, notes David Maister, must seek to achieve a balance between four fluctuating factors: 1) organizational structure; 2) economic structure; 3) the market for professional staff; and 4) the market for professional services.

The relationship between a professional services firm's organizational and economic structure has already been demonstrated.

The relationship between the two external markets is as follows:

- Clients will only employ a professional services firm if they believe that it has sufficient numbers of staff of sufficiently high caliber to deliver the appropriate level of professional service.
- Professionals will only join and remain with a professional services firm if they can see a sufficient flow of interesting and lucrative client work and reasonable prospects for advancement.

If staff members leave or are promoted, the organizational and economic structure of the firm is inevitably affected. To mitigate this, the professional services firm must recruit and train new staff to an appropriate standard so that those moving up or out can be replaced. If the professional services firm does not compete successfully in the market for professional staff, it risks losing its ability to compete effectively in the market for professional services.

In a 1998 article (*see* Suggested further reading), Tim Morris and I develop further the Maister basic model of the balanced professional services firm (*see* Figure 2). We argue that the two sets of demands that emanate from the market for professional services and the market for professional staff are linked by a third consideration – the knowledge base of the professional services firm.

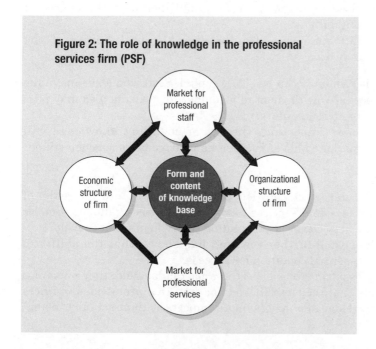

Figure 2: The role of knowledge in the professional services firm (PSF)

The knowledge base represents both an input and an output. How this knowledge is created, articulated, disseminated, and renewed has implications for the recruitment and training of staff, as well as the definition and delivery of services to clients.

The form and content of the knowledge base affect the level of fee rates a professional services firm charges and the degree of leverage it achieves.

The knowledge base thus connects its two external markets to its organizational and economic structure.

Managing knowledge

In accredited professions like engineering and architecture, all members share a common body of codified knowledge acquired through professional training. A large part of their competitive advantage, therefore, derives from possessing a unique base of expertise.

Traditionally, professional services firms have been regarded as organizations of highly trained, extremely clever technical specialists, who apply their esoteric knowledge to the creation of innovative and sophisticated solutions to clients' complex problems. It is certainly true that some firms operate successfully in this way. However, in reality there are not that many extremely clever people to go round and most clients' problems are not that sophisticated.

As a result, most highly expert professional services firms remain small and specialized "boutiques." Firms such as McKinsey would like us to believe that they are exceptions to this rule. But such claims should always be treated with caution.

A professional services firm wishing to grow large must learn to codify the esoteric and tacit knowledge accumulated by experienced staff and disseminate this throughout its organizational structure. If this knowledge can be expressed in terms of established procedures and applied to a wide range of client problems, the potential for leverage increases. Codification relaxes some of the more stringent constraints of the apprenticeship model of knowledge transfer. Increasing the number of juniors supervised by a senior professional increases the degree of leverage and, therefore, profitability.

But the process of codification can also threaten the profitability of the professional services firm in two ways:

- First, knowledge that is codifiable can be easily copied. Staff who leave may take their knowledge of procedures with them to a competitor. Clients also may pass this intellectual capital on to competitors.
- Second, and perhaps more important, the act of codifying knowledge will ultimately diminish its market value as codified knowledge becomes demystified.

Managing perceptions

As we start to explore the nature of knowledge here, we move into the realm of smoke and mirrors. Do professional services firms really possess valuable esoteric knowledge, or are they just very clever at persuading their clients that they do?

Mats Alvesson (*see* Suggested further reading) has shown that the ability to manage perceptions is an essential condition for success.

It is not enough for professionals to be expert in a particular field; they must also be able to persuade clients that they are. Indeed, for staff in a professional services firm, "seeming" to be knowledgeable may be more important than actually "being" knowledgeable.

The importance of managing perceptions derives from the fact that professional services firms operate according to a credence-based model of service acquisition.

Clients hire professional services firms because they believe they have complex and significant problems beyond their own capacity to resolve. How do I design a new head-office building? How do I defend myself in a takeover battle? How do I avoid bankruptcy?

But the client cannot sample the product of the professional services firm before acquiring it. Indeed, clients may not be able to judge the success or failure of the professional service they have purchased until many years after the project is completed. The client's purchase must be made on the basis of trust.

This trust is derived from two primary sources: 1) the relationship that develops between the individual client and the professional during the sales process or through previous experience of working together; and 2) the reputation that the individual professional and the firm as a whole have developed in the external market.

Typically, professional services firms have been quite discreet in their marketing activities and secretive about the internal operations of the firm.

The recent trend for major professional services firms to launch high-profile marketing campaigns and to allow academics to conduct research into their organizations can be seen as an attempt to disseminate the image of professionalism to a wider audience.

In the early stage of a firm's development, high-quality clients confer status on it. If the firm succeeds in developing a high-quality reputation, it can return the favor by conferring status on its clients. A corporate headquarters building designed by the Richard Rogers Partnership, for example, carries cachet and prestige far beyond that which can be explained purely by the physical structure of the building.

So when management writers cite McKinsey and Andersen Consulting as models of best practice, they are making an incalculable contribution to the revenue of these firms by advancing their mystique and reputation in the market place.

The positive benefits feed through to the market for professional staff and to the market for professional services. It is no accident that year after year these firms feature among the most popular potential employers for undergraduate applicants.

Professional v. commercial

For some years, writers have speculated that the drive for commercialization among accounting and law firms may be undermining some of the underlying principles of professionalism.

Professionalism implies a dedication to the delivery of high-quality client service and careful management of client relationships.

This is not inherently inconsistent with the concept of commercialism. However, professionalism also implies that the individual remains dedicated to maintaining professional norms over and above the demands of the employing organization and the ability to pursue work that is intellectually satisfying or socially beneficial, rather than merely profit maximizing.

Professionalism has also typically been associated with the concept of partnership, although this organizational form is by no means universal among professional services firms. In a partnership, a group of senior professionals combine the roles of owners, managers, and core producers. They also share unlimited personal liability for each other's actions. This engenders mutual trust and collaboration among senior colleagues. In this respect also professional services firms can be taken as models for organizations in general.

On the downside, the partnership model implies a slow and potentially risk-averse approach to strategic decision making, because of the need to build consensus within a diffuse authority structure.

Partly for this reason, professional services firms are increasingly abandoning the partnership form of governance, or are seeking to accommodate more conventional managerial structures within the partnership form. It is ironic that, at a time when manufacturing and retail companies are being encouraged to emulate professional services firms, many professional firms are starting to adopt management practices more often associated with manufacturing and retail service firms.

A future role model

Professional services firms embody many of the qualities that organizations in general are encouraged to emulate. In theory at least, they are relatively efficient mechanisms for developing and disseminating knowledge; they create an environment in which highly motivated individuals can enjoy a reasonable degree of autonomy; and they place dedication to client service above all other considerations. All this occurs within a non-bureaucratic organizational environment, which enshrines mutual trust and collaboration within the professed value system.

It is important, however, not to confuse rhetoric with reality.

While professional services firms may aspire to achieve all of these qualities, the extent to which they succeed varies widely. By fastening on the professional services firm as an ideal archetype, management writers risk overlooking the considerable diversity within the sector and the threat to traditional professional practices posed by increasing commercial pressures.

Professional services firms now represent a large and rapidly expanding segment within most industrialized economies.

According to statistics from the Organization for Economic Cooperation and Development, the professional services sector accounts for 17 percent of all employment in the US and major western European countries. The sector has enjoyed annual growth of 15 percent in revenue terms over recent years. Accountancy firm PwC, for example, is now the single largest recruiter from UK universities. With 155,000 professional staff worldwide and annual revenues of $15bn, PwC, if publicly quoted, would qualify as a Fortune 100 company.

To focus on the professional services firm as a model for organizations in general is to lose sight of the fact that these firms are now an important phenomenon in their own right.

Summary

Professional services firms like McKinsey and Andersen Consulting are increasingly held up as a model for other businesses – but according to **Laura Empson** the picture is more complex. In this article, she describes how such firms operate and how they are organized. She explains the key concept of "leverage," which not only underpins their knowledge-management strategies but drives profitability. And she argues that they need to be particularly adept at managing market perceptions – "seeming" knowledgeable may be more important than "being" knowledgeable. There is much diversity within the sector; the fact that these firms account for 17 percent of all employment in the US and Europe indicates that they are an important phenomenon in their own right.

Suggested further reading

Alvesson, M. (1995) *Management of Knowledge-Intensive Companies*, Berlin: Walter de Gruyter.

Lowendahl, B. (2000) *Strategic Management of Professional Services Firms*, 2nd edition. Copenhagen: Handelshjskolens Forlag.

Maister, D. (1993) *Managing the Professional Service Firm*, New York: The Free Press.

Morris, T. and Empson, L. (1998) "Organization and expertise: an exploration of knowledge bases and the management of accounting and consulting firms," *Accounting, Organizations, and Society*, 23 (5–6); 609–34.

Scott, M. (1998) *The Intellect Industry: Profiting and Learning from Professional Services Firms*, Chichester: John Wiley & Sons.

STRATEGIC
ALLIANCES

13

Contributors

Jeffrey J. Reuer is assistant professor of strategy and management at INSEAD in Fontainebleau, France. His research interests include international joint ventures, alliance dynamics and corporate flexibility.

Arie Y. Lewin is professor of management and director for the Centre for International Business, Education and Research (CIBER), Fuqua School of Business, Duke University.

Will Mitchell is Jack D. Sparks/Whirlpool Corporation Research Professor, professor of corporate strategy and international business, University of Michigan Business School.

Toby E. Stuart is an associate professor of organizations and strategy at the University of Chicago Graduate School of Business. His research interests include strategic alliances and technology strategy. He has been a consultant to a number of Fortune 1000 companies.

Mitchell P. Koza is professor of international strategic management and director of the Centre for International Business, Cranfield School of Management. He was on the faculty of INSEAD for over ten years.

David Faulkner is tutorial fellow at Christ Church College, Oxford University, and MBA director of the Saïd Business School. He focusses on corporate and competitive strategy, including strategic alliances and joint ventures.

Contents

Introduction

In a world where speed to market, geographical reach and convergent technologies are often beyond the resources of a single firm, it is no surprise that alliances and other forms of collaboration have mushroomed. Many of the justifications given for alliances, though, are the same as those used to support acquisitions, so managers need to compare the alternatives before embarking on what can be a hazardous course. This module deals with that issue, as well as pre-alliance planning and how to foster the necessary corporate capabilities for this sort of activity. Attention is also given to the various types of alliance – those with easily identifiable revenue objectives and those probing for new market opportunities, for example – the development of alliance networks and the role of trust in making joint ventures work.

Collaborative strategy: the logic of alliances

by Jeffrey J. Reuer

Executives engaged in alliances, as well as those more reluctant to try their hand at collaborative strategy, are keenly aware that success does not come easily. Failure rates often run as high as 70 percent. Yet a quick glance at business newspapers and trade journals reveals that alliances have recently experienced something of a renaissance across many sectors of the economy.

It seems extraordinary that so many companies should choose to pursue such an apparently risky strategy. So what are the fundamental drivers behind today's so-called alliance revolution? Do alliances have an underlying economic rationale that companies can turn to in evaluating their investment opportunities?

Executives often respond by referring to globalization, synergy needs, industry convergence and consolidation, opportunities for scale economies, and product life-cycle compression. New organizational forms circulating under the labels of "virtual organizations," "networks," and "heterarchies" seem to rely heavily on alliances.

All of these explanations are indeed important. It is hardly a coincidence that alliances have blossomed at the same time as these economic and organizational developments.

At the same time, the factors associated with the diffusion of collaborative ventures often underlie other types of economic activity as well. In fact, many of the drivers of alliances also figure prominently in companies' acquisition proposals.

Consider synergy. In 1995, Crédit Suisse and Winterthur combined their banking and insurance expertise in an alliance offering joint services through both parties' customer networks. Yet much the same logic underlay the merger between Citicorp and Travelers, in which the two sought to combine their banking and insurance services.

In the petrochemicals industry, BP and Mobil united $5bn in refining and marketing assets in a pan-European joint venture initiated in 1996. By pooling their downstream operations, they aimed to achieve up to $500m in pretax cost savings in their joint petrol and lubricant businesses. Yet the acquisitions that followed shortly afterwards – resulting in BP–Amoco and Exxon–Mobil – were prompted by similar synergistic ambitions.

If a company can attain synergy in alliances as well as acquisitions, what determines the route it takes? For every successful alliance – such as the GE–Snecma aircraft engine joint venture – that brings together companies with complementary resources, there seems to be another – such as Lucent–Philips, Olivetti–AT&T or Renault–Volvo – that fails to realize its potential.

Similar problems crop up when one looks at the other common explanations for alliance investments. Capitalizing on scale economies, for instance, is a common justification. Airline alliances such as Swissair's Qualiflyer Group count on joint procurement and fleet maintenance savings. Pharmaceutical alliances aim to share large research and development expenses for blockbuster drugs as well as marketing costs. But the same is at least as true for acquisitions. Economies of scale

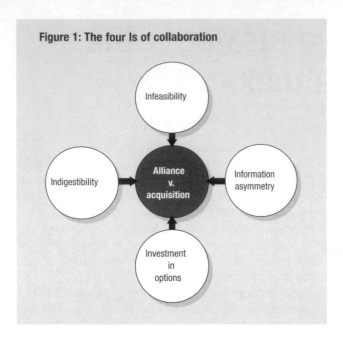

Figure 1: The four Is of collaboration

have been an important justification for many recent deals, especially in consolidating industries.

Executives overseeing the implementation of alliances are even uncertain as to whether they are necessarily quicker than other corporate investments. Many market-entry ventures in China took a long time to generate profits for Western parents, if they did so at all. Like acquisitions, many alliances falter at the juncture between signing the contract and actually building the relationship.

Thus, beginning to understand the strategic logic of alliance investments amounts to first appreciating when alliances are justified *vis-à-vis* other corporate development options. Only when these alternatives have been evaluated in a rigorous, comparative fashion can executives proceed with a more refined consideration of specific forms of alliance and with the design of alliance processes.

Because an acquisition is often the next best alternative, it can serve as a benchmark for probing the economic logic of an alliance before investing. Articulating the specific benefits of alliances in relative terms is more difficult than expressing why an alliance is attractive on an absolute basis.

When can companies justifiably turn to an alliance as the investment vehicle of choice? When should they ally rather than acquire?

A framework comprising what might be termed the "Four Is" of collaboration – infeasibility, investment in options, indigestibility, and information asymmetry – provides a useful first step in formulating collaborative strategy (*see* Figure 1). Each "I" is discussed below.

Alliances versus acquisitions

Infeasibility

Infeasibility is a common reason why companies have invested in strategic alliances rather than acquisitions. Taking on a local partner was the traditional entry fee for countries with restrictions on foreign direct investment, such as China, India, and

Russia. Focussed, horizontal alliances between large rivals such as Toyota and General Motors can be used when antitrust concerns arise. The number of airline alliances within Europe and overseas attests to the usefulness of alliances in overcoming legal and regulatory barriers. Alliances also populate politically sensitive industries such as defense and telecommunications.

While the feasibility of an acquisition can sometimes be clear cut, it is often a matter of judgment and requires revisiting. For instance, according to Mergerstat, a tracking service, the total value of merger activity in the US in 1991 was $71.2bn for 1,877 deals. Now, the value of a single transaction can surpass this figure. Investment size is no longer a binding constraint for many corporate combinations. Changes in the legal and regulatory environments in many countries suggest that companies can choose an alliance today and an acquisition tomorrow.

Investment in options

If acquisitions enhance value through commitment, flexibility seems to be the watchword for alliances. Alliances are therefore prevalent in uncertain industries such as biotechnology, which require companies to alter their bets or reverse course. Alliances also facilitate entry into distant geographic markets by allowing companies to stage their commitments. Should a particular technology or market prove to be especially favorable, the company can step up its investment subsequently.

Companies such as Siemens have argued that having a call option on an international joint venture can be one of the most important parts of the agreement. A call option confers on a company the right, but not the obligation, to expand its equity stake at a pre-specified price at some later point in time. Such an agreement enabled Siemens to strengthen its control over its Siemens Allis Power Engineering venture with Allis Chalmers.

If joint ventures provide companies with options that can enhance flexibility, they should enable companies to capitalize on emerging opportunities while avoiding losses. However, my research with Michael Leiblein of Ohio State University has found that domestic and international joint venture investments increase rather than reduce companies' downside risk in general. And a separate study has found that, unlike companies making acquisitions, those investing in international joint ventures face difficulties in using sell-offs as a corrective mechanism.

Despite the fact that flexibility and risk reduction are frequently offered as motives for entering into alliances, companies often do not seize these potential benefits. Alliance investments do not in themselves guarantee enhanced flexibility and risk reduction; collaborators should seek ways of improving the odds through appropriate alliance design and by managing alliance implementation with flexibility in mind.

Indigestibility

Post-acquisition integration costs represent one source of transaction costs in acquisitions. They emanate from the acquiring company's need to "digest" targeted assets. Indigestibility problems can be severe when the acquiree is located in a foreign country with a different culture and management systems. They can also be far from trivial when the targeted assets are deeply embedded and shared in a large, complex corporation rather than isolated in a single business unit.

When indigestibility would be substantial, alliances can prove attractive because they allow the companies to link their resources selectively as needed. Unlike acquisitions, alliances do not require companies completely to extract desired assets from others or to shed unwanted assets after the investment has taken place.

Nestlé, for instance, established a joint venture for breakfast cereals in Europe with General Mills. The parties' other businesses remained separate from the venture. It also teamed up with Coca-Cola to combine Nestlé's brand equity in coffee and tea with Coke's global distribution system. The companies remained competitors in Japan, a market in which new product introductions are frequent, and over the years Coke built a substantial market share in vending-machine sales.

While resource indivisibilities and cultural differences contribute to higher integration costs if a company makes an acquisition instead of forming an alliance, indigestibility has another important effect: it makes it more difficult for acquirers to judge the value of the combined entity in the first place. We next turn to valuation problems in assembling strategic resources.

Information asymmetry

Information asymmetry, when some parties know more than others, affects many types of economic exchange. A classic example is the market for used cars. Often the seller will know much more about the vehicle's quality than does the buyer. The seller may also have problems credibly conveying the vehicle's true value. Accordingly, the buyer often discounts the offer price to reflect this uncertainty over quality.

A similar problem confronts the corporate development office. Even with thorough due diligence, the acquiring company may be very uncertain about the targeted assets' true value. This is likely when the acquirer and the seller manufacture different products in different industries. Information asymmetries also arise when targeted assets are embedded and shared in the target company.

Alliances can mitigate these valuation problems by enabling companies to combine complementary resources on a limited basis. Companies get a much better idea about the assets' true value through repeated interaction with the partner. Once this learning occurs, the company can increase its commitment or quit the relationship as appropriate.

Whirlpool, for example, entered a joint venture with Philips as part of Philips' attempt to divest itself of its domestic appliance businesses. Whirlpool obtained a call option on the venture, which it acquired less than three years later. During that time, Whirlpool learned the businesses' value, received help with the transition from Philips, and convinced itself that the dealer network would be effective with the new management.

My research with Mitchell Koza of the Cranfield School of Management confirms the value of investment in domestic and international joint ventures under conditions of information asymmetry. In a large-scale analysis of US companies' joint ventures, we find that the stock market tends to reward companies investing in joint ventures when information asymmetry is present. When information asymmetry is not problematic, equity investors tend to react negatively or insignificantly to announcements of joint ventures.

Corporate strategy and alliances

If the adjective "strategic" that typically precedes "alliances" means anything, it indicates that alliance investments have important implications for a company's market position and deployment of resources. It suggests that a company will confront important trade-offs when investing in alliances and needs to appreciate when not to use alliances.

The following are some of the primary tasks for decision makers:

Use alliances selectively

No doubt some of the observed failures in alliances and acquisitions are due to investments in alliances when acquisitions would have been preferable and vice versa. The spread of alliances across many sectors of the economy does not alter the basic proposition that alliances are useful in some investment contexts and should be avoided in others.

Think about alliances in relative terms

Decision makers need to pin down the benefits as well as the costs and risks of an alliance in concrete terms *vis-à-vis* an acquisition. Considering issues such as scale economies, globalization, synergy and so on can certainly be an important part of the decision-making process, but the logic of collaborative strategy is inherently a comparative one.

Weigh the risks

The Four Is framework provides broad guidelines for choosing between alliances and acquisitions.

If an acquisition is feasible, and the value of commitment exceeds that of flexibility, and targeted assets are readily digestible, and the value of targetted assets can be appraised relatively easily, an alliance is not likely to be the best way forward.

In other cases, some criteria may favor an alliance while others point toward an acquisition. For these investments, the company needs to assess the risks of selecting an alliance when an acquisition would have been better and vice versa.

Such an exercise can prove difficult. When a company faces significant uncertainties and its close competitors are turning to alliances, managers will find imitation more attractive than breaking industry ranks to pursue a commitment-intensive, less reversible investment such as an acquisition.

Anticipate alliance evolution

The framework has been discussed as a way to evaluate market entry decisions, but it can also be used to manage alliance investments over time and to analyze possible trajectories for a relationship. Alliances may be an enduring feature of a given industry as new sources of uncertainty surface over time, but particular alliances will not often be equilibrium solutions for particular companies. All elements of the framework are dynamic, and companies need to revisit the underlying economic logic for an alliance. Collaborators close information asymmetries. Trade-offs between commitment and flexibility can change with technological and market developments. Experience with a partner or in a host country attenuates indigestibility problems in culturally distant countries. Improved access to capital or a changing legal environment can make the infeasible possible.

Develop alliance competence

Information obtained from benchmarking rivals can provide valuable inputs into an alliance investment decision. Information on their strategic rationales, partner selection criteria, alliance design choices, and best practices can help novices and more experienced partners.

For companies engaging in multiple alliances, it can be useful to establish databases, websites and seminars to extract and disseminate knowledge about earlier alliances for future investment decisions. Companies such as Xerox and Hewlett-Packard have used these tools in an effort to institutionalize alliance skills and move beyond the usual *ad hoc* approach to managing alliances.

Position alliances within corporate strategy

The connection between alliance investments and the company's corporate strategy is the ultimate standard by which collaborations should be appraised. Many writings on intercompany collaboration treat alliances as ends in themselves rather than as instruments of a company's strategy for developing and deploying resources.

As in all corporate investments, the managerial challenges posed by alliances and the factors influencing their effectiveness are many. Clearly, deriving value from alliances requires companies to select the right partners, develop a suitable alliance design, adapt the relationship as needed, and manage the end game appropriately.

The foundation for these activities and decisions is a solid understanding of the economic rationales for alliances in comparison with other corporate development tools at the company's disposal.

Summary

Many of the justifications that companies give for alliances – synergy and scale economies, for instance – could equally apply to acquisitions. According to **Jeffrey Reuer**, managers should therefore carefully compare these strategic alternatives before embarking on an alliance. If an acquisition looks feasible, the commitment this involves appears to outweigh the advantages of flexibility, the targetted assets are readily digestible, and their value can be appraised relatively easily, it is likely to be better not to proceed with a joint venture.

Suggested further reading

Reuer, J.J. and Koza, M.P. (2000) "Asymmetric information and joint venture performance: theory and evidence for domestic and international joint ventures," *Strategic Management Journal,* 21 (1): 81–8.

Reuer, J.J. and Leiblein, M.J. (forthcoming) "Downside risk implications of multinationality and international joint ventures," *Academy of Management Journal.*

Alliances: achieving long-term value and short-term goals

by Will Mitchell

What do the alliance strategies of a faltering electronics manufacturer in Japan, a failed software developer in the US, and an out-of-business pharmaceutical company in France have in common? Answer: each company went into decline after forming an alliance with another company. Each decline occurred because the other company learned enough about their business to be able to compete directly, while the three in question failed to learn enough to counter this competition.

What do the alliance strategies of an insolvent hospital information systems company in Britain, a dissolved auto components supplier in Germany, and a failed telecommunications company in the US have in common? Answer: each tried to operate independently, avoiding alliances, but had to exit their industry because they could not develop a strong enough set of internal capabilities to continue successfully.

The simple message from these cases is that alliances are both risky and necessary.

In their 1999 book *Cooperative Strategy*, Pierre Dussauge and Bernard Garrette show that alliances provide the access to other companies' capabilities that are needed in order to enter new markets, introduce new products, acquire new components, learn new methods of producing goods and services, and learn new ways of organizing.

Many readers of this book spend part of their daily working life in activities that intertwine with those of corporate partners and other organizational allies. Yet poorly managed alliances are also killing companies.

Some large-scale research studies reinforce this message. For example, Kulwant Singh and I (*see* Suggested further reading) have shown that hospital information system companies using alliances as part of development and marketing strategy are more likely to survive than competitors trying to operate independently.

However, companies that use alliances are at high risk during industry shocks that strike at the core purpose of an alliance and are susceptible to losing key partners. In addition, Pierre Dussauge, Bernard Garrette, and I (*see* Suggested further reading) show that link alliances (ones in which the parents contribute different types of resources) commonly lead to takeover or reorganization in favor of one of the partners – the result of partners learning from each other.

This article outlines ways of managing alliances effectively, to gain strategic advantage while reducing risk. It focusses on how to achieve both short-term and long-term alliance goals. An alliance's primary short-term goal is to obtain immediate access to the capabilities of one's partners. The primary long-term goal is to learn as much as possible about a partner's capabilities and competitive environments.

Successful alliance-management strategy depends on three elements: pre-alliance planning, post-alliance education, and corporate alliance-management capabilities.

Pre-alliance planning

Too often, we rush into alliances as if they were risk-free short-term relationships. This is the ignorance-is-not-bliss mistake. Even the briefest business liaison can have a long-term impact on corporate life. A company must undertake a systematic approach to alliance planning that addresses several key questions.

The questions include the following

What do you want to achieve in the short run? Identify the customer-oriented strategic position that you want to occupy in your market. Identify the competitive context for the goods and services you will offer your customers. Determine what capabilities you will bring to the alliance and what capabilities you will need from an alliance partner to achieve your desired position and products.

Who can best help you achieve the goal and what do they want to achieve? Identify potential partners. Identify the functional capabilities that the alliance must develop and/or that each partner must contribute for the alliance to achieve its strategic position. These functional capabilities may include development, production, marketing, distribution, financial, information, proprietary protection, managerial, and others. Assess the goals of the alliance from each partner's point of view. The ideal partner is one with all the capabilities you need, but nothing unnecessary. Such companies are best placed to help, while least likely to evolve quickly into direct competitors.

What can you learn from your partner for the long run? Identify as many long-term learning opportunities as possible. Because many learning opportunities emerge only as an alliance evolves, you must scan continually to identify new learning opportunities.

What do you want to keep your partner from learning? Identify capabilities that you want to shield from your partner and develop protection strategies. It is particularly important to ensure that people who participate in alliance activities know what capabilities you do not want to share.

Who needs to know about the alliance? Communicate key information about the alliance to all people and units who will be involved in alliance activities. Too often, corporate staff negotiate an alliance and then leave business-unit people who are lower down the managerial hierarchy to carry out the day-to-day activities, without telling their subordinates why the alliance was formed and how it fits within a broader set of objectives. Almost always, such cases either end in complete failure or, at best, realize only a small proportion of potential value.

How should you organize to attain short-term and long-term goals? Develop an initial organization for the alliance. The contractual terms, structural units, management systems, and people must meet both your corporate needs and those of the alliance. An alliance organization needs to be simple so it does not trap you within it. Too many companies attempt to reproduce subsidiary-like structures and systems for the alliance. They then become snared by the complexity of a failing or unnecessary alliance over which they cannot exercise independent control.

In summary – knowledge is the basis of alliance strength. You need to determine what you want from an alliance; which will be the most appropriate partner; what you can gain from your partner in both the short and long term; and how you should organize your relationship. Diving into an alliance assuming you will figure it out as you go along is the fastest way to drown.

Post-alliance education

It is a mistake to think that a good alliance, like a good marriage, is for ever, and that we can grow into our capabilities together with our partners. This is the tomorrow-may-not-come mistake. It causes us to underemphasize the immediate need to learn from our partners. I must stress that alliances between companies are fundamentally different from marriages between people. Even the best alliances will end and you must manage them accordingly, through effective education. Alliance education involves learning from your partner and teaching people in your own business. The approach to alliance education needs to address the following questions.

Who will be responsible for learning from your partner? Assign people from your company to be responsible for learning from your partner. Explicitly identify your learning goals to those people who will be involved in the alliance. In addition, provide people with enough information about your long-term strategies and objectives so they can take advantage of unexpected opportunities for learning from the partners that will help your company advance.

Be prepared to take advantage of unexpected opportunities to learn from a partner. For example, I was recently involved with a project where students were the first on-site visitors to a key plant of a company with which their sponsor had just formed an alliance. We gave the students clear directions concerning what they might learn from the new partner while also, of course, informing the new partner about the students' goals. The student team then provided a detailed assessment of the new partner's skills in a business system that the manufacturer was developing and planned to implement in its global manufacturing operations.

Who will be responsible for teaching people in your own business? Teaching what your employees learn from an alliance is at least as important as the process of learning from your partner. Set up explicit teaching opportunities, such as job rotation, cross-disciplinary seminars, and extensive communication systems. Teach the skills to a critical mass of people, rather than hoping that the new information will diffuse implicitly via discussions among a few individuals. Press your people to learn both expected and unexpected skills from your partner, while they meet the day-to-day demands of the alliance. Then press them even harder to teach what they have learned to other people within the company.

How will you reward alliance education? Simply telling people to undertake alliance education will almost always fail. Instead, explicitly set up job evaluations and personal incentives to take into account your employees' success with alliance learning and teaching. Then expressly review and reward job performance in terms of both current activities and alliance education results.

How is the alliance changing? Alliances change even before the partners begin to work together, often in completely unforeseen ways. Continually assess changes in the strategic position of the alliance, capabilities of the alliance and your partner, and the alliance organization. Then identify how to modify your education goals to respond to these changes.

What is your partner learning from you? Too often, we ignore the potential for our partner to learn from us and become our strong competitor as it learns. Just as you need to assess what you are gaining from an alliance, you need to assess what your partner is learning and whether the competitive losses are worth what you are gaining. As part of this assessment, determine whether there are ways in which you can block the partner's access to your key capabilities without unduly hampering the activities of the alliance. However, do not forget to intensify your efforts to learn from your partners. Blocking tactics almost inevitably provide only short-term solutions to competitive losses. While blocking tactics are necessary, it is much more important to become good at alliance education.

Can you get out if you have to? Your company can fail if it becomes trapped in a floundering alliance or snared by a dominant partner. During the course of an alliance, you will inevitably develop business routines and systems that intertwine with your partner's capabilities. If you lose access to key systems, either because your partner disappears or because a dominant partner blocks access to capabilities that have become critical for you, your business performance will suffer. As a result, even as you use alliances as key parts of your strategy, you need to develop and maintain sufficient autonomous capability to operate independently or, at least, be strong enough to attract a desirable new partner. Developing such independent capabilities in parallel with alliance activities often requires additional investment. These may seem expensive in the short term, but evaluation should measure both long-term value and short-term cost. Inevitably, assessment of long-term value involves greater ambiguity and requires greater judgment than does identification of short-term cost.

Who is the best partner now? Although your current partner may have been the most appropriate one when you formed an alliance, a new company may now have capabilities better suited to your current needs. Although you can sometimes help a current partner improve, you need to be prepared to switch partners if a better one emerges. Otherwise, you risk losing ground to a competitor that may gain access to superior capabilities. Constantly be on the lookout for a new partner who might put your current partner out of business. If we mistakenly think that business alliances bear a resemblance to marriages between people, this prescription may sound cruel and unethical. However, once we recognize that business alliances are part of dynamic corporate strategy rather than stable family relationships, the fairness of the advice becomes clear. Your corporate partner has ways of protecting itself. In part, an initial alliance agreement can restrain partners from taking unfair advantage of each other. In greater part, companies have the responsibility to maintain and develop skills so that they continue bringing value to the alliance.

In summary – education creates alliance strength. You need to learn from your partner and teach yourself as quickly as possible, from the moment you begin to interact with the other company. Alliance education requires both personal action and business systems. At their contact points, learning and teaching are individual activities, as people interact in daily jobs and responsibilities. Many companies stop at individual learning and fail to create channels for teaching the new skills throughout their business organization. The learning and teaching processes require thoughtful business systems that identify education goals, create education incentives, and provide education channels.

Corporate alliance-management capabilities

Finally, a successful alliance strategy requires the corporate capability to manage alliances coherently. Alliance-management capabilities involve two main functions: managing alliance portfolios and distinguishing alliances from subsidiaries.

Too often, we treat each alliance as if it were our only relationship. This is the kaleidoscope mistake. Fragmentation among our alliances creates a fragmented view of the competitive world. The kaleidoscope mistake generates two types of problems. First, we often create conflicting business systems to manage different alliances, risking conflicts among different alliances as they compete for resources and markets. Second, we miss opportunities to share alliance education throughout the company. Therefore, it is critically important to create a dedicated alliance-management unit, with corporate and business staff involvement. The alliance-management unit must take the lead in assessing the composite needs and opportunities that arise from a portfolio of alliances, as well as the needs and value of each alliance.

A second mistake in managing alliances is to place alliance management in a business-development function focussed on mergers and acquisitions. This is the alliances-aren't-subsidiaries mistake, because it treats alliance partners as if they had no more strategic autonomy than a corporate subsidiary. Far too often in my conversations with corporate managers, they will say: "We recognize how important the alliance has become to the company and therefore treat it as though it is one of our subsidiaries." This issue is particularly acute with middle managers who carry out daily activities involving the alliances, but even the most senior managers can fall into the alliances-aren't-subsidiaries trap. The common result of this, of course, is that an alliance partner does something that harms you but that you cannot prohibit, such as beginning to compete in a new market or withdrawing from the relationship before you are ready. Thus, it is critical to create a dedicated alliance-management unit, rather than simply treating alliance management as a minor part of a corporate development unit. Acquisitions and alliances staff must communicate and interact in a way that recognizes the different challenges of acquiring subsidiaries and managing partnerships.

The key point in managing alliances is that alliance strength requires specialized corporate muscle. A company must develop a corporate alliance mindset, which all individual members of the company must share, and which recognizes the strengths and risks of the full set of its alliances. A corporate alliance-management unit plays a key role in developing such a mindset.

Conclusion

As a concluding point, I draw an important distinction between contracts and contacts in successful alliances. Good contracts are essential parts of all alliances, whether they are formal and detailed descriptions of responsibilities and rights, or informal ones providing a shared understanding of the alliance purpose and operation. However, no contract can fully define all of the current world, let alone anticipate all future opportunities. In addition to contracts and, in my view, far more important, the personal contacts your people develop with the people at your alliance partner and with others throughout your company will determine the success of an alliance. These contacts are the primary channel for gaining access to your partner's capabilities, using those capabilities to serve your current customers better, and learning from your partner so that you can service customers better in the future.

Summary

Alliances are risky, but they are a fundamental necessity of both short- and long-term strategy, says **Will Mitchell**. Here he urges companies to undertake a systematic approach to pre-alliance planning, to introduce effective education systems and incentives, and to develop corporate capabilities for managing alliances by setting up a dedicated alliance-management unit. The author draws a distinction between contracts and contacts in successful alliances – both are important, but people and the knowledge they gain are ultimately the key. Unlike good marriages, alliances are not for ever and companies should be prepared to exchange partners if a better one emerges.

Suggested further reading

Dussauge, P. and Garrette, B. (1999) *Cooperative Strategy: Competing Successfully Through Strategic Alliances*, New York: Wiley.

Dussauge, P., Garrette, B. and Mitchell, W. (2000) "Learning from competing partners: outcomes and durations of scale and link alliances in Europe, North America, and Asia," *Strategic Management Journal*, 21 (2): 99–126.

Singh, K. and Mitchell, W. (1996) "Precarious collaboration: business survival after partners shut down or form new partnerships," *Strategic Management Journal*, (Summer) 17: 95–115, Special Issue on Evolutionary Perspectives on Strategy.

Putting the S-word back in alliances

by Mitchell P. Koza and Arie Y. Lewin

The last years of the twentieth century witnessed the emergence of a business rivalry paradox – cooperative competition. Its hallmark was the rapid rise in popularity of all types of alliances, so much so that some popular business writers refer to it as the era of alliance capitalism.

A well-recognized if surprising feature of alliances is their high rate of instability and failure.

When asked, managers offer plausible but diverse reasons for entering into an alliance. These can include: gaining access to a restricted market or overcoming barriers to entry, gaining market power, maintaining market stability, acquiring technologies, products or new skills, pooling resources, reducing uncertainty, sharing risky research and development projects, speeding up entry into new markets, deriving new incremental sources of revenue from combining complementary assets, and so on.

When asked why an alliance was dissolved or why it failed, managers often cite: lack of cooperation and trust, inadequate advance planning, too much detailed negotiation and too little managing of the actual alliance, lack of organizational capabilities and resources to manage cooperative relationships, strategic mismatch, size mismatch, cultural mismatch, change in strategy of one partner, wrong choice of partner or wrong initial strategy, and so on.

Statistics show one inescapable conclusion – alliances are tough to manage. Studies have reported that two-thirds of all alliances experience severe problems in the first two years and reported failure rates range as high as 70 percent.

At first blush, alliances are a very seductive concept. They represent an obvious simple solution to a range of strategic dilemmas. In reality, they can end up as disappointments. Our experiences and research with countless alliances of every type have led us to conclude that the root cause of alliances failing to meet expectations is the failure to grasp and articulate their strategic intent. This includes failure to consider and recognize alternatives to entering into an alliance to begin with.

The second most common reason involves lack of recognition of the close interplay between the overall strategy of the company and the role of an alliance in that strategy. Just as the corporate strategy evolves over time, so will the strategic intent for an alliance.

This happens as the alliance progresses and changes as company strategy changes. In short, the first lesson is – put the *strategic* back into alliances.

Exploitation or exploration?

Why enter an alliance? First, it can offer a source of incremental revenue from pooling complementary resources that neither partner is interested in developing on its own. These exploitation alliances generally will be implemented as joint equity ventures. Prior to the mid-1970s, exploitation alliances were by far the most prevalent.

Dow Corning, the US maker of silicone-based products, for example, entered its first joint venture exploitation alliance in 1937 and by 1988 had been involved in more than 20. In 1983, Corning derived 2.4 percent of net income (after taxes) from such alliances.

The performance goals for exploitation alliances will generally be stated as measurable operational objectives, which simplifies monitoring progress through outcome controls.

Second, alliances are useful as the strategic and organizational vehicle for probing or co-developing new markets, product, or technological opportunities.

These exploration alliances are generally implemented as open-ended co-development joint venture projects. They are intended to accomplish learning of previously unknown technologies, new geographic markets, or new product domains. In short, exploration alliances are best for prospecting strategies. But their performance goals will be stated in much less specific, more open-ended terms, such as the acquiring of new capabilities and the learning of new technologies. This greatly complicates the monitoring of progress and performance outcomes. Often, the failure of an exploration alliance can be traced to the reliance on outcome controls and the failure to develop appropriate process controls.

Mismatch

The seeds of alliance tension and instabilities are sown from the outset when alliance partners fail to recognize a mismatch in strategic intents.

An exploitation/exploration asymmetry raises the odds for ultimate dissolution or failure, with the notable exception of licenses and franchises. The two partners may have symmetrical strategic intents when they enter into the alliance, but may fail to observe the emergence of asymmetry.

The emergence of asymmetry is also a major cause of alliance failures and dissolution. This occurs for several reasons. The overall strategic direction of one partner changes as the company evolves over time and the initial strategic intent for entering the alliance becomes redundant.

Another example relates to the evolution of the alliance itself. It may very likely develop in directions that are at variance with the strategic intent of either parent and once again lead to dissolution or buyout. It is only natural that alliances evolve over time and that they develop their own direction and identity.

Similarly, it is to be expected that the strategy of the parents could over time diverge from the direction of the alliance. Therefore, high dissolution rates or instabilities are always present and should be anticipated. Long-term success will occur as an outcome of continuous mutual adaptation, recalibration, and reaffirmation of strategic intents of the alliance partners.

Understanding difference

Not surprisingly, this exploration/exploitation logic produces three basic kinds of strategic alliances. Each of these embodies a unique strategic intent and each demands a unique alliance-management process.

Learning alliances bring together companies with strong exploration intents, but with limited or no exploitation intents. These alliances have as their primary strategic intent to reduce the ignorance of the partners.

Learning alliances can be about:

- *markets*, including local competition, regulations, customer tastes and habits, marketing infrastructure, and the like;
- *core competences*, such as just-in-time processes, negative working capital, one-on-one marketing, and mass customization;
- *technologies*, such as competence-destroying innovations, new complementary technologies, as well as franchising capabilities like the Pizza Hut brand.

Regardless of the specific learning outcomes, learning alliances seek to reduce information asymmetry among the parents. Thus, many market access alliances actually begin as learning alliances in which companies unlock information about local context prior to committing fully to an entry approach, such as greenfield investment, equity joint venture, or outright acquisition.

The critical success factor in learning alliances is the ability of the partners to design, manage, and continuously adapt organizational processes and informal linkages that keep the alliance on track.

For example, failure to recognize and adjust for imbalances in differential learning rates gives rise to learning races. Here one party disproportionately captures value and then moves to dissolve the alliance.

Business alliances link companies with strong exploitation intents, but with limited or no exploration intent. Typically, these alliances seek to establish a position in a geographic or product market or market segment. The sole object of a business alliance is to secure additional incremental revenues.

Many successful business alliances are structured as equity joint ventures (EJVs) and designed to produce a child – that is, a distinct legal or administrative unit – for pursuing alliance activity. CFM International, a jet engines venture between General Electric of the US and Snecma of France, is one such example of a business alliance structured, at least initially, as an EJV. European Vinyls Corporation (EVC), first set up in 1986 as a joint venture between Imperial Chemical Industries of the UK and Enichem of Italy, is another.

A critical success factor in EJV business alliances is the existence of a strong corporate identity for the "child." This helps facilitate both recognition in the market place among customers, suppliers, and the like, as well as loyalty among alliance managers.

Moreover, loyalty to the alliance can have the added benefit of reducing the ever-present possibility of tribal warfare within the alliance.

Business alliances structured as networks represent a new trend. A network is a form of collaboration among multiple companies in which, typically, the network members are each specialized, bringing a unique value-adding resource to the network such as market access or skills. Usually, the network members include a subset of these activities within the network, but maintain their autonomy in other matters. The Star alliance in the airlines business consists of several carriers who list one another's flights in a "code sharing" arrangement.

Critical success factors for a network business alliance again include a strong identity, for the reasons mentioned above. In addition, the collective benefits from the network must be able to overwhelm any benefits that individual members would gain from defection. As collective benefits or benefits captured by an individual member decline, the tendency to defect will increase.

Hybrid alliances represent a third type. These join companies with strategic intents that incorporate both strong exploration and exploitation objectives. In these alliances, the companies seek simultaneously to maximize opportunities for capturing value from leveraging existing capabilities, assets, and the like, as well as from new value creation through learning alliances. For example, the pre-Novartis Ciba-Geigy alliance with Alza, a California biotech company, was designed not only to ensure that the companies would go to market with lower-risk products, but also to facilitate Ciba-Geigy's learning of the advanced drug-delivery system technology known as ADDS.

Thus, hybrid alliances begin as a combination of business and learning alliances. Success in the market place facilitates the longer learning process. On rare occasions, hybrid alliances will result in a major transformation. Historically such outcomes have been serendipitous, but strategically can be planned for, to increase the odds of dramatic gains.

Managing for success

These three types of strategic alliances differ on five dimensions:

- The *loyalty* of managers in a strategic alliance may reside with one or other partner, or with the joint venture itself. In a learning alliance, the loyalty of the managers must remain with the parent company. Should an alliance manager transfer loyalty to a partner or to the alliance, repatriating learning becomes problematic. In a business alliance, loyalty should transfer to the "child." This will reduce the tendency for tribal warfare between partners and alliance managers when major conflicts arise. In hybrid alliances, loyalty must also remain with the parent; however, it is loyalty to a new and improved version of the parent. In the Ciba-Geigy–Alza alliance, Ciba-Geigy managers remained loyal to Ciba-Geigy, but also internalized a new vision of Ciba-Geigy that included ADDS as a critical competence.
- *Control* in business alliances should utilize output controls. The strong exploitation intent of a business alliance can be best measured and rewarded based on financial and market performance. Learning and hybrid alliances require process and behavior control as change in behavior and assimilation of

new knowledge become the crucial outcomes. However, the intensity and organizational complexity of process controls will increase as the partner companies recognize the opportunity to obtain transformational outcomes.

■ *Ability to absorb knowledge (AAK)* is especially important in learning and hybrid alliances, because their success depends on the reduction of information asymmetry. However, in hybrid alliances the challenge is to anticipate and mediate the mixed performance signals that managers will receive from the interaction of outcome measures and process controls. In business alliances, AAK issues can also become relevant when the alliance partners must facilitate the transfer of a strategic capability between the partners and the "child."

■ *Time horizon* – strategic alliances vary in the stability of the alliance over time. Learning alliances tend to be short-term relationships, extending only to the length of the learning cycle. For learning alliances, the main challenge is to recognize when to end the relationship. Business alliances tend to extend to the industry cycle, as long as a business opportunity exists. The challenge of these alliances is knowing how to maintain continuity and in the face of success over time. Hybrid alliances tend to extend into the mid-term, as these alliances must first accumulate performance before the learning agenda is executed. The challenge is to maintain focus on the intent for change, and not allow it to decay into a business alliance.

■ *Success criteria* in learning alliances require that partners benchmark each other. A problem with benchmarking oneself is the self-fulfilling nature of such evaluations, which explains why virtually all learning alliances are reported to be successful up to the moment of dissolution. In a business alliance, periodic reviewing of the business plan and the appropriateness of the business model becomes important. Managers must guard against the complacency that accompanies market success. In a hybrid alliance, both partner benchmarking and performance must be measured and evaluated. The challenge of hybrid alliances is to recognize the potential for a true transformational outcome. This can occur if dramatic change in the mental maps of managers is encouraged and permitted to happen. As we said, transformation outcomes are rare and mostly serendipitous. One company, for example, assigned a junior manager to count at lunch the number of references to a new technology being internalized, and classify the comments as either positive or negative. Over time, the total number of comments as well as the number of positive comments increased dramatically. This suggests the need for creativity in monitoring and assessing the real effects of hybrid alliances on the thinking of managers.

The most relevant issue for raising the odds of success in strategic alliances is recognizing that they are embedded in the strategy of the parents. In this article, we have tried to present a framework for strategically approaching the alliance decision and management process. Our experience documents that this simple yet powerful framework will work to raise the odds of a successful strategic alliance.

Summary

Alliance capitalism is a buzzword describing the modern paradox of businesses simultaneously competing and cooperating. More often than not, however, alliances end in disappointment. According to **Mitchell P. Koza** and **Arie Y. Lewin**, companies frequently fail to consider alternatives or to understand the complex interplay between their overall strategy and that of the alliance. A crucial difference is between exploitation alliances, which tend to have easily identifiable revenue objectives, and exploration alliances, which are typically used to probe for new markets and technology opportunities. To improve the chances of success, companies entering strategic alliances should be cognizant of the strategic intent of the alliance and the interdependence of the alliance with the strategy of the parents.

Suggested further reading

Balakrishnan, S. and Koza, M.P. (1993) "Information asymmetry, adverse selection and joint ventures: theory and evidence," *Journal of Economic Behavior and Organization*, 20 (1, January).

Dierickx, I. and Koza, M.P. (1991) "Information asymmetries: how not to buy a lemon in negotiating mergers and acquisitions," *European Management Journal*, 9 (3).

Koza, M.P. and Lewin, A.Y. (1999) "The co-evolution of network alliances: a longitudinal analysis of an international professional service network," *Organization Science*, 10 (5).

March, J.G. (1991) "Exploration and exploitation in organizational learning," *Organization Science*, 2 (1).

Reuer, J. and Koza, M.P. (2000) "Asymmetric information and joint venture performance: theory and evidence from domestic and international joint ventures," *Strategic Management Journal*, 21 (1): 81–8.

Alliance networks: view from the hub

by Toby E. Stuart

Companies establish strategic alliances, such as joint ventures, product-development partnerships, and formal technology exchanges, for many different reasons. Motives to enter alliances include: 1) to unite complementary assets, such as when a biotechnology start-up and a pharmaceutical company establish a marketing alliance in which the latter sells and distributes a therapeutic developed by the former; 2) a desire to keep abreast of emerging technologies that may affect a core business, such as when a telecommunications equipment company takes a minority equity position in a provider of internet-based telephony or a producer of a novel switching technology; 3) to share the expense and risk of a major capital outlay, for example when two semiconductor producers create a joint venture company to build a new chip-fabrication plant. This of course is a very abbreviated list; the incentives to establish intercorporate partnerships are many and varied. The increasing incidence of alliances – to the point of near ubiquity in the technology sector – is evidence both of the strategic importance of these partnerships and the diversity of inducements to establish them.

This article addresses the benefits an organization may capture when it establishes a portfolio of strategic alliances, as well as guidelines for partner selection and network management. Metaphorically, companies with many strategic partners act as the hub of a network. To be clear about the scope of the article, the focus is on companies that enter many bilateral alliances that amalgamate to form a network. I will not address a related organizational form, the consortium. The distinction between alliance networks and consortia is that, in the latter, all of the participants work together on a unified project. Examples of consortia include Iridium, the beleaguered, Motorola-sponsored satellite phone service, and Sematech, the US semiconductor research consortium. Whereas an alliance network is characterized by one company at the center of many bilateral alliances, a consortium exists when many companies work together in the same alliance.

Why create an alliance network?

The alliance network has gained prevalence particularly in high-technology industries. Among other well-known companies, IBM, Fujitsu, NEC, Intel, Microsoft, Merck, Netscape, and Monsanto have established networks of strategic alliances in recent years. Why?

First, alliances can be an extremely important strategic tool in the digital economy, particularly when standards (i.e., a set of coordinated product designs enabling the components of a system to work together) play a vital role in industry dynamics, such as in computers, software, telecommunications, and video games. The importance of alliances in standards-based industries stems from an essential characteristic of competitive dynamics in such markets: these industries often end up being dominated by a single standard, for example in the way that the Microsoft/Intel platform known as Wintel controls the major share of the PC market. The reason for this is that the advantage of using a particular standard is an increasing function of the number of others who have adopted it, and thus early gains in the installed base of users yields a snowballing advantage for that platform (so-called network externalities were discussed in Module 2). Alliances can influence market dominance precisely because, when a standard begins to gain market share against a rival approach, it tends quickly to accrue additional momentum until it occupies the major share of the market. Thus, anything that affects early gains in market share can have a dramatic effect on the final outcome in standards-based competitions. When many organizations ally to sponsor a standard, they collectively have the power to convince would-be adopters that, when the dust settles, their approach is likely to win the market. This perception among potential adopters can create enough early gains in market share to establish eventual dominance.

Second, alliance networks can be a very useful tool in responding to the difficulties that most large, relatively old companies experience when attempting to introduce major changes in their core business activities. Organizations that are industry leaders tend to be relatively large, highly complex bureaucracies that experience difficulty in making fundamental changes in product market and technology strategy, in large part because size, experience, and a history of success all conspire to create a level of comfort with the status quo that hampers change. Aware of this fact, many market leaders rely on alliances with small and young companies to ensure that they are not left out of the next technological revolution. Alliance networks can be structured to link the hub company to the developers of an array of emerging technologies, allowing the hub of the network to experiment with different technical, operational, and strategic approaches through external linkages. These partnerships are both much easier to implement and less risky to undertake than are major, internal strategic changes. Third, alliance networks are vital in areas experiencing technological convergence. These are industries in which many formerly distinct technologies evolve toward increasing interdependence or convergence, and no single organization has mastery over all of the technical capabilities to compete in the emerging domain. We have recently observed this phenomenon in areas such as multimedia, telecommunications, and drug discovery. Monsanto, the life sciences powerhouse, is an excellent example of an organization that has used an alliance network to spearhead the transformation from an old-line chemicals concern to the cutting edge of biotechnology, and then to cope with the recent, rapid technological convergence in the life sciences.

Designing the network

The first issue in designing an alliance network is the selection of appropriate partners. When making judgments about potential partners, it is essential to possess a deep understanding of the relevant area of business, including knowledge of different technological, operational, and strategic approaches. In an influential article, Westley Cohen and Daniel Levinthal introduced a concept called absorptive capacity, which they define as the ability of organizations to assimilate new ideas and innovations from external sources. Cohen and Levinthal's important insight is that learning is a cumulative activity: the more you know about something, the easier it is to acquire, appreciate, and put to use additional information about it. The relevance of this insight for selecting alliance partners is that there must be some overlap in the business endeavors of a company and its potential alliance partners for the focal company to be able successfully to discern quality differences among potential partners and to learn from its collaborators. This is particularly so in a high-tech context because judgments must be made about the attractiveness of early-stage technical approaches, and these are impossible to make without a thorough understanding of the relevant technical area. Monsanto implicitly understood the importance of absorptive capacity: before launching into any biotech-related collaborative ventures, it first invested more than $150m to build up an internal group of biotech researchers – a group that could be called on to assist in partner selection and due diligence.

Second, alliance prospects should be screened with the same rigor and much of the same logic as one would apply to any corporate scope decision. The tools of corporate strategy are as applicable to making decisions about strategic partnering as they are to informing M&A activity. Modern theories of corporate scope place a premium on coherence: the activities performed by an organization should be sufficiently related that opportunities exist to leverage economies of scope (colloquially known as "synergies") across the units of the company. The implication is that alliances should be established only if they relate to activities performed elsewhere inside the company. Again, Monsanto serves as an example: the company has treated bio-technology as a platform technology, seeking out alliance partners to cultivate an expertise in this area that could then be leveraged into each of the end markets in which the company competes. Thus, in theory the company's biotechnological expertise had served as a central resource exploited by each of the company's operating divisions.

Third, all else being equal, organizations with prior collaborative histories are likely to make better partners. Companies that have done a number of alliances in the past have demonstrated an understanding of the logic of alliances and have acquired skills in the difficult task of working in an intercorporate context. More important, a recent paper by the author establishes that the length of the record of past alliance activity of a potential partner is a good indicator of the likelihood that the company intends to do more alliances in the future, and thus the premium it places on maintaining a reputation as a fair and reliable partner. Therefore, companies with significant, prior collaborative experience typically make good partners.

Managing the network

All companies that plan to enter multiple alliances should give serious consideration to creating the position of alliance manager, probably at the vice-president level, to oversee all of the organization's partnerships. Alternatively, companies may follow the lead of an organization like British Petroleum, which has created a committee, including the managers, which oversees company alliances to facilitate the exchange of ideas and transfer of learning in alliance management. The value of having this position or committee is demonstrated by the poor experience of an entertainment conglomerate that entered a dozen or so alliances in the multimedia area in the early 1990s, but did not have a coordinated alliance strategy. These deals were driven by the organization's fear that developments in multimedia could threaten its core businesses in music, film production, and print. Each division in the company responded by forming a number of alliances with small multimedia companies, the result being a confusing array of partnerships and an inability to consolidate learning across deals. Even within a particular division, there was a lack of communication between different levels in the management hierarchy about the objectives and priority of the division's alliances, which impeded the company's ability to perform its contractually specified role in the alliances (for example, to market some of the interactive CD-Roms developed by its partners). Many of this organization's strategic partners felt poorly treated by it, and the company's reputation as a partner was tarnished.

Problems like these can be solved, and strategic decisions made, at the level of the network rather than at the level of the alliance, if there is a senior staff position dedicated to overseeing alliance activity. Another recent paper by the author demonstrated that companies benefit more from new alliances when they possess significant, prior collaborative experience ("benefit" in this study is measured by the magnitude of the increase in the company's share price in response to announcements of new alliances). The argument is that experienced organizations will have refined their partner selection procedures and contract negotiation skills, as well as developed a reputation for reliability that enables greater flexibility in alliance contracting in future transactions. While the latter benefit will exist merely because of the reputation that emerges when previous partners were treated fairly, the former – learning – requires proactive behavior. To capture all of the benefits from experience, an organization must consolidate, interpret, and transfer the knowledge generated by previous experience. These activities require coordination across the units of a company, and will not occur in the absence of a senior staff position designed to function as a coordinating mechanism.

Venture capital metaphor

A salient issue in managing alliance networks is determining the scope of the component partnerships. As the number of alliances in a domain increases, so does the potential for conflict of interest among partners and the importance of being clear about the scope of each alliance and establishing boundaries to minimize the likelihood of conflict between partners. The Monsanto alliance network again illustrates this point. Monsanto had an alliance covering the Bt gene (which increases pest resistance in transgenic crops) with seed companies Pioneer Hi-Bred and Northrup-King (now Novartis). A different biotech company, Mycogen, also had an alliance covering the Bt gene with Pioneer, and chemical giants Dow and Ciba-Geigy (now also Novartis). Subsequently, Monsanto sued Mycogen and its strategic partners – including Novartis – claiming infringement of its Bt patents. Sound confusing? It is, in large part because there are a number of overlapping alliance networks in the agriculture biotech area. In addition to Monsanto, Dow, Novartis, DuPont, and Aventis (itself a joint venture between Rhône-Poulenc and Hoechst) are hubs in alliance networks. Overlapping partnerships have so far caused significant confusion and litigation in this context, highlighting the importance of taking a portfolio perspective when constructing an alliance network and following the design principle of conflict minimization in selecting strategic partners.

In conclusion, I think it is useful to consider the value-maximizing strategies of venture capitalists, who in many ways can be thought of as hubs in an inter-corporate network.

First, venture capitalists (VCs) have a clear sense of the value that they bring to portfolio companies, the start-up ventures in which they acquire equity positions: VCs offer guidance, boost legitimacy, and provide connections to potential investors, customers, and business service providers. My research has demonstrated that an alliance with the hub company in a network is similarly valuable in terms of the legitimacy that it brings to partners, particularly if the partner is a relatively young and unknown organization. Because hub companies are perceived to be experienced and skilled in the partner selection process, alliances with them represent key endorsements for early-stage companies that can be parlayed into the acquisition of additional resources and strategic partners. To the extent that hub companies become attuned to this and other sources of value creation for their partners, they will be able to exploit these in negotiations over contract terms in new alliances.

VCs also always take a portfolio-level perspective when deciding which companies to finance, and increasingly they have begun to define the scope of their investments in terms of their ability to broker transactions among the companies in their portfolio. For example, Kleiner Perkins (KP), the prestigious VC company that, among others, has funded internet-based businesses like Netscape, Excite, AOL, Amazon.com, and @Home, has facilitated many strategic alliances, personnel exchanges, and cross-cutting board memberships among its collection of internet properties. For example, Excite is the primary provider of web searches on Netscape – a role that almost went to Infoseek until KP brokered the deal with Excite. These transactions among KP-backed companies have been valuable for both the individual companies involved and the network as a whole. The reason that intra-network alliances are value creating relative to other partnerships is that the network hub can effectively lower transactions costs in exchanges within the network: it can make introductions, vouch for the reliability of exchange partners, and to a certain extent police the exchange.

Moreover, it can bring additional business to portfolio companies that they would not otherwise have received. In general, the greater the benefits of the networks to its members, the easier it will be for the hub to recruit quality partners and negotiate appealing contract terms.

Monsanto's metamorphosis

Under the leadership of John Hanley, CEO in the middle 1970s, Monsanto became very interested in the promise of biotechnology – at the time a radical new scientific

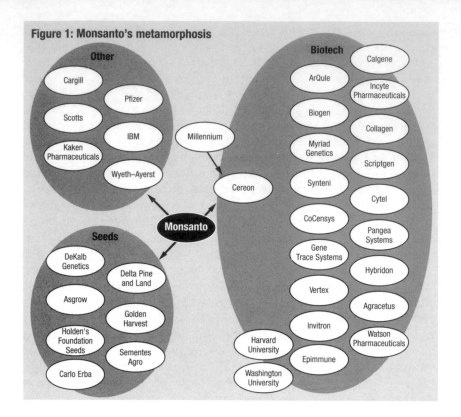

Figure 1: Monsanto's metamorphosis

breakthrough revolutionizing the agriculture business. Since that time, the company has entered over 50 biotech-related alliances (in addition to a number of acquisitions, most notably of the drug company G.D. Searle). Although the public's concern about the introduction of genetically modified organisms into the food supply may block the economic returns from Monsanto's bold strategy, the result nonetheless has been one of the most radical corporate transformations in recent business history. Monsanto has remade itself, converting from a plastics and chemical outfit to one of the world's premier life sciences companies, with deep capabilities in biotechnology and major businesses in herbicides, genetically engineered plants, and human drugs. Monsanto's collaborative history includes alliances with a diverse array of organizations: universities, start-up biotech companies, leading drug companies, seed companies, and diversified food producers. These partnerships have spanned an equally diverse set of business opportunities.

Below are brief descriptions of four recent deals and an illustration (*see* Figure 1) portraying a large section of Monsanto's alliance network:

- *Millennium Pharmaceuticals*: Monsanto committed $200m to form a joint venture company, Cereon Genomics, with gene hunter Millennium to develop genomics-based plant and agriculture products. Millennium transferred to Monsanto a range of genomics technologies for use in the development of life sciences products, including pharmaceuticals. This deal followed earlier ones in the genomics area with Incyte Pharmaceuticals, Calgene and Synteni.
- *Cargill*: Partnership to develop genetically enhanced food and animal feed.

Combines Monsanto's genetics technology with the resource base of the leading grain and food processing company, which has the capabilities to produce and deliver custom-made foodstuffs worldwide.

- *Pfizer*: Co-development and co-marketing agreement for Celebrex, Monsanto's novel anti-inflammatory compound (the first FDA-approved Cox-2 inhibitor). Among potential drug company partners, Pfizer had the largest US salesforce.
- *ArQule*: Monsanto acquired the right to use data produced by ArQule Inc. and its capabilities in structure-guided drug design, modular building block chemistry, combinatorial chemistry, and informatics. These data will be used to accelerate the identification of promising molecular candidates for the development of novel crop-protection products, herbicides, insecticides and fungicides.

Summary

When companies form many strategic partnerships, the result is often an alliance network, says **Toby E. Stuart**. The phenomenon is increasingly common in high-technology industries like the life sciences. The advantages of these networks include the influence they can exert in standard setting, the exposure they offer established companies to emerging technology, and their ability to facilitate technological convergence. The author explains Monsanto's strategy in this area and among his recommendations urges companies to appoint a high-level alliance manager responsible for all the organization's partnerships.

Suggested further reading

Cohen, W.M. and Levinthal, D.A. (1990) "Absorptive capacity: a new perspective on learning and innovation," *Administrative Science Quarterly*, 35: 128–52.

Stuart, T.E. and Robinson, D. (1999) "Network effects in the governance of strategic alliances in biotechnology," working paper, Graduate School of Business, University of Chicago.

Stuart, T.E., Hoang, H. and Hybels, R. (1999) "Interorganizational endorsements and the performance of entrepreneurial ventures," *Administrative Science Quarterly*, 44: 315–49.

Trust and control in strategic alliances

by David Faulkner

Trust and control are often cited as key success factors in alliances between companies. But do these two forces work together or against each other? Some say that good control systems foster greater trust and are necessary to achieve successful performance. Others suggest that if trust exists it makes control systems less necessary; this reduces the cost of monitoring partners and hence makes it more likely that the alliance will lead to competitive advantage.

This article looks at three case studies of international alliances that have varying degrees of trust and control. It compares the different outcomes in performance and hazards some conclusions as to whether trust and control are complementary or opposing forces. The evidence strongly suggests that managers who hold to the popular idea that control is necessary to make an alliance work are mistaken.

What is trust?

There are three ways of analyzing trust in corporate alliances:

- *Calculative trust.* One partner calculates that the other can help it and trusts the other in the hope that matters will work out well.
- *Predictive trust.* One partner comes to believe that the other will behave as it says it will, since it has been as good as its word in the past.
- *Friendship trust.* Here the partners get to like each other as people, and trust takes on a more personal aspect. Successful alliances do not need friendship trust to be successful, but if it exists alliances are likely to be more robust and flexible when problems arise.

What is control?

Control in strategic alliances is the process by which one partner influences the behavior of the other and of the alliance itself. Control must be circumscribed if the alliance is to realize its aims and the partners are to feel unconstrained, but equally if it is not present in some form the partners will not feel comfortable with the partnership.

Control can be analyzed along three dimensions: its extent, its focus, and its mechanisms. These provide a framework for analyzing the amount of control in an alliance.

The extent of control can be described as a vertical force, in that it measures the degree to which partners can exercise control over an alliance. Focus is a horizontal force that defines the functional areas over which a partner chooses to exercise control. And mechanisms are the means by which control is exercised.

Control mechanisms extend far beyond the traditional mechanisms of equity ownership and board membership, although these remain important. They also include transfer prices, information management, training and personnel development, standardization of skills, gatekeepers, and many others. Given such a variety of mechanisms, it is clearly possible – with careful management – to exercise control even from a minority shareholding position.

There is considerable dispute over the link between control and performance. There will always be tension between a company's desire to control any new venture and its willingness to trust a new partner (or partners). If one company tries to exert too much control, this can threaten the quality of its relations with its partners and harm performance. Managers must try to strike a balance between the need for control and the need for harmonious relationships.

Many managers believe that total control increases the prospects of success in an alliance. Yet this is not necessarily the case. Research into alliances between developed and developing countries, for example, suggests that performance tends to be better when the foreign partner is less dominant. The argument is that sharing control with local partners makes them contribute more. This can help the foreign partner cope with unfamiliar circumstances and result in a higher return on investment. The size of a joint venture (measured in annual sales), the amount of equity invested, and the number of expatriate personnel are important variables in the relationship between control and performance. When partners have committed large amounts of money and personnel to a joint venture they tend to want to control it more tightly; if they fail to secure such control they find the performance unsatisfactory. Yet researchers have found no consistent link between parent companies' level of control and performance. It is thus important to strike a balance between the level of a partner's "resourcing" commitment and its management control of an alliance.

Case studies

The case studies describe three different types of alliance. The first is a joint venture, the second a collaborative venture (but not one structured as a joint venture company), and the third a consortium. All face a similar challenge in the development of trust. However, the issue of control affects the alliances in different ways and to different degrees. It is likely that control will be exercised most closely in a joint venture, since there are more direct organizational mechanisms through which this can take place. Collaboration without a joint venture company on which to focus must rely on subtler methods of control. The consortium approach, where there are a large number of partners, presents multiple control problems.

The Dowty–Sema joint venture

Dowty–Sema was set up as a joint venture in 1982 by Dowty Group (which was taken over by TI Group in 1992) and Sema, with the encouragement of the UK Ministry of Defence. The aim was to create an alternative tenderer to Ferranti in the specialized market for command-and-control systems in ships.

Until its integration into Bae–Sema in 1992, the joint venture was owned 50–50 by Dowty and Sema. It obtained a lot of work from the Ministry of Defence and was a success in terms of sales growth. In ten years it grew to have 110 staff and an annual turnover of £50m.

As a company, however, Dowty–Sema suffered from a lack of independent assets with which to carry out its work. Ninety percent of the value of each contract was subcontracted back to Dowty and Sema. Only 10 percent remained with the joint venture itself, which was therefore little more than a "shop window" for marketing and sales purposes.

Trust never fully developed between the partners in Dowty–Sema. At board level relationships were good on a personal basis, but the personnel from Dowty and from Sema, two very different cultures, never trusted each other, even at the predictive level. There was at best grudging respect and basic levels of calculative trust.

Control was retained in the parent companies, with Dowty–Sema itself little more than a shell company, at least to begin with. At board level there was equal membership from both sides, to reflect the 50–50 shareholding. Joint managing directors were appointed initially, but as this led to confusion in decision making they were later replaced by a single managing director, who happened to come from Sema. He had little power, however, since when contracts were obtained the two partners merely divided them in half and took them for themselves. The joint venture only retained those activities that were neither obviously hardware (Dowty) nor software (Sema).

The shareholders had excessive concern for control, which resulted in long committee meetings – involving both the partners and Dowty–Sema's management – before any non-routine decision could be taken. As a result, potentially profitable contracts were completed late or unprofitably. The parent companies also insisted, as a further control mechanism, that all staff should belong ultimately on the payroll of one or the other parent. This made it very difficult for the venture to develop a clear identity of its own. Although Guy Warner, the managing director, reported to the board of Dowty–Sema, his performance appraisal was carried out in Sema.

There was considerable tension between the two partners in carrying out projects. Exchange of information was restricted. The extent of control by the partners was such that it tended to stifle initiative outside the sales function. The focus of control was principally on the achievement and implementation of contracts. At a functional level, Sema concentrated on setting up and controlling financial systems, while Dowty focussed on contract administration and monitoring.

Overall, a high level of parent control was strongly correlated with a low level of trust at all levels below the very top. The result was a company that was successful in sales terms but not in profits.

Royal Bank and Banco Santander collaboration

The alliance between Royal Bank of Scotland and Banco Santander of Spain was set up in 1988. It is a partial union of two medium-sized national banks in the face of the expected Europeanization of the banking industry. The two partners each own a small minority of each other's shares.

The alliance operates on many fronts. It includes joint ventures in Germany and Gibraltar, and functions as a consortium for corporate money transfer in a number of European countries. This consortium, named IBOS (International Banking Organisation Service), is to date the most successful part of the alliance, although it was not foreseen as a significant project when the alliance was created. This demonstrates the importance of allowing evolutionary forces to unfold freely in alliances. Royal Bank of Scotland and Banco Santander have learned that they can achieve most of what they wish to achieve in Europe by extending IBOS, without the expenditure and risk that would be involved in making acquisitions.

In the 12 years of the alliance's life, the relationship between the partners has evolved a good deal. Cooperation is proving to be effective in most areas of activity agreed at the beginning, and staff are now exchanged on secondment between the partners.

Trust has progressed through all three stages identified at the beginning of this article. Calculative trust was necessary to get the alliance under way in the first place. Then predictive trust was achieved through the experience of working together, through exchange of personnel, and as a result of each bank's willingness to buy more than a nominal amount of the other's shares. Friendship trust developed later. A good example is the fact that each partner is now happy to allow the other to represent its interests with third parties.

The alliance agreement, signed by Royal Bank and Banco Santander at the outset, is a very important control mechanism. However, it has not been allowed to constrain the scope of the alliance, as the evolution of IBOS shows. The partners established a surveillance committee to oversee the relationship and "gateway executives" were appointed at assistant director level. These two individuals, Walter Stewart and Jose Saveedra, have both been in the post since the alliance began and effectively control it at operational level. The banks have both put representatives on each other's main boards. Performance measures have been developed to assess the alliance's progress. In addition, accountants tot up costs once a year and compare the amounts spent on the alliance by both partners.

The extent of control operates at several levels. Strategic control is principally at the highest executive level, through the surveillance committee and board membership. Operational control is at assistant director level through the gateway executives. The focus of control is wide, but does not extend to interference in the other partner's domestic banking activities. Overall trust is high, direct control is low, and both partners regard the alliance as very successful.

Cable & Wireless's Japanese consortium (IDC)

Cable & Wireless is pursuing a strategy of becoming a global force in the telecommunications market. Given its size and relative financial power in global terms, this requires it to pursue strategic alliances.

The Japanese market is clearly important for C&W's strategy. In 1986 it decided to try to obtain the license to become the second Japanese international carrier. To gain credibility with the Japanese government, C&W decided to set up a consortium that would include big Japanese corporations. Accordingly, it founded International Digital Corporation, with C&W, Toyota, and C. Itoh each holding roughly 17 percent of the equity; 20 Japanese shareholders – including several banks and industrial concerns – shared the remainder. After a considerable battle with the Japanese government, the consortium won the license in 1987.

The alliance has undoubtedly been a success in establishing itself and C&W in Japan, gaining a 16 percent share of Japan's international telecommunications traffic. Japan has gone from having the highest prices in international telecommunications in Asia to having some of the lowest, and from having a relatively insignificant network position to being the most important hub in the area. Much of this is due to the stimulus provided by IDC.

Trust between IDC's partners is generally high, since the consortium has been forged in adversity. Partners have won trust by deeds and not words. They have gone through the calculative and predictive levels of trust, and generally reached the friendship level. Control is exercised through traditional Japanese mechanisms such as *nemawashi*, the heavy networking involved in achieving consensus decisions. As a result, individual office holders have no great individual power. There are no large legal documents, just a simple shareholder agreement.

Board membership is allocated according to shareholding. C&W provides the managing director, C. Itoh the president, and Toyota the chairman. Only a Japanese national may commit the company in writing – which does not seem to concern C&W. Almost continuous meetings ensure that there are no surprises. There is no control on the level of information movement. C&W achieves influence through its knowledge of telecommunications technology, the banks through provision of finance, and other shareholders as major customers.

Control by any one partner is bound to be limited, because IDC is a consortium with around 20 partners. However, the three partners with 51 percent between them – C. Itoh, Toyota and C&W – have most control. Extent of control in a Japanese setting is difficult to gauge, because top-level decisions are not taken without consensus. It appears that control is pretty centralized in the consortium, but that C&W has little control itself and thus has to depend on influence. The focus of control is strongly on technology and commercial relations. In typical Japanese fashion, most control mechanisms are hidden from view.

Overall, the venture comes out as being high on trust and low on control. It has been quite successful, in that IDC has achieved a high market share, but it is having trouble achieving high profits in an increasingly competitive industrial arena.

Conclusion

Figure 1: Trust, control and performance

	Type	Trust	Control	Success
Dowty–Sema	Joint venture	Low	High	Limited
Royal Bank/ Santander	Collaboration	High	Low	Very successful
C&W	Consortium	High	Low	Quite successful

In all three cases a high level of trust appears to be important to effective operation. In both the very successful and the quite successful alliances, a high degree of trust is evident between the partners (*see* Figure 1). Its absence in the case of Dowty–Sema clearly damaged performance.

In the three cases we have looked at, the less control there has been, the better the performance. However, it is important to remember that in case studies of this kind it is difficult to factor in changes over time. Different control mechanisms develop over time, as do the extent and nature of trust. Performance also varies over time. To draw hard and fast conclusions from this analysis would therefore be foolhardy. But at least one can be very suspicious of the suggestion that the best way to run an alliance is by tight control of one's partner's actions. The importance of trust in achieving performance is clearly validated.

Summary

Is it better to secure control in a strategic alliance, or is it more advantageous to build up trust? Proponents of the former view argue that control is necessary for successful performance. Supporters of the latter say that trust reduces the need for control systems, hence lowering cost and enhancing opportunities for competitive advantage. Using three case studies, **David Faulkner** argues that the conventional focus on control may be counter-productive.

Quote?

STRATEGY AND KNOWLEDGE

14

Contributors

 **Laura Empson** is a fellow of St Anne's College and lecturer in management studies at the Saïd Business School, Oxford. She has previously worked as a strategy consultant and an investment banker.

 **Joanne Oxley** is First Chicago/NBD Corporation Assistant Professor of Corporate Strategy and International Business at University of Michigan Business School. Her current research interests include technology and knowhow transfer in strategic alliances, and the emergence and organization of e-commerce markets.

 **Laurence Capron** is assistant professor of strategy at INSEAD. Her research interests include mergers and acquisitions, foreign entry, modes of acquisition of new competences, and corporate development in the telecommunications industry.

 **Anthony Hopwood** is Peter Moores Director and American Standard Companies Professor of Operations Management, Saïd Business School. He focusses on changing patterns of organizational control, information and control processes in new organizational forms, and organizational and social analysis of accounting.

 **Will Mitchell** is Jack D. Sparks/Whirlpool Corporation Research Professor, professor of corporate strategy and international business, University of Michigan Business School.

Contents

Introduction

Knowledge management has been a major growth industry in the last five years – this reflects the fact that understanding and exploiting knowledge is an increasingly vital part of underpinning strategy. This module explores the nature of knowledge, the difference between tacit and explicit knowledge, and the question of how it can best be managed. Too many companies, it is argued, are looking backwards, using information to measure and control internal processes rather than shaping the future and influencing market trends. Bad corporate habits are still ingrained but coming business generations are likely to be a mass of overlapping and conflicting information flows. KM is more than the latest management fad.

The challenge of managing knowledge

by Laura Empson

Airport bookshelves are crowded with management texts claiming to be the "definitive" guides to knowledge management. In the past five years, management consulting firms have created a multibillion-dollar knowledge-management industry. No fewer than 78 percent of major US companies in a recent survey claimed to be "moving toward becoming" knowledge based, according to research by Richard Huseman and Jon Goodman (*see* Suggested further reading). Clearly, the knowledge-management bandwagon is on a roll. Why is this happening and what do we really know about the subject?

A growth business

At a practical level, the current emphasis on knowledge management can be attributed to two distinct but related developments. Throughout the 1990s, capital- and labor-intensive industries in developed economies continued to decline, while the relative importance of technology and information-intensive industries increased. At the same time, rapid advances in information technology enabled companies in even the most traditional industries to develop sophisticated systems for capturing new sources of information and disseminating and exploiting this information more effectively.

At a theoretical level, two concurrent developments have contributed to an increased emphasis on knowledge in the strategic management literature. The first is the popularity of the resource-based view of the company. This clearly identifies knowledge as potentially the primary source of sustainable competitive advantage. The second is the development of postmodern perspectives on organizations that have challenged fundamental assumptions about the nature and meaning of knowledge within companies, industries, and society as a whole.

Traditional strategy models, such as US management writer Michael Porter's five forces model, focus on the company's external competitive environment. They do not attempt to look inside the company.

In contrast, the resource-based perspective highlights the need for a fit between the external market context in which a company operates and its internal capabilities. A company's competitive advantage, according to this view, derives from its ability to assemble and exploit an appropriate combination of resources. Sustainable competitive advantage is achieved by continuously developing existing resources and creating new resources in response to changing market conditions. Writers such as Robert Grant (*see* Suggested further reading) argue that knowledge represents the most important value-creating asset.

The primary function of the company is to create conditions under which many individuals can integrate specialist knowledge in order to produce goods and services.

The resource-based view, therefore, suggests that knowledge, like any other asset, can be stored, measured, and moved around an organization. Postmodern perspectives on organizations challenge this assumption.

Writers such as Frank Blackler (*see* Suggested further reading) argue that knowledge does not – and cannot – exist in any absolute or objective sense.

What we recognize as legitimate knowledge, and how we choose to interpret and apply that knowledge, is determined by the social and organizational context in which we operate. The "not-invented-here" syndrome is one example of this phenomenon. An innovative proposal that is perfectly valid in the eyes of an external observer may still be rejected by those inside the organization because it fails to conform to their mental model of what constitutes valid or useful knowledge.

If knowledge is a social construct – that is, it emerges through interaction – it follows that it cannot be formally managed. Like culture, knowledge exists only in a highly abstract form within organizations. It may be represented by certain physical artefacts and it may be affected by managerial action. However, its fundamental nature can change only gradually over time, through a process of interaction between the many and various individuals within the organization.

Managers need not be too concerned with some of the more arcane aspects of the debate between these opposing theoretical perspectives. They are interested in results, not philosophical debates. However, before agreeing to pay a management consulting firm a substantial fee for installing a knowledge-management system, managers should at least understand what they are buying. Perhaps we should be asking whether knowledge can be managed at all.

What is knowledge?

Knowledge itself is a flexible and often elusive concept. It is perhaps the ultimate conceit of management academics and management consultants that they should now have appropriated and exploited a term that has perplexed and preoccupied philosophers for several millennia.

Think how different the history of western philosophy might have been if only Plato and Aristotle, Descartes and Hegel had been able to subscribe to the *Harvard Business Review*!

In the context of strategic management, it is perhaps easiest to understand knowledge in terms of what it is *not*. It is not data and it is not information. Data are objective facts, presented without any judgment or context. Data becomes information when it is categorized, analyzed, summarized, and placed in context.

Information, therefore, is data endowed with relevance and purpose. Information develops into knowledge when it is used to make comparisons, assess consequences, establish connections, and engage in a dialogue. Knowledge can, therefore, be seen as information that comes laden with experience, judgment, intuition, and values.

According to this definition, most IT-based "knowledge-management systems" are merely sophisticated and efficient mechanisms for filing and disseminating information. Systems similar to the *Yellow Pages* business directory, identifying who knows what within a company, simply provide information about where knowledge resides. They are not sources of knowledge in their own right. Ultimately, most knowledge resides within individuals.

Our knowledge base is a little like an iceberg. Most of what we know is hidden below the surface. We each have a limited stock of explicit knowledge, which we find easy to codify and articulate to others. Books we have read, reports we have written, and advice we have given to colleagues or friends all fall into that category. However, most of what we know is not explicit, but tacit.

Tacit knowledge, in its purest form, cannot be articulated. A green-fingered gardener cannot explain to a novice precisely why his plants always thrive. A successful salesperson cannot tell a junior colleague exactly how to close a sale. This kind of knowledge can only be transferred through observation and practice. The traditional craft apprenticeships system recognizes this. Professional services firms continue to employ the apprenticeship model of tacit knowledge transfer between partners and employees.

However, the distinction between tacit and explicit knowledge is not absolute. Much of our knowledge remains tacit simply because we have not attempted to make it explicit. And it is this unarticulated, yet articulable, knowledge that presents the greatest opportunity for knowledge management within organizations. The primary goal of knowledge-management systems is to identify the valuable knowledge that resides within individuals and disseminate it throughout the organization. However, experience suggests that this seemingly straightforward process is in practice fraught with difficulties.

Why should I tell you what I know?

One reason is that knowledge represents a source of power for an individual. By sharing valuable knowledge with a colleague, you run the risk of diminishing your value to the company. Potentially, you are no longer indispensable. Why should you do it? Tom Davenport and Larry Prusak (*see* Suggested further reading) argue that there are three conditions under which, as an employee, you will agree to your colleague's request:

- The first is *reciprocity*. Your time and energy are finite. You will only take the time to help a colleague if you think you are likely to receive valuable knowledge in return, either now or in the future.
- The second is *repute*. It is in your interest to be viewed as an expert within your organization: if you do not have a reputation for expertise, your knowledge cannot represent a source of power. In this case, you need to be certain that your colleague will acknowledge the source of this knowledge and will not claim the credit for himself.
- Davenport and Prusak identify the third condition as *altruism* (although the motives may be more akin to self-gratification). There are some subjects that we find fascinating and important and we simply want to talk to others about them.

Davenport and Prusak's analysis leads them to argue that within an organization there is, in effect, an internal market for knowledge. Knowledge is exchanged between buyers and sellers, with reciprocity, repute, and altruism functioning as payment mechanisms. Trust is an essential condition for the smooth functioning of the market. This trust can exist at an individual level, through close working relationships between colleagues, or at an organizational level, by the creation of a cultural context that encourages and rewards knowledge sharing and discourages and penalizes knowledge hoarding.

Barriers to understanding

The concept of the internal market for knowledge is fundamentally an economics-based model of the organization. As such, it can yield some useful insights, but does not fully explain the complexity of reality. If we accept that much of what we know does not exist in an absolute and objective sense, then we need to understand how individuals conceptualize and value knowledge. If individuals construct knowledge

[handwritten margin note: If no basic in knowledge in area – expert vs. take time to explain]

in fundamentally different ways, they are unlikely to be able to share their knowledge with each other.

It is easiest to learn about things that we already know. It is very difficult to learn from an expert if you do not have a basic grounding in the topic. The expert must take time to explain the context and translate the jargon. The barriers to communication in organizations that arise between engineering and marketing departments, for example, typify this problem. These problems can be ascribed to differences in the content of the knowledge bases.

Differences in the prevailing form of the knowledge base can also lead to problems, as a recent study of mine (*see* Suggested further reading) demonstrates.

The study examined a series of mergers between professional services firms, where knowledge transfer was an explicit objective of the merger. It found that consultants in particular were reluctant to share their knowledge with their merger partner colleagues when the fundamental nature of their knowledge bases differed substantially.

Consultants who relied on highly codified explicit procedures for conducting their work viewed the tacit knowledge of their merger partner colleagues as insubstantial and even unreal.

Consultants in companies where knowledge was primarily tacit viewed the codified knowledge of their merger partner colleagues as simplistic and illegitimate. In this context, consultants were reluctant to share knowledge with their merger partner colleagues because they perceived that they would receive knowledge of lesser value in return. This study, therefore, highlights the need to understand the context within which individuals evaluate and legitimize each other's claims to knowledge, and the effect that this can have on the functioning of the market for knowledge within an organization.

Common sense in transfers

Much can be done within an organization to encourage knowledge transfer. IT-based information-management systems provide a necessary infrastructure, but will not be used effectively unless certain other conditions are also in place. The importance of trust has already been identified. IT-based interaction is no substitute for face-to-face contact when seeking to build strong interpersonal relationships. Time is also important. Exchanging information at speed may be efficient in some circumstances, but tacit knowledge in particular cannot be discovered, articulated, and disseminated in a hurry. Creating a common language for talking about knowledge can also help, either through specific interventions, such as joint team training and staff rotation, or more informally by encouraging staff to think and talk about what they know and what they need to know. Much of this is common sense. As Davenport and Prusak explain, the good news about knowledge management is that, if you sit down and think carefully about it, you can probably design a perfectly adequate knowledge-management system yourself.

The difficult part is getting it to work. It is not enough simply for companies to manage existing knowledge. In order to achieve sustainable competitive advantage, the knowledge within an organization must adapt and evolve continuously in response to changing market conditions. But organizations cannot create knowledge. Individuals create knowledge, not organizations.

When an individual is in the initial stages of developing a new idea, he or she may

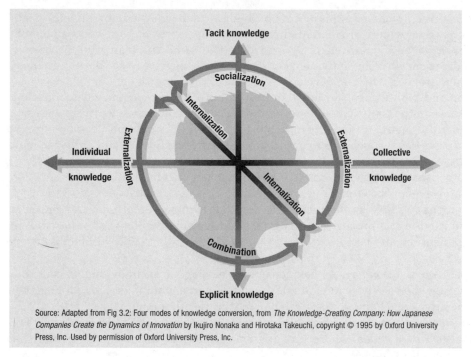

Figure 1

not be able to articulate it effectively. By working in isolation, this individual may develop the idea into an explicit form. For example, the lone inventor working in his garden shed may, in time, develop a patentable innovation. Within organizations, individuals can draw on the insights and expertise of their colleagues when developing new ideas. Knowledge creation in this context can be seen as a process for converting tacit and individualized knowledge into explicit and collective knowledge.

Ikujiro Nonaka and Hirotaka Takeuchi, in their landmark book *The Knowledge-Creating Company*, identify four inter-related processes by which knowledge flows around the organization and transmutes into different forms (*see* Figure 1).

Socialization is the process of communicating tacit knowledge that resides within individuals to a broader organizational context. Individuals share experiences, demonstrate skills, and model behavior in such a way that they can be observed and copied by others within the organization. The apprenticeship model is formalized socialization, but the socialization process of tacit knowledge transfer may also occur at an unconscious level.

Externalization is the process of converting tacit knowledge into explicit concepts. This can, for example, take the form of models and metaphors, which express a subtle, complex concept in a highly simplified form.

The diagram is, in itself, an example of externalized knowledge.

Externalization may occur at an individual level or at a collective level, depending on the range of constituents involved in the process. Once an individual has externalized his or her tacit knowledge, it is more easily combined with the knowledge of others. Combination is the process of analyzing, categorizing, and integrating the explicit knowledge of a set of individuals in order to create new explicit knowledge, which can be disseminated more widely within the organization.

These three processes explain how individual tacit knowledge transmutes and flows until it is widely disseminated around the organization, but it does not fully explain how new knowledge is created. The final link in the process is internalization, whereby individuals absorb explicit knowledge so that it becomes a firm foundation on which to develop new forms of tacit knowledge.

On an individual level, internalization is akin to the concept of unconscious competence in the context of skill acquisition. For example, when learning a musical instrument or sport, we first have to absorb formal training and develop our own basis of expertise through practice before we have the confidence and ability to move on to the next stage in the skills-acquisition process.

If we accept the logic of Nonaka and Takeuchi's stages in knowledge creation, what can we do to encourage the process?

They identify five key conditions. The first is *intention*. Senior management must be committed to accumulating, exploiting, and renewing the knowledge base within the organization, and be able to create management systems that will facilitate this process.

The second is *autonomy*. As new ideas first develop at an individual rather than organizational level, those individuals must be given maximum scope to follow their own initiatives and explore unexpected opportunities that emerge.

This process of exploration can be further encouraged by the third condition. This they call *creative chaos*, where flux and crisis cause us to reconsider established precepts at a fundamental level.

The fourth is *redundancy*. This means that knowledge should not be rationed (or hoarded). Instead, opportunities should actively be provided for even unrelated individuals to exchange knowledge.

The final condition is *requisite variety*. In order to respond creatively to changing conditions, an organization's internal diversity must match the variety and complexity of the external environment in which he or she is operating.

A skeptic would sound a note of caution. The knowledge-creating company that Nonaka and Takeuchi describe is far removed from the organizational reality that most of us experience.

Chaos and crisis, for example, are just as likely to stifle as to promote creativity, by provoking anxiety and insecurity. Here the term "redundancy" will have a very different meaning from that envisioned by Nonaka and Takeuchi. Employees are unlikely to forget that the last major management fad, business process reengineering, was associated with massive restructuring and large-scale unemployment.

What is known

What do we really know about management knowledge? The truthful answer is, not a lot, yet. We just know that we ought to be doing it better. Although 78 percent of major US companies surveyed claim to be moving toward becoming knowledge based, the majority are in practice "nowhere near" achieving it, according to Huseman and Goodman, who conducted the survey.

Certainly, the phenomenal success of the Nonaka and Takeuchi book has helped to create the "intention" within organizations, but it may take many years to convert rhetoric into reality.

There are no short cuts, in spite of what some management consultants and writers might suggest.

In seeking to understand how to manage and manipulate knowledge, writers run the risk of being either grossly simplistic or frustratingly vague.

Much of what management consultants currently sell under the guise of knowledge management is simply information management rebranded.

The problems arise because we are trying to incorporate the inherently ambiguous, fluid, and abstract concept of knowledge into mental models, which have been shaped by highly structured, static, and systematized forms of organizations.

As Thomas Bertels and Charles Savage (*see* Suggested further reading) comment, the dominant logic of the industrial era is a barrier to reaching an understanding of the knowledge era: "Perhaps we are again standing with Galileo, realizing the contradictions of conventional wisdom and reaching for a new order." Others might say, perhaps not.

Certainly, companies seeking to become knowledge based have embarked on a journey with no clear destination and only a rudimentary understanding of the preliminary stages. No doubt they will encounter many setbacks and false trails. Academics can only really begin to perform meaningful research into knowledge management by observing the discovery process undertaken by just such companies.

Let us therefore hope that knowledge management does not come to be considered as another gimmick destined for the junk heap of management fads. Potentially it is far too important and exciting for that.

Summary

Much of what consultants are selling as knowledge management is, says **Laura Empson**, simply a re-branding of information management. So before paying someone to install a knowledge-management system, it is legitimate to ask if knowledge can really be managed at all. The author here articulates the important difference between tacit and explicit knowledge, describes some of the difficulties associated with collecting and distributing knowledge throughout the organization, and suggests some simple ways of encouraging its transfer. Companies seeking to be knowledge based should persevere – KM does not deserve to be remembered as the latest management fad.

Suggested further reading

Bertels, T. and Savage, C. (1998) "Tough questions on knowledge management," in von Krogh, G., Roos, J.L. and Kliene, D. (eds) *Knowing in Firms: Understanding, Managing, and Measuring Knowledge*, London: Sage.

Blackler, F. (1995) "Knowledge, knowledge work, and organizations: an overview and interpretation," *Organization Studies*, 16 (6).

Davenport, T. and Prusak, L. (1998) *Working Knowledge: how Organizations Manage What They Know*, Boston, MA: Harvard Business School Press.

Empson, L. "Fear of exploitation and fear of association: Impediments to knowledge transfer in mergers between professional services firms." To appear in *Human Relations (Special Issue): Knowledge Management in Professional Services Firms*, Empson, L. (ed.), forthcoming.

Grant, R. (1996) "Toward a knowledge-based theory of the firm," *Strategic Management Journal*, 17, Special Issue.

Huseman, R. and Goodman, J. (1999) *Leading with Knowledge: the Nature of Competition in the 21st Century*, Thousand Oaks, CA: Sage.

Nonaka, I. and Takeuchi, H. (1995) *The Knowledge-Creating Company: how Japanese Companies Create the Dynamics of Innovation*, New York: Oxford University Press.

Recreating the company: four contexts for change

by Laurence Capron, Will Mitchell, and Joanne Oxley

In today's competitive environments managers constantly have to recreate their companies, drawing new knowledge from both internal and external sources. The starting point for such changes is dynamic leadership and highly capable people throughout the organization. However, even the best and brightest need to choose modes of change that suit a particular context, and then manage the change process in a way that suits these modes.

This article outlines the four primary modes for changing businesses: internal development, discrete resource exchange, interorganizational alliances, and business acquisitions. Our research, along with that of colleagues, suggests that these four change modes suit different change contexts, each offering unique advantages as well as raising particular risks. In addition, each change mode offers organizational processes and incentives that fit the mode the company has chosen for gaining new knowledge.

Figure 1 summarizes our core framework. We start by assessing internal development, which is the first mode that people usually consider when they recognize the need for change. This assessment serves as a useful benchmark for analyzing the progressively more complex external modes, including discrete

Change mode	Superior change context	Mode advantages	Mode risks	Key processes	Key incentives
Internal development	Relevant resources exist within the company	• Speed • Coordination • Protection	• Irreversible commitments • Path dependence • Low-powered incentives	Cross-functional coordination	Change-focussed individual and group rewards
Discrete resource exchange of people and physical assets	Active market for new resources	Low cost & low confusion via targetted resource acquisition	• Limited availability • Limited coordination of external exchange • Limited protection of on-going exchanges	• External search • Internal integration	• Search rewards • Integration rewards
Inter-organizational alliances	Moderate market failure for resource acquisition	• Shared costs • Quick access to complex resources • Hands-on inter-organizational coordination • Partially retractable commitments • Bilateral protection	• Coordination confusion • Internal conflict • Proprietary loss	• Partner search systems • Interfirm coordination • Internal commitment • Loss protection	• Aligned partners' incentives • Aligned internal incentives
Business acquisitions	High market failure for resource acquisition	• Extent of resource acquisition • Depth of integration • Protection	• High cost • Slow integration • Low-powered incentives	• Pre-acquisition search system • Post-acquisition reconfiguration systems	Aligned internal incentives of new employees and existing employees

Figure 1

resource exchange, alliances, and acquisitions. A comparative analysis highlights the main trade-offs involved in selecting modes. In practice, of course, it is common to combine some or all of them in order to make necessary changes.

Internal development

Change via internal development involves building on existing resources, such as technical skills, production processes, marketing systems, and managerial expertise. Internal development is most feasible if a company already possesses the needed resources and must "simply" recombine these to implement the desired change. A common example is using an existing distribution system in one market to sell an existing product, typically after refining product features and production techniques to suit the new market. Another example is developing an incrementally different version of an existing good or service to sell in a current market segment.

The key advantages of internal development are speed, coordination, and protection from competitors. First, internal development offers a quick way of undertaking changes when a company possesses the relevant resources, because its people already have substantial knowledge and understanding of the situation. Second, the shared knowledge and common communication "code," although often taken for granted and frequently unnoticed within the company, helps ensure coordination of the change activities. This coordination is particularly important when changes involve the active, on-going participation of many people and functional areas. Consequently, a key organizational process supporting change through internal development is cross-functional coordination. Effective cross-functional coordination creates communication channels, providing people who have different skills and responsibilities with the ability and motivation to work together. Third, internal development also helps protect the proprietary value of change activities, because existing resources and new resource combinations stay within the company. Hence, internal development offers the potential both to protect existing resources and develop new proprietary resources.

The downside of internal development is that it is often costly and difficult to develop resources that are new to an existing repertoire of skills. Cost issues arise because internal development requires irreversible commitments for new resources that have uncertain value. These and other uncertainties can result in powerful inertia, leading in turn to a general unwillingness or inability to envision and enact change outside currently accepted arenas. Moreover, breaking through this inertia is difficult, because internal development often suffers from what institutional economists refer to as "low-powered incentives." Low-powered incentives arise because individual change agents in a company rarely benefit from the full value of a change. Therefore, managers cannot rely on economic incentives to offset the natural reluctance of employees to overturn the status quo.

Overcoming reluctance to change is the key incentive issue for the internal development mode. It is rarely possible to ensure that change agents within a firm garner most of the benefits of an internal change. However, the closer that salaries, bonuses, and promotions are tied to change activities and outcomes, the more people will commit to the change and the cross-functional work required. We refer to these ties as change-focussed incentives. Change-focussed incentives provide rewards for successful change outcomes, as well as for participation in change activities. Change-focussed incentives must address the contributions of both individuals and cooperative groups. An organizational culture that promotes experimentation and change can inject supportive non-economic incentives. Nonetheless, since radical change is almost always more difficult to achieve through internal development than through external modes, companies often turn to one of the external modes, which we examine next.

Discrete resource exchange

Changing via discrete resource exchange involves acquiring the specific resources you need in order to undertake a change. Such exchanges commonly involve new hires, equipment, and business systems. Discrete resource exchange is most appropriate when an active market exists for the needed resources, providing ample opportunities to evaluate available alternatives and negotiate reasonable terms.

Discrete resource exchange is the simplest of the external change modes and the first mode that companies should consider when searching for resources outside the company. Discrete resource exchange allows a company to target specific resources, focus resource-acquisition expenditures, take advantage of specialized suppliers, and limit the need for extensive coordination.

However, discrete exchange is not a panacea. Several types of "market failure" often limit the effectiveness of this change mode. Market failures due to asymmetric information arise when a partner is concerned that the other party might take advantage of its information. Market failures due to bilateral lack of information arise when both parties lack critical information. Market failures due to institutional illegitimacy arise when a company lacks sufficient credibility in a market to attract necessary resources. An example of this last form of market failure arose in recent discussions that we held with several telecommunications companies that are transforming their corporate client businesses. Managers of the companies told us that they would prefer simply to hire people with the right technical and marketing skills for their new businesses – but even with the offer of higher salaries and benefits, they cannot always do so. Consequently, the companies either have attempted to change internally, slowly developing the skills of existing employees, or have allied with or acquired other businesses that possess the necessary skills.

Even when a potential market for the needed resources exists, discrete exchange may not work if buyers and sellers of resources cannot agree on terms of exchange, either because of asymmetric information or bilateral lack of information. Both types of market failure arise when there is substantial uncertainty about the costs and implications of extracting and transferring a needed resource. Consider the case of a company purchasing a distribution system from another company for entry into a new market. This exchange requires separating the system from the original company's activities and adapting it to the purchaser's products and customers. The extraction and adaptation processes may be slow and difficult, requiring substantial coordination between seller and buyer. Furthermore, this on-going coordination can raise concerns about the level of dependency created between the companies, and whether the relationship will be managed equitably.

Two processes are particularly important to effect change via discrete resource exchange: external search systems and internal integration systems. External search systems identify the best available resources, whether the resources are physical assets, business systems, or people with skills that best suit the needed change. In part, external search systems also help a company learn that a change is necessary. In our view, though, most companies know when they need to change because they learn quickly through contact with customers, suppliers, competitors, and through the many forms of business media. More difficult than simply recognizing the need to change is the creation of search systems that help to identify and acquire the resources that companies need for the changes. The most successful are those that develop linkages with knowledge bases that lie well outside existing activities.

Internal integration systems are critical complements to external search processes. Simply identifying and obtaining needed resources is only the beginning of a change process driven by discrete resource exchange. Success demands that new resources be effectively integrated with existing resources. Examples of internal integration systems include individual and group training, as well as the on-going cross-functional coordination mechanisms that we described for internal development.

The need for external search and internal integration systems also creates a need for additional incentive systems, which must complement the change-focussed incentives for internal change. Indeed, the change-focussed rewards for discrete exchange must include responsibility and compensation for search and integration activities. A particular issue to watch for in designing a reward system is the "not-invented-here" syndrome. Employees rewarded primarily for new internal developments, particularly in technological areas, are unlikely to initiate or cooperate with effective external modes of change.

Interorganizational alliances

Interorganizational alliances represent the third mode of change. There are many such relationships, ranging from product licenses to complex joint ventures, partnerships, and research consortia. Alliances may involve two or more companies, or relationships between companies and social organizations such as universities and government agencies. Alliances are most likely to be effective when the resources you need for a change face a moderate degree of market failure.

Alliances offer several strengths. First, they allow companies to share development costs and other costs of change, so long as the change activities create resources that more than one of the partners can use. Second, they offer both short-term and long-term access to resources embedded in other organizations through interorganizational coordination mechanisms. This interorganizational coordination is especially important when both or all partners must change their existing resources to achieve needed changes at either company. Alliances also offer the potential for creating protective mechanisms that extend well beyond the simple hands-off market contracts available for discrete resource exchange. In addition to simple contracts, alliance partners can undertake equity investments in the alliance or each other, create forums for resolving disputes without litigation, or otherwise credibly commit to adjust terms of the agreement in an equitable way. Such protection mechanisms reinforce the intrinsic trust in each partner's good intentions.

A third potential strength of alliances is their flexibility, as companies can turn back from an unsuccessful change attempt more easily than they can when change is internal. However, it is important to remember that alliance activities rapidly create a substantial degree of irreversible business commitment. Moreover, trying to "pass off" risks to an alliance partner without appropriate compensation is rarely effective.

Alliances also generate substantial challenges. First, coordination confusion may arise between partners, either because the parties have conflicting strategic objectives or because they fail to understand each other's needs. Second, internal conflicts can arise when employees whose work is affected by alliance activities do not buy into the objectives for the alliance. Third, alliances invariably create some risk of proprietary loss, because a company is committing its resources to activities that involve another party with strategic autonomy. Even if a company selects a trustworthy partner, describes needed coordination systems, encourages internal buy-in, and creates contractual and organizational protection mechanisms, some risk of intercompany confusion, conflict, and proprietary loss will remain. Such risks become increasingly strong as market failures rise.

Effective use of alliances requires a mixture of the processes and incentives that internal development and discrete resource exchange require. Other key alliance processes include partner search, intercompany coordination, internal commitment, and proprietary loss-protection systems. Partner search systems identify potentially trustworthy allies with needed resources and determine appropriate initial conditions for an alliance agreement. Intercompany coordination systems involve careful attention to the formal and informal means by which people from the allied parties work together, exchange information about general objectives and specific actions, and learn about each other's capabilities.

The internal conflicts that alliances generate prompt the need for internal commitment systems and proprietary loss-protection systems. Effective internal commitment systems emphasize extensive communication of both the objectives of the alliance and the opportunities that the alliance will create for existing units and people. The systems must then realign incentives accordingly. Creating loss-protection systems, on the other hand, involves identifying the points at which you may lose proprietary information and market opportunities to your partner. You can then specify contractual terms and organizational commitments that will limit the potential losses. Close attention to loss protection is important both at the beginning of an alliance and as it evolves, disclosing unexpected opportunities and risks.

Business acquisitions

Business acquisitions are the fourth change mode. Business acquisitions involve purchases of entire corporations or business units. Acquisitions become increasingly attractive when market failures increase beyond a level that can be worked out in an alliance. Acquisitions provide a quick way to obtain an extensive set of new resources, while offering control over integration and protection of the resources needed to undertake a change.

However, acquisitions can create substantial disadvantages. Outbidding other potential acquirers, for example, can drive the price of an acquisition much higher than anticipated. Even more importantly, post-acquisition integration costs often far outweigh even the most optimistic expectations of pre-acquisition analysts. Vast amounts of money and time can be spent on extracting and adapting resources, eliminating unwanted resources from the target business, and disposing of resources that you no longer need in your existing business. The notion of the "winner's curse" commonly arises in discussions of acquisitions, as the successful buyer discovers the true difficulties and costs of post-acquisition integration. As with internal development, acquisitions face the issue of low-powered incentives.

Nonetheless, despite their costs and difficulties, acquisitions are a critically important means by which companies change. Indeed, this may be the only feasible way of changing when companies need rapid access to a complex set of resources that would take a long time to develop internally, and a level of business integration that an interorganizational alliance cannot achieve.

As with alliances, business acquisitions call for a mixture of the processes and incentives needed for internal development and discrete resource exchange, as well as additional processes and incentives. The two key acquisition processes are pre-acquisition search systems and post-acquisition reconfiguration systems. Pre-acquisition search systems identify relevant targets and determine appropriate prices. Unfortunately, this pre-acquisition process is often the main focus of acquisition activity, leading many companies to struggle with the post-acquisition process. Post-acquisition reconfiguration systems must identify needed resources and then coordinate the redeployment of resources to and from the target and acquiring businesses. In addition, they must identify unneeded resources in both the target and acquiring business and find the most valuable new uses for them, and either apply the resources to new business opportunities or divest them. A critical point here is that successful change via acquisition typically requires substantial reconfiguration of both target and acquirer to overcome the costs and difficulties of acquisition.

Like alliances, acquisitions require internal alignment of incentives. Alignment involves identifying and rewarding the changes that you want from new employees coming from the target company. Realignment of incentives also extends to existing employees who may need to change their activities to combine with the resources that the target has provided. Far too many acquisitions fail to realize the full benefits of change activities because employees from the target and acquiring businesses continue to view themselves as members of their original organizations, and to act as though they still work for independent organizations, often for many years after "integration" supposedly has occurred.

Conclusion

We have described four modes of change, their advantages and disadvantages, and the processes and incentives needed to support change in each mode. The relative weight of the advantages and disadvantages depends, of course, on the competitive environments in which you operate, the characteristics of your business, and the changes you face. Nonetheless, our contact with business managers has convinced us of the power of analyzing the specifics of a particular change context within the more general framework proposed here.

We end by reiterating a point we made earlier. Successful change requires recognition of the need to change and an organizational commitment to the change. We believe that recognizing the need to change is the easy part. Identifying appropriate change modes and then committing to change implementation is much harder, particularly in large and complex business organizations. Managers who take a systematic approach to assessing the change modes that best suit their change context and creating processes and incentives to suit the modes they choose will be the successful change agents of tomorrow.

Summary

There are four basic ways to change a business: internal development; discrete resource exchange (that is, obtaining specific outside resources); interorganizational alliances; and business acquisitions.

Recognizing the need for change is the easy part, say **Laurence Capron**, **Will Mitchell**, and **Joanne Oxley**. Identifying the most appropriate change mode and committing to its implementation is much harder, particularly in large and complex business organizations. The authors set out the advantages and disadvantages of each mode and the context in which it is likely to be successful. They suggest that managers who are good at dealing with change adopt a systematic approach, matching processes and incentives.

Suggested further reading

Capron, L. and Mitchell, W. (1999) "The impact of relevant resources and market failure on four modes of business change," University of Michigan Business School working paper, May.

Capron, L., Dussauge, P. and Mitchell, W. (1998) "Resource redeployment following horizontal mergers and acquisitions in Europe and North America, 1988–1992," *Strategic Management Journal*, 19: 631–61.

Oxley, J.E. (1999) "Institutional environment and the mechanisms of governance: the impact of intellectual property protection on the structure of inter-firm alliances," *Journal of Economic Behavior and Organization*, 38: 283–309.

Oxley, J.E. (1999) *Governance of International Strategic Alliances: Technology and Transaction Costs*, Amsterdam: Harwood Academic Publishers.

Strategy and information: time to look out

by Anthony Hopwood

Just as no history of pottery would be complete without mention of Wedgwood, so no history of management would be complete without mention of the company's founder. Josiah Wedgwood was more than a potter; his remarkable gift for strategy and entrepreneurship ensured that the company he founded in the eighteenth century remains synonymous with fine pottery to this day.

Students of strategy today would do well to consider the disparate preoccupations that underlay Wedgwood's genius. He kept abreast of the changing technology of materials and himself engaged in scientific inquiry. The knowledge he acquired enabled him to create innovative products and to transform production technology. Attuned to shifts in aesthetic taste, he reshaped the social significance of dining. He was acutely aware of the shifting social dynamics of a newly emergent bourgeois society, and recognized within those changes the potential to create a new sphere of consumption – and hence of profitability.

Wedgwood was clever, entrepreneurial, successful – and informed. An obsessive analyzer, he invested in understanding and then changing his costs. Ascertaining the changing nature of his sales, he managed them carefully to create a new regime of consumption. Production methods were equally analyzed and changed on the basis of his deep knowledge of them. For Wedgwood, an active concern with information and understanding was a vital ingredient of his strategic stance. He was a prototype for the "reflective practitioner," consciously striving to learn. Knowing and being informed were key components of his approach to management.

That there is nothing inevitable about such a constellation of concerns is illustrated by the Wedgwood of today. The contemporary Waterford Wedgwood, an Irish luxury goods company, is more noted for its traditionalism than its innovative potential. No longer associated with new developments in materials, not obviously attuned to the changing sociology of eating and consumption, and not calling on the design skills of a David Hockney or Damien Hirst, the young British artist, it is more of a self-regarding than an analytical organization. It is as if the links between analysis and information on the one hand, and strategy on the other, have been pulled apart.

The information on which effective strategizing must be based cannot therefore be taken as read (although many companies still seem to treat it that way). It needs to be actively constructed and carefully maintained. Recognizing the importance of getting the link between information and strategy right, this article focusses on two questions:

- What factors constrain the development of an effective informational basis for strategy formulation?
- What is needed for the processes of informing and strategizing to work together in a productive manner?

Informational constraints

The wrong information at the wrong time in the wrong place can clearly have an adverse effect on strategy formulation. Both experience and a growing body of research suggest that the following factors can seriously constrain the development of a proactive information strategy:

- *Too dominant a control orientation.* Control is important, but if corporate information systems and approaches place too exclusive an emphasis on it, other opportunities can be lost. In many corporate information systems too much emphasis is put on history, conformity, and constraint. Information is not allowed to develop a surprise value. Learning is seen as less important than conforming. The organization that operates this way may be efficient, but it is less likely to be effective in the longer term.
- *Performance myopia.* We live in times when performance has become a dominant cultural value, inside and outside organizations. Enormous attention has been paid to measuring outcomes at more and more organizational levels, on more and more dimensions, more and more frequently. Organizations have become observational entities, focussing on the measurable and the quantifiable.

  In the rush to do this, much less emphasis has been put on providing the detailed informational underbelly on which performance advances. Better performance is fine, but how do you get it? The information that reaches the surface in organizations has become unbalanced. It emphasizes what the result is, instead of the more valuable question of how the result has been achieved. But real change requires the latter.

  Take costs, for example. Performance reports focus on the statics of what a company's costs are. Control approaches are similar. A more strategic perspective emphasizes the need for more dynamic understandings that can help to induce change – to make costs what they are not. Why are costs as they are? What can change the level and structure of costs? How do costs relate to other decision areas?

■ *Newly poor behavior*. Such tendencies become visible and worrying when companies face crises. A common response to financial difficulty is to intensify internal information flows. Reports become more detailed, more pervasive throughout the organization, and more frequent. That is fine and often necessary. But if nothing else is done, this only serves to increase the company's internal focus at the very time when it should be facing outward. If your problems are external, in the market place, increased navel gazing is not going to help you. There is a very real danger that the company will become ever more detached from its external environment and consequently fail.

To succeed in such circumstances, companies need to learn more about themselves at the same time that they are learning even more about the external contexts in which they operate. Companies in crisis need to become more information intensive, looking outward as well as inward.

■ *Internal orientation*. As the previous point makes clear, traditional inclinations among information specialists too often result in companies examining themselves rather than their contexts. Costs become more visible than sales revenues – but it is the latter that ultimately tell you more about the group that really matters, namely the company's customers. Financial performance outcomes are given more emphasis than progress in new product introductions, shifts in market position, and changes in market context. Information designers too easily and too frequently forget that strategy involves managing the relationship between the company and its setting. That management requires a company not only to know itself but also to know its competitors, its collaborators, and the market settings in which they operate. The company of today is a company that needs to look out.

New clothes

There is no doubt that practice in the information field is starting to free itself from the constraints just outlined (*see* Figure 1). More attention is at last being given to the needs of strategy formulation. Learning and understanding are beginning to complement control as the driving force behind the supply of information to

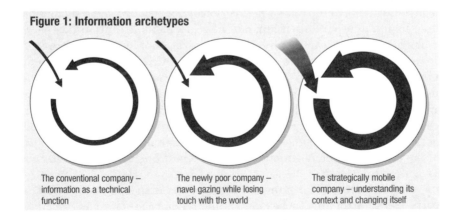

Figure 1: Information archetypes

The conventional company – information as a technical function

The newly poor company – navel gazing while losing touch with the world

The strategically mobile company – understanding its context and changing itself management. Performance measurement is starting to be looked at in more complex ways that can readily be related to strategic – as opposed to just accounting – concerns. And there are encouraging signs that companies are now making the market and its customers more visible and thereby more salient.

But innovations still need to be treated with some caution. Old wine can easily appear in new bottles. Take activity-based costing (ABC), which aims to calculate the true cost of a product or service in terms of all the business processes that have contributed to it. Seemingly, this is an exciting new approach to internal financial reporting. But in practice it still largely operates on the basis of allocations rather than analysis. It still tells you what costs are, rather than trying to help the company make them what they are not. It focusses only on giving the most bureaucratic of insights into why costs are as they are. Although the claims of ABC are often ambitious, the reality is a technique that still has difficulty operating in a strategic rather than an accounting context. I am sure that before too long we may come to see ABC as a technique of the past.

The same may be said for "balanced scorecards," another consultancy-led innovation. These aim to apply performance metrics that capture not only the financial situation but also such things as how the company is regarded by customers, and how innovative it is. But while multiple performance measures may be preferable to one, to orchestrate them through a single report may create as many problems as solutions. A vibrant, successful organization relies on multiple information channels, the balance of which varies across time and space as the nature of the organization's problems shift. To be dynamic, information flows need to have the potential to compete instead of being bureaucratically coordinated.

Both ABC and the balanced scorecard are adaptations of the past. They derive from abstract reasoning, rather than experience and the frontiers of practice. People claim they are better, but offer no convincing evidence that they are. It is not as if successful companies are known to have different costings or balanced scorecards. In fact, they don't. Successful companies have much more innovative approaches – often messier, usually less bureaucratic, sometimes more temporary, and almost invariably linked more directly to practical learning and experimentation. Innovators such as Benetton and Hewlett-Packard are known for the extent to which they invest in temporary, *ad hoc* and multiple information channels.

Emerging trends

With sometimes amazing speed, a number of new developments (*see* Figure 2) are starting to change the way in which information is regarded, managed and deployed as a strategic tool:

- *The diffusion of information expertise.* Where information was once the preserve of the accountant and the IT expert, it is now being much more widely diffused. Accountants know this, and are worried, as they should be. With information being collected, analyzed and used throughout the organization, a form of corporate information democracy is emerging. Information can now be anywhere – in operations, in marketing, in finance, in distribution, in development, and so on. In fact, it is now more likely to be where the action is than where the bureaucrats are. Information, one might say, is starting to come alive. The company is emerging as an informational entity in its own right.

  Such trends offer enormous possibilities for changing the way information

Figure 2: Emerging trends in information

	The conventional company	The strategically mobile company
Location of information expertise	Accounting MIS	Dispersed information expertise
Roles of information	Control	Learning & control
Knowledge being created	Counting outcomes	Understanding causal processes and how to change them
Organizational focus	Internal visibility	External & internal visibility
Time dimensions	Still the past	Nearly always the future
Action orientation	Conformity	Change

permeates corporate life – from operations to strategy. Information designers and users can now be the same people. People who ask questions can often answer them. Because information is more widely diffused, the predominant control orientation of the past is starting to decline. Learning is finally in vogue.

- *Analyzing rather than counting.* This process of diffusion is starting to shape the way information is used in companies, not least strategically. Take sales information. In the past, it was passed through marketing on its way to the accountants. There it was counted to arrive at a revenue figure, plus an allowance for bad debts. And often that was it. Increasingly, it is being recognized that sales provide the informational linkage to understanding the customer – who buys what, where and when. A US mail-order business, for example, was able to identify which customers bought the average product at the earliest time by analyzing sales. Those people now receive new catalogs early, while purchases from suppliers are delayed. The company looks at what the "vanguard" buys and adjusts its purchasing accordingly. Inventories and non-sales are now lower and profits higher. Likewise, UK retail chains are identifying the potential for e-commerce, finding out who repeatedly buys the same things. These companies are using sales information to understand, appeal to, and shape customers' tastes over time. And in the airline sector, which has pioneered revenue management, such analysis drives marketing campaigns and different approaches to customer segmentation.

But in a changing world it is vital to move beyond analyzing what *is*. Even with regard to sales, it is important to push analysis and understanding to the point where it is possible to appreciate what drives change. What *might be* is becoming a more significant focus for information collection and analysis. How are wider cultural, economic, and social changes affecting consumption? How are emerging lifestyles creating new possibilities for consumption? Wedgwood recognized the centrality of such questions more clearly than his successors. In today's more mobile, consumer-oriented companies, the drive for such understanding is the basis on which information and analysis can focus on the future.

Information thereby introduces an important dynamic of change. It takes the company forward. What was once ignored is emerging as a strategic resource. Understanding and inquiry are replacing counting and control. As this happens, (ac)counting is becoming less and less significant.

Similar – albeit slower-moving – trends are observable in the cost area. Counting continues, as the fascination with ABC demonstrates. But more and more companies want to know why their costs are as they are, so that they can change them. Traditional costing does not do that; nor does ABC. What are required are detailed probes, conducted locally by people who know the technology, the product or service, and the market.

Once again, information is being diffused. Bureaucracy is being sidelined. What is usually at stake is combining information, understanding, and specialist management and technical knowledge. Insights emerge dynamically where the action is. Given such developments, accountants have even more to worry about.

- *Sucking information* in. Internal information needs to be interpreted in a wider context, an imperative reflected in popular concerns with benchmarking. Comparisons provide a basis for being uneasy or otherwise with the status quo. They introduce a rationale for learning, for understanding causal relationships, and for making things different. Good comparisons generate action.

Sales are related to market shares, market trends, key competitive products and related products. Costs can be compared not just with the cost levels but also with the cost structure of competitors. Different cost structures can suggest different competitive options.

Informing the future

As the above costing examples illustrate, the focus in the new informational world is on making the future what it otherwise would not be rather than knowing what has happened in the past. Information is needed to act on the world. A new action-oriented dynamic has entered the world of information. Information, strategy, and action now go forward together.

Josiah Wedgwood would have been familiar with all of these ideas, albeit in simpler forms. That his successors may not be should highlight the fact that an effective informational economy needs to be actively created; it is not something that is simply revealed. Although many of the emerging trends might appear obvious, survey after survey suggest that most companies still reside in an informational past.

Take the analysis of sales records – a seemingly obvious area. Even the US is lagging behind in this vital field. A recent survey found that over two-thirds of companies there were failing to explore the knowledge potential that was sitting in their own records. They did not necessarily know which clients to target, where they were gaining from their competitors, and where they were losing to them.

The future company is nevertheless likely to be more information oriented. New technologies are part of the story. But they only provide potential: that potential has still to be recognized and exploited. I sense that recognition and exploitation are more likely to emerge as informational expertise, curiosity, and experimentation are diffused around the company. Rather than having the informational quasi-monopolies of the past, the company of the future will be characterized by a mass of overlapping and conflicting information flows.

The order that emerges from this will be one of process and action – a more market-oriented order – rather than one of bureaucratic form. The future company is likely to be one that will have a multitude of scorecards, the balance between which shifts over time. Dynamic companies require dynamic informational economics, not static bureaucratic ones.

Summary

Too many companies are living in the past when it comes to information, says **Anthony Hopwood**. Instead of using it merely to measure and control internal processes, companies should see information as a means to shape the future and influence market trends. The author highlights bad corporate habits that typically constrain a proactive information strategy – including, controversially, activity-based costing and "balanced scorecards" – but concludes optimistically that a sort of corporate information democracy is developing. Coming business generations are likely to be a mass of overlapping and conflicting information flows.

STRATEGY AND
OPERATIONS/
MANUFACTURING

Contributors

Steve New is lecturer in management studies at Saïd Business School and fellow of Hertford College, Oxford. His research focus is on operations management.

Fiona Murray is a university lecturer in management technology at the Saïd Business School, Oxford, and is currently visiting assistant professor at the Sloan School of Management, MIT. She focusses, among other subjects, on the organization of R&D and the impact of science and technology on industry evolution.

Mari Sako is deputy director of research and the Peninsular and Oriental Steam Navigation Professor of Management Studies (international business) at Saïd Business School, University of Oxford. She is a fellow of Templeton College and focusses on comparative business systems, supply chain management and labor management relations.

William S. Lovejoy is the John Psarouthakis Research Professor in Manufacturing Management and professor and chair of operations management at the University of Michigan Business School. His research is centered on the cross-functional aspects of company operations.

Contents

Introduction

Strategy and operations are separated in many organizations, a division reinforced by the teaching style of many business schools. This module, however, begins with a stirring rebuttal of that notion and of the idea that products, markets, and prices in the right combination can generate a business system that delivers the goods. Those at the top, by contrast, need to dirty their hands in the complexity of operations if they are to take advantage of new strategic opportunities. For example, cutting-edge information systems delivering corporate-wide integration – notably Enterprise Resource Planning – offer huge opportunities to secure competitive advantage through superior operational skill, though companies need to consider whether they should use centralized or decentralized management control mechanisms. The module concludes with a discussion of "modular" strategies in product design and production with reference to the computer and automobile industries.

Operations strategy: why bosses must dirty their hands

by Steve New

In a famous political squabble Michael Howard, Home Secretary in a former Conservative government in the UK, faced a chorus of calls for his resignation. A series of escapes from high-security prisons had caused massive embarrassment, and the media and opposition ensured that his head was on the block. Was he not ultimately responsible for the parlous state of the nation's penal system? Were not his decisions on funding and staffing the root cause? Howard rebuffed these assertions with an argument that goes to the heart of a major problem in our understanding of management. "Don't blame me," he implied, "I'm policy – and this is an operations problem."

The presumed divide between the strategic and the operational is a vital issue for organizations of all sorts, public and private sector alike. It is central to the very nature of professional management. For many organizations, it reflects an important assumption about the focus of intellectual labor. Strategy = brains, operations = muscle. Strategy specifies, operations delivers. It is a split mirroring the divide identified by Frederick Taylor between planning and execution in the workforce. But does this separation of operations and strategy match the demands of business in the contemporary world?

In a recent interview Robert Lutz, chief executive of Exide Corporation, the automotive battery maker, talked about the need for team leaders on major projects to be some way down the corporate hierarchy. He wanted "people who are sufficiently junior that they understand how the company actually works." What is going on here? How have we reached a point in the development of corporations when seniority is perceived as a barrier to understanding the fundamentals of how operations are supposed to operate?

In this article, I argue against the separation of strategy and operations – although the divide is hardwired into many large organizations, and reinforced by the standard teaching of business schools. I go on to discuss one particular development, the emergence of Enterprise Resource Planning (ERP), which requires the fusion of operations and strategy and makes new assumptions about the jobs of senior managers. First, though, it is worth sketching out some background ideas that link strategy and operations.

The idea that the operational function is of strategic importance has been vigorously argued by a number of leading academics. The two most influential are probably Wickham Skinner and Terry Hill (*see* Suggested further reading). These pioneers have shown that the business of strategy is about much more than selecting the right combination of products, markets, and prices. Macro-level analysis cannot of itself generate a business system that actually delivers the goods.

A key problem, Hill argues, is that "operations people" tend to be psychologically oriented toward making things happen and solving problems. If top management ignores their concerns, operations people, rather than bristling against this neglect, just get on and make the best of things. So, instead of entering a strategic debate about how sales are managed, a factory manager who has been asked to fulfill an unrealistic customer order will work away at trying to make the impossible happen. The cart may be put before the horse, but this horse just treats it as another challenge.

Much work in operations strategy, then, has focussed on "promoting" operations to the realm of strategic decision making, to ensure that operational issues get a fair hearing in the boardroom. Three main issues (although there are others) have framed the way organizations have sought to accomplish this match. They are all to do with the idea that there are trade-offs between variety, inventory, and quality. Following a model of strategic decision making that emphasizes rational analysis, the idea is that senior managers should consider the rewards and penalties of different options and select the operations strategy that best fits the market and the company's own internal capabilities.

Boiling down operations issues in this way makes the analysis easier and allows what seems like a simple and straightforward process of decision making. But this apparent simplicity is deceptive, because the trade-offs the company makes conceal hidden levels of complexity. These can have counter-intuitive results.

Economies of scale

First, organizations have to consider the variety of their product offering – do they want a bespoke product for each customer, or do they want customers to choose from a restricted range of options? The trade-off here seems simple: cost is normally reduced by a higher degree of standardization. The temptation for businesses is always to move in the direction of product uniformity, driven by the compelling logic of economies of scale. After all, did Henry Ford not win in this way, with his famous rallying cry: "Any color as long as it's black"? The answer is of course, yes – until Alfred Sloan of General Motors started offering a wider range of choices more suited to an increasingly fragmented market place.

As a general business problem, this issue is well understood. We all know that there is a difference between a suit from Savile Row, the exclusive London tailoring district, and an off-the-peg item from Marks & Spencer, the UK retailers. There is a world of difference between a meal at Mossiman's, a select London restaurant, and one at McDonald's. The operations issues, though, are not so straightforward. Moving to large-scale production of standardized products may reduce product cost, but it also reduces the flow of information about customer requirements to a company's decision makers.

The scale of investment in infrastructure that such a strategy assumes can tie companies to inflexible production patterns for years. Finally, fickle customers can shift their attention from price to other product characteristics, with the risk that a decision to go for scale leaves a manufacturer high and dry. Trading off volume and variety, then, should only be made after taking into account detailed knowledge of operations and marketing.

The second type of trade-off relates to the way that the operation balances the costs of holding inventory against the advantages of production stability. Long product runs secure economies of scale and reduce time spent flipping from one product to another. But long runs also incur cost in the shape of higher inventory requirements. One of the key lessons from Japanese manufacturing is the high hidden cost of holding stock.

Traditional calculations use an inventory cost based on 1) the cost of working capital, and 2) the immediate expense of warehousing stock. A key insight from the production system of Toyota Motor, the Japanese industrial group, is that this method massively underestimates the true penalty of holding inventory. This is because high inventory levels also affect managerial behavior.

As inventory acts as a buffer between the organization and the uncertainty of its external environment, it tends to disguise problems of reliability and quality in its operations. Surplus inventory hinders the solving of problems. For example, if you operate a low-inventory, just-in-time system, failures by suppliers or equipment can rapidly escalate into a crisis, forcing managers to focus their attention on the root problem. In a system buffered by inventory, however, problems can be shelved rather than solved. As they get worse, the need for inventory buffers becomes even greater. The Japanese production guru Shigeo Shingo describes this as the "narcotic" effect of inventory.

The third trade-off, which also relates to ideas from Japanese management, links the concepts of cost and quality. Traditionally, high quality has meant high cost. Exacting production standards come with a corresponding bill. Japanese experience has led to a reformulation of this problem, in which quality is recast as a measure of how a product or service matches the needs and expectations of the customer, rather than, as it were, the amount of gold plate it involves.

So, while on one score there is an obvious difference in specification between an Aston Martin DB7 and a Toyota Corolla, the latter may well keep its new owners happier than the former. Furthermore, if quality is measured in terms of defects and reliability rather than specification, it is perfectly possible for the cheaper car to beat the more expensive one. As far as product quality goes, the trade-off with cost depends on how the notion of quality is defined.

With process quality, the issue is even more important. Just as Japanese production systems focus on the hidden costs of inventory, so there is a parallel emphasis on the hidden costs of errors, scrap, and waste in the production process itself. Here the relationship between cost and quality seems counter-intuitive. But it may rest on the idea that it is nearly always sensible to invest in preventing quality problems before they arise. Defective production, when all the costs are added up, works out to be surprisingly expensive. So the trade-off between quality of effort and the cost of failure is not straightforward. It needs to be made with a full realization of the extraordinary scope for "prevention better than cure" production economics.

Basis of manufacturing strategy

These three sets of trade-offs form the basis of most work in manufacturing strategy. Decisions about those trade-offs can only be made by a detailed analysis of exactly what it is that secures orders from customers. Approaches to strategy that fail to address these issues run the risk of becoming disconnected from business realities. They fail to exploit competitive advantages that can be opened up in operations. But is even a more expansive approach enough? The emergence of ERP suggests otherwise. It points to a fundamental reconfiguration of the idea of operations strategy.

The last few years have seen an unprecedented growth in the implementation of company-wide information systems that have replaced fragmentary isolated systems. Leading ERP software companies such as SAP, Baan, and Peoplesoft have produced systems that provide support to almost all key aspects of an organization's operations. Of course, the promises these systems make have been the basis of computer salespeople's patter for the last 30 years. Managers are rightly cynical when an IT company dangles before them the prospect of fully integrated systems that "do everything." Technological progress and the standardization of communications and interfaces do, however, mean that systems can now be developed in a relatively stable and scalable framework.

Effective implementation of ERP opens up an incredible range of opportunities for the refinement and improvement of a company's operations. Rather than a static process of analysis that produces the "right" answer, the process of manufacturing strategy becomes instead the continuous application of intelligence to the business processes.

Correctly handled, the ERP systems become tools of unprecedented power for informing process and performance decisions. They also open up the prospect of new product and service offerings to the market. If you have comprehensive company-wide stock systems, why not open these up to the customer? If you can collate performance data at a highly detailed level from plants across the world, why not use this to introduce permanent benchmarking? The increased availability of data improves the scope for analysis. Product offerings can be refined and enhanced, smaller market niches identified, and more complex sets of customer preferences accommodated.

A good riposte to this argument is to point to the many examples of companies that have come seriously unstuck with ERP systems. Surely the promise of these systems has been massively overstated? The answer is that implementation failure with ERP occurs only when computer systems are superimposed on poorly understood business processes, or when insufficient effort has been made to understand the detail of how an organization operates. The potential of ERP is limited by the amount of brainpower that has been expended on fundamental business processes.

Use of internet technology

The ability of companies to manage product variety changes as the costs of coordinating production with customer needs rise and fall. Using internet technology, for example, companies are able to ameliorate the risks of large-scale production. Similarly, management of inventory becomes easier if you have effective information systems that enable the organization to hold only that which is needed. This is much more than having a system that simply logs stock levels; the new information systems allow a sophistication of control and analysis that simply has not been available before. In 1999 Ford announced that it planned to trade used car parts over the internet, a development that will both give the organization more influence over the secondary car market, and meet environmental and recycling objectives. As for the third trade-off, the ability to account more accurately for the costs of quality by more systematic tracking of performance is a major opportunity.

All these opportunities share a common theme. The arrival of ERP systems opens the way for a quantum shift in the sophistication of operations management. The role of operations in the formulation of corporate strategy also becomes much stronger. The problem, however, is that as long as operations issues continue to be perceived as too detailed or too mundane for high-level strategic thinkers, the potential for improvement is likely to be squandered. The only viable solution to this conundrum is a wholesale recasting of the intellectual responsibilities of those at the top of the organization so that they are mandated to grapple with the challenge of understanding the increasingly complex systems in their charge.

The conclusion, therefore, is that the separation of strategy and operations is not tenable in the new business environment. The arrival of information systems that can genuinely deliver corporate-wide integration means that the possibility of securing opportunities for competitive advantage through superior operational skills is too great to be ignored. The challenge for organizations is to grasp the complexity of their operations at the most senior level. Senior management can no longer be left to stand aloof from the detail, and pass the buck for failures in operational issues.

Summary

In today's business environment, strategy and operations can no longer be separated, argues **Steve New**. Cutting-edge information systems delivering corporate-wide integration – notably the emergence of Enterprise Resource Planning (ERP) – offer huge opportunities to secure competitive advantage through superior operational skill. The author charts the ways in which companies have historically made the link between boardroom "brains" and shopfloor "muscle." He concludes, however, that those at the top need to make new effort to grasp the complexity of operations.

Suggested further reading

Clark, K. (1996) "Competing through manufacturing and the new manufacturing paradigm: is manufacturing strategy passé?" *Production and Operations Management*, 5 (1): 42–58.

Hayes, R.H., Pisano, G. and Upton, D. (1996) *Strategic Operations: Competing Through Capabilities*, New York: The Free Press.

Hill, T. (1995) *Manufacturing Strategy: Text and Cases*, London: Macmillan.

Skinner, W. (1978) *Manufacturing in Corporate Strategy*, New York: John Wiley.

Modular strategies in cars and computers

by Mari Sako and Fiona Murray

The automobile industry was the source of major strategic thinking throughout the twentieth century. Ford's moving assembly line, for example, first standardized work, while Taiichi Ohno's Toyota Production System and, more recently, lean production techniques were important managerial innovations. The design, manufacture, and distribution of the automobile capture the key strategic challenges associated with a complex and technologically sophisticated product, with the result that companies in other sectors have sought inspiration and lessons. Now the focus of many European and American manufacturers is on so-called modular strategies in product design and production. This article assesses the success of this new development and its value as a strategic weapon in the search for new sources of competitive advantage in manufacturing industries.

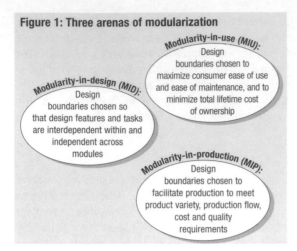

Figure 1: Three arenas of modularization

Modularity-in-use (MIU): Design boundaries chosen to maximize consumer ease of use and ease of maintenance, and to minimize total lifetime cost of ownership

Modularity-in-design (MID): Design boundaries chosen so that design features and tasks are interdependent within and independent across modules

Modularity-in-production (MIP): Design boundaries chosen to facilitate production to meet product variety, production flow, cost and quality requirements

What is a modular strategy?

A modular strategy is a strategy that leverages the advantages of modular product architecture. A modular product is a complex product whose individual elements have each been designed independently and yet function together as a seamless whole. This kind of product has been rapidly adopted in the computer industry, where the modules might be thought of as including hard disk drives, operating systems, and microprocessors. By adopting a modular strategy, International Business Machines was able to achieve dramatic reductions in the lead times for designing and manufacturing its System 360. However, the definition and subsequent standardization of the modules led to the success of Microsoft and Intel, as value was captured not by the architects of a modular strategy but by the modular suppliers. Nevertheless, the distribution of the profits resulting from the adoption of a modular strategy is driven by different industry-specific characteristics, as the following contrast between computers and automobiles shows (*see* Figure 1).

Drivers of modularity: computers v. autos

The main impetus toward modular computer products was modularity in use: consumers were demanding compatibility, upgradability, and retention of elements of their existing computer systems. This starting point led to much investment of time and effort in the creation of global design rules and standardized interfaces between modules. Modular product architecture, in turn, led to a modular business organization with independent design teams. In the US at least, the eventual disintegration of the industry into modular suppliers was facilitated by the availability of venture capital for start-ups and the mobility of technical labor between firms.

By contrast, in the car industry the impetus to adopt modules lay in production, rather than demand. The attraction of modular production systems is that they reduce the complexity, capital assets, and cost of assembly. In modular assembly, production tasks are broken down into separable elements that can be carried out independently. The final product is then assembled from these large subassemblies. While Fiat adopted an in-house modular production system in the 1980s in order to increase automation in the face of labor problems, it can also be used as a step toward the outsourcing of production. Outsourcing shifts complexity, assets, and

Figure 2: Why create modules?

	Computers	Automobiles
Catalyst for modularity	MIU MID	MIP MID
Organizational adaptation	Modular design teams & start-ups first, outsourcing later	Outsourcing, tiering & consolidation of suppliers
Labor markets	Mobility in technical labor market	Wage differentials between OEM and suppliers
Capital markets	Venture capital for start-ups	Investment banking advice for M&A

cost to suppliers. The next logical step after modularity in production is to design products with modularity in mind. Modular design separates the design task into separable units, which may or may not follow the same elements as the separable production units. These clearly defined product boundaries also present the ultimate manufacturers with considerable opportunities to outsource the design process and reduce the complexity of the design activity (*see* Figure 2).

In response to this pressure from vehicle manufacturers, suppliers in the automotive industry are consolidating to create a broader and deeper base of technical knowledge and financial resources. Companies such as Delphi Automotive Systems (formerly General Motors' parts division) have expanded their technical capabilities to incorporate fiberoptics, multimedia, energy systems, and electronics. Some suppliers are changing their business strategy in order to provide much greater levels of technical expertise than they have done traditionally, so as to become involved in the design of modules. These companies are also increasingly involved in the production of modules and subassemblies. Rather than shipping components to the manufacturer's plant, they are setting up subassembly product lines that are off site but typically only a few kilometers away from the final assembly site. In Alabama, for example, Delphi assembles the cockpit for the Mercedes M class car with a 120-minute window for assembly and delivery on to the final assembly line. Until it reaches the line, the cockpit is still owned by Delphi and it is Delphi that remains responsible for its quality.

In short, there are two quite distinct stages in the shift toward modular products. The first is to separate the product into discrete modules either for design or for production. The second is to consider whether to outsource these activities to suppliers. The separation of the car into distinct production elements is relatively straightforward. Indeed, there has been an on-going process of simplification and separation since Henry Ford first adopted the principle of standardized work on his moving assembly lines. However, the design process is more difficult to separate because the car is at once a group of physically contiguous subassemblies and a series of systems – climate control, safety, electronics, and so on. System integration is essential to performance and yet systems may criss-cross physical subassemblies to a degree that renders their separate design almost impossible without sacrificing performance.

The contrast with computers is instructive in comparing the strategic outcomes of creating modular products. As noted earlier, the main catalyst for modular computer products was modularity in use. Design work at IBM strove to meet this goal. IBM found that the electromechanical system was susceptible to separation without significant performance reduction (although it is interesting to note that the most high-performance computers are not designed with modular hard drives, operating systems, etc.). Modularity in production was not a major driving force in the computer industry, and IBM's conscious decision to outsource the development and the production of the operating system to Microsoft and the chip to Intel for personal computers came much later than its decision to adopt a modular product architecture.

Despite significant differences between the two industries, the IBM experience also raises important lessons in the possible consequences for industry organization, industry power, and profits that can come from the changing shape of product architecture. The value added from computers shifted rapidly from the overall product architect, namely IBM, to the designers and producers of modular system elements, such as Intel and Microsoft. Are the same trends likely in the auto industry and in other industries? And what are the strategies that the auto manufacturers and suppliers ought to follow?

Modular strategy and competitive advantage

The strategic choice facing original equipment manufacturers or OEMs is whether to remain integrated or to become modular. Integrators will retain control of the entire design and production processes. They will continue to make a wide range of investments in both capabilities. Close control over the entire design process gives an integrator the advantage of retaining technological leadership. This will be hard to manage if technologies become standardized and controlled by dominant module suppliers. An integrator will also control the entire production process and therefore has control and oversight of quality and complexity.

The problems with this strategy are the problems that OEMs typically face as the automobile comes to incorporate a wider range of technologies – overly stretched R&D, problems associated with technical diversity, costly capital investment in new plants, and complex production. One step toward alleviating these problems is to retain technical control of R&D and design, but to shift to highly modular production processes with a considerable reliance on suppliers. Mercedes seems to fit this model. It conducts substantial R&D in-house while shifting production complexity to large suppliers who produce modules and make investments close to final assembly plants.

Modularizers lie at the other end of the spectrum. They will shift the complexity of production to suppliers and in so doing also follow a path toward modular design that facilitates modular production. They will then increasingly rely on suppliers to provide not only production expertise but also design and technical expertise. Modularizing OEMs will lose technical leadership and may risk undermining the source of value added as technical control shifts to the suppliers. OEMs' retention of "shadow engineering" in-house attests to this fear. However, modularizers can retain value through brand, customer service, product styling and innovative overall product concepts (the Smart car, Mercedes' entry into the small car sector, is a good example here). They can also retain value through global presence, facilitated by the reduced investment that outsourcing enables them to bear. In fact, modularizers might be primarily interested in adopting modules as a cost-cutting or asset-minimizing strategy.

To summarize the OEM's strategic choice, sustainable profits come from the control of assets and market position. Competitive advantage may derive from a number of sources, including technological innovation, standard setting, and brand management. But in the shift toward modularization, the source of control is not yet clear in the global auto industry. It is too early to say whether there has been a decisive shift in the balance of power within the industry.

Where do these strategies leave the suppliers? We often think of company strategies in isolation from the rest of the industry. But in fact, supplier and OEM decisions are inextricably linked. Major European and US suppliers are making active decisions to pursue a modular strategy. This means broadening the range of their technical skills, and making investments in design and system capabilities and R&D, in order to be able to bring a unique range of design concepts to the table well in advance of specific design competitions. For these strategies to pay off, modular suppliers must first target the modularizing OEMs. They will be their early customers.

If modular suppliers start to own intellectual property that can shape the industry, they will have greater leverage over the integrators. The reason that IBM was forced to abandon the operating system market was because the supplier of the operating system "module" – Microsoft – owned the industry standard. Only a few suppliers, however, can earn their living by designing modules and setting standards. Whilst a first-tier module supplier that trades directly with OEMs can earn higher profits than lower-tier suppliers, the latter may be component suppliers that have a separate competitive advantage in the shape of its focussed R&D and specialist knowledge. Just as an OEM integrator requires the cooperation of specialist component suppliers to realize its strategy, a modular supplier also relies on strategic alliances with other suppliers that have complementary technical capabilities.

Implementing modular strategies

Modular production has been largely pioneered in greenfield site projects. In the absence of existing constraints from plants, labor contracts, and local suppliers, modular suppliers can be brought together around the production plant, as seen in the Smart plant and VW's Resende plant in Brazil. With brownfield sites, existing physical and human assets inevitably limit the extent to which modularity can be used in production. Union opposition to outsourcing is a typical constraint faced by many OEMs.

Even in a greenfield site, however, modular design needs to be organized by engineers and R&D managers from the core organization. Modular design changes the roles of these individuals, from one of part design and part specification to one of high-level systems integration and module performance specification. Despite recent moves toward integrated product development teams, functional specialization ("chimneys") still exists in some OEMs. For example, the design of a cockpit requires at a minimum technical capabilities in plastic molding, electronics, audio, and electrical engineering. In the same way that greenfield sites have provided an opportunity to experiment with modular production, so modular design at companies such as BMW (with the Z3) and Mercedes (with its M class and Smart models) has tended to start life as innovative non-core projects.

Organizational history necessarily influences how modular strategies are implemented. These different paths ultimately lead OEMs to retain, develop, and discard different capabilities. Take a car manufacturer that has a non-modular product design and whose production is highly vertically integrated. This car company has a choice of three trajectories for moving from the current position to the ultimate position of modular design and outsourced production. The paths are: 1) by designing modules and producing them in-house first before outsourcing them; 2) by outsourcing non-modular components before moving toward modular design; and 3) by simultaneously implementing modular design and outsourcing. Each path leads to a different set of capabilities and performance outcomes for the supply chain.

In the first path, modular design is likely to be adopted only if it brings about significant performance improvements and solutions to problems arising from ergonomics and complexity. By the time modules are outsourced, suppliers would benefit from the solutions found by the car manufacturer. In the second path, outsourcing rather than modularization is the initial driver, and it is unclear whether the car manufacturer or the suppliers will end up taking a lead in proposing modular design and the integration of components. In the third case, a simultaneous implementation of modular design and outsourced production may not necessarily lead to the reduction of complexity if the task of dealing with complexity is merely passed on from the car manufacturer to the supplier.

Thus, is the overall level of complexity in the supply chain reduced as a result of modularization and outsourcing, or does it remain the same as the car firm externalizes complexity down the supply chain? The answer depends on the boundary of the organization for which the architect has optimized objectives. A car company that produces modules in-house or has solutions to be implemented by suppliers is likely to benefit from an overall improvement as a result of modularization. By contrast, a car firm that outsources modules without an in-house set of solutions may end up not reducing the amount of complexity in the total supply chain and therefore pay more dearly for the modules than if they were produced in-house.

In Japan, the production of components was outsourced a long time ago. But so far, Japanese companies within Japan are generally very cautious about outsourcing modules. While modular assembly is being considered by some OEMs, it is largely kept in-house (i.e., Path 1 in Figure 3 is dominant). In Europe, by contrast, the outsourcing of components is a relatively recent phenomenon, and there is sufficient push by some car manufacturers to outsource modules to suppliers (Path 3 in Figure 3). Also, some existing component suppliers are asked to form a consortium to supply a module (thus completing Path 2).

The global forces that lead to modularization – the need to make large global investments without expanding fixed costs dramatically, and the problems of managing complex global organizations – may well have different implications in different regions. It need not automatically lead, as some commentators argue, to homogeneous managerial styles and industry structures. For example, our research sponsored by the International Motor Vehicle Program (IMVP) shows that in Europe and the United States, suppliers are making significant investments in order to compete as module suppliers. They are spurred on by the demanding requirements of the financial markets and the need to raise their contribution to the value added in automobile development and production. This suggests a possible shift in these regions from adversarial supplier relationships to ones of active

Figure 3: Three paths combining modularization and outsourcing

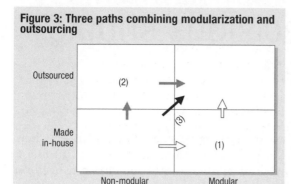

contracting based not solely on price per part but on innovation, speed, and access to intellectual property. In contrast, our Japanese colleagues have found limited willingness on the part of Japanese OEMs to embrace modularization. They prefer instead to stay with the close but hierarchical supplier relationships that they have built up over a long period. However, as they too expand globally and build greenfield sites overseas, Japanese OEMs are also becoming modularizers, or at least production modularizers.

We might therefore see strategies that vary by country of origin of the OEM, with Japanese companies following a different path to US or European ones, predicated on their history and embedded capabilities. However, the pattern is complicated by the geography of operations. In other words, OEMs may follow one strategy in established plants, but use greenfield sites and new car models as opportunities to experiment with modularity in production and/or modularity in design. This leaves a complex tapestry of industrial organization and company strategies. The strategy of OEMs will be contingent on country of origin, country of operation, and country of the suppliers. Profitable suppliers must be sufficiently flexible to offer a range of modular options, from production only to a complete design and production package, catering for multiple OEMs.

Summary

The focus of many European and American companies is currently on "modular" strategies in product design and production. A modular product has individual elements that are designed independently but function together as a seamless whole. In this article, **Mari Sako** and **Fiona Murray** compare the experiences of the computer industry – where modularity was consumer led – with that of the automobile industry – where the impetus for adoption has come from cost and complexity reduction. They discuss the strategic choice between integration and modularization for original equipment manufacturers, note the changing role of suppliers, and conclude by describing recent research highlighting regional differences.

How many decisions should you automate?

by William S. Lovejoy

Major industrial testimonials and rapidly increasing sales of integrating business software systems make clear the virtues of Information-Age solutions to classical business problems. Such systems enable data to be current, uniform, automatically updated, and available to all. Changes in demand patterns or resource availabilities will be automatically translated into the required tactical responses either for the parent company or a supply chain partner. Production will be scheduled for the right amount, at the right time, to maximize customer service with minimal waste in excess capacity and/or inventory. Sales of such software are climbing rapidly, and major consulting firms are advising on their implementation. Clients are already reporting impressive gains in inventory turns, delivery lead times, and on-time delivery.

Do the above statements describe the Enterprise Resource Planning (ERP) and Advanced Planning and Scheduling (APS) products made by the likes of Germany's SAP? No, in fact these claims come from 1970s articles about Materials Requirements Planning (MRP) systems, which, in their extended form (called MRP-II), shared the same vision of optimizing business processes through information technologies. MRP-II promised to integrate business planning, marketing and sales efforts, engineering and product design, finance and accounting, and materials/manufacturing issues through a communication network and an integrated database. Also, MRP-II used a modular approach in which software building blocks could be locked together as the system developed. Over 25 years ago, MRP-II promised what ERP/APS is promising now. Current software vendors may object to these broad characterizations. However, for the purposes of this article the similarities in vision, potential capabilities, and implementation of ERP/APS and MRP-II outweigh their differences. The central issue explored here is how much decision making in a company should be automated. Regardless of which software suite from the above list a company considers, this question is a critical one.

Notwithstanding the enthusiastic performance claims cited above, MRP bashing had become common by the 1980s. Stories spread about long implementation times without the accompaniment of the promised benefits, unsuccessful implementations, and general disillusionment. MRP systems were castigated as costly mistakes. The popular press, which had earlier championed MRP, veered to the other extreme by suggesting that anybody investing in MRP systems was behind the times. The most significant business process development of the 1980s turned out to be just-in-time (JIT), a low-tech, visual management system that depends not on a computer but on humble cardboard cards to schedule production.

As we survey the current testimonials about ERP/APS systems, an intense sense of *déjà vu* is unavoidable. Have we learned anything from the MRP era, and if so what, to help us avoid a similar fate?

The answer is, yes, we can apply some venerable, long-standing concepts of organizational design to the question of what manner of functionality should be embraced in an ERP/APS system. In short, it is almost always desirable to integrate databases so that everybody reads off the same page when discussing critical performance parameters (such as forecasts, shipping dates, accounts, or engineering change orders). This makes information more complete and more readily available. However, integration does not address the decision-making process (how the information is translated into decisions). It is in the process of making decisions that companies need to be very careful about how much of the optimized planning and scheduling solutions they include in their information system upgrades.

ERP systems can stop at the level of integrating databases, or they can be extended with modules that use the information automatically to make decisions. Do you want your software to forecast sales? Maybe and maybe not. Do you want your software to schedule production? Maybe and maybe not. Do you want your software to usurp decisions or simply inform them? Do you want your software to find and implement "optimal" decisions? Maybe and maybe not. The volatility in your competitive environment is the key to understanding how much of the ERP/APS vision to embrace.

It is important to distinguish between decision support and decision making. Feeding information in various forms to a decision maker in order to calibrate and augment his or her judgment can be quite helpful. Replacing human judgment with an automaton may or may not be helpful. Broadly speaking, in rapidly changing environments, decision making should reside with people and not computers, while in stable environments automating decisions makes sense. This is because people are better at creative problem solving, while computers are better at rapid repetition of known and preset plans.

Volatility and control systems

"Volatility" in the competitive environment refers to rapidly changing technologies, competition, and/or market preferences. High-tech companies at the cutting edge of technology in emerging markets operate in a volatile environment. A stable environment is one in which technologies and customer preferences are relatively fixed over a long period of time. Process industries such as paper or steel that supply commodity products with standardized features operate in a relatively stable environment. Process industry representatives striving to compete and survive might not think that their environment is stable, but in relative terms it is. This does not mean that the challenges of management are less difficult, but they are different.

How one organizes the decision-making process in a company depends critically on the level of volatility in the competitive environment. In a stable environment, the major product and process design challenges have already been met and analyzed, repeatedly, and relatively good solutions are already in hand. Capacities, costs, and customers are well understood, and accounting data are more complete. In short, the ingredients needed to model the processes of the company are in place. Under these circumstances, system models can be relatively accurate and optimal or near optimal plans determined. Individual employees are required to implement the recommended actions. This strategy is efficient in a stable environment. If the best response to a given challenge is already known, why would a company tolerate individuals departing from that known solution? Steel and paper companies commonly load their plants and schedule their production using large optimization algorithms. This is appropriate in their relatively stable environment. Taken to its logical conclusion, we would see uninhabited, lights-out factories in which all processes are controlled by computers, with pre-programmed responses for all contingencies.

In volatile environments, many of the challenges that need to be faced are novel, and there is no track record for them within the organization. Capacities, demand rates, revenues, quality levels, and other critical process parameters are unknown and/or constantly changing. The individuals closest to the action are those at the lower levels of the organization, who are in daily contact with customers and the technology. Since these people are best positioned to solve many of the daily challenges the company will face, it is better not to tie their hands with plans based on outdated or incomplete information. Granting employees the latitude to make their own decisions about how best to proceed is the most efficient way to operate, providing those individuals have the ability and incentive to make decisions that are good for the company.

Root out sleeping information

One potential benefit of ERP systems, however, is available to companies regardless of the competitive environment. Makoto Komoto, president of Nippon Otis, a subsidiary of Otis Elevator and part of the US United Technologies group, once said that the key to process improvements was to root out sleeping material and sleeping information. Sleeping material is easy to see and interpret – it is inventory lying around tying up cash. Sleeping information is more difficult to see, but is just as insidious. The supplier division of one multidivisional manufacturer on the US West Coast scheduled its production based on historical orders from the buyer division. The supplier treated orders as if they were being generated by some random demand process, and variations in order levels were buffered with safety stock and surplus capacity. In fact, the orders released to the supplier division were determined by the production schedule in the buyer division, which was known weeks in advance. A simple transfer of production plans from one division to another would have reduced the need for expensive buffer inventory and capacity. This is an example of sleeping information, useful information that is resident in the system but that nobody bothers to communicate. ERP systems that replace islands of data with easy-access, system-wide information will almost always add value, because they will help reduce the levels of such information in an organization.

In short, supplying information to decision makers so that they can make better decisions is different from presuming to make those decisions for them. The latter presumption should be avoided in volatile environments.

"Optimal" decisions

While increasing the integrity and availability of information in an organization is almost always beneficial, the Advanced Planning and Scheduling (APS) modules in ERP systems are more appropriate in stable than volatile environments. Software should not "optimize" (usurping decisions instead of simply informing them) any decision for which the basic parameters (inputs, capacities, quality levels, etc.) are changing. In a rapidly changing world, the decision-making module will be outdated long before anybody using the system realizes it, and the end result will be decisions based on a model of the world that is out of touch with reality. In short, the module will make poor decisions.

I recall visiting an engine plant in Mexico in which some important parts previously sourced from Brazil (with a long lead time) were switched to a local supplier. Nobody updated the MRP system, which continued to order these parts as if they would take many months to arrive. The result was a mountain of inventory in the warehouse, which was not picked up for more than a year. Eventually, the company initiated a JIT effort and the mountain became visible.

While software vendors can and do make clear that the models running a company need to be updated frequently in a rapidly changing environment, for several reasons this is seldom done in practice. First, the optimization models internal to APS systems are not transparent or easily understood. Thus, after the crush of consultants leaves, it is likely that nobody in the organization has the knowledge or inclination to take real ownership of the software. Also, the models are invisible, crunching away behind computer screens, and problems (as in the Mexican engine plant) are often hidden. Finally, since the use of these systems is disempowering (workers simply do as they are told), the tendency is to do what the computer says, no matter how silly it may seem, rather than buck the system. Alternatively, workers can ignore the system and get the job done in spite of it. This can be a rational and constructive action.

When the world changes, somebody has to tell the model that things have changed. Historically, this conceptually simple task has often not been done quickly enough to keep the model relevant. Worse, the underlying model may be incorrect in some fundamental way (as in the assumption of fixed delivery lead times in MRP systems). The end result is a system that gradually (and sometimes not so gradually) deteriorates as an accurate model of the world, because changes in the world outpace changes in the model. Buyers at one Silicon Valley high-tech company knew more about the current market and the state of their suppliers than was coded into the company's MRP system. As a result, they routinely ignored the MRP reports and did their job in a parallel, but more effective manner. The company was left paying for the overhead to keep up an information system that was largely ignored, although nobody would say so too loudly in public.

In 1980s retrospectives of what went wrong with MRP systems, an almost uniformly voiced conclusion was that failures were tied to lack of "worker discipline." In other words, workers were not disciplined enough and kept doing *ad hoc* things that did not conform to the requirements of the model. Workers refused to behave precisely as the system demanded. Rather than being a problem, this was most likely the result of rational workers doing the best they could to help the company in spite of obviously obsolete software recommendations. Over time, the system was circumvented more and more, until parallel informal systems of management made the MRP system unheeded and unneeded.

Volatile environments

Volatile competitive environments call for decentralized control systems that allow employees to exercise their judgment in choosing appropriate actions, based on their richer knowledge of relevant issues. The real challenge in this environment is in allocating the decision rights, and providing the incentives, to make those decisions properly. That is, the formal organization and incentive structure represent the key design issues.

A salesperson whose sales quota is based on his or her forecast will have an incentive to bias the forecast low, regardless of how complete his or her information is regarding actual sales potential. The sales vice-president may recognize these biasses and amplify the forecasts to be consistent with current earnings targets. The manufacturing vice-president may recognize this potential for forecast inflation and, being responsible for excess inventory, reduce the estimates again. This game of mutual deception goes on, with all parties recognizing its nature but unwilling to deviate from it within the existing incentive structure. The cascade of distortions will continue apace even if all share their information seamlessly with others.

The difference between supplying information and making decisions with that information cannot be overemphasized. It is theoretically better for product designers who are working in parallel to have access to the most current design configuration. Real-time updating of design changes can be beneficial. However, there is no guarantee that more complete information will result in better design decisions. In the presence of incentive conflicts among parties on the design team, advanced information systems may accelerate the rate of conflict and gridlock among team members.

ERP systems that make data uniform and readily available to all can add significant value because decentralized decisions can be improved when information is more complete. However, the real challenge in decentralized systems is in organizing the human resources so that they are willing and able to use that information appropriately. That is, the real challenge is in managing people. Advanced information technologies can help, but are not the biggest part of the answer. In volatile environments, the hard task of managing people is still center stage.

Conclusion

The vision portrayed by ERP/APS systems repeats the promises of MRP-II systems in the past, and will eventually fall prey to some of the same criticisms. ERP systems that make data consistent and easily available to all can generally add value to companies. Advanced production/distribution planning and scheduling modules that promise to optimize tactical decisions can add value in relatively stable competitive environments. However, in more volatile environments (rapidly changing technologies and markets), these centralized decision modules should be avoided, because the world will most likely change more rapidly than the internal models, resulting in poor-quality automated decisions.

In volatile environments, more decentralized methods of coordination are appropriate. Subordinates need to be empowered to make and implement decisions, and to be given the information they need to make those decisions. The major challenge is in designing the human organization so that employees have the appropriate incentives to use information wisely. Managers expecting that the technological fix will be sufficient will be disappointed. In a volatile world, human creativity is still the most valuable resource, and managing people remains the greatest challenge.

Summary

Enterprise Resource Planning (ERP) and Advanced Planning and Scheduling (APS) business software systems can undoubtedly add value to companies. But the false promises of MRP-II systems a generation ago should serve as a warning. According to **William S. Lovejoy,** the volatility of the competitive environment is a primary driver of whether companies should use centralized or decentralized coordination (management control) mechanisms. In more volatile areas, centralization should be avoided and subordinates empowered with sufficient information to make and implement decisions. The key challenge is to design the human organization with appropriate incentives.

Suggested further reading

Lovejoy, W.S. (forthcoming 2000) *Integrated Operations*, South-Western College Publishers.

FRESH CHALLENGES
FOR THE FUTURE

16

Contributor

Dan Schendel is founding and current editor of the *Strategic Management Journal*, published by John Wiley and Sons, as well as the founding president and current executive director of the Strategic Management Society. He is professor of management, Krannert Graduate School of Management, Purdue University, and Dean, German International School of Management and Administration.

Contents

Introduction

This final module sums up the main themes of this book, addresses some of the current controversies, and offers pointers to how the field may develop in coming years. The core message is that those who fail to keep up with the best in strategic management risk losing their businesses and losing their jobs. The cases of failure cited throughout the book underline the point.

Fresh challenges for the future

by Dan Schendel

Mastering Strategy has offered readers a wide range of ideas from some of the best writers working in the strategic management field today. My congratulations to the authors and editors for a job well done. Their work shows the complexity of strategic management today, its speed of development, and its significance to competition and success.

As a consultant, teacher, and research worker, I have been a student of this field for nearly 40 years. Over that period, the technical content of strategic management has expanded and its influence grown. I am impressed with its contributions, both as a field of learning and as an applied field of practice. Few developments in management have been so influential.

But we all must be concerned about facile, inappropriate uses of the language, concepts, and theories of strategic management. Too often, assertions and unsupported opinions pass for supported learning and knowledge.

The field of strategic management today is complex, rapidly developing, and with influence that could not be imagined all those years ago. In 1960 the term "strategy" was not in use, although the ideas basic to it were developing, and of course, by today's definition, organizations even then had a strategy, whether good or bad.

Then and now, the basic notion behind strategy is that a successful, high-performance business requires a distinctive competence or competitive advantage. This fundamental notion means that the product or service offered by the business has the largest profit margin relative to its environment, including costs, market price, competition, and perceived buyer benefits. Without an advantage, without competence, went the logic, the business would struggle at the margin, perhaps fail. At best, the cost of capital was met, along with the costs of the input factors, with no excess return available.

Given the long history of its importance, it is surprising how often the term strategy is used today without any reference or relevance to this basic formative idea in the development of strategic management as a field. Everything, and nothing, is strategy for too many.

If you are willing to exclude the work of Chester Barnard, the management writer, it was not until the second half of the twentieth century that management studies distinguished between concerns over operating a business and those of determining just what the business was to be relative to its environment. Before then, the main advance made in managerial labor specialization, the breakdown of the manager's job, had been functional. Specialists in marketing, finance, manufacturing, and so on, the functional elements of business, represented a split of the overall managerial task, and allowed larger organizations to develop and grow. Under functional specialization, the general manager's primary job was to integrate the functional activities of the business, to ensure that the business used its resources efficiently in pursuit of a purpose understood as unchanging. While the multibusiness company existed, it received little early attention – it was only later that the distinction between separable businesses within the same legal entity came to play an important role in the field of strategic management. As the field would come to understand and later explain, organizational forms and processes were centered on and adapted to function within the notion of a single, continuing business.

However, this functional view of organizations and managerial work was changing under pressures of rapid advances in technology and other elements of the environment of business. For more than 100 years, ever since the launch of the Industrial Age and the large accumulations of capital and labor under one legal entity required by developing technologies, management students and practitioners working with large business organizations had been concerned with efficiency: with using less, with making more. As for strategy, managers had to be concerned with competitive advantage and the search for the lowest relative cost for conditions specified, usually assumed and understood to be static.

The time-and-motion studies of those involved in the science of work began in the nineteenth century with the advent of large-scale organizations. No well-managed company today is run competently without understanding such matters as cost accounting, variance analysis, planning and control systems, and so on – all managerial tools concerned with efficiency. Competitive advantage would not be possible without such understanding and such skills. Unfortunately, regardless of the quality of the strategy used, many companies still fail because they are inefficient.

I once heard this progress referred to as the "science of shoveling" (mainly because it involved physical work such as shoveling coal). Concerns with this aspect of management practice had a 100-year headstart on the "science of strategy." It was not because there was no such thing as competitive advantage, or strategy, or even strategic management.

Change strategy is not new

Read the early history of steel and Andrew Carnegie, or autos and Henry Ford, to see that new strategies did come along and revolutionize industries, just as they do today. Such change is not new, despite those who tell you it is. What is new is the frequency of change that alters existing competitive advantage, and with it the upset in the static structure of an industry. Such change increased dramatically after the Second World War.

With change came the normal upset to existing business. Peter Drucker, the venerable management guru, said it well. "Doing things right," or efficiently, could not save the company when it was not "doing the right things." Strategic management worries about doing the right things; that is, the science of strategy. Operations management worries about doing things right, the science of shoveling. Both operations and strategic management must be done well to be successful, to gain and maintain a competitive advantage. Do one of them badly, and you fail.

It was the realization of these twin tasks of management that led away from functional specialization to more complex organizational forms and managerial processes needed for the development of strategy and strategic management as we see it now. Functional specialization was no longer enough. Need gave rise to invention and eventually to new opportunities, this time in the technology of management which, if unrecognized and misunderstood, leads to failure or its modern equivalent, the takeover or merger. Cases of failure are well documented and many have been cited in articles in *Mastering Strategy*. This has been the message throughout the book. If you wished to be a successful professional manager, you had better understand what the field of strategic management was offering and how it was changing your job, or you could face the ultimate risk of losing your business. Obviously, if you were not learning what the field of strategic management was learning, your competitor might be. And your competitor could come in different technological forms, not necessarily obvious or visible.

But recognizing that the field of strategic management exists is not the same as understanding it or keeping up with its developments. This was once easy, but daily it becomes harder. What *do* you know about alliances, barriers to entry, competitive advantage, diversification, economic value added, first-mover advantages, globalization, horizontal scope, innovation, knowledge management, learning organizations, market power, networks, and option theory? New concepts, new ideas, new theories crop up every day, and this book has cited many, although certainly not all of them. Furthermore, not every concept is valid, and there seems to be no immunization – short of detailed understanding – to save you from the charlatan, the guru, the quick fix, the misleading, the erroneous. What is a manager to do?

Some have compared development of the knowledge of management to the stage that medicine had reached when it believed in bloodletting as a universal cure for all ailments. If sound, professional strategic management practice is to develop, the field needs – indeed, all of the subfields of management need – to take on the trappings of science where theory, replication, and accumulation of knowledge characterize learning and development. That means that teachers, researchers, and practitioners alike need to seek evidence and reasonable proof that their advice can work if taken and applied. For those in the workplace who read this, the question is: "How do you judge whether the advice you receive or take from management writers, gurus, teachers, consultants, and the like is good advice, capable of resulting in sound, workable practice?" Extend the question: "What is it that a professional manager needs to know to take advice from those who offer it?" A further question: "For those who entrust their assets or future to a professional manager, what assurances should you receive that the best practice is being used to preserve and grow your assets?" Unfortunately, the answers to these questions are neither obvious, nor simple. Too little emphasis has been given to finding their answers.

One controversial theme discussed in this series – and reflected in the literature of strategic management – is the importance of the resource-based view of the company and notably its role in explaining the performance and success of businesses. The resource-based view is often contrasted with the market structure or market power view of success. It is too early to say how this issue will be resolved, but what is necessary is that it should depend on the evidence of peer-reviewed studies published, examined, and argued by others who do further work. Replication is important and necessary to any field that proceeds as science proceeds, with evidence.

Such arguments and the literature in strategic management that contains them are largely inaccessible to practitioners (and I am afraid to many teachers and researchers as well) who are unable or unwilling to take the time and effort to understand them. This is an interesting aspect of practice. Should society allow competition to erase those who do not keep up? Is this efficient? Or, should professional managers be required to demonstrate understanding of the basic ideas we have learned? Society does not allow medicine to be practiced without proper attention to sound, informed procedures. Professional managers, on the other hand, are allowed much more leeway in this respect than other professions – from plumbing to pharmacy – for whom examination and licensing are necessary prerequisites.

Improving practice

Evidence is growing, even as the complexity of strategy and its management grows, that it is possible to improve practice. Some achievements we have seen in the last 40 years are significant, for example the advent of the capital asset pricing model (CAPM) and modern portfolio management in financial economics. These developments have, among other things, reduced the growth–share matrix made famous in the 1960s by the Boston Consulting Group to a diagnostic tool, but not one that provides the answer to what businesses should be included in a company's composition. The growth–share matrix (and its clones) was once purchased through consulting firms as the solution. However, the CAPM calculus is now well established in sound practice; indeed, the concept of abnormal return defines competitive advantage. Similarly, option theory as it is developing is replacing more traditional capital budgetting approaches, even as the latter is being adopted by those who are only now developing an understanding of the role of cost of capital. The dynamic view of strategy is taking the field into concepts that allow for understanding how companies must adapt to environmental change. How many professional managers, even teachers and researchers, can follow these fields and their application? Too few, I am afraid.

What is being learned in the field of strategic management is as much about what *not* to do as it is about what to do. The creation of those conditions that lead to competitive advantage is still more art form than science. Even if this is true, however, the avoidance of the traps that lead to failure is a significant accomplishment. Here, the field can help.

Predictability, as much as causal explanation, will serve practice so long as the underlying assumptions, including assumptions made about the environmental context of the business, are identified and evaluated. The field's ability to predict, if not explain, is growing.

The usage of strategy, its implementation, is perhaps more readily accessible to the manager regarding prescription and predictability. It is the nature of management that strategy creation must be done *ex ante*, while absent much possibility for experimental design so fundamental to the physical sciences. To learn, strategic management must make do with *ex post* studies of outcomes and inference using multivariate statistics, databases, and complicated empirical studies, as though actual experiments had been conducted. This is perilous ground for the uninitiated researcher, or the reader incapable of detecting flawed work. Unfortunately, too many are incapable of either doing the work required or detecting the flaws. Much too much is ignored because it is too hard. But that is how it is: either understand it or take those consequent risks that attend ignorance.

My own view of the field is that it has advanced well, and has been well served by proper application of scientific method. But it needs to go further. We don't know anywhere near enough about some things. And we don't practice enough replication of work already done. Here are some examples of where I think we do need to know more:

- The resource-based view and market structure explanations of success may not be about mutually exclusive explanations of success, but about contingent, specific, identifiable conditions of a life cycle of a technology set underlying products or services. Is there a dynamic life cycle at work? Can it be separated into phases and must research take into account the contingent conditions characterizing each phase?

- Much is being written about alliances, networks, and new organizational forms, but they all seem variants on the theme of why companies exist and why markets fail. Is there a dynamic process involved that explains the different legal forms that have cropped up to control different activities in the value chains creating goods and services for society?

- Does the technology of management change and how do new managerial processes themselves change viable strategies? How much of recent explanations of success is in fact owed to management practice rather than invention of products or services?

- The role of innovation in change is huge, but little understood. The role includes not only entrepreneurship, new ventures, and job formation, but how well an economic system can adapt to change and competition. Even underlying theory does not develop innovation's role in private companies' or the public's interest. Economist Joseph Schumpeter may have had it right, but is theory developed well enough for us to understand and manage innovation?

- In improving the practice of management, how much can be taught in a formal way, how much must be experienced? Can strategic managers be taught, or must we simply wait for the Jack Welches of the world to appear while bad managers waste assets?

- Has the day arrived that professional managers must be examined and licensed for proficiency? The assets that some managers control are greater than those of entire countries, yet there is much about management succession and control that receives only the check of the market place, often an inefficient control mechanism. Should society pay more attention?

There are many other issues and problems in the strategic management field that could be cited. The field will sort them out over time, as will experience. The significant challenge for all of us is to keep up with that field and understand its development and applications.

Subject index

Organization index

Name index